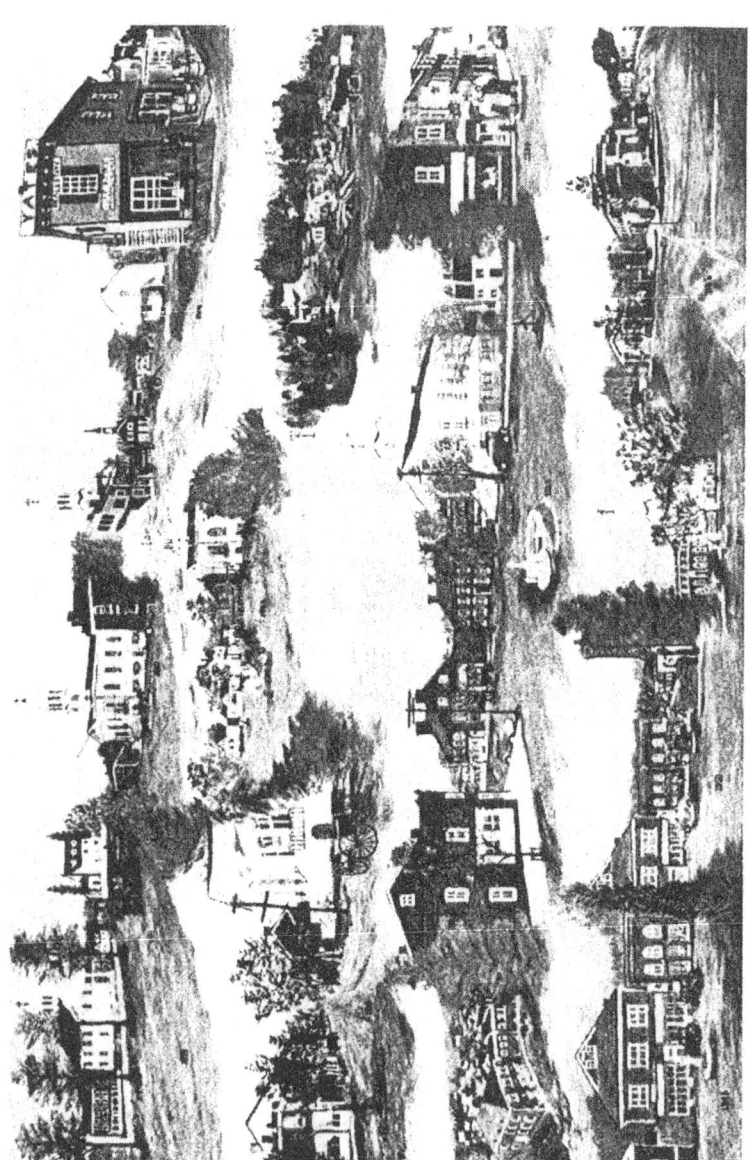

Painting by Lee Moffett, portrays the many faces of Court House Square.
Courtesy of Mrs. R. J. Hockensmith, Warrenton, Va.

The Diary of
Court House Square:
Warrenton, Virginia, USA

FROM EARLY TIMES THROUGH 1986,
WITH 1987–1995 REFLECTIONS

—Revised Edition—

Lee Moffett

HERITAGE BOOKS
2012

HERITAGE BOOKS
AN IMPRINT OF HERITAGE BOOKS, INC.

Books, CDs, and more—Worldwide

For our listing of thousands of titles see our website at
www.HeritageBooks.com

Published 2012 by
HERITAGE BOOKS, INC.
Publishing Division
100 Railroad Ave. #104
Westminster, Maryland 21157

Copyright © 1996 Lee Moffett

Other Heritage Books by the author:
Those Who Were: Annotated Inscriptions of Two Thousand People in Warrenton, Virginia Cemetery, 1811–1998

Original cover artwork by Lee Moffett

All rights reserved. No part of this book may be reproduced or transmitted in any form or by any means, electronic or mechanical, including photocopying, recording or by any information storage and retrieval system without written permission from the author, except for the inclusion of brief quotations in a review.

International Standard Book Numbers
Paperbound: 978-0-7884-0544-0
Clothbound: 978-0-7884-9228-0

INTRODUCTION

It is said that in the past 100 years, the world has progressed farther and faster than in all the time preceding. Whatever the age, the way each of us remembers living in our childhood has disappeared. However, it doesn't matter if the times were happy or sad, those by-gone days are not lost. "The Good Ole Days," they are called. We usually think of events when this is said, but what made them good are the people who are remembered. The people or person made the event happen. Without people there would be no happenings.

In this writing I have tried to involve not only the people here now, but people of the past, all who have made things happen at Court House Square and in the surrounding area. Some events reported occurred far from The Square, but they had some influence there.

Some people were: the delightful Mr. Albert Fletcher who said what he thought about things, or the distinguished looking Mr. Ford Anderson in his high collars. Mr. John Thoma loved children and fed them goodies. Mr. Earnest Pappas, a man from Greece, did not hesitate in helping his fellowman. Several people tried to climb the Courthouse steps by various methods other than by foot. Children picked apples along Main Street as they went to school, watched fights, or played marbles when they shouldn't. The train was met either for business reasons or just to pass the time of day, as there seemed to be more time then, and people could relax, enjoying what they saw in nature. A few people passed The Square whose minds had been affected by a terrifying experience. During droughts dust was kicked up as old and young came to the Courthouse well for their water, and in winter, others might have great fun in front of the Courthouse while playing in the snow.

Carnivals were held in The Square and parades still pass by. People sat on benches around a bubbling fountain to attend concerts, sermons, song festivities, celebrations, or just to rest from the chores of the day. Not everything was fun and gaiety for there were funerals and disasters. Fires occurred, the one of 1909 being especially bad, while epidemics and storms were among other sad times.

Traffic along the roads has been from the footfalls of the Indian, the sound of horses' hoofs, and the jingle of sleigh bells to the smell of exhaust from the horseless carriages. The things that happened to people when they tried to drive those first cars was something to see! After they were supposed to know how to drive, they still put their cars through windows, on lawns, had fires in them, bumped them together, knocked down signs, or as one lady did—hooked her bumper on a parking meter, and then tried to take it with her.

Like everything else, changes come, sometimes not for the good. New roads were built to eliminate traffic on The Square and did such a wonderful job that about 12 or 14 stores on Main Street became vacant at the same time. After things picked up and traffic problems began all over again, the fact was discovered that some things never change.

Because of the Courthouse, the Jail, the Theater, the Library and stores of all types located around The Square, each one has its own distinctive story to tell and the people who ran them had their gratifying triumphs and disappointments. At one time nearly everyone in business along Main Street was related. But, what happened to those families and their businesses? What has happened to the many, many people who walked along Court House Square or lived and worked in its neighborhood? How many ghosts walk the streets on dark nights? How have all the different businesses changed the face of The Square and Main Street? And, how is it still changing?

Some of the answers to these questions is what has been attempted in *The Diary Of Court House Square* as The Square tells its story in history. Some answers have been lost forever and the imagination must then go to work.

Warrenton may have been called a "sleepy community," but after all the things that have happened around just this one section of town—The Square—has it been? Is it now? It seems to me, once awakened, The Square really hasn't had time to sleep again!

I wish to thank the many, many people who took so much of their time to talk with me and to find pictures or articles that would help with this work. Thanks to Dr. A. R. Anderson Jr., Ralph Appleton, Arabelle Arrington, Mary Ashby, James Austin, Nancy C. Baird, Lucy Barbe, Betsy Bartenstein, Jack Bartenstein, Charles Beach, C. H. Braun, Amy Brown, Wayman Carter, Margaret Cornwell, Luther Cox, Lawrence Craig, W. M. DeCross, Nellie Downs, Madeline Fletcher, Sallie Fletcher, T. N. Fletcher Jr., Elizabeth Furr, E. M. & City Garrett, Irvin Garrett, Rudy Gill, W. H. Goldthorp, John Gott, Welton & Frances Hansbrough, Mr. & Mrs. Sam Harder, William Harris, Mary Hartsell, Maxwell Harway, Dr. J. O. Hodgkin III, Mary Ellen Hudson, Clifton Hurst, Tom Hutchison, Elizabeth I. Hutton, Phil Hyde, Margaret Jacobs, Charles Jeffries, Frost Jeffries, Joseph Lawler, Robert & Edith Lunceford, Mabel Martin, Robert McClanahan, Chilton McDonald, Rachel Mills, Frank Moffett, Susann Moffett, Mildred Moser, Angus Myers, Phil Nelson, Blanche O'Connell, Martin Joseph O'Connell, Earnest & Virginia Pappas, Marguerite Piel, Nancy Price, Frances Carter Ritter, J. Albert Robinson, Dorothy Rust, Sallie Sadler, D. D. & Margaret Sanford, Anne Brooke Smith, Tom & Virginia Stafford, Louis & Edna Stephenson Jr., Mildred Sudduth, Ruby Sweeney, Bob Teates, Florence Thayer, Hallie Thorp, Wallace N. Tiffany, Harold F. Timberlake, Eloise Trainum, Mrs. Joseph A. Whitmore, and to any others who gave bits of information.

The Diary of
COURT HOUSE SQUARE
WARRENTON, VIRGINIA

1600's

In 1612 the Susquehannock Indians used The Plain Path to the east when trading with those in the Carolina area for furs and skins to take to Dutch merchants on Manhattan Island.[2] Later the war-loving Iroquois drove them out and became known as "the Senecas" in Virginia and Carolina. Charles II granted territory to his followers, 1649, their heirs being able to grant, give, sell or do whatever they wished with the land, thus beginning what was called "Proprietorship". A treaty in 1679 gave the Indians the Piedmont and the trail was renamed "Shenandoah Hunting Path". Grazing buffalo and other animals gathered in areas the Indians burned off in order that grass could grow back, so animals would be easier to kill.[3]

Perhaps the first white men and horses to enter lower Fauquier was a party led by Col. John Catlett, 1670.[4] Because the Iroquois did not keep the treaty but robbed houses, killed stock and so forth, in 1686 Brent Town Block House (not far from present Sowego) was built along the Shenandoah Hunting Path. Not wanting to be watched, the Indians changed their path a little. When landowner, Lord Culpeper died in 1689 his daughter, who was married to Sir Thomas Fairfax, inherited his holdings.

1700's

As more people began to come into the territory, in 1712 George Neavil built a mill and an ordinary on Cedar Run where the Indian Path, also called Carolina Road, met the Dumfries Road. The settlement became Auburn.[4] An ordinary or inn in this country was similar in looks to those in England, with a front porch the length of the house and almost covered with hand bills—the more the better, for that meant it was a popular place. It would take its name from the person keeping the house for the profession of inn-keeper was more respected here, and hours were different, for they stated a certain time for meals. Several beds were in every room and they said it was a good thing the sheets were mostly brown in color, as seldom were they changed.

During the summer of 1713 the Knights of the Golden Horseshoe crossed the future Fauquier County on their way to the Valley. Through an agent Catherine Lady Fairfax, the sole proprietor of the Northern Neck of Virginia, granted land to Col. Edward Barrow, November 10, 1717 (to become Fauquier Springs).[5] Disposal of the land was not made directly by a proprietor. With the exception of the manors, the land was granted with the right to collect quit-rents. If the rent was not paid, the proprietor could reclaim it. In 1718 a grant was given to Thomas Lee.[4] Lady Catherine died 1719 and her son, Thomas, the 6th Lord Fairfax inherited from her.

A colony of Germans had settled in what would become Culpeper County and in 1720 they traveled over the Carolina Road to settle on Licking Run while the Indian and backwoodsmen occupied most of the land. A treaty in 1722 said the Indian would never come east of the Blue Ridge again, so their trail was moved to the Shenandoah Valley and the Carolina Road became an immigration route for the white man.

1723 found more grants by Col. Robert Carter, (who had so much land he was called "King Carter"), manager for Lord Fairfax and Thomas Lee, gradually working their way up the Rappahannock River as well as along its runs.[4] He had the idea of establishing his manors with Scotch-Irish immigrants who had come as indentured servants, had served their time and were looking for permanent homes. By 1727 most of the land in the southern end of the county was taken and the western movement toward the Pignut and beyond was underway.

Prince William County was formed March 1731 from Stafford and King George counties. The 'Parish' was division coming from England through which taxes and other things were collected or decided.[4] Hamilton Parish of Prince William would include the future Fauquier. Before the western boundaries of the Fairfax land was surveyed, Col. Carter died, 1732, thus Lord George William Fairfax came in 1735, to ride over the property during the survey, selecting certain land as his own calling it the Manor of Leeds, part which would be in Fauquier.

Around 1742 it was discovered the 'savage' Indians had been traded for something almost as bad along the Carolina Road. Horse and cattle thieves driving their stock through the county often drove off the animals of people whose lands they passed. When animals became mixed together, the thieves said they could not separate the two groups.[2] An Act of the Virginia Assembly was passed requiring cattle-drovers to carry a bill of sale of all their cattle. This helped stop some cattle thieving, but the following year horse stealing was on the increase. The name "Rogue's Road" was given to the old path, (its bad reputation lasting for the rest of the century). Lord Fairfax returned the England, 1737, but came back to Virginia in 1747. He met 16 year old George Washington, who was employed the next year to survey his holdings west of the Blue Ridge. On their way to the Valley, March 1748, they stayed at George Neavil's Ordinary.

A 1754 map shows the Fredericksburg-Winchester Road taking a more direct route over the hill that was destined to become the Courthouse Village.[4] This was planned as the shortest route for troops to be moved between the two towns. It was the policy of Glasgow merchants who controlled the tobacco trade of the Upper Piedmont and the Valley to promote the building of roads and to establish stores at convenient points where their agents could distribute merchandise and buy tobacco. After the Dumfries' Road passed Neavil's Tavern, it forked. One, called the Rappahannock Road or Lower Dumfries' Road (went past what would be Turkey Run St. Mary's Episcopal Church, 1½ miles from the present town) crossed the Marsh Road. Alexander Cunningham, a Dumfries' merchant, built his "Red Store" along this road. (It was located on Lot #2[6] - back of where the fire house would be at 4th and Main Streets.[1]) The building had two rooms, one above the other with the steps on the outside. (It was moved at an unknown date to 162 Main Street to be incorporated in the Pretlow House.[7]) Shortly after the road passed the store it came to where I am located (and Water's Tavern would be built), then on down through the hollow (just north of present cemetery) and proceed to the mouth of Carter's Run (Waterloo) on the Rappahannock River.

The Upper Dumfries' Road went (to the present Chestnut Forks, where it crossed the future Alexandria Turnpike, to Bethel and on) through Ashby's Gap of Rappahannock Mountain to the Valley. Culpeper Road led over the ridge to the southwest (west of its present course, passing the site of the present Episcopal Church) and reached Main Street near the Red Store.[8] Troops marched over the new road going west to fight the Indians. Major General Edward Braddock, in charge of British forces in America, had George Washington as an aide. Braddock's mission was to drive the French from the frontier territory claimed by Great Britain. He came to Virginia in 1755 and his troops dug several wells in the new village of future Fauquier County. One, (on what would become Main Street near the present 3rd Street) was called Braddock's well. Possibly they also dug the well where I am (in front of the future Courthouse).[9] It is said the British did not take Washington's advise as how to fight the Indians, but marched in close formation with flags flying and music playing, thus they were ambushed July 9, 1755, south of Fort Duquesne. (Pittsburgh, Pa.) Braddock was wounded, his men fled, and he died two days later.[10] In October 1755, in fear of the French and their Shawnee allies settlers from the west fled over the Blue Ridge. By April 7, 1756 the Militia wanted volunteers to fight the Indians. A fort was built at Winchester for the protection of nearby inhabitants.[4]

Things were really becoming busy around me. The population was growing and May 1, 1759 the County of Fauquier was formed from Prince William. People said it couldn't have been a prettier time of year. The lavender-pink of the Red Buds were just about gone from the forests and the white Dogwoods were taking their place. The act creating the county was passed at the first assembly held by Francis Fauquier, Lieutenant Governor of Virginia, after he had been appointed in January 1758. Perhaps this was why the county took his name.

The First Court held May 24, 1759 was in a private house on the Marsh Road at the junction with Frogg's Road. (About ¾ mile northwest of present Morrisville.)[11] The Justices decided the place for a courthouse should be closer to the geographical center of the county, which was the plantation of John Duncan whose land included the junction of the Marsh Road and Lower Dumfries' Road. When the county was formed, the system of rough roads were maintained by tithables under the supervision of road surveyors, who were appointed at the First Court. But, June 13, 1759, the governor told the Second Court to meet in the house of William Jones. They met as planned on June 28th at Duncan's home, then moved to the newly built log-house of W. Jones, located on land belonging to Richard Henry Lee, son of Thomas Lee. R. H. Lee's political influence evidently had been used to secure his land for the future settlement. The Jones land lay northwest from the Duncan house and within half a mile of the crossing to the 1754 road and the Dumfries' Road where the Red Store was located.[4] The Justices decided the county needed a Jail and a Courthouse, so the first Sheriff, Joseph Blackwell who was appointed at the May meeting, was to advertise for workmen to build them. The Courthouse was to be of wood and the Jail the same size as Stafford County had. John Bell, William Eustace, and Yelverton Peyton or any two of them would receive the bids.[12]

At the July 26, 1759 session, the Court directed that two acres of land belonging to Richard Henry Lee be for the county buildings, which were located east of Culpeper Road and below the Rappahannock Road on a rocky knoll (that would become the town cemetery) in a wood-land. The area was called Fauquier Court House. Indians picked their way along a ridge so they could see in the distance and avoid attack. This could have been a reason for the location of the settlement, as it is 675 feet above sea level. Since more and more people were stopping for the night—it was a two day drive from Winchester to Falmouth or from Charlottesville to Alexandria—a blacksmith shop, more houses and another tavern were built. At this session a license was granted for Andrew Edwards' Tavern near the Courthouse.[11] With all the people walking about or stopping to talk, I found that a lot of things happen in this world.

Some people persuaded the Court, June 27, 1760, to build a larger Courthouse of brick. This was finished prior to July 26, 1762, located a short distance east of Culpeper Road (in the rear of the present Lucien Keith-Richard Payne House) about ¼ mile south of the Dumfries'-Rappahannock Road. At the September 23rd meeting, Lord Fairfax was present as Joseph Blackwell presided.[1] Major William Eustace was named Sheriff, September 1, 1769. The Parish of Leeds was established this year in the northern end of the county due to the increase in population.

A map of the year 1770 mentions the name "Fauquier" and the position of the Courthouse is shown.[169] An addition was built onto the Courthouse in 1771.[11] In August 1773 J. Valentine of Fauquier County delivered to John Likly in behalf of William Cunningham & Co., merchant of Glasgow, 700 head of cattle, one white mare, 16 head of "hoggs", one servant woman named Agnes Smith, one featherbed and furniture, all of his household stuff as well as a crop of tobacco and corn.[161] That was a variety of things. While a surveyor, George Washington traveled throughout this area. March 15, 1774 he recorded a deed at the Courthouse.[13]

The first Minute Men were from Virginia so named because they were "raised in a minute, armed in a minute, marched in a minute, fought in a minute and vanished in a minute". Although some were armed with rifles, others carried tomahawks and scalping knives in their belts. The motto 'Liberty or Death' was inscribed in white letters on the front of their green hunting shirts and their hats had buck-tails on them. The men, about 100 from Fauquier, included Thomas Marshall (father of Chief Justice John Marshall).[12] The Fauquier Militia of Volunteers that had organized in 1761, served in the Revolutionary War,[1] as Culpeper Minute Men.[186]

Around 1775, the Red Store had competition with one across the street run by Martin Pickett. He married Ann Blackwell in 1764 and about now built a house on Winchester Road (part of what would become "Paradise"). Thomas Maddux's Ordinary was in the village.[14] Towards the end of the 18th century the public stage was introduced. The Red Store was a stage stop and as it approached the store, the driver announced themselves by blowing a horn. After the Battle of Bunker Hill, June 17, 1775, a school building named "Warren Academy", was built (on what is now Academy Hill). Rev. Hezekiah James Balch organized the school[99] that was named for General Joseph Warren, who in trying to reorganize the retreating militia in the battle was killed by a cannon ball. They also say he started Paul Revere on his ride.[8] One result of the hostilities was that in 1777 the Commonwealth abolished feudal land tenures and lands were exempted from further payment of quit-rents.[4] They had been paid annually on the first day of St. Michael the Archangel in September.[1] As of April 15, 1778 the Presbyterians were also using the Turkey Run Church.[99]

By March 5, 1786, Spicer gave the Warren Academy two acres of land.[168] Then a larger school was built, probably, November 28, 1788.[4] William Horner came from Maryland in 1786 to open a business in the house (eventually belonging to William A. Pattie, 1869), and later opened a business at the stand opposite the Courthouse (that still bears his name).[15] There does not seem to be a record of reasons, but frequent orders for repairs on the 1762 Courthouse were given. Although only 27 years old, Court was not held there in 1789, but at the house of Thomas Maddux.[11]

The first census taken 1790 had a total county population of 17,892 that included free whites, free colored, and slaves.[1]

Now I am truly going to be the center of attention. April 27, 1790, it was decided to move the Courthouse (to its present location). The brick building to be 52 feet long and 30 feet wide in the clear, 16 feet at one end to be divided into 2 rooms one of which is to be 20 feet wide and 16 feet long. Two rooms above to be finished for jury rooms within the walls. The partition wall to be of brick.[1] The county purchased, May 26, 1790, Thomas Maddux's life lease, planning to build there the Courthouse, Prison, Pillory, Whipping Post, and Stocks.[4] [*See below & page 8.*] Richard Henry Lee gave land for the town of Fauquier Court House, directing James Routt, December 4, 1790, to lay it off in relation to the new Courthouse.[11] There were to be 12 lots on either side of Rappahannock Road of ½ acre each, all to face Main Street as that section of the Rappahannock-Dumfries' Road was straightened and renamed. The street was widened to 55 feet 7¼ inches and was intersected by cross streets 30 feet wide, into one of which the old Alexandria-Culpeper Road was diverted, which then proceeded west by Main Street.[12] The Red Store was on Lot #2, William Horner was on Lot #3 (later the Presbyterian Church), Dr. Gustavus B. Horner was at Lot #4 (later the Grenville Gaines property and owned by Vincent Jacobs).[16]

DEED Book 10, Page 304   Teste, Brooke CC

This Indenture made the twenty sixth day of May in the year of our Lord Christ one thousand seven hundred and ninety (Between Thomas Maddux and Elizabeth his wife, Thomas Nelson and Rachel his wife, and Joseph Nelson and Jane his wife, of the one part, & William Grant, William Edmonds, Jeremiah Darnall, James Bell, John Moffett, John Blackwell, Martin Pickett, William Pickett, Thomas Keith, Aylett Buckner, Charles Chilton, Edward Digges, Thomas Digges, Francis Triplett, William Neale, Samuel Blackwell, John Thomas Chunn, Benjamin Shackelford, Joseph Blackwell, Original Young, John Blackwell junior, Robert Randolph and John Peyton, Harrison Gentlemen Justices of the County Court of Fauquier of the other part; Witnesseth that the said Thomas Maddux and Elizabeth his wife, Thomas Nelson and Rachel his wife and Joseph Nelson and Jane his wife, for and in consideration of the sum of five shillings to them in hand paid by the aforesaid Justices at and before the

305. sealing and delivery hereof, the receipt whereof they do hereby acknowledge and thereof do acquit and discharge the said Justices and their successors by these presents, Have granted, bargained, sold, aliened, enfeoffed, released

and confirmed, and by these presents do grant bargain sell alien enfeoff release and confirm unto the said Justices and their successors a certain piece parcel and lot of ground situate in the said County of Fauquier and on which the prison of the said County now stands, which said land is bounded as followeth to wit, Beginning at a stake standing twenty five links from Thomas Maddux's cellar door thence running South 35½ West 12 poles and sixteen feet to another stake in the road that leads to Culpeper Courthouse, thence North 55½ West 16 poles to another stake in Nelsons lott, thence North 34½ East twelve poles sixteen feet to a stake standing two chains from Bowens store door, thence South 55½ East sixteen poles to the Beginning, containing one acre and forty seven poles, together with all and singular the rights, members, Privileges, whatsoever thereunto belonging or in any wise appertaining, and also all the estate, right, title, interest, use, possession, property, claim and demand whatsoever of them the said Thomas Maddux and Elizabeth his wife, Thomas Nelson and Rachel his wife, and Joseph Nelson and Jane his wife, or either of them, in law, equity or otherwise whatsoever To have and to hold the said lot or parcel of land and premises hereby granted unto the aforesaid Justices and their successors for the purpose of erecting thereon a Courthouse, prison pillory, whipping post and stocks and for no other use, intent or purpose whatsoever. In Witness whereof the said Thomas Maddux and Elizabeth his wife, Thomas Nelson and Rachel his wife and Joseph Nelson and Jane his wife have hereunto set their hands and seals the day and year first above written.

Sealed and Delivered
in presence of
Augustine Jennings,
William Edmonds jun:
Elias Edmonds jun:
James Headley jun:

Thos. Maddux .... L.
Elizabeth Maddux .... L.
Thos Nelson .... L.
Rachell Nelson ...... L.
Joseph Nelson .... L.
Jane Nelson .... L.

At a court held for Fauquier County the 25th day of October 1790. This Indenture was proved to be the act and deed of the said Thomas Maddux, Thomas Nelson and Joseph Nelson by the oaths of Augustine Jennings, William Edmonds junior, Elias Edmonds junior and James Headley junior witnesses thereto and ordered to be recorded.

Teste, H Brooke CC

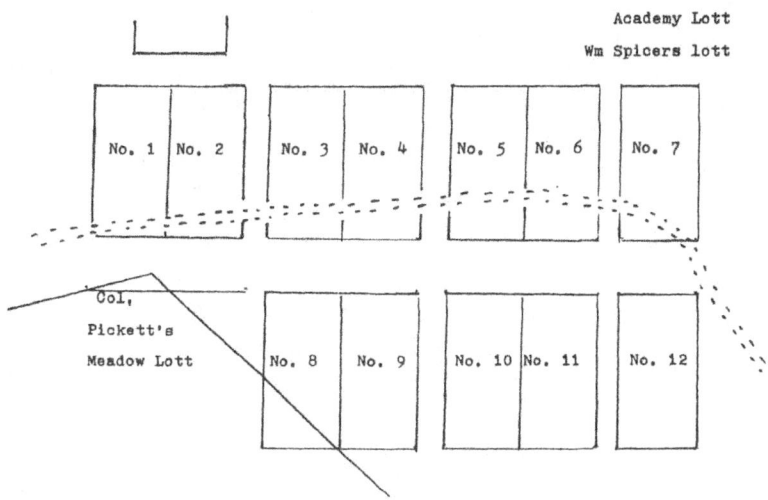

The Routt platt, found in Deed Book 17, Page 397, has the following explanation. "Vigt. S Hnss (?) is the lot adjoining Mr. Francis Scott. No. 2 includes the Store and so on to No. 7 which borders in or near the line of W. Spicers' Lott, also near the Academy Lott. No. 8 adjoining Col. Picketts Meadow Lott & cornering in the same, takes off the Low Lott one tenth of an acre and leaves just double that quantity of Land between said lot the meadow lot & the Main Street. The width of the Main St. is a chain 34¼ links which is 55 feet 7¼ inches. The width of the cross street or alley is 30 feet except that between the first lott and Mr. Turner, which is only left 20 feet wide in order to prevent the Division line between the first and second lotts interfering the Red Store. Each half acre Lott is 6 ch. 16¼ lk in length and 3 ch. 8 1/8 lk wide. The bearing the Main Street is South 50° East and the bearing of the Cross Streets or alleys No. 34° East. Surveyed for Col. Thomas Lee Esq. by direction of Col Pickett." It is signed by P. James Routt Devc and dated Dec. 4, 1790.

1782-1790 more affluent families using wheeled vehicles, but most people still traveled by foot or on horseback. The Carolina Road began to loose its importance and the location of the National Capital decided upon in 1790, had something to do with this as other roads from the south were more direct leading to it. Also about this time the town of Alexandria began to put out several turnpikes, taking more traffic from the road.[2] Among business now were the ordinaries of Edwards and Waters, grog shops, blacksmiths, saddlers, cabinet maker, millinery shop, clock making and tailoring.[14] Recorded in the Clerk's office, June 3, 1793 was that Johnzie Tongue bought the house (present 4th and Main Streets) from Martin Pickett and Anne his wife for 7 pounds 10 shillings.

From Deed Book 11 - Page 453:

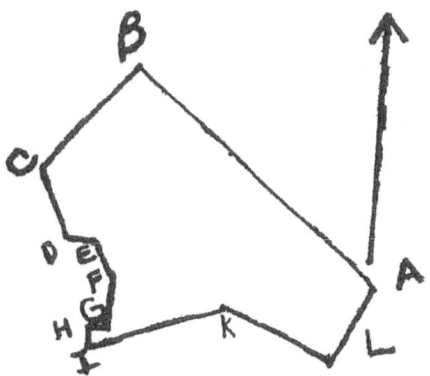

"Prison Bounds-Surveyed—lot of land Laid out for the purpose of Prison bounds, & is bounded as follows vis. Beginning at A the Northwest corner of the Old Bale House, that formerly belonged to the Red Store House lott, extending thence Nth 50 Wt 58¼ poles to B a red oak on the east side of the great road, opposite to Wm. Horners Store & dwelling house, thence crossing the said road, & including the said Horners store house Sth 37 Wt 25½ poles to C a chestnut tree in Joseph Nelsons yard, thence S 32 E 12¾ poles to D, the northwest Corner of Col. Martin Picketts yard fence, thence along the said Picketts yard fence S 65 E 5 poles to E, S 28 E 4 poles to F S6 (?) W 10¾ poles to G NS (?) 6 W 3 poles to H, a corner on the Northwest side of Col. Picketts Well, thence including the said Well S 4 E 2¾ poles to I, a dead chestnut tree thence N 77 E 29 poles to K, a stone corner, thence S 68 E 17 poles to L, a dead red oak saplin, with grape vines on it, thence N 25 E 15½ poles to the first station containing ten acres

James Routt
September 4, 1793"

The Warren Academy had been mentioned in an ad 12/29/1791 as being at Fauquier Court House[17] and again in the Columbian Mirror and the Alexandria Gazett on 1/6/1794.[18]

The Court agreed March 1795 to build a Clerk's Office for the county of brick or stone.[1] Not until 1795 was the new brick Courthouse approved for use. This third building was brick stuccoed and had in its steeple a bell in which silver was incorporated with other metal. Not long after the town was laid out, it became known as Warrenton in honor of the hero of Bunker Hill. The exact date is unknown, but a local deed in 1797 mentioned it as "Fauquier Court House now called the Town of Warrenton."[4] Progress was showing for in 1799, 60 coaches and 16 chaises were owned by local people.

1800's

Ah! the calendar rolled over into another century and October 27, 1801 there was an order "that after January Court next no person shall be permitted to reside in the Courthouse".[11] Could this mean the old Courthouse of 1762 or did someone live in the new one? So long ago—oh, well no matter really. We had a hero in 1805. Presley Neville O'Bannon had been born in the county and this year he led a group of Marines in a successful attack on a fort along "the shores of Tripoli".[1] In 1806 gold was begun to be mined in lower Fauquier County. October 28, 1808, a brick jail replaced the wooden one being built next to the Courthouse,[19] (now Old Gaol Museum). June 1809, Richard Thompson & Sally, his wife, bought "in consideration of 100 pounds current money", from Peter and Ann Glascock, a lot at the Courthouse on the south side of Main Street, "and all houses, buildings, orchards, ways, water courses and appurtenances,[20] (to become #32 Main or the Sweeney Building).

The name, Town of Warrenton, became official when it was incorporated January 5, 1810. The town included 71 acres May 8, 1811 and old roads were now streets. The Fredericksburg-Winchester Road was straightened (to become as it is today) and renamed Winchester Street. The Dumfries-Rappahannock Road as it went past the Courthouse, changed to Jail Street (later Waterloo). The road to Culpeper Court House became Culpeper Street, Churchill's Road that led to Churchill's Mill on Cedar Run, existing as early as 1768, now became Court Lane and was adopted as the line of the new Alexandria Turnpike. This area around the Courthouse is becoming more popular, more grown-up all the time. Diagonal and Horner Streets are two of the oldest ones in town.[16] During 1811 James Barnett opened a school in a room of the Martin Pickett mansion (now site of Warren Green). It's unknown when the house was built on the crest of The Square but Pickett, a merchant, also had a store near the corner of South 5th & Main Streets.[168] In 1811 there was a survey of boundary lines and roads. A map was made (later) showing the relationship of that survey with the one from 1790. [*See map with the correction, page 12A.*] (Can be seen in the old Gaol Museum.

Bishop Meade came to Hamilton Parish in 1812 to find no house of worship of any denomination in Warrenton, so he preached in the Courthouse instead of at Turkey Run Church.[98] Deed Book 18 for 1808-13 - Page 468 - shows a survey dated June 22, 1812 with the following explanation. "Site of Laid Town-from A to a stone in the edge of the Winchester Rd. west of Daniel Withers House—above alley between Withers & Sakens Lots to B a stone. Thornhills house to C a stone in Col. Wm. Edmonds woods near a small oak & hickory to D a small pile of stone in William Horner's meadow—to E a stone between Braggs Shop to F a stone in east corner of Academy Lott to G a stone in Mrs. Marshall's meadow-to H- a stone corner to Doc Horner to I a stone in Mrs. Marshall's meadow near a large pile of stones. No. 1 begins a corner Lucketts No. 3 begins-corner Wm. Horner & heirs of Septimus Norris No. 4 begins corner Dr. G. B. Horners Shop now occupied by Richard Baker No. 5 begins corner Norris Tavern No. 6 begins corner between Jennings Glascock So. 1st begins corner Mrs. Marshall's lot So. 3 begins corner near Marshall's corner to a chestnut Stump corner to Tongues So. 4 begins corner Fisher's house So. 5th begins at corner of the brick store So. 6 begins corner of Glascock So. 7 begins west end of the jail. . Court Lane begins corner Wm. Horners Store lot & goes to public Square—Winchester- begins on Court Lane at corner of James W. Wallaces Lot. Diagonal St. begins at Drums. Smith begins corner of Joseph Blackwells to Jail. Chestnut begins corner of Sakens Lot." [*See map for this, page 13.*]

The Presbyterians and Episcopalians both meeting in the Turkey Run Church, in September 1813 wanted to buy a lot in town. November 9th they found one on the south side of East Main Street (probably the site of the upper side yard of #170 Main, a block or so from present Baptist Church). The small building known as the Brick Church was used jointly by both denominations.[99]

The British took Washington August 24, 1814 and on that day and the next, burned the city. A treaty signed 12/24/1814 brought peace.[10] The mails were irregular, but someway things became known and as they walked about, people talked "it over". By 1814 the school of James Barnett had closed.[168]

In January 1816, the Warrenton Seminary, operated by Wesley and William T. Cowles opened.[1] George B. Pickett sold a house (to

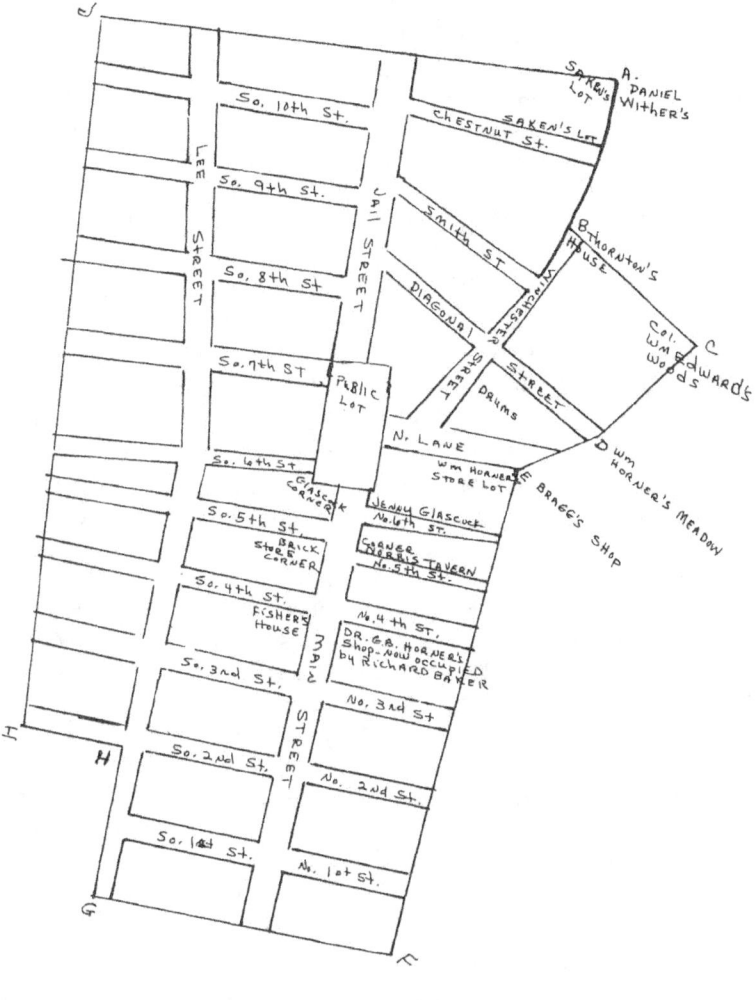

become "the California House") to William Lakeman for $600.00.[21] The Episcopalians wanted to have their own place of worship, so built the first St. James Church of wood in 1816 on Alexandria Turnpike (site of present First Baptist).[1] However, they continued their interest in The Brick Church.[99] Reverend George Lemmon was the first Clergyman at St. James.[98] At the June 6th Court, a discussion was planned for the next Court meeting regarding a new Courthouse,[22] which evidently were not completed until July 28, 1817.[11] The old Courthouse was now twenty-two years old.

Someone who turned out to be rather important came to Warrenton in 1817. James Caldwell, born in Winchester, worked in a printing office there. When he came here, he established a newspaper called The Palladium of Liberty. This weekly was the first newspaper published in Fauquier County. The print shop was located at Jail & South Seventh Streets (now Ashby).[23] This had been the property of Martin Pickett and then it belonged to Congressman Love. T. Norris bought it from him.[168] The issue for July 26, 1817 had an advertisement by Thaddeus Norris for "proposale for the making and laying 150,000 Bricks". He also wanted shingles, plank, scantling and Locust posts. He was beginning to work on his Ordinary that would be built behind the Courthouse. Another ad that day announced the practice of physic by Dr. John Drish.

Deed Book 22- Pages 209-211- February 13, 1818 tells of the boundaries for the Public Square being determined. *[See copy, pages 15, 16, 17.]* The Methodist Episcopal built their first church building, which was wooden, in 1818 on South Fifth Street (now 2nd, about where the Black & Gold Inn is), continuing to preach in the Courthouse until their building was built. Slavery was becoming a major issue in the U.S. and the church on a national level was becoming divided on the question.[24] Construction began on the new Courthouse August 24th.[11] During this time the Court met in Mr. Tongue's house. Near the end of a summer day in 1818 a stranger walked into the village. Being covered with dust he didn't look very important, especially as he had a cane across his shoulder from which was hung a handkerchief with his possessions. The Frenchman stopped in front of Turner's Tavern to talk with a man on its steps, but he stayed as a guest at Water's Tavern. He had a note for introduction that read, "The celebrated historian and naturalist, Volney, needs no recommendation from G. Washington."[8]

An advertisement in The Palladium of Liberty for Friday, January 15, 1819 told of a happening nearby, and it would be one of many. It said, "FOR SALE, On Monday the 25th inst. being Court day will be exposed for sale several LIKELY NEGRO GIRLS from twelve to eighteen years of age for cash. Further conditions made known on the day of the sale. RICHARD THOMPSON".

The house (to be known as Carter Hall after 1900) was built in 1819 as the home of Inman Horner of Richmond, Va., a member of the U.S. Senate and a lawyer, he was the oldest brother of Dr. Brown Horner (who later bought the property and lived there).[25] Perhaps it was July 26th when Thaddeus Norris began building his

Scott &c
to
Pickett

24/309

This Indenture made this 13th day of February 1818 between John Scott, Thornton Buckner and Thomas Ingraham of the County of Fauquier and State of Virginia of the one part and George R. Pickett and Stephen Pickett of the County and State aforesaid of the other part. Whereas by an act of the General Assembly of Virginia passed on the 4th February 1817, entitled an act concerning the public Square in the Town of Warrenton the above named John Scott, Thornton Buckner and Thomas Ingraham, together with Ann Gurne and Thomas Fitzhugh, were appointed Commissioners with power to any three of them, to Act, to survey and ascertain the proper Boundaries of the public Square in the Town of Warrenton, to be attended by the County Surveyor for that purpose, with power to omit in Survey such part or parts of the said Square as might appear to them to interfere with the Uniformity, the Convenience and the Beauty of the Streets of the said Town and Convey such parts thereof, as might be omitted as aforesaid to the original proprietor, or proprietors or their Representatives with a proviso in the said Act that nothing therein contained should be construed as to authorise the above mentioned Commissioners to make such Changes or innovations in the said Square as will be injurious to the public, that in pursuance of the said Act the said John Scott, Thornton Buckner and Thomas Ingraham three of the above mentioned Commissioners on the 11th August 1817 being attended by the Surveyor of the County of Fauquier did Survey and Ascertain the proper boundaries of the public Square in the Town of Warrenton and they being of opinion that the part herein after described does interfere with the uniformity the Convenience and the Beauty of the Streets of the Town of Warrenton and that the Omission of the parts herein after mentioned will not be injurious to the public and the said John Scott, Thornton Buckner and Thomas Ingraham three of the Commissioners above named by the said Act are Authorised to Execute a Conveyance for the said parts hereinafter mentioned they have agreed to Execute these presents. This Indenture Witnesseth that the said John Scott, Buckner and Thomas Ingraham are of opinion that the Boundaries represented on the plat are

15

of William McCoy Deputy Surry of Fauquier County hereto annexed by the lines and Letters Black A from them along the Black line to Red F thence along the red line to Black C, thence along the black line to Black D thence along the black lines to the beginning at A are the true and proper boundaries of the said public Square We are further of opinion that the part of the said Square represented on the said plat by the following lines and letters to wit, beginning at A thence along the black line to Red E, thence along the red line to red H thence along the red lines to red G thence along the black line to the beginning at A whilst it remains a part of the said public square does interfere with the uniformity, convenience and beauty of the streets of said Town of Warrenton and that a Conveyance of the said part to the representatives of the original proprietor will not be inconvenient to the public. Wherefore we the said Commissioners in consideration of the premises and in pursuance of the power vested in us by the said recited act have granted and Conveyed and by these presents do grant and Convey unto the said George B. Pickett & Steptoe Pickett their heirs and assigns all that part of the said public Square last mentioned and described on the said plat by the said lines and Letters black A red E red H red G and thence to A. Containing eleven perches To have and to hold the same to the said George B. Pickett & Steptoe Pickett their heirs and assigns for such Estate as we the said Commissioners may Lawfully Convey. In Testimony whereof we have hereunto set our hands and Seals this 13th day of February 1818.

Wm. Scott
Wm. Von Buckner
Thomas Ingram

Witness:

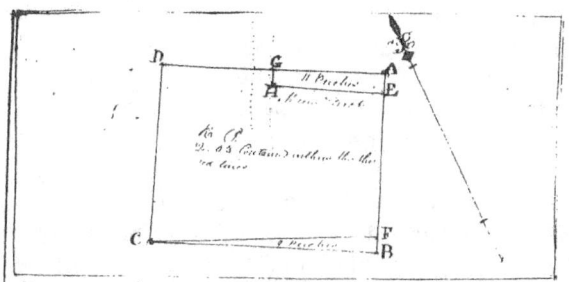

Winchester Frederick County House, August 11th 1817

By the decision of John Lock, Thornton Buckner and Thomas Ingram Esqrs (Commissioners appointed to execute an Act of the General Assembly of Virginia for the purpose of laying off and establishing the Boundaries of the publick Lott) I began at A, a Stone one pole from the Cellar door of the House now belonging to R. John Bruiser thence along South 6° West S 54½ W 12 22/25 po. to B, a Stake thence N 57½ W 11 po to C a Stake west of the Sore, thence N 34½ E 12 25/25 poles to D a Stone by the Office door of E. E. Cook Esqr thence S 56½ E 11 poles to the Beginning.

The red lines show the parts cut off the Lott, as originally run. The courses and distances of which are as follows Beginning at E, a Stake 1 25/25 po from A, thence S 5½ W 10 25/25 po to F a Stake thence thence N 57½ W 11 po to C, thence N 34½ E 12 25/25 poles to D. thence S 56½ E 7 22/25 poles to G, a Stake on the edge of the Court lane thence with it S 31 W 1 25/25 po to H a Stake thence S 55½ E 7 22/25 poles to the Beginning.

Williams McCrey D.S.F.C.

At a Court held for Frederick County this 16th day of March 1818 This Indenture of Bargain and Sale was produced into Court and acknowledged by the said John Lock and Thornton Buckner to be their act and Deed and was proved as to Thomas Ingram by the Oaths of Alfred Harris, ____ McKinlee, and Robert Richard Henry Subscribing Witnesses thereto and Ordered to be Recorded.

Teste Daniel Wilber Clk

Examined & delivered to F.W. Brooke, one of the present owners of the property conveyed by the deed. this 15th Jany 1837.
Jas Smith, CFC

This Indenture, made this 25th day of October in the Year One thousand eight hundred and seventeen Between Peter Catlett of Green up County in the State of Kentucky now of the Town of Alexandria of the one part, and Thomas brick tavern,[26] for "he right worthily carried out his conception, and mason & joiner and even Mr. Baker, the old silversmith at the corner of Main & Culpeper Streets, who had a penchant for taming mice, heartily seconded and encouraged it. The old gentleman's contribution was a thin plate of silver with the date the work began (found later beneath the cornerstone)."[27] The new Courthouse was finished August 23, 1819, the second on this site, and the first Court was held in it. People thought it was a waste to tear down the old one and rebuild. The now famous Red Store was sold this year, too. Its advertisement was in The Palladium of Liberty for Friday, September 21st, which read: "Valuable Property For Sale—Will be offered for sale at public auction on Monday the 25th day of October next; at Fauquier Courthouse, on the premises, the house and Lot belonging to the estate of Septimus Norris dec'd, and long known by the name of the RED STORE LOT, containing one acre. It is intended to sell the same on the Main Street opposite Mr. Tongue's on which is the STORE House, and in which the Court lately sat. . . . Thaddeus Norris, Admr." William B. Cordell was constable for Fauquier County in 1814-1821 as well as having a watch and clock-making shop. In 1820 he advertised that he had removed his shop to a new brick building opposite the residence of William Horner, Esq.[183]

Norris' Tavern   Courthouse   Jail   Palladium   Water's
                                        Office   Tavern

Central View in Warrenton.
C. 1819 (Picture in Old Gaol)

The newspaper was busy with advertisements and notices. How did anyone know what was going on before The Palladium came into being. For example, Friday, March 16, 1821: "Entertainment. Thomson Ashby, having removed to that elegant and commodious brick building just back of the Court House, lately built by Thaddeus Norris tenders his thanks to his friends and the public generally for the liberal encouragement he has received. The House is large and comfortable; with a new stable, which will hold forty horses. Travellers are invited to call, and nothing on his part shall be wanting to give general satisfaction." A notice Friday, May 8th was given about "a NEW JAIL. For this county, or adding to, and repairing the present jail. . . . . . ."

The Court Records, October 22, 1822, had "Kemper & Co. contracted with the jail commission to add 50 x 24 feet on the outside, 2 stories high, each story divided into 2 rooms with 8 foot passageway. The first story outside walls to be 3 feet thick and the building to have no chimney's. The addition to be placed 8 feet from the present jail & enclosed with a stone wall 50 x 50 feet, 25 ft. high and 2 feet thick, well secured on top with iron spikes. The old jail is to be repaired". Completed by 1823, the new jail was built behind the old one with an enclosed courtyard connecting the buildings. Now the stone kitchen was added and the old building used as the residence for the jailor and his family (and would be until 1965), his wife being responsible for feeding the inmates. The Court ordered on June 1, 1824 that a pillory, whipping post and stocks were to be installed at the jail.[28]

The Court levied, June 28, 1825, $715.71 for a new brick addition to the Clerk's Office, 13 x 19 feet, 2 stories high. August 22nd, the Courthouse was open so the General LaFayette Committee could make arrangements for his visit,[28] and next day the town was privileged to see The Marquis de LaFayette. Ex-President James Monroe, Congressman Charles Fenton Mercer and others accompanied him in a procession of open carriages, guarded by a troop of Fauquier Cavalry and infantrymen. People were everywhere along the road as they came from Culpeper. Men called welcome greetings, women and children wearing white threw flowers and kissed his hands.[2] Along Main Street to the Courthouse portico they marched with artillery and the Marine Band from Washington. There must have been 5 or 6,000 people to hear the speeches. Thomas L. Moore, a professional orator, rattled the Courthouse windows with his welcome speech.[14] After the General's brief reply, the party moved on to rooms prepared for refreshments and resting at Mrs. Norris' Tavern. At 4 p.m., the group had dinner on the Tavern lawn where there were toasts and music by the band until after sundown. Then, at 7:30 a reception, lasting until almost 10 p.m. The following day at 9:00 a.m. the General and his company set off.[1] The Carolina Road was just as wild as the Culpeper one had been, as they continued on to Monroe's home in Loudoun County.

The first mention of an election being held was in the Court records March 26, 1826, that was for re-electing a delegate to the General Assembly from Fauquier County. June 26, 1826, there was "Ordered commissions appointed for an addition to the Clerk's Office, do contact for a post and rail enclosure around the public square with as many gates or stiles as may deem necessary." October 23rd, "Court ordered commissioner contact a suitable person to pave so much of Main St. in Town of Warrenton as runs up on and in front of the public square."[28] The road that was Court Lane (Alexandria Turnpike) was completed in 1826. By January 29, 1827 the new road had two stages a week going between Alexandria and Orange Court House.[4] Another newspaper is being published in Warrenton—The Virginia Gazette.[29]

While enroute from "The Hermitage", Nashville, Tenn. to Washington, President Andrew Jackson stopped unheralded at Norris' Tavern. He was the 7th president and was inaugurated March 4, 1829. A Gazette advertisement mentions that October 24th there would be a sale of Negroes in front of Norris' Tavern at public auction. Wonder if there was a 'slave block' there, or was a horse mounting block used.

Late at night wolves might be heard howling in the high mountains, but they, like all creatures were becoming less and less as more people came to live in the county. The Bull Run Mountain may be the last place for the wolf to live on this side of the Blue Ridge. September 28, 1829 the Court allowed a reward of $10 for each wolf and $5 for each young wolf that was killed in the county.[28]

March 30, 1830 the town bought a lot for $200 from William Bell, Trustee and Margaret Glassell, on the corner of Main and No. Second Streets. There, during the fall and winter, a Market House was built. Large trees stood behind it where the carts and wagons parked, which went past me loaded with all sorts of farm products and other items. The upper part of the building was used as a Town Hall.[30] Property at the corner of Main and Culpeper Streets, a part of a larger tract belonging to the Horner family, was sold to John Macre, who built a large brick house and sold it to George Lemmon who was one of the early Rectors of St. James Episcopal Church.[31] The Court of August 27th gave the ladies of Warrenton and its vicinity permission to hold a fair at the Courthouse during the next Warrenton races. The county population is now 12,950 whites and 13,136 Negroes, a total of 26,086.[12] James Caldwell bought land from John A. Cash, which was on Smith Street, near his printshop, and built a home of fieldstone in 1831. (It is now called Walraven House[23] and occupied by his descendant, Michael Welton and family.)[182] Erasmus Helm had purchased land from John Walden and, it seems it was this year, he built a store building at the corner of "Cow Alley" and Main[32] (now North 1st Street). During the fall of 1832, "Old Hickory", President Jackson, again quietly stopped at Norris Tavern as he went through town.

Someone said, July 25, 1833, that a Commission was appointed to build a whipping post, pillory and stocks in the Public Square.[28] But they did that June 8, 1824. Why did they do it again after nine years? I can't remember—was there a mistake of the time? James Caldwell sold his print shop property to Henry V. Pope, [23] and by 1833 it had become The Farmers' Hotel. An advertisement dated September 21, 1833, but in Warrenton's third newspaper, The Independent Register of May 3, 1834 stated, "The subscribers having formed a partnership in keeping the above establishment, beg leave to notify the public that they have instituted a regular system of improvement, both in and out of doors, by which it may be expected that the comfortained convenience of visitors will be much inhanced. They have enlarged the yard immediately about the house, and cleared away much rubbish, so as to remove sources of nuisance and increase the free circulation of air—added to their stables and carried its yard much further from the house.—They mention this because the chief objection to this establishment (that of being too confined) is thus obviated. In other respects they are satisfied their efforts will meet the public wishes. Their bar is good, and their general arrangements for the cooking and table departments are equal to any in the country. They are willing to stand or fall by the fair test of public opinion, which can only be afforded by a due proportion of public patronage.—DUDLEY FITZHUGH and THO. L. FITZHUGH".

Andrew Jackson paid off the National Debt January 18, 1835 by selling off western land. (I think this is the only time we've been out of debt.) A report this year showed how fast Warrenton was growing when it was described as "containing 200 neat and closely built dwelling houses; three houses of public worship, Methodist, Presbyterian and Episcopalian: four primary schools, three taverns, four private boarding houses, two printing offices, each issuing a weekly paper; four wheelwrights, one coach maker, three saddlers, one hatter, two boot and shoe factories, two cabinet makers, five house carpenters, four blacksmith shops, two tailors, two clock and watch makers, three bakers, one tanner and currier, three breweries, one tin plate worker, two milliners, one mantua maker, one house and sign painter, and two plow manufactories. The village had a regular market (built 1830) which was held in a neat little building, the upper part of which was used as a town hall. Population, 1300 of whom three were resident ministers, nine attorneys and eight physicians."[12] At the death of Chief Justice John Marshall, July 27th, the county resolved to cherish his memory.[28]

In 1836 John A. Saunders founded a funeral home on Main Street (to become Sudduth's). William Horner was appointed a commissioner, April 1, 1836, to have a pump placed in a public well in Warrenton. The wooden pumps didn't last long. May 22nd the Court gave permission to the Baptist denomination to preach and hold worship in the Courthouse when it was not being used by the public, and they must keep it clean. The Courthouse was a "mission station", used to preach The Gospel and to see if there was enough interest in the town to begin a church.[182] This year, the William Lakeman Estate was sold to Benjamin R. Wallace.[21] More newspapers in town, as 1836 saw The Jefferson and 1837 had The Warrenton Times. John M. Jacobs, a watchmaker and jeweler, had a shop next door to George E. Yeatman's in 1839.[183]

In the Saturday, September 26, 1840, issue of The Jefferson was a notice concerning the Farmers' Hotel. "Trust Sale Of House & Lot. By Virtue of a deed of trust, executed in the subscriber by Edward E. Cooke and wife, and now on record in the Clerk's Office of Fauquier County Court, I shall sell, on Monday, the 26th of October, before the front door of the Courthouse of Fauquier County, the store-house and lot, adjoining the tavern lot of the Farmers' Hotel, known as Norris' and now in possession of John A. English. Terms will be made known on the day of the sale. Sam'l. Chilton, Trustee". It was also in 1840 that Henry Clay met with a group of his friends and admirers on the east portico of the Warren Green Hotel. They were congratulating and wishing him well as he was again a candidate for the presidency.[26] (Although sure of the nomination, the dream did not come true.)[10] This year Abraham Rindsberg, born 10/01/1809 in Uhlfeld, Bavaria, Germany, began a store in a small building on Main Street (to be torn down later and rebuilt to adjoin the Jeffries Drugstore).[33]

Another newspaper was published for Warrenton in 1842, called The Flag of '98.[29]

It was 1844 that the first organized steeplechase ran at the site of Fauquier White Sulphur Springs.[34] Some people want to move the County Seat to Salem (now Marshall), as they feel the distance is too great to travel to the county seat from such places as Paris and Upperville.[182] A petition had been to the General Assembly in November 1795 and now there was another. Both times it was rejected. The son of James Caldwell, Lycurgus W., was the person who worked the first telegraph May 24, 1844, for Samuel F. P. Morse' message- "what hath God wrought".[1] Joseph H. Watson bought the stock and shop of John M. Jacobs announcing November 1, 1844, that he would continue the clock and watchmaking business as well as having jewelry, silver spoons, etc.[183]

A book published in 1845 said of Warrenton, "A beautiful village in the heart of the County, adorned with shade-trees, standing upon an eminence commanding a fine view of some of the spurs of the Blue Ridge. It contains about a dozen mercantile stores, 1 Episcopal, 1 Presbyterian and 1 Methodist church, a fine male academy where ancient and modern languages are taught, a female academy in excellent repute, a newspaper printing office, the county buildings among which is a handsome court-house, and a population of about 14,000. An excellent macadamized road leads from here to Alexandria".[184] A little different description than it was ten years ago. The house that Benjamin Wallace bought in 1836 was sold to John Smith and William H. Gaines in 1845, being described as a house and lot occupied by Daniel Warner with barber shop.[21] George Lemmon, the owner of the house on the corner of Main and Culpeper Streets, died in 1846. Shortly afterwards, the property was sold to Samuel Chilton.[31]

February 20, 1847 Charles Hutchinson, clock and watchmaker was located on Main Street, opposite Bronough & Fant's Hotel, and one door above the post office.[183] I'm not sure just where those places were. November 20, 1847 the town of Warrenton sold to Charity Lodge 27 of the Odd Fellows, the Market House lot together with the first floor of the brick building for $856. The Masons and

Odd Fellows then used the second floor together. This year Joseph H. Watson bought the lot and house on Main Street "running to the centre of the alley between the silversmith shop now occupied by said Watson and a saddleryshop."[183] The brick church on Alexandria Pike was built about 1848.[1]

The Methodist Episcopal Church continued to have problems over issues, which by 1849 caused a separation and two Methodist churches resulted. In 1849 land was given by Richard M. Smith for a building site on the corner of Lee and Culpeper Streets and August 13th the Warrenton Methodist Church South bought the adjoining lot from Smith. He had purchased the Norris' Tavern property from the heirs of Thaddeus Norris and had a school for boys there, called the Warren Green Academy. The building the church built (later The Wallach Building) had the sanctuary on the second floor with Sunday School rooms below.[24] The Gazette, January 13, 1823 had a notice that Miss Mariah A. Kemper opened a school in Warrenton for ladies.[1] Wonder if she was related to Miss Eliza Kemper who sold her home on Culpeper Street, across from the Methodist Church, to them for a parsonage.[16]

I heard two versions as to why or how the Baptist came to Warrenton. The first was that on August 11, 1849, seventeen members were dismissed from the Broad Run Church near New Baltimore. They later built a church here.[35] The second reason was that nine white and six colored members separated themselves from the Broad Run Church for the stated purpose to organize a church in Warrenton. August 27, 1849 they had their official meeting with twelve members present, in "Miss Swift's School Room", located in the Odd Fellows Hall.[36] November 22, 1849 the Episcopalians sold out their share of the church to the Presbyterians for $150 as they wanted to build their own.[99] Perhaps at this time they also sold the frame church on Alexandria Pike and bought the land on Culpeper Street.[98] By 1849 three more newspapers were being published in town, which are the Warrenton Republican, the Warrenton Whig, and The Piedmont Whig.[29]

In 1850 a tornado destroyed the Warren Academy and the Presbyterian Brick Church.[38] Only the pulpit with the Bible remaining on it was left. Land at the corner of North 3rd and Main Streets was bought from Inman Horner (but the deed was not recorded until May 18, 1893).[99] The Warren Green was returned to its former state this year,[26] when Richard Smith discontinued the Academy and sold the property to Becham & Payne. A small group calling themselves the Methodist Episcopal Church North bought the site across North 3rd Street from the Presbyterians. The contract signed July 20, 1850 stated they would, "build a stone and brick work, a house of worship . . ., the dimensions . . . to wit: fifty-five feet long, 40 feet wide and 23 feet in pitch, the front and gable ends to be built according to a plan . . . (to be) completed by the 15th of September, and also that the front wall of said house shall be built of brick similar and equal to the front of the Baptist Church in Warrenton. . ."[24]

Part of a map in Deed Book 55 - Pages 449-455 - March 11, 1850 Warrenton extended its boundaries, so was remapped. Beyond the town limits Winchester Street is called Winchester Road and it turned east at the foot of the hill. Jail Street beyond the limits is Chester Gap Road, Court Lane is Alexandria Turnpike the change being at Horner Street. Main Street turned off at East Street and Falmouth continued on.

When the main line of the Orange & Alexandria Railway (Southern) was laid out, it was not wanted here, so was re-routed and only the branch came to Warrenton.[39] The Warrenton, Calverton and Washington line was built in 1851 and a small place down the line was named Three Mile Switch (later Melrose, then Casanova).[40] Construction may have begun 1851, being completed 1853.[182]

April 9, 1852 the Town Council amended the Town Charter and By-Laws of the Cooperation of Warrenton. The Council met in Mayor James V. Brooke's office Monday, May 3rd. They ordered three dozen fire buckets to be placed around town in convenient places, and had a patrol or fire guard on duty at night.[41] John R. Spilman was the Fire Chief. Merchants were ordered to store their powder in a place of safe keeping. The many water pumps over town were to be examined and repaired if necessary. The next week, Monday, May 10th, William A. Pattie was appointed Commissioner for the pump on Winchester Street near Joseph Horner. Ladders made for the use of the town, were stored in the Public Square and William A. Pattie was to see that they were protected from the weather. A Committee was appointed to examine the condition of the house near the Public Square which belonged to the estate of William Waters. June 9th they reported the Waters' house as in danger of falling down and being a nuisance. Such a lovely old place it was once with its double front porch.

Plans were made for people to vote in a poll at the Courthouse regarding the Sperryville and Rappahannock Turnpike Co. The question concerned the willingness to leave the route of the road the same if it joined with the Warrenton & Springs Turnpike. The point of the junction should not be further from the town than 200 yards beyond Kettle Run.

Wednesday, June 23, 1852, and again on August 21st the Council met at the Courthouse. $4000 was set aside for the Sperryville & Rappahannock Turnpike to extend the road, which was 18 feet in width and at least 9 inches in depth through the corporate limits along said street, through Public Lot, to its intersection with Main Street. Then it was to go down Main Street to intersect with South 4th, along that street to its intersection with Lee Street, then up Lee to South 6th or Culpeper Street so it could go in either direction. June 17th the Council decided to sell the Waters' house to Dr. Ambrose Hord for $28.56¼, but he must not have settled because on Wednesday, November 17th an order was given to clean up the Waters' lot and Joseph Horner was to remove the chimney and any other material that was part of the building. With the train coming to town now, Wednesday, December 22nd the Council spent $25.00 to make a sidewalk of plank and ties from the railroad depot to a suitable point on Culpeper. A. Rindsberg built and moved into a store at the corner of So. 5th & Lee Streets.[159]

January 19, 1853 the Town Council meeting in the Municipal Building discussed the Waterloo-Warrenton Road crossing Watery Mountain. May 23rd disaster struck the Town! The Courthouse was destroyed by fire reported to have been 'the wanton act of an incendiary'. Nothing of the $18,000 building was left standing but a portion of the walls.[11] Thursday, May 6th the Town Council selected someone to act as a night watch or patrol to be on duty every night from 10 o'clock until after daylight, to be paid $1.00 a night. It was decided June 25th to widen the street from Main to the depot at a cost of $150. But, which street was that? So. Fifth Street (now 3rd) was the most direct going there. I also can't remember where Dudley M. Pattie's shop was. He was allowed to put a platform in front of it with side steps, but they were not to be more than 3½ feet wide. During 1853 the brick Episcopal Church was consecrated.[98]

In August 1853 the Court sessions were held in the basement of the Methodist Episcopal Church South on Culpeper Street.[11] September 7th the drain from the Warren Green towards Henry Fants to Lee Street had to be repaired so as not to be a nuisance. October 25th found the Council planning to have a crossing made from the corner near—was it Waterman's?—store to the House known as "Five Points". This house sat almost opposite the Courthouse with Court Lane going on one side of it and an alley between it and W. A. Pattie's store. It was planned, December 12th, to pave South 2nd Street from Lee to the Railroad depot. It was to be 16 feet wide 9 inches deep.

1854 was a busy year. Miss Harriet Swift continued with her girl's school on the lower floor of the Odd Fellows' Hall.[42] At the corner of Main and No. 3rd Streets (now 4th St.) the Northern Methodist built their Church on the lot that was bought about six years ago.[11] Stores along Main Street included Ruel H. Ross' bakery and grocery store. A Mr. Pipenbring also had a bakery with residence above and ovens in the basement. Trees in front of the bakery and along Main Street had metal cages about them for protection and were used to tether horses. There was a mounting block in front of the bakers and its windows were barred.[43] On the corner of Main and Culpeper was located the firm of Latham & Green,[44] or was it now?

Wednesday, January 1854, the Town Council planned to have the crossing near the Clerk's Office at the head of Culpeper Street repaired. They also discussed the Orange-Alexandria Railroad Co. By Monday, April 24th, meeting, John Q. Marr was Mayor. May 17th meeting was held in the Sergeant's Office. The cleaning and repairing of wells was discussed and the wooden pumps were still being used in town. At a meeting held July 19th, the Council planned to examine the house on Winchester that belonged to Mrs. Catherine Waters and if it was a public nuisance, to have it removed. The next day, July 20th, they levied $200 for the Town Clock to be placed in the tower of the Courthouse, now being erected on the previous ones' foundation. It was being patterned after the Parthenon, the marble temple of Athens, Greece. Actually, the clock cost $400, but the town paid half and the county half. It won't be installed until next year. Again August 16th, the Council met at the Sergeant's Office. It was reported that the Waters' house was sold for $11 at public auction and it is to be removed. It was valued at $20.00. The Committee on Streets was advised October 19th to contract for repairs of the street leading from Culpeper Street to the Depot and that they make such disposition of the loose stones lying near the "Five Points" as shall to them appear best. The annual value of the "Waters' Hotel" (torn down 1852) lot at the corner of Jail Street and The Square was fixed at $70.00.

In 1854 there were two small tenements that set back on the corner of Court Lane and Main Street; about the center of that block on Main Street was Elkon Lyon's General Store; S. M. Voss lived above the Beckham & Voss store in the building thought to have been built in or before 1847, by Erasmus Helm (later Kloman-Jeffries Building); and, Helm continued to live in the one he built in 1831 (to be the Hilleary Building). Across the street was the general store of Madison J. Follin (later Anderson & Allison), who lives above the store. Inman Horner's home, office and stables at the north corner of Winchester and Diagonal Streets had two small tenements next to it on the site of the Doram homes. Thomas R. Lunceford's store was across the street. William S. Clark dwelt on the northeast corner (Winchester and Court Lane) and had a livery stable in the rear, opposite the Horner's vacant lot.[45]

The Presbyterians began building their church on Main Street in 1855 at a cost of $4,901, the other one being destroyed in a tornado five years ago. The Reverend William Wall was pastor at the time.[46] The house belonging to Catherine Waters that was sold and pulled down under orders from the Council last year is again in the news. February 21, 1855, they ordered that she be allowed $25.00 for it. That was more than its value. April 30th saw Charles T. Green as acting Mayor and then Edward M. Spilman took over as Mayor. September 5th Cyrus Cross was appointed to wind, regulate and keep in order the Courthouse clock, commencing the first of November. He is to receive $12.50 per year for this. Many new laws put on record September 26th. It would now be unlawful to fire any gun, pistol or firearm in the corporation limits, to make unnecessary noise, cursing, swearing, etc., to ride or drive at any speed other than ordinary pace or trot or on the side pavement, to injury a pump, hay scales, or public burying ground, to keep dead animals on lots in town and so forth, as well as for misdemeanors committed by slaves they would be "punished with stripes".[47] From all that you'd think we were quite a rowdy town! A will dated, 1849 concerned the house John Smith and William H. Gaines bought in 1845. But it was the will of William Henry Smith and James C. Smith, leaving the property to a William Smith for Mary Amelia Smith stating that they were about to embark upon a dangerous and hazardous journey—supposedly to the California Gold Rush—. The William Smith is thought to have been Gov. William Smith locally known as "Extra Billy". However, one of the brothers did not return and his money was used to build, about now, a three story brick residence, giving it the name, California Building.[21]

During December 1856, someone began a rumor, as it turned out, that the slaves would revolt on Christmas Day, so the Town Council appointed some men to be night-watchers. Since all had been quiet over both holidays these special policemen were dismissed shortly after the coming of the New Year.[158]

One of the important things to happen in 1857 was the erection of a three story, 12,000 square foot building as a girl's boarding school, called Fauquier Female Institute, located on Lee Street.[48] December 16, the Town Council meeting had a decision to fill up the drain at the intersection of Beckham and South 5th Streets near the Depot and to McAdamize the same for $25.00. Both things were a little away from The Square, but would have their effects.

During 1858 the Town Council continued to approve work on several streets. The property at the corner of Main and Culpeper

Streets was sold this year to Berkeley Ward, to be held in trust for the two Ward daughters, Mary Anne and Grace, and rented as a residence.[31]

Poor Mr. Smith A. Jeffries approached the Town Council on March 11, 1859 with his problem. He had a horse to become mired in mud on South 5th Street in February and the horse died as the result. He asked the town to pay him $15.00 to cover the loss, which they did. Charles Bragg was elected Mayor in a poll taken in the Courthouse basement, April 29th. President John Adams had appointed John Marshall as 3rd Chief Justice of the United States January 20, 1801. When the 1854 Courthouse was built, space was left for a large portrait of Marshall because at the age of 25 he had been admitted to practice law at the Fauquier County Bar August 28, 1780. The painting, executed by William D. Washington, was ready June 27, 1859.[49]

The Methodist Episcopal Church, North, received financial aid from the national headquarters, but they did not do well at all. In an 1859 sermon, a minister said the church "might as well be turned into a dance hall."[24] Is this a prediction?

An advertisement dated October 4, 1860, was still appearing in Thursday, June 27, 1861 Warrenton Flag of '98, describing The Farmers' Hotel. "The subscriber having leased and taken possession of the above named Hotel, respectfully solicits a liberal share of the traveling customers. It is his determination to have the House thoroughly cleansed, refitted and well furnished, and he will at all times be happy to accommodate his old friends and acquaintances of this and Rappahannock counties, as well as the public generally, with clean, comfortable beds and the best market will afford, on most reasonable terms. The rooms will be kept clean; the Table bountifully supplied, and the STABLE under the management of an experienced and trusty ostler. The BAR will be supplied with the best of liquors.

It is the intention of the subscriber to keep an orderly, well conducted house, and to charge only moderate prices, so that all persons traveling or coming to the Court-house, may find a comfortable hotel with a good fare, without having to pay the exorbitant prices now generally charged.

Persons registering at the Hotel will only be charged with what they are furnished.

Drovers, and witnesses attending court, will be charged moderate price, and Jurors, for themselves and horse will in no case be charged more than the compensation allowed them.

The subscriber respectfully solicits the public patronage, confident from past experience, that he can keep a house to suit the people and the times, and assuring all who may be inclined to stop with him satisfaction in every respect or no charge whatever will be made. ALBERT R. SINGLETON"

Another article in the same paper gave the rates for the Warren Green Hotel . . . Board per month $25.00
Board by the week $8.00
Board by the day $1.50
Single meals 50¢

The first Catholic Church was built on Lee Street this year,[50] 1860.

In 1861, Warrenton prepared to fight for the Southern Cause in the Civil War. Eleven Companies were formed in Fauquier County with a strength of 1100 men.[51] Robert Eden Scott, who was too old for military service, organized and equipped a company of infantry called The Warrenton Rifles.[52] The Black Horse Troops organized and aligned themselves on the street facing the Warren Green as they prepared to leave for battle.[26] All those black horses and the riders with a black plumb in their hats looked rather pretty.

John Quincy Marr, Captain in the Warrenton Rifles was killed at Fairfax Court House, May 31, 1861, being the first Southerner to die. His father John Marr had built a home in 1830 on Culpeper Road (now #342). When news of his death reached Warrenton, the Confederate flag was lowered to half-staff. His remains reached town Saturday evening, June 1st, between 6 and 7 o'clock, being met and escorted into town by the Lee Guard and a great number of sadden citizens. Sunday afternoon at 5 o'clock, after a service to his memory by Rev. O. S. Barten in the Clerk's Office yard, with about 1500 people there, he was buried in full dress uniform, with the honors of war, in the town cemetery.[51] With battles so close and armies on the march, people were afraid the Marshall painting might be damaged. It was cut from its frame and sent to Chicago to be kept in a vault until The War ends.[49] But, did I hear someone say it went to Cincinnati to the Kemper family residing there, for safe keeping with them?[182]

The First Battle of Bull Run or Manassas was July 21, 1861. I heard it said that the Federals almost were victorious until late in the day. Then Confederate reinforcements routed the Union Army and won this first important engagement of the Civil War.[10] August 2, 1861 the Town Council ordered that the school room of Mr. Lindsay which was the Town Hall, be, with his consent, appropriated for the wounded and sick soldiers. Also, churches, Bakers, Bechaur & Voss' Store, the Courthouse, depots 1 & 2, Odd Fellows Hall, Rindsberg's Store, and White & Smith's Store at the corner of Culpeper and Main Streets were used.[53]

1862

On January first of each year both the Negroes and the white people would meet in Warrenton to settle accounts of the past year and to make arrangements for the new one. It was called the "hiring day". On this date in 1862, President Lincoln proclaimed that all Negroes shall be free.[51] The Confederates retreated from Centerville early in the spring of this year and the Union Army came into Fauquier.[51] The Town Council met May 1st, but did not enter notes in their Minute Book. August 25th, The Springs was the scene of a battle for the bridge across the Rappahannock River. Either then or a few days later, the two large hotels were burned to the ground.[5] I'm not sure when, but during a Battle of Bull Run, a railway engine was taken off the tracks at Warrenton station, hauled overland to Salem (Marshall) and used on the Manassas Branch.[39] Now that was quite a feat, with all the gruntin' and groanin' and crackin' of whips! Troops and supplies were always traveling on 'the cars' as the railroads were called. August 30th became the day of the Second Battle of Bull Run or Manassas. From August 16 to September 2nd the Confederates had 9,100 casualties,[10] many of them brought to Warrenton. What a busy time! What a sad time! The buildings that had been planned for, as well as private homes, were filled with wounded and dying. Every woman became a nurse. The many who died, mostly from South Carolina and Georgia, were buried in the town cemetery. A small wooden cross with the person's name marked each grave.[51]

Pictures were being taken of the town, some by Matthew B. Brady, the official military photographer for the Federal Government.[10] A picture of Alexandria Pike looking up the hill towards the Courthouse, called it the dirt road that was a major highway between Washington and Warrenton having a large flow of traffic and trade traveling to the busy crossroads. Another picture shows an 1863 scene with the Clerk's Office to the left of the Courthouse, and a two

ALEXANDRIA PIKE IN 1862.
T.A. O'Sullivan, a free lance photographer, took this picture during the Civil War looking up Alexandria Pike toward the Fauquier County Courthouse. There is a covered wagon in front of the courthouse.
(–Library of Congress Collection)

FAUQUIER COUNTY COURTHOUSE – 1863
U. S. Military History Institute   Timothy H. O'Sullivan, August, 1862

**McCLELLAN'S FAREWELL TO HIS OFFICERS
AT WARRENTON, VA. — 1862**
(From collection of John K. Gott)

story brick building to the right and across the street. Could this have been the George Booth home?[64] General Ambrose Burnside had headquarters at the Warren Green at one time. General George B. McClellan gave his farewell speech to the troops from the front porch of that hotel, on November 2nd, as he was removed from Command of the Army of the Potomac on November 11th.[26] While the Union soldiers, The Ninth Regiment of New York Militia, occupied Warrenton, they took over the presses of The Warrenton Whig and printed their own newspaper called The New York Ninth.[29] An issue for July 31, 1862, said, "our opinion of Warrenton is that it is one of the prettiest towns we have seen. . . Pleasantly situated on a high ridge with views on every side of surpassing loveliness. It is . . healthy and in every way desirable as a place of residence. It has 2000 inhabitants. A Courthouse is very finely situated at the terminus of the Warrenton & Alexandria turnpike . . . wish their reception by the inhabitants had been more cordial. We consider ourselves fortunate in our present quarters. Maj. Gen. Pope, Commanding to Army of Virginia, arrived last evening and has taken quarters at the Female Seminary building of Dr. Bason on Lee Street." The price of the paper was 3¢.[54]

I suppose it is like everything else. There is always good and bad. As the article said, most of the inhabitants stayed away from the Union forces, some though, with businesses had to attend them. Many times the Union soldiers or officers were kind and considerate of the citizens and there were stories of friendliness on both sides. All churches were used as hospitals except the Episcopal whose structure was not suitable, so all denominations met there for worship. The Baptist church was destroyed by the Union troops.[51] The Presbyterian sanctuary was used as a hospital by Federal Troops with the basement being a stable. A large hole was cut in the floor above so food could be thrown down to the horses. The pulpit and benches were burnt for firewood and the steeple was a lookout post.[99] With so many men gone the women didn't go out by themselves unless forced into it. They had to work the land if it was done. There were questions, too, as what to eat for the soldiers on both sides needed food—not just the extra, but what the people themselves needed.

WARRENTON, VIRGINIA,
LATELY OCCUPIED BY THE ARMY OF VIRGINIA.
Sketched by Mr. Davenport
(Picture in Old Gaol)

Although the majority of people joined the Confederacy without question, some did go with the Union, either openly or in secret. Colonel John Mosby and his men had hit and run tactics against the Yankees and many times someone told where they were staying. One story was told about the ride of Roberta or "Bert" Pollock, a first cousin of General Lee and quite a horsewoman who lived at Leeton Forest just outside of Warrenton on The Springs Road. She was in town one winter evening when she overheard a Negro telling Union soldiers where they could find Mosby hiding near Marshall. She immediately mounted her horse, rushing off to warn the Confederates. Only a servant was with her as they went across View Tree Mountain, over a spur of Wildcat Mountain, getting lost a couple times and was almost shot when seen by one of Mosby's pickets. During this time Janet Weaver, a young girl, (later Mrs. Norman V. Randolph) lived in the house that had been built by Horner in 1819 at the corner of Diagonal and Winchester Streets. She and her sister would lie awake at night listening to horsemen riding along the road under their window. If the clank of sabers or other military equipment was heard, they knew it was Union soldiers. If they heard only the foot falls of a carefully guided horse, they knew it was their own men. Even though they could be arrested for helping the southern cause, people did it.[51] In the still of the night, intrigue went on around me. No one would know what would happen next.

1 8 6 3

Now came a terrible winter. The Yankees occupying Warrenton needed wood to burn and since the crosses in the cemetery were convenient, they were used for firewood. That left all those graves nameless. The train engines burned coal as long as they had it, but when that ran out anything along the tracks made of wood was used. In January 1863, Stuart marched through Warrenton on his way towards the Rappahannock. Stoneman was camped near town for a while.[55] April 5th, Easter Sunday, had 9 to 10 inches of snow with a temperature of 31 degrees. It stopped about noon, with some melting by night. But there were no buds on the trees and no planting had been done. It was the "dreariest, coldest, wettest, saddest winter followed by the latest spring within the memory of man," someone said. Even on May 1st, people still wore winter clothes, gardens were not cleaned, trees still did not have many leaves and, of course, the corn wasn't in nor much grass to be ready for hay.[51] Some wondered if it were a punishment for their actions. Was the Almighty unhappy with the country? The Warrenton Baptist Church minutes had nothing written in them from January 23, 1862 until February 1863 when they met. It was then recorded that the country was "invaded by an invading Army of Northern Fannactics". July 26, 1863 Meade's headquarters were in Warrenton.[12]

1864-1866

All during the months of 1864 and 1865 people fought even though they were hungry, cold or perhaps homeless. For four years the armies marched across Fauquier again and again. Fences, buildings, crops, and livestock were destroyed.[51] The Town Council met on September 30, 1864, but recorded no minutes. November 14, there was a meeting of citizens requesting the Cooperation to make some immediate arrangement for the relief of the suffering poor of the town during the coming winter. A meeting December 5th again left no notes. After the 1850 tornado the Warren Academy had been rebuilt, but it was destroyed by Federal soldiers in 1865.[38] Again the Council left no record of their meeting April 4, 1865. Then came the fateful day, April 9th, when General Robert E. Lee surrendered to General Ulysses S. Grant at Appomattox Court House. People walked past me with their heads down and hearts heavy. They felt that never again would Fauquier be as green or lovely as it once was. But this was the spring season of new life and so people picked themselves up and began again. Another Town Council meeting was held July 31, 1865 without being recorded. However, August 23rd it was "ordered that the mayor inform the proper military commandant at this Post that an election has been held for corporation officers under order from Gov. Peirpoint; and that said officers were anxious to restore municipal law; etc." September 5th a report was given of the Mayor and Mr. Brooke's visit to the Provost Marshall. They "were taken to the quarters of Col. Commanding the Federal Forces at this Post; they assured the Mayor that the military was here to aid the civil authorities to restore law and maintain order; and that they would cheerfully guard civilian prisoners, or render other needful assistance if requested to do so- and if all that transpired he was persuaded no conflict would arise between the Municipal and Military authorities, if the police ordinance touching negroes was modified so as to conform to the laws both State and Federal under which we do now live."

January 4, 1866 found the Town Council busy. One law they passed said the snow must be removed from pavement in front of people's residence and business within 24 hours. Some of them didn't like that. A meeting March 16th recorded an incident of the night before. Stones were thrown into the room occupied by Miss Fannie Wood as a school room and where she was at the time, conducting her school for freedmen. The persons are to be punished and if necessary she may request protection. Her school was named after

John Greenleaf Whittier.[158] This is really something quite new for before the Civil War, the education of colored people was prohibited. No wonder some were upset.[175]

At the April 4th, 1866, meeting the Council accepted the proposition of C. A. Tavenner who offers to donate that part of his lot lying parallel with Culpeper St. and running from the corner of the M. E. Church South to the corner of the street leading to the front of his hotel and the California House to have built on said street a brick or stone wall high enough to keep the dirt from his yard washing onto the street pavement. It said Mr. Tavenner's hotel. Now when did he acquire the Warren Green? Flagstone was provided July 25th, for the pavement to be laid between the Clerk's Office and White & Smith's Store at the mouth of Culpeper Street.

1867-1869

During the Reconstruction era, newspapers returned. The Palladium of Liberty became known as The True Index.[29] People were still getting back on their feet in 1867—trying to be normal again. Sometimes one wonders what normal really is. June 22nd, 1867, the Town Council minutes report that after "consultation with Lieut. Chase, Military Commandant at this place, the following proceedings were adopted." All voters were to register, and 6 special police were to be hired to help the regular municipal authorities. It will be unlawful on Monday next, the 24th, which is Court Day, for a bar to be open or to have drinks sold. No weapons will be allowed to be carried, either.

May 30, 1868 Decoration Day (Memorial Day) was originated. May is "the season of smells", not only from all the blooming flowers, but also the soil—as gardens and fields have their freshly turned earth. During 1867 and 1868, The Market House at Main and No. 2nd Streets had a school for boys, taught by Dr. Winter Payne. The First Baptist Church was founded this year.[56]

B. M. Campbell was mentioned as Mayor in the April 12, 1869 Town Council minutes. Dogs were having their problems, the "Dog Days" of August seeming to be true, for to cut down on rabies, on April 22nd, a law was passed requiring all dogs to wear a muzzle during the month of August. Also there was a dollar tax on all dogs and spayed sluts, with $2.00 on all sluts not spayed. Things were improving street-wise for on September 20th, it was planned to extend the pavement on Main Street in front of Dr. G. R. Horner's store house and continue the same from the corner of said Horner's lot across Alexandria Street and connect with the pavement running in front of W. A. Pattie's store house, which had been mentioned in 1786. The crossing is to be 4 feet wide with heavy curbs and paving stones to be not less than 5-6 inches thick and laid in sand. The Northern Methodist Church, at Main and No. 3rd, in which services had been held since 1854, had a deed of trust closed on it. William H. Gaines bought the property.[11]

1870

April 9, 1870 the Town Council minutes recorded R. Taylor Scott as Mayor. The First Court of the county held with a judge was April 25th, the judge being Thomas Smith. Before this Justices had presided at the courts.[57] The minutes for June 30th reported John B. Withers as Mayor. It was October 1st that the Mayor presented no report upon the purchase of the 5 Points. The facts having been made known of a sale of the said 5 Points to H. C. Yates the Council directs H. Sheppard to wait on H. C. Yates and see upon what terms he will sell the same and to report back. But, on October 5th Mr. Sheppard was not present. It appeared though that Mr. Yates intends to begin building a house on said lot. The Council thought best to notify the intention of the council, which said, "It being the opinion of the Council that the lot of Sand within the corporation, belonging to H. C. Yates and known as the Five Points is needed for the purpose of said corporation, it is hereby ordered that with a view to the condemnation of the said Sand the Mayor of the Corporation to apply to the County Court of Fauquier Co. at its next term to appoint five disinterested freeholders for the purpose of ascertaining a fair compensation for Such Sand and said Mayor is further ordered to cause at least ten days previous notice of such application to be given to Said H. C. Yates." Oh, Boy! all that legal talk.

Another sad day. At a meeting October 13th, it was reported that General Robert E. Lee died at 9:00 Wednesday, October 12th, at his home in Lexington, and a decision made for the Community to close all places of business from 1:00 this day until the next morning. Also the bells of the town tolled from 1-2:00. The Council ordered on October 15th that H. C. Yates be permitted to put a flat cellar door in front of his House now under construction on Winchester Street, so as not to obstruct the passway. October 31st a proposition was made for the purchase, by the Corporation of Warrenton, of the property known as the Methodist Church on Main

Street, and recently purchased by W. H. Gaines; for the purpose of a Town Hall, and it being reported that Gaines is willing to sell the property to the Corporation at the price of $2250. Another problem to be solved came before the Council November 19th. The Pump Committee was requested to study and report back as to the best method of protecting the pumps against the abuse of watering horses around them.

1871

A Committee was requested February 4, 1871 to examine the old Methodist E. Church recently purchased by the Council and to report back as soon as possible. The True Index ran an advertisement April 22nd for A. M. Brodie, Tailor on Main Street, whose business sign hung on a building (later G. A. Vose's Store).[20] That building was built about 1856 by John G. Beckham, the contractor who rebuilt the Courthouse in 1855. At the corner of Main and Culpeper Streets the building was valued on the tax books in 1871 at $4,500, the highest valuation of any property in town. White & Smith were still there.[58] Free public education began in Fauquier County this year when the first free school was opened, being located in what had been the Episcopal Church building of 1816 on Alexandria Street.[38]

May 6th, 1871, the Town Council had the Sergeant see about the lamp at H. C. Yates' place and put it in order. It had been broken this week by "Rowdies". The treasurer is to pay the bill. Repairs to the new Town Hall May 31st, included the sealing of the room, erecting a stage, repair of windows and doors so the place would be in a condition to be used by the Town Council and also to rent whenever an occasion presents itself. A law on June 10th said that no hog or pig-pens or hogs to be raised within 100 yards of the following streets- Main, Culpeper, Winchester, Jail, Lee, South 5th, 4th, and 3rd. But it was decided June 24th that because so many people rely on next year's supply of meat from the ones raised, and also they sell many, the law will not begin until January 1872, but the pens must be scraped and swept daily. Horner Street was now added to the list. 600 tons of White Flint Rock, called Pavement, was ordered July 17th. The California House was mentioned, August 26th because they had to help pay for the stone laid near them. December 1st a bill was presented by the Sergeant for killing and burying Dogs and Cats and for the labor performed. It was $85.38. Guess there were a lot of unwanted animals around.

1872

A survey was ordered April 13, 1872 to see what had to be done and what cost would be to supply the town with water. Fire extinguishers had been bought by the new Hook & Ladder Company, and on April 20th they were tried out on the Public Square, a large fire of combustible material having been made. When the fire was burning brightly, they were demonstrated and found to be just the thing to put out fires. It was decided that two be left in the Mayor's office and the remaining five be given to "good and responsible men in different parts of town" and that the town provide 35 charges of the chemicals with the extinguishers. The seven of them cost $250. Volunteers are wanted for the Hook & Ladder Company of Warrenton that is to be formed soon. This will be the first of its kind here, and John R. Spilman was appointed to be the Fire Chief. On April 27th the Council planned to buy a 4-wheel truck with ladders and Buckets, this being "the proper equipment". May 11th, they paid $850 for the truck and other things.

Well! it seems as though someone decided to help the Sergeant with the dog problem. Only this wasn't a very good idea. On June 8th, 1872, there was a $25 reward for the apprehension of the person or persons who distributed poison in private lots and on public streets, and as someone said, "this is a great annoyance to some of the dog owners." Children, too, could find some of the poison. Wonder if that is thought of when it is put out. July 6th found John H. Rixey the Mayor. The Council recommended a Health Officer for the town and Dr. John Ward was appointed. More laws were put into effect July 20th. It is now unlawful to fire off a gun, pistol or other firearm in the town limits unless it is on ones own lot and then only to kill something deemed a nuisance or for protection, or for slaughter or with a written permission. Plans were being made August 17th to repair Alexandria Turnpike. November 20th an election was held in the basement of the Courthouse. The free school moved from the Episcopal building to the old Methodist Church or new Town Hall.[38] The Town Council made plans December 4th to purchase Academy Hill lot and erect a school house on it. The lot was bought December 18th for $600. Plans were for a free public school building of four rooms to be built.

1873

The Town Council on January 8, 1873 prohibited the sale of Intoxicating Liquor on the Sabbath within the Town limits.

The True Index ran an ad for the Farmers' Hotel February 22nd, 1873 for "Jas. H. Maddux, Proprietor. . . . I have to inform my friends and the traveling public that I have leased the above hotel lately occupied by Mr. Hutton and formerly by Thornton Withers. It has lately been fitted and rendered more attractive than it ever was. Everything that a landlord can contribute towards the accommodation and comfort of guests shall be found there—the best fare, the best chambers and the most polite attention. My stables for the care of horses, are ample and supplied with grain, hay and reliable hostiers." Also an interesting notice was in the same paper. "The Washington D.C. Masonic choir, composed of accomplished musicians, have kindly volunteered to give a grand concert in Warrenton at the Town Hall on the 1st day of next March Court at 7½pm, the proceeds of which will be handed over to the benefit of the Order in this place."

Concern was felt for those 600 graves without their wooden crosses, now being nameless. March 19th, the Town Council had a Memorial from the Ladies of "The Fauquier Memorial Association" asking aid from the Council in order to remove the remains of the Confederate Dead from the cemetery to a point in the Public Square where they propose erecting a "monument". Plans were also discussed this date of providing a cistern on the Public Lot, and to clean up the burnt part of Town, repairing the pavement on Main Street at the site of the burnt Hotel. Now what hotel was that and where on Main Street was it—near the drug of E. F. Kloman? He was advertising in the True Index February 22nd that he had a town lot for sale, fronting 25 feet on Main Street, and having the largest most productive garden on that square. The building had been mostly destroyed by fire.

April 2, 1873 the Council, feeling it was unwise to disturb the dead, decided to let the ladies make the decision on the Square or the Cemetery for the Monument. An advertisement in the True Index, May 3rd, was for fresh garden seed at Stephens & Jeffries, Druggist, in the building built by Erasmus Helm in 1847. Joseph Arthur Jeffries had returned from the Confederate Army in 1865 and become partners with Dr. J. H. Stephens. The building became known as the Stephens Building.[59]

The Warrenton Hook & Ladder Company was getting off to a good start. Alderman Spilman reported to the Council, May 22nd that it had been organized and the truck and fixtures were to be turned over to them. May 30th it was resolved that the County would allow the privilege of keeping the Town Truck, Ladders and other fire equipment under the Front Portico of the Courthouse, and also allow Doors instead of gates to be placed in the arches, to allow the Fence to be moved so as to leave the archway or the west side, out in the street and that the Fire Co. be allowed to use the Basement for their meetings and that a rope be attached to the fire alarm in the Steeple—the bell—and extend down so as to be rung from the basement or under the front porch. Pictures during the Civil War do not show a fence. June 4th, Charles T. Green was Mayor of the Council that approved a solid door to be made in the archway of the Courthouse and the fence was removed so the truck could be carried out, and also timber was to be laid on the floor of the archway so it would be easier to run the truck in and out.

$210.00 was approved by the Council July 2, 1873 for the purchase of musical instruments for the Warrenton Riflemen of 22 April 1860. I thought they were organized in 1861. It was in July that Erasmus Helm sold his store building on the corner of Main and "Cow Alley", to William Perry Hilleary, thereafter giving it the name of Hilleary Building.[32] The Steeplechase which had been interrupted by the Civil War, but had become an annual fixture almost immediately afterwards, was described this year as one of the nations most thrilling sport.[34] November 12th, the owners of the lots in the burnt district facing onto Main Street, were to fence in those lots on line with the street. People with cellar windows opening on the sidewalks of town were to cover them with a grating or other "cover of a substantial character". With Christmas coming, the Saturday, December 20th meeting the Council decided from now on it will be unlawful to explode on the public street any firearm or other instrument charged with "explosure compound and fire crackers, cannon crackers, Roman Candles, Rocketts or such like mechanical" device. A $1 or $5 fine will be given. The exception to this ordinance was during Christmas Day until 10pm, upon New Year's Day until 10pm, and upon February 22nd and July 4th until 10pm. All persons, especially boys, shall have liberty to set off upon the public streets, fire-crackers, Cannon crackers and such but not what are known as fire-balls. It was the custom from one of the "old countries" to fire guns on Christmas from the front door. Some people still think of Christmas celebrations as being strictly pagan. Also at this meeting the Sperryville and Rappahannock Turnpike was mentioned.

1874

The Town Council minutes for June 19, 1874 gave an Ordinance to prevent the Destruction of Birds. From now on it will not be lawful for any person to hunt, shoot, catch, trap, or otherwise to cause the death of Mocking Birds, Sparrows, Blue Birds, Wrens, Robins, Martins, or any other inseasonal bird or to rob their nests of eggs or younglings. These birds were used for food, especially in pies or dumpling stews. Robin pie was a real delicacy. Anyone guilty of this misdemeanor was fined not less than one nor more than five dollars for each offense. They could even pay a fine and Court costs and be committed to the County Jail for 10 to 30 days. July 10th the Council made it unlawful to throw stones or other missels by means of a sling, gum spring, or in any other manner at any person, Bird, or thing with the intent to kill, mame, injure, or deface the same within the Corporation limits. More excitement and destruction in town. The Warren Green was destroyed by fire in November of 1874.[26] The sycamore tree at the corner of Hotel and Culpeper Streets was partially burned, but left to see if it would grow again.[8]

1875

In January 1875 the Town Council ordered a plank walk to have a stone crossing at the intersection of Horner and No. First Streets. Sidewalks were mostly plank and stepping stones used to cross the streets, being spaced so wagon wheels had no trouble going between them. The March 6th issue of the True Index told of a house and lot on Main Street occupied by Jacob Mytinger that would be sold at Public Auction on Monday, March 22nd. It adjoined the dwelling of H. C. Yates, Esq. and the Town Hall. But, the ad "closer to home" was about the 5-Points Store of H. C. Yates having "cheese and macaroni for sale and a choice of Family Groceries as well: Pure Wiskeys, Brandies and Wines for Family and Medicinal use; It is the largest, cheapest and the best." The sale of the Warren Green was announced. The "main building had recently been destroyed by fire, but there still remains a commodious brick and frame building containing 16 rooms, stable stalls for 40 horses, kitchen, cistern, Ice House and all necessary appurtenances for a first class Hotel. Also a fine garden with fruit trees and grapes." James M. Rixey and George S. Carter leased it, planning to remodel. At the corner of 5th and Main Streets was the business house of Uhlfelder.[168]

At the Town Council meeting on March 29, 1875, the St. James Episcopal Church asked to rent the Town Hall until their building was repaired, due to damage during the Civil War.[100] Sometime after the war the Methodist Episcopal Church closed for repairs and held their services in both the Presbyterian and Baptist Churches. It had broken windows, blood-stained floors, walls and doors had been removed and used as operating tables and furniture was either damaged or lost during the time it was used as a hospital.[24]

Mr. B. F. Rixey appeared before the Town Council on May 4th asking that in consideration of the loss which the Firm had sustained by the burning of the Warren Green Hotel that their tax be abated to some extent. $33.95 of their license was refunded. August 20th the Council wanted to find out the cost of relaying the sidewalk between the Courthouse and the cemetery. August 21st The True Index ads included Kloman's Drugstore on Main Street opposite the Courthouse with Dr. J. O. Hodgkin's office in the Stephen's Building next door, and for the Warren Green with James H. Maddux, Lessee-saying, "I have leased the Warren Green Hotel property and assure the traveling public of a warm welcome, comfortable accommodations, and polite attention. To more permanent guests I promise to make my house a home. My table shall be good, my chambers tidy, and my services always at the command of patrons. My bar shall be stocked with good liquors and everything calculated to give satisfaction shall be if possible supplied. To my County friends and the public generally I extend the right hand. Encourage me." September 13th was a big day for the Town. There were no street lights until the napha (petroleum or any of several volatile inflammable liquids) street lights were used.[60] On this date the Committee of Lighting the Town purchased six lamps and 12 tubulas (having the form of a tube) burners. $150 was the estimate to light them for the year.

1876

1876—The Centennial Year. What did happen that year to celebrate? What do I remember? There was a Centennial Exposition in Philadelphia celebrating the signing of the Declaration of Independence. Some people must have attended and returned to talk of it. Some service must have been held here, but I can't think of a thing now. Of course there were fireworks on that July 4th, maybe more than usual. The first 100 years have been good overall, with so many new inventions each year. The next 100 must be even better. Fashions had more colors now, people enjoyed regular picnics or "dancing picnics". A wooden platform was built under the trees for them and "square dances" were called. Sometimes two girls or a girl and her brother would be brave enough to waltz, but as a rule waltzing was frowned upon. Mountain climbing was a pasttime and in the fall hunting parties were held to find nuts.[2]

But I'm getting ahead of myself, for it was on January 28, 1876 when the Town Council appointed a committee to solicit subscriptions for the Lee Monument, so people were busy with the project. May 1st the tax on the Warren Green Hotel was reduced to $30 for the fiscal year ending May 31, 1876. Before the Civil War George B. Cochran went to San Antonio, Texas where he became a successful merchant. After the war he sold out and returned to his home in Salem, buying several farms as well as the Warren Green. For a time he also owned the Fauquier White Sulphur Springs.[182] This year he erected a new Warren Green with a stone telling of it, which can be seen from the side facing Main Street.[26] March 6th, The True Index ran an ad saying that Jas. M. Rixey and George S. Carter had leased the Warren Green Hotel.

June 28th, 1876, the Council proposed that the Waterloo Turnpike to be made a County road. A brick gutter was mentioned from First Street to the Menefee Pump on Main Street, and it was not to exceed 4 feet at any point. People were buying town pumps but with the understanding they were not to be used as septic tanks. The town was sinking new wells, too. As of October 20th it was unlawful to roll any wheelbarrow or other wheel vehicle- except children's carriages- on the sidewalks of town. It was in 1876 that Joseph A. Jeffries bought out the drug business of Dr. E. F. Kloman.[39]

1877

The Solid South newspaper began publishing in Warrenton during 1877.[29] An advertisement in it announced the next session of the Fauquier Female Institute on Lee Street would begin September 3rd.[61] Although several blocks from the Courthouse, it involved The Square, for on pretty days the girls would be walking about. There would be at least two together, never one being alone. Of course there were entertainments and dances held at the school with local residents attending.

An advertisement dated March 1, 1877 was in the True Index,[62] which stated, "Having dissolved my partnership with J. H. Stephens and bought out the stock and fixtures of E. Felix Kloman,[186] I am now afloat in my own canoe. My stock is large, and will be complete in every particular and kept so. Of Drugs, Medicines, and Chemicals. I shall keep none but the best. After an experience of over twenty-two years, I flatter myself that I know the wants of the Warrenton drug trade, and shall use every endeavor to satisfactorily supply all who will give me an opportunity. From want of ready money I shall have to sell for cash and to promp paying Fancy Goods, I will sell them very low. I am at E. F. Kloman's old stand, opposite the Clerk's Office. Joseph A. Jeffries, Druggist." Kloman moved to Culpeper Street. J. H. Stephens and Son continued as Druggists in their same building.

The Monument to the Confederate Dead was completed in 1877. The tall marble shaft was placed in the cemetery over the common grave dedicated to "Virginia's Defenders" and proclaiming "Here they sleep as sleeps a hero on his unsurrendered shield".[51] It was dedicated by General Wade Hampton[63] whose ancestors came from Fauquier.[186] The town allowed $250 for it and the rest of the cost was by contributions.

The Council minutes for June 29, 1877 had A. W. Utterback as Mayor. By July 14th the Masons had completed their Hall at #9 Culpeper Street and moved there from the Odd Fellows Hall or old Market House. July 31st there was a petition to citizens and tax-payers living on Main Street asking that the noise along that street between the Courthouse and 4th Street, especially at night and on the Sabbath, to be stopped. September 7th plans were made to lay pavement on the Alexandria Turnpike.

1878

It was in 1878 that a company was formed to rebuild the hotel at The Springs so it could again become the center of summer life with germans, entertainment and people "taking the waters". Tournaments were held there with knights, jousting, and the crowning of a queen. The manager then was named Tenny.[5] From the intersection of Alexandria Pike - or Court Lane - east along Main Street were three vacant lots. The January 26, True Index had a notice that Charles W. Smith had established a Marble Yard, called the Fauquier Marble Works, where "he is prepared to execute in the best style all kinds of monuments, Tomb and Headstones, Mantles, Stand Tops, and also Brown Stone work, such as Door and Window Sills." Shop & Yard were at the California Building.

April 6th the issue of the True Index gave a brief history which might be interesting to relate refreshing the memory. "1817 the County seat of Fauquier by act of Assembly became an incorporated town, and Berkeley Ward, then Clerk of the "Superior" Court, was elected the first mayor. 1762- Alexander Cunningham was the King's Hi-Sheriff. He appears to have been a Scotsman, and is believed to have been a partner of the firm of Cunningham & Co. of Glasgow, which had a branch at Dumfries. His warehouse here was the nucleus of the residence of Wm. Bootwright; back of Town Hall. At that time Warrenton was a struggling settlement built on the land of R. H. Lee and along the forks of the highway running from Winchester to Falmouth. One of these forks passed in front of Turner's saddler's shop; after Wards the 'Warrenton House' and now the livery establishment of Galloway and Everhart. There it curved to the left —passing through Suddith's lot to the North side of Cunningham's store, and on through the Presbyterian church lot; and the lots on which the Odd Fellow's Hall and the Baptist Church stand to Jenkin's Corner, where it continued on what is now Main Street. This old merchant does not appear to have lived here much over a decade, for we find John Likly, his agent and factor, titled in 1774; and in a little account book charged with 5 pounds cost by him a wager with a planter as to the price he had paid for tobacco the previous year. Deeds of record in the county court also show that Likly was in the habit of extending credits, and transferring lands obtained for goods and money from persons moving away. The close of his employers contained 6 acres running North towards the foot of the hill, where he had a bath house and spring. He took vast pains to cultivate mint, and as every morning that he bathed he brought back with him a bunch of pungent sprigs, he is believed to have been the first to introduce juleps among early settlers. Before that time and ever after, juleps had to compete with punch (lemon and not the Moffett innovation) for popularity—the court at each sitting ordering a bowl of punch and annually levying for the same. . . In 1786 Wm. Horner, a native of Maryland, came hither and commenced business first in the house in which Wm. A. Pattie now lives and after Ward conducted business at the stand which still bears his honored name opposite the Courthouse occupied by Mr. Franks. . . 1817, Gaskins & Diggs was opposite the P.O." Now the thing is remembering where all those were. On an 1878 map, the P.O. is on Winchester Street next to W. A. Pattie's. [*See maps on pages 49 and 50.*]

  Town Council minutes had many improvements for the comfort

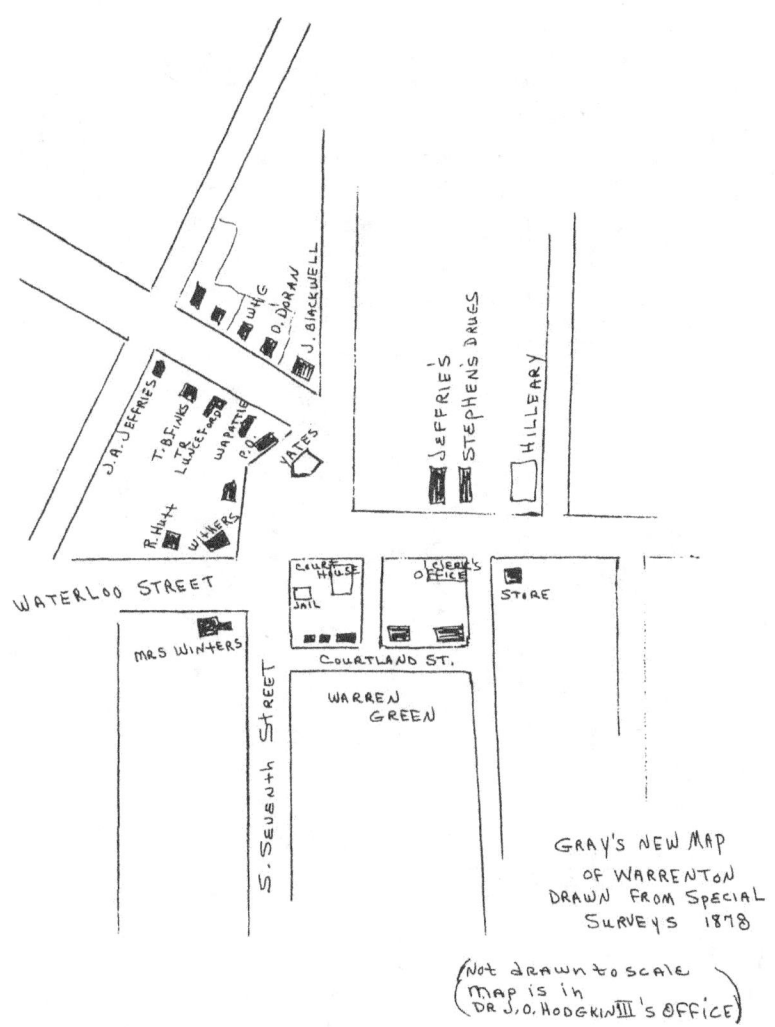

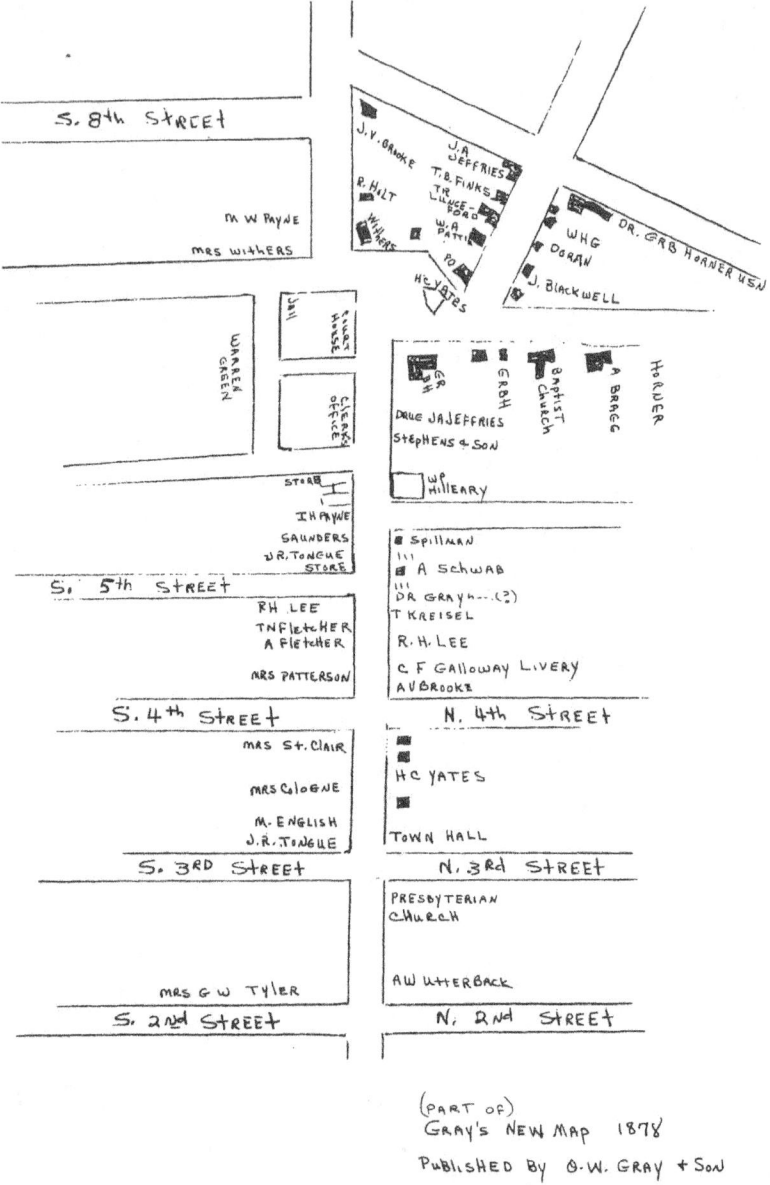

of the people. April 19, 1878 a pavement was to be laid on Lee Street of Flagstone and they had all the specifications recorded, too. The stone was not to be less than 2¼ inches thick nor less than 12 inches square or its equivalent. The outer curb to be set 4 feet from the fence and to be 2½ inches thick, setting 12 inches in the ground . . . not less than 8 inches wide at the end. The inner curbs may be 4 inches less, the pavement to rest upon a bed of sand at least 2 inches deep. That all took a lot of work and care to put in. July 19th the width of the sidewalk was to increase in width from Main Street to Mr. Braggs on Alexandria Street to 4 feet with 2 curbs and from Braggs to Horner Street 3 feet with like curbing. But Dr. G. R. B. Horner was having a problem August 28th. The Council wanted to have his steps removed on Alexandria Street and within 24 hours, too! Or the Sergeant was to have it done!

1879

Memorial Day, 1879, was celebrated by a crowd so large that the head of the procession was at the cemetery as the rear of the column was passing the Courthouse. Little girls were followed by little boys, then came the young ladies and youths, matronly looking females and fathers—all marching according to age, to the cemetery, where the talk was at the Memorial.

The Town Council, September 5th, had 25 loads of white flint stones placed on Main Street and the Public Square where they can be broken by violators of the Law who are convicted, but do not have the money to pay their fines. The many pumps and wells of the Town and their platforms are to be cleaned and repaired. Always something to be done. Of course, the Town Clock needed winding and repairs at times, too. December 19th, Joseph H. Watson, a watch maker and jeweler, was paid for the job.

1880

The Committee on the Cistern reported January 16, 1880 to the Town Council regarding the building of a cistern on the Public Square at the joint expense of the Town and County. It was first mentioned in 1873. So, The Square is to become more and more involved in the town's activities. By March 5th, the contract for the Cistern had been signed and May 8th, the Committee guaranteed the county that "The Town of Warrenton" will keep the Cistern in good order and would establish proper regulation for its protection. The county paid $350 towards the Cistern, and therefore they do not pay any more. The streets were lighted, someone said—by coal oil. However June 28th, the Sergeant was requested to have the Street lamps lighted between the hours of 8pm until 11pm until the 1st day of October.

Officials of the town now had to sign statements, giving an oath not to fight a duel or knowingly be involved in dueling during their term in office, which Mayor James V. Brooke, Jr. and the Aldermen did. Very few formal duels were fought in the U. S. after the Civil War, since the war ended a way of life that had such action. In fact several years ago John S. Mosby and John B. Withers almost had a duel over a political issue, but Judge Keith put both men in jail until they cooled off. And, again in 1874 due to political differences, Mosby and Capt. Alexander Dixon Payne planned a duel to be in Maryland to avoid the penalties of Virginia's anti-dueling law, but it was moved to Buckland. However, before it happened, they were arrested and Keith again settled it. After this Mosby moved his office to Washington.[185]

A disturbance must have occurred at the depot because at the July 2nd meeting a special policeman was to meet the trains and maintain peace during June, July, August and September. A new lamp was placed at Alexandria and Jefferson Streets, August 6th, with plans to have a brick pavement on the Northeast side of Main Street between 3rd and 4th Streets. It and the old curbstone will cost 90¢ a square yard.

During 1880 Joseph A. Jeffries and his family were living above his drugstore. He bought from P. W. Hilleary the vacant lot next to the Stephen's Building. Other business were Mr. Hilleary's Dry Goods & Notions' Store at the corner of Main and Culpeper Streets and B. F. McConhie's shoemaking and repair shop next door. Along Winchester, between the Five Points Building and T. E. Pattie's General Merchandise Store was a 20 foot lane or alleyway. Next, was the Pattie residence with stable in the rear. The house next to it was built flush with the street and owned by Theo. Krisel. William C. Marshall owned and lived in the corner house. All the buildings were of frame. Opposite Patties' was Miss Jane Blackwell's house where Mrs. Kemper and her family lived. On the same lot was a small frame house that was sometimes used as a store. Going from Winchester towards Jail Street, sort of behind Patties' was a small frame building where William Morgan and his family lived. He was a

Negro preacher who ran an eating place in the same building. Although the floor was dirt, when swept daily it might be cleaner than some places where cracks between planks collected dirt. Beside it, the vacant lot was used by horse traders on Court Days. George Booth had his two story brick home near the corner. On the same lot was the brick home of Mrs. Lula Sowers Jennings. Across the street was the Farmers' Hotel run by "Louie Lyon". Continuing on along 7th Street, behind the hotel was their garden and ice house. Next came the Livery Stable of James Flynn, and then the Warren Green Livery Stable,[64] where men liked to go to sit and talk. They said it took three people to work on a horse, — one to catch it, one to hold it and one to shoe it.

1881-1883

March 15, 1881 D. S. Delaplane asked the Town Council to pay the cost of repairing his wagon that had been broken on the town street when his horse was frightened by firecrackers. Wonder what date that happened—was it February 22nd? It was alright to explode them then, according to the 1873 ordinance. That same date they allotted $200 to be given to the Warrenton Rifles for new uniforms as their existence tends to the preservation of the peace and good order of the Town and Security of its citizens and their property. On July 6th the Council was informed that Company A of the Washington Light Infantry will visit Warrenton on Tuesday the 19th while enroute to Fauquier White Springs. It was planned that they would be met and have a reception at the Town Hall. September 7, 1881 had the highest September temperature ever recorded in Washington, which was 104 degrees. That meant it was HOT here, too.

S. S. Shaffer was taking care of the Town Clock, as of May 1, 1882. A. D. Payne became Mayor on May 29th and at the June 30th Council meeting, $40.62 was paid for a brick pavement over the top of the Cistern. The building at the corner of Main and Culpeper Streets was now occupied by Latham and Green Chemical Merchandise store.[31] During this year the New Baltimore Journal was first published.[29] The True Index reported, September 3rd, that Kloman purchased the drug establishment of Mr. J. C. Johnson on Culpeper Street.

The Town Council appointed Horace Pattie, on June 29, 1883, to "be authorized and empowered to act as special police for the protection of the Cistern," as the town told the county they would do when planning for it.

1885-1886

H. C. Yates was mayor, June 30, 1885, but June 29, 1886, the mayor was Charles M. White. The Warrenton, Plains, Alexandria Telephone Company was recorded in the Clerk's Office as being organized the 28th of June 1886. William Beverley from Broad Run was president; J. P. Jeffries, treasurer; C. F. Galloway, vice-president; and H. N. Brawner, secretary. The first central office was in the store of H. C. Yates in 1886. It was a service known as the Fauquier and Upperville Telephone Co., which was not the same as the WPA Telephone Co., although it was formed the same year (and was to operate for many years).[66]

We were getting to sound like a big city, and perhaps in more ways than one, for one night there was a big disturbance to the peace of the town. The July 13th, 1886 meeting of the Town Council offered a $20 reward for the arrest of the party or parties who exploded the bomb or ball in the streets of Town on the night of July 12th. Someone was still celebrating the 4th. The Warren Green's condition has become a nuisance and the Council feels it must improve. October 1st, Mr. Menefee moved to reconsider the petition of Miss Mary Smith, which had been rejected on September 17th. She is asking for payment of damage done to the California Building when the bomb exploded. It was decided that she be allowed the amount of $11.75 to pay for the repairs.

1887

Some things stay the same, some things change. In 1887 the northeast corner of Main and Court Streets continued to be a vacant lot. Next in line was a frame building of considerable age sitting back about 30 or so feet from the street where in 1885, R. E. Foley opened a bar-room, then Jeffries Drugstore, and the Stephens' Building that had the ground floor divided into two store-rooms. William E. Gaskin's Real Estate and Insurance business was in the first room while the drugstore of Dr. J. H. Stephens & Son continued in the second room, with Albert Stephens manager and dispenser. A vacant lot was next. In the Hilleary Building on the corner was the grocery store managed by C. F. Gaskins. Across "Cow Alley" was the dry goods and grocery store of J. A. Spilman. Adjoining it was the dry goods and grocery store of A. W. Utterback. Along Main Street was Aaron Nusbaum's men's clothing store, a small frame building of H. N. Graham's merchant-tailor business, Theodore

Krisel's bakery and candy store, a two story frame building occupied by Miss Julia French's residence and Millinery Store, a frame building with John P. Wyer's Drugstore, another frame building sitting back about 20 feet from the street was C. W. Smith's marble works, on the corner of 4th Street was the Livery and Sale Stable of C. F. Galloway. On the opposite corner was the toy store of Captain Julian P. Lee. Along the south side of Main Street was Miss Cornelia St. Clair's Millinery Store with Dr. J. O. St. Clair, dentist, in the rear; the small two story frame home of a colored woman called Aunt Ellen; a brick building where Henry Lee and family, colored, lived and had his merchandise business; and an old stuccoed building on the corner of South 5th Street with L. T. Hout's Jewelry Store. On the other corner is a large frame building with Joseph H. Nelson's hardware and furniture store. Next came John Saunders' Undertaking and Furniture Repairs business with Thomas E. Saunders' Boot and Shoemaking in the following frame building. Then, Dr. G. W. Hunton's Drugstore and the butcher shop of William Shepherd beside it. Charlie Madison had his Barber Shop, B. F. McConchie's Boot & Shoe Repair Shop with R. W. Hilleary's Dry Goods Store on the corner of Culpeper making up the rest of the street.[67] Or, was this when William Perry Hilleary's Merchandise Store was there?[31]

Along Hotel Street in 1887, is the Stag Annex to Warren Green Hotel called Rowdy Hall and connected to the main building by a covered plank walkway. In the basement of the California Building, was Fisher Brothers' Bar. The Post Office was now somewhere on Culpeper Street. Winchester Street continued to extend to within 50 feet from the corner of Main and Court Streets. Diagonally across the street from Patties' was the large dry goods and grocery store of Jim Doram and his wife, who were colored.[67] It was also in this year that a charter was granted by Judge James Keith to the Warrenton Hunt, with James K. Maddux as Master, making it the first Hunt in Fauquier.[29]

Joseph A. Jeffries was granted his request to the Town Council on February 1, 1887 for a crossing to be laid across the Main Street to the Clerk's Office from his store. He also asked for relief from pig pens near his residence. The Council decided that no minors or parties were to gather on the streets in Town after 10pm, unless the minors have written permission from their parents or guardians, as there is too much disturbances when they do so. February 7th, the Plank Walk leading to the Creamery was to be repaired, but not beyond the Corporation limits. Was the Creamery at the foot of Alexandria Pike at this time? There were other Plank Walks in town such as the one from Horner Street through Hayti (Haiti). A crossing was planned to be laid across Winchester Street to James Doram's Store and a brick pavement to be laid in front of his property. He was to pay part of the cost. A new brick pavement was also to be laid on Waterloo Street from the Corner of "Lewis Lion's"- as the Council Minutes called him- Restaurant to the corner of what is known as the Warren Green lot. Mayor White resigned March 7th. The Council ordered that Culpeper Street be widened, which was to be done by removing the Clerk's Office fence and filling up the entry to the basement of Gaines' Law Office. Joseph H. Nelson was elected Mayor March 24th.

April 12th the Council was planning to enclose the grounds of the Clerk's Office again with an iron fence. They also made a ruling prohibiting the playing of ball or other games within the Corporate limits on the Sabbath. If so, the fine was to be no more than $10.00. A room was rented, April 22nd, over Shepherd's Butcher Shop, but is now Hunton's Drugstore to be used as a Council Chamber, for $50.00 a year. A Town levy of 40¢ a head on all male persons over the age of 21 was put into effect. An ordinance now prohibited the washing of vehicles on Main, Winchester, and Culpeper Streets with a $10 fine for doing so. The Fauquier Telephone Company was mentioned, which was different from those in 1886. Maybe it was still the Fauquier-Upperville Company, but they just used part of the name. In the opinion of the Council June 10th, "it would be to the interest of this town as well as to the interest of the Pennsylvania Globe Gas, Light Company" to have a lamplighter appointed. It was done, June 24th, Charles Marshall being recommended for the job.

July 1, 1887 J. W. Shirley was selected Sergeant for the coming year to end June 30, 1888. Mr. Hilleary is to purchase the proper uniform for him. July 22nd was a busy day for the Council. A new pump had to be ordered for the well on Smith Street. A brick pavement was to be laid from Town Hall east of the Odd Fellows Hall, and one at the end of "Cow Alley" next to Main Street reaching the new stone pavement. Also, Arthur Schwab and A. M. Brodie were notified that unless they rebuild the broken privies on the lots owned by them on "Cow Alley" before August 25, 1887, steps will be taken by the town to close them up as nuisances against the health and decency of the Town. August 4th, it was made unlawful to ride, drive, lead or hitch any horse on or across any pavement or sidewalk in Town or to ride or drive on any street in Town at a greater speed than that of an ordinary trot or pace with a $10 fine if so done.

November 11th the weighing of stock cattle was 3¢ per head and fat cattle was 5¢ a head. Revenues came to the town through the Hay and Cattle scales. There was a well, too, near the Hay Scales close to the Planing Mill (located off the present So. 5th Street on the dirt road running along the railroad from the overpass). The loaded wagons were pulled onto the scales and weighed, then pulled off to be unloaded. After that they were weighed again. The Cattle Scales, Union owned, were at the regular railroad yards (later to become the Co-op on Washington Street). Cattle were brought in to be unloaded there as well as being shipped out every week or so. Mr. Shirley did the weighing for a time. (Later the scales would be at present Warrenton Supply.)[68] December 9th the Pennsylvania Globe Gas, Light Company was notified that another Lamplighter was needed.

1888

In the building where R. E. Foley had his bar-room, the next tenant was Ben F. Martyn's Tin Shop, probably in 1888.[67] People were still requesting stone pavement as was shown in the Town Council Minutes for March 9th when Mrs. George G. Booth wanted it adjacent the Jail and crossing to the corner of the Warren Green. July 25th, the Superintendent of Streets is to pay special attention to the privies and hog pens, as owners are to keep them clean and limed. If not, the work will be done at the cost of the delinquent party. If this is not done, then they will be destroyed. From now on, too, it will be unlawful in the Corporation to use profane or obscene language or urinate on any Public Square or place where the act may be offensive to persons passing or in any bar-room or public building, or make indecent exposure of his person, or be found upon any public street or Square in a state of offensive drunkenness. The fine for language is $100; for the other it is $10 and or 30 days in jail. All of this going on in poor little innocent Warrenton. Can you believe it? November 20th Joseph Nelson resigned as Mayor and John R. Spilman became Mayor-elect. The Council considered establishing a public market for the town and having another artesian well to supply water for the town. The purchase of a fire engine called, "The Little Giant", was discussed December 5th. It was not to cost over $75.00. Now it is unlawful for any cows, bulls, or steers to run at large in the town between sunset and sunrise, as they had been doing damage.

1889

In 1889 Charles B. Horner erected the building on the corner of Main and Court Streets (which is still there, but has been remodeled). When built, the Post Office moved to it. The entry to the building was on the Main Street side with a window on the angled-corner and a small window on the first floor side of Court Street. William Strother was the Postmaster then.[64] On January 25th, cases of Typhoid fever were found in town. A public meeting was called February 8th, in order that Dr. R. I. Hicks could give advice on the disease. Also, that date, the Domestic Fire Engine & Pump Company asked the Town Council to order two Little Giant Engines with 100 feet of hose for $125.00. The request was approved. A dozen leather buckets at $30 was ordered from the Boston Woven Hose Company. At the March 22nd meeting it was decided that one Little Giant Engine, No. 1, and Hose Reel was to kept at the Courthouse under the front portico. Engine No. 2 was to be kept wherever the Mayor and the new Chief of the Fire Department, John Robert Spilman being the first chief, thought best.[49] John R. Spilman, a builder and carpenter, worked on the Baptist Church steeple. One of his workmen said it was too high to be up on. Spilman, it is said, climbed the steeple and stood on his head.[68] The Town Council on this date also ordered the Sergeant to clear the streets of all women of notiously disrespectable character, known to be common prostitutes and after notifying them that after the hour of 10pm to withdraw from the public streets, they refuse, they are to be jailed and could be fined up to $5.00 and or given 30 days.

The Ladies of the Presbyterian Church asked the Council April 5th, 1889 to put the horse rack across the street between the Town Hall and the Church in order to protect their fence. People are still complaining that there is too much noise on Main Street at night. No one in jail will be asked to work on the street, it was stated June 7th, if he did not pay his fine, but if he did work, he would receive 75¢ a day to help pay off the fine. After June 28th no alcohol is to be sold between 10pm and 5am during January, February, March, April, May, October, November, and December; or 11pm to 5am during June, July, August and September. It was on the Sabbath that none was to be sold in 1873.

It was decided November 11, to allow the citizens to have a jollification bonfire, fireworks, the firing of the cannon, among other things, on Friday night, November 15th, but there were to be no fireballs. What a fateful decision that was and what a disaster that

Friday night turned out to be! The celebration was to be for the Democratic victory, the defeat of Governor "Billy" Mahone by Fitzhugh Lee, and the election of Grover Cleveland as President.[49] The festivities closed with fireworks and a bonfire on the Courthouse lot. What made the bonfire especially good was that all the empty wooden boxes in town had been piled on it and everything in the stores seemed to come in wooden boxes. General Mahone was burned in effigy. Shortly before 9 o'clock the Courthouse building was burning, too.[11] Bird nests on top of the pillars and eaves caught fire from the sparks of the bonfire. For the second time John Marshall's portrait was removed from its frame. John Carter, Richard N. Brooke, Eppa Hutton, Jr. and others took it to a safe place.[49] Someone said that while a bucket brigade was formed, an elderly man, John Ashby, stood and watched. He was told to find a bucket and help, but he said he came to see a fire and a fire he was going to see—as he continued to watch.[146] Thus, the second Courthouse on this site was gone! The Town Council called a meeting November 19th to see what could be done until a new Courthouse could be built. The County and Circuit Courts would be held in the Town Hall.

During the year of 1889 Johnnie Tongue bought the business and building that was the dry goods and grocery store of J. A. Spilman. Dr. G. W. Hunton bought the drug store of Dr. Stephens and moved across the street to the Stephens' Building.[67] The oath of the Mayor and Alderman this year said they had not fought a duel with a deadly weapon since the 1st day of May 1882, or sent anyone to or accepted a challenge to fight a duel either within or beyond the boundaries of the State, or knowingly conveyed such challenge or aided or assisted in any manner in a duel. 1880 was when the oath was first noticed in the Council minutes. (It would be included for several more years.)

1890

Mr. Parkinson, Superintendent of Streets, January 7, 1890 was ordered by the Town Council to inspect the Courthouse Cistern, and if necessary to thoroughly cleanse it at once. The well in front of Mr. Caldwell's house had to be cleaned out and he was to do whatever was necessary to make the water better. About March 5th, Rappahannock Station village was changed to Remington. April 1st the springs on Watery Mountain could be used for the town water supply. It was May 13th that the Sergeant was instructed to rid the town within the next 24 hours of the presence of two women who were offensive prostitutes. The Baptist Church was damaged by a storm, and June 3rd was allowed to hold services at the Town Hall until it is repaired.

In July 1890, the Court sessions were back in the new Courthouse's finished basement room. This is the third to be built on that site, being rebuilt on the old walls and same plans. The only difference in the two buildings was a shortening of the portico, east and west. In the former building it was of equal width with the main structure.[11]

1891

February 3, 1891 Alderman Jeffries reported to the Town Council regarding the organization of Alert Fire Company. A committee was appointed to find a suitable place to build a cheap house for the fire apparatus. It was reported of securing the Gaines' land at the head of Main Street for the ground rent of $15, but the building was subject to removal on his motion. Yates' stable could be had for $12.00. The Council ordered the riding of bicycles on sidewalks be declared a misdemeanor punishable by a fine of $1.00 for the first offense and $5.00 for the second. March 8th, Daniel P. Wood and 19 others formed the "Alert Hose Company". The hose, reel, hook and ladder, truck with other items were turned over to them and they were given full power to use the bell in the Courthouse as a fire alam. Fire was usually announced first by someone yelling "FIRE"! and the cry taken up by others until the bell was rung. With all the coal or wood burning stoves and frame houses there were many fires, especially in winter. Just about everyone went to fires day or night. All the men helped with fighting it or removing the contents of the building. Sometimes the women helped save clothes or other household items. At times the outfits people threw on in the middle of the night, as they rushed out, were something to see. The two-wheeler was under the Courthouse steps. Disaster occurred once when a frog was caught in the hose nozzle, and at times a hose broke to cause trouble.[41]

The First Baptist Church was thought to have been completed in 1890,[69] but June 2nd the Council approved the "First Baptist Colored Church to use the Hall the second Sunday in each month". They also allowed a dancing school to be held in the Town Hall. July 14th, Granville Gaines was mayor. October 6th he was requested to notify Dennis Kelly that better attention must be given to the street lamps, or a change of lamplighter will be made. There is something a little romantic about the dusk falling, especially in winter, and the man making his way down the street with his ladder, sitting it against the lamp post, climbing up to light the lamp and then going on his way to the next one, greeting people as they pass by. Just one of the activities that makes this a pleasant time.

1892-1893

It seems that Mr. Kelly didn't improve in his job, for Ed L. Sheppard was elected Lamplighter February 2, 1892. April 26th, the people at Bethel Military Academy were busy planning to have their 25th year reunion and hoped people of the town will make their guests "welcome and joyful". The Council on June 7th appointed a committee on Gas and Electric Lights.

Someone must have been getting a little out of hand for February 7, 1893, the Town Council had to pass an ordinance to protect the "inmates" of the Female Schools. From now on there will be no more whistling, coughing or other noises while the pupils are walking. May 2nd Gen. Eppa Hutton wanted a fireplug in the rear of his dwelling. Special attention was to be paid, as of June 6th, to people selling liquor on Sundays.

1894

Things finally fell into place for the Town Council. August 7, 1889 they first began talking about a new Municipal Building and February 17, 1891 they discussed land belonging to Gaines and Yates. At last on February 26, 1894, in order to erect a town building for the use of the Fire Department, they would purchase the lot belonging to Mrs. William H. Gaines, at the end of Main Street, which has a 30 foot front by 90 feet deep, situated next to the property owned and occupied by Mrs. A. A. Booth and the Public Cistern. The price of the lot is $700. It is planned that a brick building 28 feet by 42 feet with two stories will be erected. Each story will be 12 feet high. The ground floor being for the use of the Fire Department will not be "furnished further than to have brick pavement for the floor and joints struck, with white washed walls." The top floor will be divided into two rooms for the use of the Council, so will be plastered and furnished in the usual way. This will cost about $1600 so it will all total $2300 more or less. The Town Council Building will stand nearly upon the site of the old "Waters Tavern" whose ruins had been removed in 1852. Some of the Tavern's terraced gardens still remain.[11] The steeple of the building would be used to hang up the fire hose to dry after being used, so there would be no bell. The frame building behind the Post Office at Court and Main Streets, was now occupied by J. White.

The True Index for December 1, 1894 Editorial said, "We have some funny conceits. For instance: That old ugly gap between the P.O. and Jeffries' drug store made Main Street look to us like a pretty girl minus a front tooth. Now that Jos. A. has filled the cavity, Main Street may smile and receive compliments. Mr. J. expects to fill one of his new stores with holiday goods." There were also ads for Aaron Nusbaum at the corner of Main and S. 4th Street, and that Follen & Jeff Jolly bought out S. W. Smith's Marble Works on Main Street (next to present P.O.). They were working for Smith in 1887 as marble cutters. Dr. J. O. Hodgkin's Dentist office continued over G. W. Hunton's Drug Store in the Stephen's Building, but as soon as Jeffries finished his new building, he moved into it. Dr. R.R.O. St. Clair, Dentist, was still on the other side of Main Street.

1895

An ad in the True Index April 20, 1895 was for the City Drug Store. J. P. Wyer bought and remodeled the store on Main Street above C. F. Galloway's Livery Stable (now Post Office), the store formally being occupied by B. F. Martyn, the Tinner. L.T. Hout, Jewelry was opposite Galloway's, on Main Street. A. Nusbaum's Clothing store was on the corner of Main and South 4th Streets. Miss C. St. Clair's Millinery was on Main and T. R. Schwab opened a family grocery in the Schwab Building. W. E. Bishop put in a refrigerator to keep all the fresh meats, but still carries salted meats. June 2nd Council minutes reported John R. Spilman continues as Mayor. Again December 7th, the True Index reported two small items of interest in general. At the Council meeting, December 3rd, it was resolved that the owners of improved lots shall be assessed one-third of the cost to the whole town for building or repairing plank or other walk ways. It was also ordered that the price for weighing cattle shall be 5¢ per head on and after January 1, 1896. The Courthouse Meetings will be resumed next Sunday afternoon at 4 o'clock. The singing will be supplemented by music from cornet and a splendid new organ. Everyone is invited. Wonder if this was the "Courthouse Mission" or The Gospel Wagon? (Both were around the following year.)

1896

Lots of things happened during 1896 as recorded in the True Index. Good ole newspapers that help bring back memories. A. M. Brodie, Merchant-Tailor's ad now has him over the Post Office. Pants are $4 and suits begin at $15 and up. Speaking of the Post Office, L. C. Yates was then Postmaster. Names of people who had letters awaiting them were published in the newspaper. February 29th it was reported that Sullivan & Bro. have had several offers for their interest in the Farmers' Hotel and are thinking seriously of disposing of it. It is hoped their successors will give equal satisfaction and thrive. April 11th, W. H. Gaines and J. S. Gaines advertised saying, "Gaines & Bro.--Bankers, Notes, Drafts and Checks collected from all parts of the U. S. Special facilities for collecting overdue. Notes, Loans, negotiated Deposits and Collections solicited. Scotland, and all parts of Europe. Strict attention given to all banking business. Satisfaction guaranteed. All we ask is a trial. Office west side of Culpeper St. Next to the Public Square." Gaines' Bank at 12 Culpeper St. opened 1891. May 9th paper said The Courthouse Mission meeting the past Sunday was led by Richard N. Brooke, and attendants enjoyed both his exhilaration to holier life, and the instrumental and vocal music. These Sunday services are growing in popularity.

E. S. Turner and J.A.C. Keith, Fire Insurance Agents bought out the insurance business of the late H.C. Yates, as reported May 30th, 1896. Their offices were in the Payne Bank Building at the office of Scott & Keith in the rear of the Courthouse (Hotel and Culpeper Streets). The past Saturday had been Memorial Day. Even though the clouds lowered threating rain, the young Cadets and a larger number of citizens than usual gathered in town. The Town Hall was filled to over-flow for the services there. Patriotic memories will never die. John Spilman, a Civil War veteran sometimes led the parades as did Alex Rose some years. He was not a veteran, but he always wore a business suit of Confederate gray color.

James H. Maddux gave notice June 6th, 1896 that he had bought the Warren Green Hotel. Many activities happen at the Town

Hall. June 13th reminded people not to forget to hear live, "Life", on Monday night for the benefit of the Fire Company.. W. C. Weeks, Fire & Life Insurance Company, on June 20th had the office over Gaines & Bro's Bank, were agents for the Northwestern Mutual Life Insurance Company of Milwaukee. The Gospel Wagon reached Warrenton Friday morning. Someone said, "It will do more good than McKinley's band wagon." It was a church on wheels, being a large surrey-like wagon drawn by 4 or 6 horses. The wagon was a large square with an open top and sides that let down. Chairs were placed on it for the people and there was a small reed organ.[70] Miss Nannie E. Kemper, June 27th, had an Ice Cream Saloon on Winchester Street opposite T. E. Patties' store. The ice cream was made with skimmed and sweet milk. She said she would be thankful for patronage from the good people of Warrenton and vicinity. Commissioners Scott & Keith, on the previous Monday, "sold Court under decree in Randolph vs Weaver's admr. & c. the house and lot on Winchester to C. M. Pattie for $4330."

One of the things for sale cheap at Patties, July 4th, 1896 was a "Second Hand Refrigerator in good condition." Boy! Excitement at the Warren Green July 18th. Galloway's one horse fix was standing in front of the Hotel when the "horse began to kick at flies, missed his perpendicular and fell heavily. Thoroughly ashamed of himself, he jumped up and ran for his stable. Entering it, he broke both shafts. Galloway put him to another fix, and his customers drove away. The Moral to that is—don't bob a horse in fly time." The Ladies of The Warrenton Baptist Church announced July 25th that they will give a Musical Concert at the Town Hall. The Play of "Woodcocks" was there for two evenings. December 1st a report to the Town Council was made of the hog-pens and hogs, and it was estimated there were 285 hogs raised annually within the town.

1897

The Warrenton Review announced in 1897 something sort of funny - Kaptain Kotton's Komikal Kompany was giving an entertainment in the Town Hall. Sounds as though it'd be fun. Court met the fourth Monday in the month according to the weather. Usually it was too bad during the winter to meet, so when March came it might have been a looooong time since a person had been to town. This year there seemed to have been more people for March Court than have visited the County Seat for many years. The weather was ideal and everyone seemed to have been in fine spirits. The dress parade of fine horses down Main Street, some imported and some down in the stud book, was the center of attraction as all eyes watched it. The "scrubs" and cows under the hammer had little notice and brought low figures. The vacant lot between the Municipal Building and William Morgans' Eating House was the site of the horse auction. Sometimes western ponies were brought in by the car loads. The saloons were well patronized, but disorder and drunkenness was less than usual. Two arrests made, but those were late at night. I don't remember when it happened but at one time Reuben Rowzie rode his trained horse up and down the Courthouse steps. That attracted a crowd, too.[71] The True Index, March 27th said the bank building of Gaines & Bro. was "taking on a fresh suit at the hands of Jolley & Kirby."

May 4, 1897 the Council said it would now be unlawful to put or place upon any street, lane, alley, or public place any ashes, glass, crocking, scrap iron, nails, tacks, or any other article which would be liable to injure or damage the feet of children or animals or the tires of bicycles or other vehicles that have rubber or pneumatic tires. People had not been too careful before as to where they threw their trash, but as tires coming more prevalent, new laws came.

Fauquier's Memorial Day was May 29th, being a "movable feast" because the date was decided when the most flowers were in bloom, so it could be May or June, but usually was close to May 30th. Children dressed in white had home-made wreaths around their shoulders. Girls carried baskets of flowers and older people had bouquets. All so pretty! The occasion always opened with a speaker. If bad weather, it was held in the Town Hall, but if it were nice, as this day was, the speaker stood on the steps of the California House that was the home of Miss Amelia Smith. The people sat or stood in the grassy plot back of the Clerk's Office Building. Horse drawn vehicles were tied all over Town as the Livery Stables were filled. After the ceremonies, everyone marched to the cemetery to honor the 600 unknown Confederate dead. There would be the Bethel Academy boys, the Confederate veterans in their grey uniforms, the Daughters of the Confederacy, Sons of Confederate Veterans and many others—all marching along. They sang "The Bonny Blue Flag", "Tenting Tonight" as well as other Confederate songs. The service at the cemetery ended with the playing of Taps.[72] This year Rev. G. Nelson, Rector of St. James Church and also a Confederate soldier, was the orator, speaking at 5pm that day.

D. H. M. Clarkson, County Superintendent of Schools for Prince William, "a delightful versifyer and scholar" read an original poem.

It was announced June 12, 1897 that Mrs. May Mosby-Campbell was the "postmaster" as Mrs. Yates was leaving. Recipients who received letters in the Post Office are still published in the newspaper. The Warren Green Hotel was under new management, June 26th. Mills and Roche were now proprietors of the newly and neatly furnished place. On all Court days, first class meals will be served for 35¢. The night of July 24th had an odd but interesting thing to happen. Sort of spooky—and I'm glad it wasn't Halloween. The little dog called "Tex", to the surprise of all inmates of the Farmers' Hotel, brought in a "cunger bag" which contained one peach seed, one snake egg, and a left hind leg of a graveyard rabbit. It was "supposedly lost by some old colored man". The owner of the bag could have it "by coming forward, proving the property and paying the cost of storage".

The Town Council was given credit, August 21st, 1897 for the nice new brick pavement just completed by contractor Hall, that extends from Mr. Nusbaum's residence to that of Messrs. Gaines and also for the sandstone crossing at the Farmers' Hotel on Waterloo Street. December 4th, Hurst's Jewelers did not want people to forget his store was between Jeffries' and Hunton's Drug Store, as Christmas was coming soon, so Santa needed that information. A few days before Christmas it was announced that Mr. A. Nusbaum, who had a store on "Schwab's Corner" (present 3rd and Main and Streets)[58] purchased the large store house at the corner of Main and Culpeper Streets from the Ward family. Because he will be moving to the new location, he is now offering goods at "prices without regard to cost". This year too, the Warrenton Daily Banner was published.

1898

The cry, "Remember The Maine" broke over the country after it was destroyed in Havana harbor on February 15, 1898. Congress approved President William McKinley's request to recognize Cuba's independence from Spain and a state of war between the United States and Spain existed.[10] During the Spanish-American War days there was a popular song that had a refrain, "There'll be a hot time in the Old Town tonight!"[73]

March 5th, 1898, the True Index announced that Dr. C. S. Carter bought the brick house and lot on Winchester Street for a residence. This, the old Inman Horner house, would become known as Carter Hall. At sometime Mrs. Murray Forbes lived in this house and kept "guests".[74] Although the Masonic Lodge Building was at 9 Culpeper Street, there was a notice September 10th of the Masonic Fair being held at the Town Hall. The Warrenton Review newspaper also told of a theologian that was to preach in the Town Hall on the doctrines of the Universalist Church. The Hall was a busy, well used place.

Mr. Eddie Pattie was described as a fat, bald headed man with candy in his pocket which he gave children, one of them being Sallie Wood (Sadler). Another child who was fascinated with Pattie's store was Nellie Sudduth (Downs). Her family came to town to shop and went there. She saw something strange. . . and because she always received an orange for Christmas, she thought this was an orange. . . but it was really the first time they had seen a grapefruit. This time—in the 1890's or just before the turn of the century—was called a "warm time", with an innocence in the world, things not hurried, people spoke to one another, and took time to talk. It seemed a nice time to BE, no matter where you were.

1899

January 10th, 1899 Mr. H. R. Moffett petitioned the Council for damages to his wagon and horses that happened Christmas Eve. The horses were frightened by firecrackers and ran away while he was dealing at a store. The ordinance that resulted said it was now unlawful for anyone to set off firecrackers or cannon crackers or such on public streets even if it is a holiday. Those fireworks gave the Town 'fits'. The Treaty of Peace from the Spanish-American War was ratified February 6th. The 18th of February was a Burrrrrrr Day! The fierce snow storm ended in a blizzard of several feet deep.

March 4th, the True Index reported that two wagon loads of tramps, alias Gypsies, caught in the woods during the blizzard had two horses to freeze. They said they were going from Richmond to Washington, but some felt that no doubt they had heard the story about help extended to the distressed Gypsies found on Lee's Ridge and they promptly came too. They were told to "move on", some feeling they "ought to go to Cuba and share free rations with the victorious army of Gomez." During the Spanish-American War, Jose

Miguel Gomez fought in Cuba.10 Gypsies weren't too welcome around here. March 18th Joseph A. Jeffries engaged messrs. Jolley & Kirby to make his old store and dwelling correspond in beauty with his new additions, as he realized the importance of having everything around him look as fresh as daisies in Spring.

The vacant room on the floor of the Council Chamber was rented April 4th, 1899 to R. N. Brooke for an art gallery at $2.00 a month rent, with the provision that he drive no nails in the walls. A committee reported on the claim of H. R. Moffett who has asked for damages in January, saying it lacked merit under the ordinances of the town. Also, in January, G. W. Hurst may have moved his office to the floor above the Post Office. May 13th six street lights were broken by Partridge egg-sized hail stones. People scattered to get indoors when it began. The rain was welcome even with the damage. G. G. Booth presented a petition to the Council, July 11th, for a walk-way from his hotel to his stable, and for a horse rack using two sides of the Jail.

August 12th, 1899, the newspaper reported that the weekly Germans in the Town Hall continued to surpass any held in the state. What a social life Warrenton seemed to have! The Vaudeville at the Town Hall was also a delightful entertainment.

It was planned, September 5th, 1899 to have additional police during the celebration of Emancipation Day and in an emergency to close all sales of liquor. September 22, 1862, President Abraham Lincoln had announced that he would declare free all slaves as of January 1, 1863.10 However, the next week, September 11th, the Council decided that due to the expected large number of people to be in town on the days of September 22 and 23, that all bar-rooms would be closed from 12:00am the 22nd to 12:00am on the 23rd. I don't remember when the first automobile came to Warrenton but it came to the state of Virginia this year.104

About the turn of the century an old man, Mr. G., died in the old gaol.75 He owned and lived on a farm in the upper part of the county, but thought relatives wanted to take his property. He tried to prevent it by burning the house and himself. After being rescued, he was arrested for attempted suicide and arson, and put into jail. There he caught pneumonia and died, and he wanders through the place.76

WARRENTON'S MAIN STREET
(Municipal - Firehouse in center)
Circa 1900

1900's

A brand new century! 1900 is here! The 20th Century! Population of Fauquier County has grown to 23,374.[77] And, another February Blizzard! The snow and wind began the 13th about 3pm, continuing until the evening of the 15th. The snow had a hard top— a sheet of ice. Snow drifts were as high as 10 feet, covering wood piles and fences. People could ride their horses across the fields and right over the top of fences with no problem. They didn't need the roads. A good thing, perhaps, for it took a while to clear them as each citizen and land owner was to do it.[78]

The railroad passenger shed in Warrenton was a center of social and business activity. When passenger trains came in the porter from the Warren Green, and perhaps other hotels, met them and carried the baggage for the guests. Most stores sold drinks. The Dorams on Winchester did, as well as Ullmans Department Store and Bar-room on Lee Street. Across from it, Albert Fletcher's store had a bar in which was sold three kinds of brandy from the same barrel. Someone asked him about this and he said, it didn't make any difference, it would all make you sick. He was also a private banker who had access to banks in the city as well as having the Electric Company. He lived on the corner of Main and So. 2nd Streets (now Surles' Parking Lot) and had a house on Waterloo Street (near the District

Nursing Home). Around Ullmans was called "The Flats" and next to that was "Fishtown". Along an alley off Lee Street was Jack Holmes' Bar (destined to be the last bar in Warrenton).[182] Another was on Culpeper Street and especially on Saturday nights they were filled with Black people.[68]

The sounding of the approaching train whistle made people run to the station to see what was going on and to get the news. The Post Office on the corner at The Square was a good gathering place, too. Warrenton, a true summer resort town, had lovely ladies strolling around town to shop or go to church. There were several boarding houses, such as Carter Hall, where summer boarders came, especially from Washington. Many Warrenton girls married the out-of-town boys and of course the girls who came to visit found the "country boys" attractive, too. The Springs, the horse shows, the schools, and perhaps because it was cooler here than in the city, all brought many visitors. After the finals at Bethel Military Academy and The Fauquier Institute, boys and girls, and the bands that played for their dances, all left on the same trains.[39]

Near the corner of "Cow Alley", sometimes called Hilleary's Lane,[79] and Main Street was a vacant lot owned by R. W. Hilleary. The Fletcher Brothers bought it in 1900, building on it (later Peoples National Bank). Next to it on the corner continued R. W. Hilleary's Grocery, managed by C. F. Gaskins.[67] Actually the groceries were in the back of the store and a dry goods and clothing section was in the front. Edgar Ramey worked the groceries. Clerks seemed to be concerned that they sell good products to their customers. Eggs were sold "loose" and Edgar would always examine each one when checking them out. If he thought one was bad, he wouldn't let the customer take it. Shelton Cropp was in the clothing part. Lucy Fewell worked inside a small booth as cashier. The customer checked the article in with her. She put the money in a container, pulled a cord and the money went in a mechanical device to the office, returning with change if it was needed. A Mr. Williams delivered groceries for the store.[144] There was a new Ice Cream Saloon on Culpeper Street now.

1901

The Town Council, February 5, 1901, decided to notify the Globe Gas Light Co. that the lighting of the Town was not satisfactory. The Council suggested a new lamp-lighter to be appointed and that the Company put new burners on the lamps as the light is now very poor. Ed J. Martin was appointed lamp-lighter March 5th to replace Ned Sheppard who had the job since 1892.

Ladies did not go on the streets when March Court was in session or if they did have to do it, they were well escorted. After the Parade of Stallions was up and down Main Street at noon, owners then made up the books for the season. Some of the churches provided a dinner for the large crowd. Tim Bray, a giant of a man, was called "King of the Free State". Then came Charlie Ashby to claim the title. The Free Staters were responsible for most of the fist fights and pranks that went on during this day. Sometimes a group of boys hid behind Yates' Five Corner Building and yell—"Fight!". A crowd would come running, but by then the boys were on the other side and they would yell again. The crowd ran there, but the boys were ahead of them on another side—and so on. The bar-rooms were filled and when tempers arose the fists, sticks, and even stones were used to fight. One year they said a fight went all the way to New Baltimore and baseball bats were used in it. But, when the sun went down it was soon all quiet again. Perhaps one reason for this being that the jail had more occupants than usual.[80]

CORNER OF WINCHESTER AND MAIN STREETS
WARRENTON, VIRGINIA

The Gospel Wagon was still making its rounds. The place of service was announced from the pulpits of those churches whose ministers took turns holding services in the different communities. Because many places had no church, the church had to go to them.

May 14, 1901 found the Town Council purchasing apparatus used by physicians for disinfecting houses of contagious diseases. They requested, July 5th, that all ice ponds be emptied to help rid the county of contagious diseases, and August 6th, the Board of Health was organized. August 20th diphtheria, one of the dreaded diseases, and its cases were discussed. September 5th a deodorless cart was purchased. Also an ordinance was put into effect saying, no more dead animals were to be left on lots to decay, water closets and garbage was to be regulated, also cellars, cowsheds, etc., to be cleaned, no more night soil was to be collected by buckets in an open cart - they will use the new one -, water closets are to be limed and persons dead of contagious disease will be buried privately and as soon as possible. There will be no burning of refuse or paper in the streets from now on. Houses with disease in them will be fumigated with the items purchased May 14th. The only fire equipment in 1901 was a 2-wheel hose cart and about 500 feet of hose.[81] Wonder what happened to the 4-wheel hose cart they had in 1899.

1902-1903

It was decided to enlarge the corporation limits, March 4, 1902. The Fauquier National Bank opened for business this year in a room at 33 Culpeper Street[82] in the Payne Building. September 18th the Town Council felt that ½ of the cost of crossing or stepping stones should be paid by the owner of private residences when the crossing leads to their place. The Upper Fauquier and Warrenton Telephone Company advised the Council, December 2nd, they wished to have an exchange in town and wanted to use the poles of the Electric Light Company.

The Fauquier National Bank bought the lot behind the Courthouse from James V. Brooke April 11, 1902. He had his law office there, the bank began building the first banking house in town, moving into # 10 Court Street, January 13, 1903. The Warrenton Telephone Exchange was organized January 17, with Joseph A. Jeffries as president; J. Brad Beverley, vice-president; Edward S. Turner, secretary; and C. E. Tiffany, treasurer. The office was in a building on Main Street with Mrs. Jessie Caldwell Walraven, operator in charge. There was a small switch board and it was operated with a hand crank.⁶⁶ Wonder if this was the same company or part of it, that asked the Council about using the electric poles.

As of May 5th, 1903, the Town was to be systematically vaccinated against smallpox. It came to the Town Council's attention, June 20th, that there was a building on the property of William Morgan, adjoining the Municipal Building and Fire House, which was of such nature as to be dangerous and likely to burn. They ordered Morgan to remove it. But, July 9th, he came up with a change in specifications to meet the requirements and they allowed him to build or rebuild the shed.

The streets were so bad in town in 1903 that sometimes a spring would break or wheels went deep into the mud.⁸³ The Warrenton Horse Show brought many people not only to Warrenton, but also neighboring towns, all which were filled to overflow. Extra trains ran out of Washington and the roads leading to town were filled at sun-up on that day. It seemed that anything on wheels was there; coaches, four-in-hands, and large wagons filled with straw. Everyone had guests and luncheons were the order of the day. Of course special outfits were bought for the show which lasted two days. There were afternoon and night sessions, a public address system, several rings and many invocations.

1904-1905

A water meter system was adopted by the Town Council, April 26, 1904. Among the horse racks in town was one at the Presbyterian Church on Main Street, which was brought up at the Council meeting, December 4th, as needing improvements. Probably this year G. A. Vose opened his grocery store on Main Street in the building where Brodies' Tailor Shop and other¹⁶⁷ businesses had been.

April 4, 1905, the Council Rooms were being refinished by papering and painting. July 1st, John Thoma came to take over the Krisel Bakery that opened 1854.⁴³ Thomas C. Thornton was Mayor as of December 5th. Every Friday night there was a German at the Town Hall, and one for a Horse Show Ball and one called a Ladies' German, when the women asked the men. Women wore beautiful evening dresses while men went in white tails and black ties or tucks. It was a lovely sight to see! There were also private dances and card parties. Favorite meeting places in town continued to be the Post Office and drug stores. December 16th The Fauquier

Democrat newspaper made its appearance,[131] the 23rd Warrenton paper. It was in the building where the Warrenton Telephone Exchange was located, which sat back a little from the street and had a step or two up to the door.[84] (About where Carter's Furniture Building is now.[84]) Thomas E. Frank formed the paper from the True Index.[85]

1906-1908

March Court in 1906 was still a rough and rowdy time. Can you believe May 10th there was a slight snow fall! Talk about shrivering, but at least it didn't last long. C. G. Horner petitioned the Town Council, June 6th, for a new sidewalk on Main Street in front of the Post Office. Wednesday, August 8th, a new crossing was requested from the Post Office across Alexandria Street to the head of Winchester Street. Trees along the streets continued to have metal cages around them and were used to tether horses. The Warrenton Review reported that the Warrenton Rifle Company was organized in Warrenton December 1906. But the Town Council gave money to them in March 1881. Maybe this means they reorganized or recruited more members.

January 3, 1907 found the Town Council considering the improvement of the Winchester extention to the corporation limits. Another telephone company now. The Piedmont Telephone Company was seeking a franchise, June 4th. Plans were made July 2nd to repair the street crossing from Main to Winchester at the Post Office. July 3rd, the Young Men's Christian Association rented the Town Hall. There was to be a concrete sidewalk, September 3rd, be in front of and abutting C. W. Smith's property. November 5th, A. and T. N. Fletcher were granted the contract of lighting the streets of town with electricity. The Episcopal Church and Parish House were built on Culpeper Street during 1907.[87] No—perhaps it was just the Parish House.[98]

Aaron Nusbaum was joined in his clothing store on the corner of Culpeper and Main Streets by F. G. Anderson and the business was known as Nusbaum & Anderson. After Anderson bought the building, it became known as the Ford Anderson Building. Mr. Anderson was so handsome that girls, they say, come from everywhere to go into the store just to stand and stare at him.[182] During Nusbaum's ownership he brightened the streetscape by filling in the niches on the Culpeper Street side of the building with colored paintings of men's fashions.[31]

The Warrenton Library Association, a circulating library, was formed November 1, 1907. Now, January 1, 1908, they rented a room for $5 a month in the Farmers' Hotel. Membership was by subscription with a fee of $2 a year. One book at a time could be borrowed.[88] The Warrenton Germans continued to be popular as people loved to dance. The Fiday night dances at the Town Hall began about 9pm. Perhaps it was this year, March Court Day, Albert Robinson on his way to school went past Bradburn & Clatterbuck's Livery Stable on 7th Street near Lee. He saw two men fighting, and stopped to watch. Both men probably had been drinking—or else they were very tired—for they were hanging onto buggy wheel spokes to help them stand up as they continued to fight. An interesting place along this street was the meat house in the back yard of the Farmers' Hotel with its steep 4-sided roof and the cut paper tree standing guard over it.[181]

June 2nd, 1908, I. W. Jeffries and others told the Town Council they wanted to organize a Fire Company in order to better protect the town. Jeffries was appointed Fire Marshall and authorized to buy suits for the Fire Company, but not the exceed $200. August 13th, the Council made plans for enlarging and extending water pipes in the fire plugs. Fire was a dreaded thing, even with precautions. People still did not travel fast, so they had time to wave or speak as they passed. They conversed as they rode their horses or walked along. Some could even read or write when on horseback.

Behind the Farmers' Hotel, the Warrenton Skating Rink opened this year with a music box and someone to help you learn to skate.[89] Gay, laughing groups would go past The Square on their way to the rink (now site of Warrenton Supply). It was owned by W. A. Garner & Company and also had bowling alleys in the building. Elizabeth I. Hutton liked to skate with Charlie Jeffries who was a wonderful skater and Albert Robinson was also one of the boys who went to skate in the large frame building. Another thing Albert liked, were the large cinnamon sweet buns Thoma's Bakery sold for a nickle, which tasted good for lunch.

W. A. Garner owned the Farmers' Hotel, too, and W. H. Kays had a restaurant there. This was Kenny Kays' Dad.[103] The Square was in the middle of much activity. The Horse Show had its great hordes of people coming to town, some meeting after not having seen each other since the same time last year. The Wood family was driven to the grounds by carriage in the morning, then it went back home - or to the stable as did many of the carriages. Most people took a lunch and would spread their blanket or tablecloth on the ground. Sometimes several people put lunches together. One thing for certain—fried chicken was everywhere. In the late afternoon, when the show was over, the carriages returned to take their people home.

1909

Fire was on the minds of the Town Council, January 12, 1909, when they decided to formulate some plan for fire alarms in town. The next day—great excitement! The news spread fast, school let out and there were people all around. The President of the United States, Theodore Roosevelt and his party were arriving at 11:00 to have lunch at the Warren Green. Remember when Jackson came and no one paid any attention? Included in the party was the Surgeon General, P. M. Rixey, Captain Archie Butts, Dr. Cary Grayson, many Secret Service men and their horses. Excited people cheered, waved, gave them a royal welcome, and many ate lunch with the President. It was a cold, windy, grey day, so they left soon after eating, about 12:30pm to return to Washington. The purpose of the trip was to prove an order President Roosevelt had given. He said officers must be able to ride a 100 miles a day, and he as Commander-in-Chief of the Army, was trying it out. They left the White House at 3:40am and returned at 8:40pm, going through a sleet storm blowing in their faces for the last 30 miles. Each person used four horses during the trip. "His Excellency, Theodore Roosevelt" presented the Town of Warrenton with a photograph portrait of himself dressed in hunting clothes, taken from a painting by the Virginia artist Gori Melchers, with notes written and autographed by himself,[91] in recognition of the respect and courtesy shown him by the people on his recent visit. The Town Council Tuesday, March 2nd, resolved to gladly accept the memento and they ordered the portrait to be suitable framed and hung in the Council Chamber. (It later hung in the Library.)

The year seemed to be going along as usual. May 4th, concrete pavement was to be constructed on the east side of Culpeper Street from Main to Lee Street, with a curb and gutter at a cost of $2.05 per square yard. July 6th, the Ladies of the town asked for assistance in buying a sprinkler. The streets did get dusty, especially in the dry summers. The Street Committee agreed to do so, allowing $150.00 for the cost of a sprinkling wagon. But, the Fall was so very dry, and a water shortage developed.

Then came that horrible night of Monday, November 22nd, 1909. It was about 20 minutes before 8pm and a high wind was blowing. A revival was being held at the Methodist Church and several of the Volunteer Firemen, as was custom for men to do, were waiting at the Post Office at the corner of Main and Alexandria Pike as the evening mail was put up. The dreaded sound of "FIRE!" sounded. It apparently started in the hay loft of Bradburn & Clatterbuck's Livery Stable on 7th Street beyond the Skating Rink. The men were there quickly with the fire equipment— but—the water from the hose was a thin trickle at first—then— nothing.[92] What a helpless feeling those men had as they watched the flames spreading toward Waterloo, The Square, and on to Winchester Street. One good thing. The Annex of the Warren Green did catch fire, but it was put out before reaching the main building. When the call went out for everyone around to come fight the fire, one man and his sons who lived on View Tree Mountain came. The fighters were getting free drinks at the saloons in town. This particular man had, maybe a little too much, and he fell into the horse watering trough at the Cistern on The Square. He was in such a position that he had to be pulled out.[68] Some people brought their small fire extinguishers. Even the Bethel Military Academy Cadets marched double time to come. Finally it was decided to use dynamite to stop the flames. The road to Bethel was being built at this time with dynamite used on it, so the firemen took it.[103] One of the seven houses to be dynamited was that of Mrs. H. A. Parker, as was Yate's store.

How the wind carried the pieces as the houses blew up. Irvin Garrett, a small boy in the crowd of watchers was impressed as how high the papers, ashes, and other trash was blown by the wind. His family lived in one of the Brooke houses on Waterloo Street, which burned. Frightened horses turned loose from the livery stables were running through the streets adding to the confusion. Robert Lunceford, who was living in Cassanova with his family, could see the flames leaping into the air that far from Warrenton. Thirteen year old Sallie Wood (Sadler) and her sister sat on the roof of their house on Academy Hill to watch the fire which was "unspeakably horrendous to see". They had a couple of buckets of water and a cup, so when the many sparks or burning paper was carried there on the high wind, they poured a cup of water on it, as they were afraid of the tin roof becoming too hot. They had to be careful of the amount of water used, for with the drought there wasn't much to spare.

It was 11:30pm before the fire began to burn out. 26 buildings were burned to the ground, leaving 14 families homeless. One was Captain and Mrs. Edward Carter who lived at Carter Hall, moving there when they sold their farm at Bethel. He walked with a cane and crutch after being wounded at Gettysburg, and was now cashier at the Fauquier National Bank. They kept "guests", whose trunks were thrown out the windows. Everything from the house opposite Carters was also dumped in the street. The boarders and others sat on the trunks to watch the fire. With furniture piled high in the streets, Judge C. M. White and Mayor T. C. Thornton felt the Militia should be called out. When the rally call of the bugle sounded, the Warrenton Volunteers went home to get their rifles and returned marching in file. The cadets from Bethel assisted in the guard duty, however, there was no disorder. Captain Newton Collins served coffee to the soldiers and fire fighters now that the tired men could relax. Another thing of interest that burned was the Debtor's Oak, opposite the M. E. Church in front of Mrs. Robbins or Robins. This marked the boundary beyond which no debtor could go when on parole for a few hours.[181]

BURNT DISTRICT
WINCHESTER STREET, WARRENTON, VIRGINIA
(From Collection of John K. Gott)

**CORNER OF WINCHESTER AND MAIN STREETS
WARRENTON, VIRGINIA
AFTER THE FIRE OF 1909**

**RUINS OF CARTER HALL
BURNT DISTRICT LOOKING FROM WINCHESTER ST.
WARRENTON, VIRGINIA**

After the fire the people of Warrenton opened their hearts and homes to the unfortunate ones.[92] What few books were saved from the Library room were taken to the California Building.[88] People were stunned—in shock they viewed the smoldering result. For days they were standing around with their hands in their pockets, the women crying softly, or quietly talking as they looked. J. W. "Pete" Shirley, Town Sergeant had succeeded R. M. Pattie as Jailor when he died, and Henry Burke who was part of the team, had their picture taken beside the Town Cistern showing the burnt area behind them.[93] The following week, the 26th of November, when the Town Council met resolutions were made resulting from the fire. Fire lines in which frame buildings would not be constructed commenced at Railroad Street, went up South 3rd Street to Horner Street, along Horner to Alexandria Pike, then up Diagonal Street to Waterloo Pike, on to So. 7th Street going along it to Lee Street, on to Culpeper Street, along it to Franklin Street and to Green Street. It would be unlawful from now on to smoke about or in any public or private stable in town. Plans were made to go to Baltimore to inspect a chemical Engine. A small shed was built approximately where the Municipal Building had stood and the fire equipment was stored in it temporarily until the old Town Hall could be remodeled for a Municipal Building.[94] A few people returned to town after the fire to find employment in the rebuilding. William A. Downs, Sr. with his family returned from Washington, D.C. where in October he had been painting on the U. S. Capitol Building.[95] The Warrenton Review newspaper appeared this year.[160]

1910

The Town Council met in the Clerk's Office, Tuesday, January 4, 1910 to discuss building lots around the Engine House and were advised that the Bartenstein and Fletcher or Yates Lot could be purchased. January 25th The Fauquier Democrat announced the opening of The Peoples National Bank of Warrenton on Culpeper Street. Again the Council met in the Clerk's Office Tuesday, April 5th. A Bond issue was discussed for building a Municipal Building. The Tuesday, April 26th meeting was held in the Bank with R. W. Hilleary presiding as Mayor pro tem. It was May 9th that Dr. C. S. and Mary Carter sold to the Warrenton United Methodist Church, the land at the corner of Diagonal and Winchester Streets for $3000. The house and stable on it burned last year.[24] May 26th at the Clerk's Office, Mayor Thornton returned for the Council meeting. July 5th, D. P. Wood was Mayor pro tem and it was resolved to have Lucien Keith appointed as Mayor. The possible sale of the old Town Hall for $5000 was discussed. It might be used as a Post Office. Before the September 6th meeting, Mr. Thornton died. The Council felt that no vehicle should be driven on the streets at a speed of more than 8 miles per hour. For doing so, the fine would be $1 to $50 or to be put in jail for 90 days—or both. A few months after being in the California Building, the Library moved into two rooms of the Warren Green Hotel.

**WARRENTON AROUND 1910
(MAIN STREET)**
(From collection of John K. Gott)

Albert and T. N. Fletcher built a brick building near where the old Firehouse-Municipal Building had been on Court House Square, and opened a furniture store in it, called the "Fletcher Building". The brick store of T. E. Pattie on the corner of Winchester and The Square along with his house next door on Winchester were rebuilt by September 10th, 1910 for they were advertising in The Fauquier Democrat as "Busy Corner" having clothing and groceries, located opposite the Court House Square and on Winchester Street.

Offices in the second floor above the Post Office included that of Louise Evans, a Notary Public. One day two men, the crew from a Balloon went to see her. They entered the International Balloon Race from St. Louis and had come down on North Wales Farm not far from town and needed their log book notorized.[96] Once there was a young man called "Balloon White". One theory as why, was that at a circus or carnival, he took a ride in a hot-air balloon. When high in the air, the "driver" jumped out and left White by himself. What White did not know was that the man had set valve so the balloon would come down.146 Then, someone said a balloon landed at the school on Academy Hill, and White got inside to look at it. Some boys cut the ropes and White floated all the way to the Potomac before he came down. Whatever the cause, his mind was effected, and he could be seen carrying a lantern everywhere he went. During the winter, when his girls were courting, he would put the lantern in the stove so the light would shine through the glass door. The fellows thought the fire was going, but not getting warm, they didn't stay long.68 Even on the hottest summer day, he wore a heavy overcoat pinned together with horse blanket pins. His beard was always matted and unkept looking as he brought farm produce into town to sell. If several items were bought at different prices, White would sort of look up at the sky for a couple seconds and quick as a wink, tell the buyer the correct change. He really had a sharp mathematical mind. Another theory as to the cause of his problem was a horrible one—that lightning struck his home, killing one child and badly burning several others, even to melting the metal on a watch. White had a habit, when leaving town he would go along Lee Street and passing the utility pole on the corner beside Ullmans' store, he would lash out at it with his buggy whip. If someone was near the pole, as at times boys might be gathered there, White stopped his wagon up the street and waited until they moved. Then he proceeded with his ritual.146

When Martin Joseph O'Connell moved to Warrenton in 1910 he was a little surprised to find there were no paved streets. That's why the stepping stones across the main streets were so wonderful on rainy days. But with the coming of the automobiles in town, they were a hazard to them. What confusion it was to both humans and animals when these vehicles first came. In a picture of this year there is a mounting stone at the Post Office corner. It was rather a large stone, placed on an angle, about 2 feet tall and 1½ feet wide that went back and sort of curved around so buggies, and now cars, would not hit it.97 According to John D. Courtney the stone was found in Carter's Run and brought here to be used at the corner since it was a natural angle.182

An organization was introduced for young boys in 1910 called The Boy Scouts. The Methodist Manse between the Odd Fellows Hall and the Baptist Church was sold October 14, to W. E. Robinson, Jr. for $2750,24 (now site of Baptist Churchyard). The Episcopal

Church and Parish House on Culpeper Street, as well as several buildings near it, were destroyed by fire in October.[98] Dynamite was used once again to stop the flames.[92] After St. James burnt, the Episcopal congregation held services on the second floor of the Methodist Church at the corner of Culpeper and Lee Streets.[24] The Peoples National Bank moved from Culpeper Street to the Hilleary's Variety Store across from the Clerk's Office on Main Street. Population in the county this year was 22,526.[12]

1911

In 1911 the Town Council met Wednesday, January 11th at The Fauquier National Bank Building in the Director's Room. A. and T. N. Fletcher contracted to furnish lighting by electricity to the streets of town, fire house, Council room, Mayor's office, and Town Hall. All lamps and lights are to be lighted every night during the months of December, January, February and March from dark to 1am and from 5:30am to 6:30am and during the remaining months from dark to 2am, except on such nights or parts of nights when the moon is shining with sufficient clearness to light the streets.

Tuesday, March 7th, 1911, a concrete walk was to be laid from Winchester to Waterloo Street in front of the property of Pattie and A. and T. N. Fletcher's new buildings on the Square. May 2nd, a Tuesday, the Street Committee was to purchase the necessary material and construct a concrete pavement on Alexandria Turnpike from the Post Office Building to the corporate limits. It was this month that the Warrenton Garden Club was organized, the first in Virginia and the 3rd in the nation.[1]

August 1st, 1911, again a Tuesday, the Council was informed that meat and Slaughter Houses needed inspection by an Inspector of the Bureau of Animal Industry. They decided that anyone sentenced to jail may be sentenced to work upon the chain gang of the Town or do other labor under the Supervision of the Town Sergeant at 25¢ a day until his fine and costs are paid. Now there would be 50¢ on $100 for property real and personal and 50¢ as a capitation tax on all male persons over the age of 21. At the Tuesday evening meeting, September 5th, the Street Committee was requested to have Court House Square put in proper order.

Tuesday, October 11th, 1911, James Dorum made application for pavement in front of his house on the east side of Winchester Street. Jim Doran was known as the politest Black man in Town. Robert Lunceford enjoyed watching him drive his rubber-tired buggy with a dock-tailed pony. He built his home and store after they burnt and sold plenty of 1¢ candy, especially to children of the town. Ford Anderson was probably the most polite white man in town. His store sold the button shoes that needed a hook to fasten. Once when Robert Lunceford was trying to do it, he was really pinched! Mr. Anderson's trademark might be his high celluloid collar that he always wore, which came up under his chin.

The Council decided an incandescent light is needed at the west corner of the Jail on 7th Street. Tuesday evening, December 5th, 1911, the Council meeting continued to be held at the Fauquier National Bank as they had all year. Mrs. Keith suggested a light be put in the Town Clock.

December 6th, 1911, M. J. O'Connell now owned the Electric Company. There are 27 street lights in town and 50 customers. During this year the old Methodist Church and lot were sold to Paul C. Richards. (An auto sales agency and car rental were eventually operated by Richards and Mason McCarty.[24]) In place of the burned skating rink building, F. W. Hilbert built and with O. B. Calohan, opened the Warrenton Carriage Works for handling harness, buggies, wagons, farm equipment and selling carriages. Probably this year the "Warrenton Virginia", formerly the "Solid South",[8] moved from the southwest corner of Main and 4th Street, across to the northeast corner and changed its names to the "Warrenton Times".[177]

1912

The Telephone and Electric light poles opposite the Courthouse were in the way of traffic and the Town Council, February 8th, 1912, ordered them to be removed, and placed wherever the Street Committee suggests. April 2nd the Warrenton Electric Light & Ice Company was discussed. Real estate and personal property taxes were increased June 4th to 65¢ per $100. The new Episcopal Church had been rebuilt on the old foundations and a portion of the old walls which had been left standing. Rough plaster covered the brick. The first services were held there in June.[98] July 2nd the ladies of Town wanted the town to keep the streets clean of trash and refuse. All merchants are now required to put trash in suitable barrels and place them on the sidewalk or street adjoining the property between 7 and 8am on work days. The Town will remove and empty the trash, then - the barrels will be returned as soon as possible.

The town wells are being sold one by one to owners of the

property they adjoin. Of the several wells, one was on Winchester Street (near present O'Connell house), one on Green Street at which people going to the Horse Show Grounds might stop for a cold drink, one at Thurston Willis' place where East Main and Lee Streets meet and the one on Court House Square. People walked several blocks to get a bucket of water for their household. Someway The Square's cistern, which was 8-10 feet across, was constructed so the water filtered through a one brick thick wall as it drained from the roof tops into the cistern. There was also one about mid-way on the street between the Episcopal Church and the Depot. They all had horse watering troughs, and at this last one, Albert Robinson once watched a crippled Black man walking with crutches while carrying an armload of wood splints. He put them in the trough of water to soak before being used to make chair seats or backs. A lot for the hitching of horses must be found for parking is a problem on Main Street.

The new Methodist Church, and parsonage that was built as part of the main structure, was finished during 1912. A ceremony by the congregation including a choir, an organ and a couple of horns, was held Sunday, July 7th. The cornerstone was placed in the space left for it in the front wall.[24] August 6th, the crossing at Mrs. Brittons was to be laid and 1/3 of the cost to be paid by each Mrs. Britton and Captain Carter. They lived on the corner of Diagonal and Winchester Streets across from the new Methodist Church. October 1st an ordinance said that no pool or billard room keeper, alley keeper or restaurant keeper, or tin pin keeper can stay open after 11pm.

October 25th, 1912, F. D. Gaskins was to be Acting-Mayor for a while . A town ordinance prohibited the Turkey Trot, Bunny Hug, Grizzly Bear, and any kindred dances in the Town Hall.[101] All those dances had become "risque". Stuyvesant School on Winchester Street opened this year. During 1912 Wayman Carter's Dad had a butcher shop in the back of the building at the corner of "Cow Alley" and Main Street. Someone else had a grocery store in the front of the building. The butcher business was not good for people had their own animals, except perhaps for a little beef, and being without refrigeration for it was hard to keep meat in the summer. They depended on ice from the Ice House. Because of these things, Mr. Carter gave up and went into another business elsewhere.[154] Dick Schwab had a grocery store in this building.[144] Wonder if this was in 1895?

Robert E. Foley opened a restaurant in the building at the corner of Main and 4th Streets after the "Warrenton Virginian" moved out and lived above it. That building had been built sometime after 1854 on a burnt lot.[179]

1913

January 16, 1913 the Town Council planned to improve Alexandria Street by using Convict labor and on February 4th, the Road Board was allowed to connect and use Town water for drinking and cooking in the Convict camp on the Fisher lot. A plan was made to lay a 4-inch water main on Alexandria Street and have fireplugs installed as soon as possible. From now on no one is to operate a slot machine in town. Something new this month. The 16th Amendment now provides for an income tax in the nation. The offer of Mrs. Julian C. Keith was presented May 6th to the Council through the Civic League as she and her sisters would like to present the Town a fountain as a memorial to their father, Major John Barry. It was referred to the Street and Water Committees.

May 15th, 1913, it was decided to work Alexandria Street with Convicts as far as the law will allow them to work and that the other part be macadamized under the direction of the Street Committee. People feel it will be good not to be sinking ankle deep in mud. Waterloo Street will be worked on under the same terms. About this time a man from Hagerstown, Maryland came to visit Sallie Woods' (Sadler) older sister and he was driving one of the first cars to come to Warrenton. Of course, he had to spend the night after traveling so far. Mr. Wood felt the car should be put under shelter for the night, but the only building they had was the stable, so it stood outside, and attracted a lot of interest with people stopping to see it.

June 4th, 1913, the Council met at 5 o'clock pm at Court House Square to consider the application and location of the Fountain offered by the Barry family. After due consideration of plans and location, it was unanimously decided to accept the Fountain and to locate it in the center of Court House Square, subject to the approval of the Board of Supervisors. Present was Mayor Lucien Keith, F. D. Gaskins, Recorder, and Councilmen R. W. Hilleary, Edward Carter, D. P. Wood, M. G. Douglas, H. I. Hutton, J. O. Hodgkin and W. A. Garner. Although many people associated the Fountain as being where the old Town Well was located, it was farther down the hill from the well, which was almost in the center of the road, a few feet in front of the Courthouse steps. And, the Cistern is to the northwest of the Well.[103] The Council decided July 1st to diminish noise in the operation of automobiles or motors. Now they must muffle their engines or pay from $1 to $10 fine. September 2nd, the meeting was held at the Board of Trade Room in town - but where was it? October 10th, they again met at the Fauquier National Bank, and November 4th, it was in the office of H. I. Hutton.

Toll gates existed during the 17 and 1800's,[104] some being in Fauquier County and one was mentioned in the Town Council minutes of 1871 as near town. When the town roads became macadamized people in vehicles or on horseback had to pay to use the "new" streets. The exact date when they came into existance is unknown. They were not here in 1911 when M. J. O'Connell came, but shortly after that, perhaps at this time since the Convicts were working on the roads. Most of the Toll-keepers lived in a house nearby and had a small house of one room for weather protection and heat, where the pole was raised or lowered across the road. A rope was used to do that and a stone might weight it so it would stay down. The toll gate was always located on the side of the road to collect from people coming into town. One was within sight of The Square on Alexandria Turnpike, run by Mr. and Mrs. Woodzell. There were different fees for various modes of transportation. Sometimes horses were frightened by the gate and might try to jump over it. There was a gate on each of the five main roads leading into town. At the foot of Alexandria Pike, just before the Toll Gate was The Flag Factory which began either last year, 1912 or this year, 1913. There were a couple of women employees who sewed the heavy ducking or canvas type of cotton cloth to make red flags, which were mounted on poles about three feet long. The flags were sold to the railroad companies to be fitted into a container at the end of cars, especially the caboose. Mr. O'Connell always thought it was interesting to think of places where Warrenton flags might go. This was the same building that had the creamery in it—or did that come after the Flag Factory?. . . .

The Warrenton Supply Co. was incorporated December 1913 from the Warrenton Carriage Works. O. B. Calohan became president with F. W. Hilbert Vice-president. They had services for automobiles such as Studebaker, EFM, and the Allen & Stanley Steamer.[143] The garage building was located on the Lee Street side of the large building. Albert Fletcher might have been the first person in Warrenton that M. J. O'Connell saw owning a car, which was a Stanley Steamer. People were very interested, excited, but some feared it—as did some horses that backed or reared up when it came by, although it was so quiet you could hardly hear it coming. He drove it around for people to see the oddity—and they followed along behind him, walking just about as fast as he could drive. You know Albert Robinson was named for Albert Fletcher. Ed Kinchloe and Thad N. Fletcher also were owners of Stanley Steamers. They had a work clothing store in the upstairs part of the Fletcher Building near the Depot. Ed Kinchloe had a feed business in part of it, too. Albert never sat down in his store. He had a chest-high table that he used in his cashier's work. Besides having a wonderful memory, he also could be a very generous man.

Two others who were among the first people to have cars in town were Paul Richards and Elizabeth I. Hutton's father. The cars were Buicks called a "Bug", with running boards and brakes on the outside of the driver's door. Curtains were put on the open windows if it rained.[152] John Thoma probably had the first truck in Warrenton, using it to make his deliveries. It had one cylinder and was so slow, it could hardly pull the hill from the Depot to Main Street.[146] But, before when he bought flour by the railroad car load, it came in 200 or 215 pound barrels. Four men with a two horse wagon could unload, deliver and stack it up in the store in one day. They kept the horses trotting.[144]

1914

The Town Council met January 6, 1914 in the Board of Trade Room. Mr. A. Fletcher appeared before them seeking information with regard to children playing marbles in the streets of town. On motion the matter was referred to the mayor. Perhaps they can be in the way of people walking if they use the sidewalks—and some of them did have chalk marks on them. The Cistern was a place for people to stop for a drink and before the water system in town, many coming each day. One place that used its water was Madison's Barbershop on Main Street. Charlie Madison's father would send him to the Cistern for the water, but sometimes he would stop to play marbles with anyone who was around. When Charlie did return to the shop—Ohhh, that is where the razor strap was! Everyone went to Madison's not only for a haircut, but it was a gathering place to find out the news. A haircut was 25¢ and a shave was 15¢. Before there were many telephones, if someone had a message to send, they had the "taxi" deliver it, and Madison's was where the drivers 'hung-out', too.68

February 14th, 1914, the Council met at the office of Lucien Keith. All persons in the Town limits must be vaccinated or pay a $1-100.00 fine, or six months in jail or both. A copy of this order was attached to the front door of the Courthouse. April 6th the remodeling of Town Hall was decided so it would be put in a suitable condition for a Municipal Building. Another discussion on April 13th decided the office room, Council Room, Mayor's office, storage rooms and Firehouse to be in the remodeled building. In 1914 President Woodrow Wilson issued a proclamation designating the second Sunday in May as "Mother's Day". May 15th was named Clean-Up Day under the supervision of the Civic League. There were complaints about the pig pens and manure piles in town. With warm weather they do make themselves known! J. W. Shirley resigned, June 2nd as Sergeant of the Town and W. H. Burke was appointed at $60.00 per month, Mr. Shirley is to be Superintendent of Water Works, Cemetery, to look after the hay and cattle scales, and town clock since C. M. Pattie died. Bids were taken July 7th for furnishing signs to show automobiles the regulations for the roads leading into town. The Warrenton Supply has become the agent for the Model T-Ford with the Ford dealership.143

1915

The Town finally has both a Town Hall and a Municipal Building. But, the remodeled Town Hall on Main Street across from the Presbyterian Church is not the Town Hall now. It sounds confusing. May 10, 1915, the Town Council decided that it should be officially the Municipal Building, and the name Town Hall would be given to the Warrenton Improvement Company to be applied to their new building which was formerly called the Fletcher Building. July 6th, the Council met in the Municipal Building with Lucien Keith continuing as Mayor, discussing the Sanitary Cart and scale receipts. A Block Party was held this summer from the Courthouse to 4th Street (present Post Office). Proceeds from this went toward the Methodist Church Building Fund.105

The now, Municipal-Firehouse Building, had a porch raised above street level where a band played on summer evenings. Irvin

Garrett's father, Bud Kirby, Tom Frank, and a Meyers man were among those who played in it. People brought chairs to sit in or just stood around to listen. Silent movies were shown on the second floor there with a Mr. Jeffries having them. Another interesting activity was watching the Warrenton Rifles as they drilled several times a week in Court House Square. Irvin and others would sit on the Courthouse steps watching, as Irvin's Dad was also in it.[103]

Gypsy Smith, Jr. held a series of revival meetings under a large tent pitched on a vacant lot at North 4th Street (which was about the present Post Office). He brought together many creeds, classes, young, old, rich, poor—everyone, even if they weren't very religious. It was rather pleasant on the mornings after the meetings. Small groups would stand along the street talking. Once in a while you could hear a part of a hymn being sung or whistled. "Brighten the Corner Where You Are" was most popular. Happiness came to many people.[106] Robert Lunceford who played ball and shot marbles on the vacant lot that used to have Galloway's Livery Stable on it, sang the song. When the stable moved back of the Warren Green and what happened to their building is unknown. For several summers Dick Lewis—or was it Jo?—, a comedian came to Warrenton to pitch a tent on the same lot. He also used the corner of Green and Washington Streets near the town well.[146] Sometimes the circus was held on Washington Street and many times Irvin Garrett pumped water from the well to water the elephants. September 8th, A. O. Weedon was Mayor. The Town Council kept the Street Committee busy with investigating roads and making repairs. This time it was Winchester Street from "Paradise" to the corporate limits. All those racing automobiles doing damage? There were the usual bills to think about, too; the livery stable or Blacksmith, horse feed and horse or hack hire among others.

The first car M. J. O'Connell owned was a Ford in 1915. One day he went to a horse show near Marshall, but stayed until after dark and then couldn't see to drive home. The car lights were very dim, there were not any street lights, and only once in a while he'd see a light in the window of a house that sat way off in a field. He had a terrible time getting back to Warrenton. Also, between 1912 and 1915, turkeys and cattle were shipped in by railroad and then driven as they walked to their final destination, going by the main roads out of town, sometimes they passing through The Square. If the turkeys had to spend the night on the road, they would fly into the trees to sleep. In the morning their food would be thrown on the ground to get them out of the trees. After eating, they were rounded up into the flock and driven on. Then trucks began to do the hauling.

The Warren Green was always a good place for people to meet friends, to entertain others, especially for a Sunday night supper, and there was a dance floor. When homes were over-crowded, the extra guests were put up at the hotel. Summer boarders came from all over the United States and often foreign countries. There were exhibits held here and a shoe-shine business as well as a barbership in which the curtains could be drawn, perhaps a little early, so ladies could have a haircut in private. In the winter some of the local people closed their homes and took apartments there.[26] During this year the Presbyterian Church received a refund from the Federal Government for damages by the Federal Troops during the War. The repairs cost $1500.00, but they filed in 1906 for only $1200. They received $741.68.[99]

In 1915 Wayman Carter's Dad returned to Warrenton. Evidently the grocery store in the building at the corner of "Cow Alley" and Main Street hadn't made a go of it either. Roadhouse & Bunch was now there and Mr. Carter bought them out.[154] Mr. Bunch was at one time manager of the train station. He was being transferred to one between Orange and Culpeper but he didn't want to be away from home, so had joined Mr. Roadhouse.[124] I don't remember exactly when, but Bill Hicks worked a third chair in Madison's shop. Also, one day a man by the name of Dick Smith had a fight behind the shop, after which he went inside to put cold water on his head. That was the end of him—he just passed right on out.[144]

1916

After the Fletcher Furniture Store closed, 1916 was rather a busy year with many activities held in the Town Hall, or as the building on The Square was also called, "The Opera House" (later Hiden Building). The Warrenton Times in January told of the 5th Annual Exhibition of the Warrenton Poultry Association and February 10th reported the Warrenton Garden Club's Flower Show as being at Town Hall. The body of Col. John Mosby lay in state there for several days after he died May 30th.[107] Someone said he was a small man with a large reputation.

The Fauquier Democrat, June 24th, 1916, told of the Recruiting Station at Town Hall where they recruited for Company C of the

Warrenton Rifles. During training for the Mexican border they sometimes marched up Main Street. Holcombe Chamberlain would play a mouth organ as they went, one song being, "Brighten The Corner Where You Are."[106] Gypsy Smith still had his influence. Company C, Second Virginia Infantry under Captain Lew Wood left in June for the Mexican border,[108] with everyone at the Depot for their send off.

An advertisement for Moving Pictures on Tuesday night, June 27th, 1916, at 8:15 was showing "The Price of Happiness" by Mary Boland, in the Opera House. It was for the benefit of the District Nurse Fund. Admission for Reserved Seat was 25¢ with General Admission being 15¢. Martin Joseph O'Connell showed movies in the Fauquier National Bank on Court Street, for a while until he rented space in the Opera House. He felt the film was too inflammable without a fan, so did not do it until electricity was installed in the building correctly. Even with a fan, he made it so if the film broke, a shield went down. An agency in Washington, D. C. supplied him with films. They had a list for him to choose what he wanted, and mailed it to him. After he finished, he returned it to them by mail. There were portable chairs for the audience which would be pushed askew and jammed together when people left the theater. It usually took quite a while to put them right again. They sat on a platform, having the back rows raised above those in front. Miss Molly Carter sold tickets and Sam Appleton was pianist. Harry O'Brien, the projectionist, had to climb a ladder in the lobby to the projection room above. All the ladies wore hats and at the beginning of the film a sign flashed on the screen saying, "Ladies, Please Remove Your Hats".[103] Sometimes films were still shown at the firehouse. News of a picture was sent around by word of mouth.

July 1st, 1916 the Fauquier Democrat told how last Monday there floated from the Armory of the Warrenton Rifles, over the Town Hall, the flag of the Warrenton Rifles which was purchased in 1882 by the young ladies of Warrenton. The flag was painted by Richard N. Brooke, and presented to the Warrenton Rifles as they left for Yorktown to take part in the Centennial of 1882. July 8th, a sealed bid was given the Town Council for the lot belonging to the town and "fronting on the Public Square, and Waterloo Street, and adjoining the property of the Warrenton Improvement Company". . . from Lucien Keith for $2,500.00 cash. That sounds as though it is the corner lot, (now John Barton Payne Building). A Block Carnival was held Wednesday, Thursday, Friday, and Saturday, July 19th-22nd, for the benefit of the Boy Scouts. It was on

Main Street with hay wagons, motor truck with hay, booths with lemonade, cakes, candy, confetti, horns, whistles, false faces, and other things being sold. Was this at Main and No. 4th Street, too?[151]

August 12th, 1916, a Monument to Colonel John S. Mosby was proposed. The Town Council, August 14th ruled that dogs must be muzzled when on the streets, and they must wear a license tag due to the prevalence of rabies. The necessary steps to prevent the disease of Infantile Paralysis are being brought to Warrenton. The ladies of the Catholic Church held their annual Bazaar August 16th in the new Opera House. The Council, October 3rd, had the Pepsi Cola Company pay $15 for a license to use the Town water. The Council advised closing a portion of the street near the Public School, adjoining the property of Mr. Battaille and to see that the nights of the town are preserved. November 18th, the Hawaiian Trio was advertising their performance at the Town Hall on Saturday night. Admission is 25 and 35¢ with the tickets being available in Jeffries' Drugstore. November 25th, the people of Warrenton packed boxes in the Town Hall to be expressed to Brownsville to help furnish Thanksgiving cheer for Company C of the Warrenton Rifles.

M. J. O'Connell, along with the ladies of both the Presbyterian and Baptist Churches, came up with the idea of a Community Christmas Tree, with the Warrenton Electric Light and Ice Company to furnish the lighting. He felt it should be placed in a prominant place and the lawn of the Clerk's Office was chosen. During 1916 The Warrenton Supply Company bought out the Hardware stock of Hutton & Payne's Store.

It was probably during 1916 that St. James Episcopal Church had an electric organ donated to them by someone in New York.[162] They asked the electric company for and were granted electricity in order to play it during their services, then Mr. O'Connell began getting requests from people all over town for electricity during the day time so they could obtain and use the electric inventions that were coming into existence. And that is the way electricity came to the whole town of Warrenton.[150] It was this year that 11 year old Irvin Garrett "got a taste of printer's ink". His job was to carry The Fauquier Democrat papers, on his back, from the printing office on the other side of Anderson & Allison (now Little Folks), to the Post Office.[103] In the A & A building at one time Willard White had a movie theater with someone to play the piano, as well as Vaudeville shows.[187] Also, a Mr. Schwab had a grocery and Henry Brewer had a grocery with a restaurant upstairs.[155]

1917

The happenings in Europe and the fighting there seems to have become worse as the year 1917 came into existence. During March the U. S. began to mobilize for war and The Warrenton Rifles were "called to colors" again for the second time within a year. April 3rd the Council gave an order that no one would be permitted to keep a pond, barrel, or a receptacle of water within the Town limits. For having such the fine is $10. Those are places where mosquitoes like to breed. No more watching the wiggle-worms in the rain barrel. Events finally became too much and April 6, 1917 Congress declared WAR on the German Empire.[10] Even before our entrance into the World War a number of the people were involved in war work. Some of them met at Carter Hall to knit as they socialized with conversation or went to the Tea Room for a "spot of afternoon tea".[74] The kitchen was in the basement or lower floor and "guests" usually went there to eat.[109] School children, including boys, knitted for the war effort.[176]

East Main Street had its name changed to Falmouth Street on May 1st, 1917. The speed limit in Town, June 5th, for an automobile was fixed at 12 miles and at 8 miles at all crossings and/or turns. June 16th there were pictures at the Town Hall for the benefit of Liberty and a Mass Meeting, for the Red Cross, called "A Dry Uncle Sam". July 16th, said no pig pens will be allowed within the corporate limits. These hot night and days should smell better now as well as getting rid of some flies. It is felt that traction engines were damaging streets and they must remove steel or iron cleets or have them covered. July 19th the Town sprinkler was changed into a sanitary wagon. They didn't need it now that roads are macadamized. A light one-horse cart is to be provided for scavenger work. The time limit of 65 days was fixed for having open sewers in Town repaired and provided with septic tanks. A limit of 30 days is given for all privies to be put into sanitary fly-proof condition and provided with sanitary scavanger pails. Each property owner, residence or business, using the Trash Wagon is given 30 days to install metal covered garbage cans. That's putting things in order in a hurry. The Council wants a list of cesspools, sewers, septic tanks, and dry closets.

There weren't many Venders in Warrenton, but some of the men in town would buy cakes of ice from M. J. O'Connell's Ice Company and peddle it door to door. Robert Lunceford liked to watch John Clatterbuck go through town on his way to Washington.

John lived on Waterloo Pike, a little past the foot of the hill going out of town. He was a huckster who loaded his wagon with eggs and so forth, having three horses in tandem, and it took three days to reach the city, but returning with an empty wagon, the trip was only 2½ days. Once he was returning on the old dirt turnpike with his money—$500—in a shopping bag. When he arrived at his lodging place, he discovered the bag was missing. He bedded down his horses, got a lantern and began walking back to Washington. Don't remember how far he walked, but he found that bag!

During the summer volunteers worked on farms to help with the crops as many men were at war.[47] The Barry Monument had cement benches around the fountain and a watering trough for horses, with small shrubbery planted at the base, like a tiny park in the center of the road. It was a comfortable place to rest, and a gathering place to chat or hear the news. Soldiers would meet the girls there, some bringing "hardtack" from camp to share in picnic fashion for it was something new. Sallie Wood (Sadler) was one who sat there or on the Courthouse steps during the gatherings in The Square and sang "The Long, Long Trail" and other songs with the group. Everyone was trying to keep up others' courage. A "Peace Pageant" was held on the steps of the Courthouse climaxing a parade, one of several observances staged by Mrs. Julian Keith, to raise money for the war effort. The Statue Of Liberty was personified. Children, one who was Betsy Keith, carried a rainbow and were called "The Rainbow of Hope". Of course, patrotic songs were sung, with members of the Red Cross Chorus. Peace was pictured as an angel of Mercy. The Fauquier Red Cross Volunteers displayed their work beside the Courthouse on a lovely summer day.[111] People at home were doing their best to help "the boys over there". Irvin Berlin's songs, such as "Over There" were popular. Irvin Garrett not only worked for The Fauquier Democrat, but also as usher at the movie house now.

1918

January 13, 1918 was the year that Dorothy Montgomery (Rust) was nine years old and she, along with the other children in the family, had red measles. Her mother brought the children into town to board during the winter at Shadow Lawn. They had a cow with them so they could have fresh milk, however, the weather was so terrible that one day the cow slid down the icy hill to the cemetery. They sent for her Dad to come help them. He took ashes from the fireplace, using them in a path, to get the cow back to Shadow Lawn.

Many patriotic activities were happing in Warrenton. The Fauquier Democrat announced March 13th, 1918, a British War Film would be shown at Town Hall for the aid of the Red Cross. A meeting on May 18th at The Hall was to raise money for the Red Cross War Fund, and May 25th a large board was placed in front of the Courthouse with an indicator attached showing amounts of subscriptions for the Red Cross. Men, of course, were still going to war. Wayman Carter's father had his brother come and run the store when he left town. The H. B. Carter Company had been formed in 1915 with the two brothers.

July 2nd, 1918, the Town Council asked the Government to pay for damage their trucks were doing to the streets. July 13th, the Fauquier Democrat published a poem written by J. C. called TO THE WARRENTON BOYS OVER THERE. It told of the town being lonely and how deserted Main Street looks.

August 10th, 1918, the damage from an electric storm that hit at 7:30pm was reported, leaving two people dead and one injured. The Courthouse tower was struck and the clock damaged although everything looks alright on the outside. Now we are having quite a heat wave. August 17th was a County Community Carnival along Main Street and the lights in Court House Square showed it off. Volunteers are again working on the farms to help with the crops. The Second Community Sing was reported September 7th, as being held Tuesday night in front of the Courthouse. Song sheets were provided containing words of the choruses most popular. Judge Fletcher was the leader and all took part in the singing, the children being very enthusiastic. It was much enjoyed. Next week they plan to have the soldiers leading patriotic songs. September 14th the new Post Office, on the vacant lot at No. 4th and Main Streets, was completed. The Warrenton Rifles were in the front line during the Mause-Argonne Campaign in September.[108]

November 16th, 1918, the Fauquier Democrat told how the whole population assembled Monday night at 7:30 in Court House Square. All the bells in Town were ringing, every horn sounding, dinner bells ringing and even people beating on tin pans. The Boy Scouts, Stuyvesent School and the Fauquier Institute were out in force, each carrying a handsome flag and the crowd was gay with small flags and paper caps. You never heard such! Presbyterian Minister, The Rev. Mr. Chinn offered a beautiful and appropriate prayer of thanks for the blessings of peace, after which the evening was given up to "Jubilation and music". Mr. F. G. Anderson, becomingly attaired in a linen duster and a straw hat and carrying a red-white-and-blue fan, was the master of ceremonies. A parade was formed in front of the Courthouse and marched about Town. Upon returning Judge Fletcher led the singing of patriotic songs and —including "Hang Bill, the Kaiser On A Sour Apple Tree". The crowd cheered itself hoarse with cheers for President Wilson, for England, for each of the Allied countries, for Pershing, Fosh and other generals, and naturally for the Warrenton Rifles and "all the boys over there". Mayor McIntyre made a short talk on the United War Work Campaign. The celebration was concluded with the singing of "Praise God From Whom All Blessings Flow". Wasn't that a Good Day!

Because of an influenza epidemic that caught the Country napping, the Library had to close.[101] So many people died, not only here, but in the nation. The Community Christmas Tree was placed in the Clerk's Office lot, with carols to be sung around it on Christmas Eve, which had to be cancelled due to rain. Christmas Day was bright and beautiful. Plans to sing carols New Year's Eve was not to be as it rained again. Maybe next year.

1919

But, here it is next year—the year 1919, and still raining. . . . all New Year's Day and the next one, too. Another Amendment- the 18th, called "Prohibition". That's going to change a lot of businesses in Town. It had been so ladies didn't go downtown on Saturday because there were too many drunks, and if they did have to be in town, they never walked along the street where a bar was.[153] The Library reopened during January, so it wasn't closed too long. Around February 22nd an advertisement told of moving pictures at Town Hall on Friday night for the benefit of the YWCA. Mr. Frey, Manager of the Town Hall kindly consented to use his new machine on this occasion. The tickets were 35¢. Also an ad telling that the New Warrenton Theater would open March 10th. Did they do some remodeling in the 'Opera House' where they had been showing since 1916? Maybe that's what was meant when the other notice said Mr. Frey would use his new machine.

The Town Council, April 1st, 1919, ordered "auto-trucks" not to exceed the speed of 8 miles per hour upon the streets of

Warrenton and 12 miles for passenger machines. The Street Committee was requested to buy and place the new speed limit signs. May 15th the Mosby Monument began working on their collection campaign. Somewhere near Sudduth Funeral Home on Main Street, it seems there was a jewelry store where Gene Garrett (Sr.), about this time, bought a wedding ring for his new bride.[124]

June 3rd, 1919, the Council said the Poll Tax levy for the year was 50¢ for each male person over the age of 21 and the Dog Tax for a male was 50¢ with $1.00 tax for a female. The notice in The Fauquier Democrat, July 5th told of,

>"A Good Place to Eat
>The Warrenton Cafe
>Main Street   Old P.O. Bld'g
>Meals A La Carte
>Special dinner from 11:30 to 2:00
>Meals & Lunches at all hours cooked to your order.
>Unexcelled Service—Open 5AM to 1AM"

The town was jumping,—open until 1 o'clock in the morning. People have been parking in odd positions, so August 19th the Council decided to make some laws. Now vehicles of all kinds are to keep to the right and when parked it must be headed in the direction in which they would be moving, with both front and rear wheels to be six inches from the curb and on both sides only when the streets are wide enough to leave sufficient space for vehicles to pass, otherwise there will be parking on one side only. Albert Robinson bought his first car, a Model-T Ford, with its crank on the front. Sometimes it was hard work to get started, but the car was so wonderful he vowed to keep it many many years.

September 6th, 1919 the paper told of the Street Carnival that had been held in Court House Square for two nights. All through the week different features of it was on hand. Tuesday evening the Trial and Hanging of the Kaiser took place on the Courthouse steps, to the satisfaction of all. Wednesday the Calverton Band, the local string orchestra and young songsters had an impromptu concert. Everyone went home between 11 and 12pm. Captain Boyd Smith, in a ceremony, chose the spot for the Mosby Monument, selecting a place on the north side of the Courthouse lawn.

October 11th, 1919 the site of the Mosby Monument was dedicated, bringing out a large crowd. The sidewalks surrounding the Courthouse yard were crowded and there was a large number inside the buildings, as well as on the platform that had been built for the occasion. High School girls sang two beautiful southern songs. Captain Smith turned the sod for the site and marked it by a Confederate flag. Later along with Mrs. Edward Carter, he christened the ground, "Memorial Park", taking possession of it in the name of the Association. At the October 19th meeting, the Council felt the town needed to buy a horse.

At his bakery on Main Street, Mr. Thoma was thought of by school children as "the best old man", as he stood behind the counter and made sure no child left there without getting a cookie—and usually it was one in the shape of a horse. He also made his own ice cream, using a large container and transferring it into smaller ones to go into the freezer. He'd look around, counting the number of young people, and say, "You seem to know just when I'm going to make ice cream". Then, he wouldn't have enough small containers to completely clean out the large one, so the youngsters would have to eat—free—that which was left so it wouldn't spoil. There was also homemade taffy, which Mr. Thoma thought the children smelled all the way up to the high school. The secret was—he had boys and girls in school, too.[103]

1920

The Fauquier Democrat February 7, 1920 lamented the loss of sleighs. "Up to a few years ago, after every snow that covered the ground, the sleigh bells jingled up and down our streets; sleighs seemed to be always on call, through not more than one day in two, winters might afford good running. Perhaps because motoring has so largely taken the place of driving we miss this winter sport. Only one sleigh has been seen so far this winter. The team consisted of a mule, he had a rather sad look, perhaps thinking of the past, and moved at a very prudent pace. He evidently thought if he made too much noise with the bells it would arouse envy in others so he shook them as gently as possible." Main roads going out of town were not paved much farther than a mile or so beyond the corporate limits.

When Mr. Carter bought out Roadhouse & Bunch's 5 & Dime Store in 1915, they were not to open another similar business within 5 miles or 5 years. It seems they did not wait quite 5 years before they opened in the building next to Jeffries' Drugstore. In part of that building, which had a partition in the center, was George Hurst's

Jewelry Store.154 (He was father of Clifton Hurst.) Perhaps about this time, Mr. Hurst moved to the building on the far side of Thoma's Bakery.

The Town Council met in the Mayor's office on February 13th. It was decided that the town would "purchase The Hall at $14000". In 1915 the Fletcher Building on The Square was named Town Hall even though it did not belong to the Town. April 3rd, 1920, loads of stone for repairing the streets were brought into town and weighed on the Town scales as one dollar was paid for each ton. After weighing, directions were then given as to how and where to unload. The Council decided to take bids, April 19th, for trash removal from the streets. Maybe things will be a little cleaner around here. May 20th, the Red Cross work rooms in the Municipal Building have finally been closed this week and the material packed away for the use of the County Health Department. The rooms have been turned over to Mr. Clarkson, Town Manager, and the Boy Scouts will have the use of their room as before.

May 22nd, 1920, the Memorial Day exercises were reported to have included a dinner served in the Town Hall for veterans and at the memorial service "Tenting Tonight" was sung by school children and audience. Poems, speeches, list of names were read, and so forth. In 1918 a YWCA Worker first read the poem, "In Flanders Fields Where The Poppies Blow". Flanders Field is a United States Military Cemetery in Europe. This gave the idea of wearing a poppy for the dead of the World War. The worker persuaded the American Legion to adapt the poppy as its memorial flower this year, 1920.

A dance was given at the Town Hall, June 18th, 1920, for the benefit of the Mosby Monument Fund. The monument was unveiled on the 19th, which was a perfect June day. Naturally a large crowd was present. To make it more wonderful—the monument was fully paid for! It is made of a shaft of Virginia granite, 18 feet high resting on a polished granite base. Around the shaft are four medallions. One bears the bronze head of Col. Mosby when he was a young man. On the opposite side it says, "John Singleton Mosby, Lawyer, Soldier, Patriot, December 3, 1837, May 30, 1916". On the other two sides is written, "He has left a name that will live till honor, virtue, courage, all shall cease to claim the homage of the human heart", and, "This tribute is affectionately dedicated to Colonel John S. Mosby, whose deeds of valor and heroic devotion to state and southern principles are the pride and admiration of his soldier comrades and fellow citizens."

COURT HOUSE, WARRENTON, VIRGINIA
Circa 1920
(From collection of Marguerite Peil)

Although The Warrenton Pony Show may have been formed in 1918,[112] it could have been during 1920 as it was first recorded on records of the Virginia Horse Show Association then.[1] Some young boys in town had their cars "souped-up" and naturally would see how fast they could run. One such person was Irvin Garrett and his 1914 Model-T Ford. He liked to see how far he could come up Winchester Street hill in high gear towards the Toll Gate there. If there was a good start at the bottom, it might hit 10 miles an hour as a top speed.

The Town Council, July 6th, 1920, requested merchants of the town to close their places of business on Saturday night by 10:00. It will be quiet around here then. There were two nights of fun that the July 24th paper reported. The Red Cross Carnival turned night into day and transformed Court House Square into a miniature little city all its own. That was a lovely thing to see, and a nice way to talk about The Square. A public meeting, December

4th at the Town Hall was on anti-tuberculosis work and the sale of Christmas Seals. There were 32 deaths in Fauquier County during 1919. What is needed are more sanitoriums. It is hoped that everyone will use the Seals in decorating their store windows during Christmas.

Wayman Carter's father returned to Warrenton during 1920 to buy the building on Main Street in which was Newton Brooke's (Sr.) Furniture Store.[154] It was this year while still 14 years old that Irvin Garrett began to sing with the Warrenton Choral Quartet. Sometimes they gathered after hours in Madison's Barber Shop as either a single or a double quartet. Among the singers were Sam Appleton, G. L. Fletcher, Robert Foley, Biggie and Bill Hodgkin and Major McIntyre. Stores had a habit of sitting their products out on the sidewalk for exhibit, and the A & A Grocery would have a pile of watermelons during the summer to show off that way. Irvin Garrett, who worked in The Fauquier Democrat printing office next door to it, asked Mr. Arthur R. Anderson if he wasn't afraid someone would take one. Mr. Anderson was sure he'd see it if they did. The people from the printing office went to Voses' Store on the other side of the Anderson & Allison Grocery, to play a slot machine there. One day as Irvin returned to work, he pushed a melon along with his toe right on into the printing office. He kept it there for several hours before returning it to Mr. Anderson, showing him it was possible for a melon to disappear. Mr. A. said if he did miss one from now on, he'd know where to look for it. Goods really didn't disappear, except maybe a banana or so, which being in a bunch, were hung up and sold individually.[103]

1921

In February the wholesale prices had gone down and the farmland prices collapsed. The Fauquier Farmers Union held an all day meeting at the Town Hall May 21, 1921. The building was busy with all sorts of goings on. July 2nd had people talking about the windstorm which was the heaviest for years and destroyed a number of trees. They should replant "or before we realize it the Town will be stripped of one of its chief attractions. Already some parts of Main Street and other places are bare and glaring as a country Village should never be". A proposal was made for a Hitching Lot for the town, because now one must drive to the suburbs to hitch a horse or else leave it unhitched on one of the main streets. A lot is needed as a convenience and for sanitary measures. One hitching lot was at Kinchloe's Hay and Grain Feed Store, located near the Depot or across from it. Mr. Kinchloe, always well dressed, wore a high stiff collar. One of the workers usually took him home from work, going along Lee Street, in a one horse buggy.[151]

July 21st, 1921, the Town Council felt the Town force should daily clean in front of the tie rack at the Presbyterian Church, using every effort to keep a sanitary condition. They also planned to purchase a horse and wagon to use for scavenger purposes and to have improvements made on Main Street. The League of Women Voters met July 30th at the Municipal Building. The 19th Amendment in 1920 prohibited denial of suffrage because of sex,[10] so the ladies are now joining forces openly. That building was used for many things, too.

OPERA HOUSE, WARRENTON, VIRGINIA
(From the collection of John Gott)

The Carnival in August attracted a record crowd. $3000.00 was collected. When $650 for expenses was deducted, $2350 was turned over to the Treasurer of Warrenton. September 6th the Council gave thanks to the Chamber of Commerce for the Carnival as it had been done in an efficient and successful manner. The well supplying Town water and the well adjacent to it was found to be unclean September 17th, due to insufficient weather conditions. There was a light snow during the winter and it has been a dry summer, which effected the deep water supply, and the water needed to be boiled. In October the Council made plans to chlorinate the Town Well.

October 1st, 1921, the work of paving Main Street was progressing rapidly and it will certainly be an improvement. A new piece of cement sidewalk has been laid in front of Brooke's Furniture Store. The Main Street work was finished by October 29th and the roadway is in good condition except for Court House Square. The Democrats are meeting at Town Hall and urging all democrats to vote. Some ladies of the town petitioned the Town Council to plant trees on Main Street, December 22nd, but the discussion was moved to the January meeting. The first piece of motorized fire equipment was bought this year. It was a 1916 Chevrolet truck costing $2815, with a 50-gallon chemical tank and a slipping clutch which often failed on an up-hill climb. There was also a hand-driven hose reel. Charles M. Jeffries was the Fire Chief now.

The Warrenton Supply built a small service station in 1921 on the lot at the corner of Waterloo and 7th Streets,[113] where the Farmers' Hotel used to be. About now W. E. Sudduth had one of the first touring cars in town, - an open sporty type of machine that made a lot of noise and went about 20 miles an hour. Down the hill on Waterloo Street was a dairy farm (now Sudduth Memorial Monuments) and Mr. Moser delivered milk in town, one place being the home of Robert Anderson. His mother had a steel bucket sitting on her front porch into which Mr. Moser poured the milk from his container. The bucket of milk continued to sit there until Mrs. Anderson eventually took it into the house.[145] Someone said there were times when Mr. Moser might deliver the milk in the hearse.

1922

Just before February 4th, 1922, there was reported to have been the heaviest snow since 1899. An oyster supper was held at the Town Hall for the benefit of St. James Parish Aid Fund. Twice, February 10th and 23rd, the Town Council was approached by W. E. Bishop and J. L. Howard with an application to build a garage, first at the corner of Winchester and Alexandria Pike and the next time at the corner of Waterloo and Diagonal Streets. They were refused both times. Eight sportsmen met at the Fauquier Springs Club April 3rd and organized The Virginia Gold Cup Race.34   April 4th, the Council rescinded the order not to allow any pool rooms in town. Also they heard that some of the entertainments in The Hall were a nuisance.   June 6th was a perfect spring day for the Gold Cup or Steeplechase held that day on a farm west of town, so people were passing through on their way to it.34

MAIN STREET, WARRENTON, VIRGINIA
Circa 1922
(From the collection of John K. Gott)

MAIN STREET, WARRENTON, VIRGINIA
Circa 1922

CULPEPER STREET, WARRENTON, VIRGINIA

June 3rd, 1922, The Fauquier Democrat reported that the Rebel Yell was given on Confederate Memorial Day during the ceremonies, among other events. There was the usual procession to the cemetery from The Square. The Town Council decided, June 6th, that the hitching shall be discontinued in the street between the Presbyterian Church and the Municipal Building. "Main Street", a one night open air entertainment will be given in the Court House Square on Wednesday evening, September 13th. The ad in the paper September 9th told about it. . . . .

"MAIN STREET"

Grand Fall Opening

Court House Square   On Night Only

Wed. Sept. 13

Visit our complete Grocery, Our Sanitary Drug Store, Drinks, Cigarettes, and Ready-Mixed Paints.
Ten Cent Store with full line of Toys and Confetti
Patronize the Baldwin's Ridge Emporium
Come to Our Quick Lunch Stand, Dairy and Candy Kitchen
Try Miss Lulu Bett's famous cakes at the Bakery
"If Winter Comes" be prepared
Our prices are Moderate and Plenty of Fun Thrown In With Every Purchase.

William G. Bartenstein became the Fire Chief in 1922 and Lester Burke was the official bell ringer. The Courthouse Bell had a special way of being handled or else it would turn over and no sound would come from it. All available men rushed to the Fire House to take out the truck. Others pulled the hose reel, running as they went down hill, but going up hill was more like a crawl.

1923

February 24, 1923, "Her Honor The Mayor", a clever little play was presented at Town Hall by the Dramatic Club of Marshall High School. March 3rd, "To Have And To Hold" was presented at The Opera House. Wonder what made the difference since both were the same building? Maybe it was the activity—when a movie it was the Opera House and when another program, it was Town Hall. A Pageant, "The Grand Old Country" was held May 8th, as reported on the 12th. It celebrated Historical "Fauquier Day" or as some called it, "Warrenton Day". The 1½ hour parade formed

WARRENTON DAY, May 8, 1923, featured horseback riders, floats, marching veterans and school children. This scene shows the present-day H. B. Carter Furniture store at right end of the block.

at Stuyvesant School, came down Winchester Street and Main Street to the Post Office, turned there and continued to the Horse Show Grounds where they held a program. There were four group themes—Indian Life, Colonial Period, Ante-Bellum and Modern Life.[114] So many floats, horseback riders, marching veterans and school children parading to portray the themes.

June 2nd, 1923 was the usual Memorial Day program beginning at The Hall. July 16th, the cornerstone of the new Warrenton Library Building was laid, being built through a gift to the Warrenton Library Association by Judge Barton Payne, but the vacant lot was purchased with funds left to it by Mrs. Elizabeth Sharpless Keith. August 2nd, President Warren G. Harding died and Vice-President Calvin Coolidge succeeded him. By August 28th, the Town Council planned the digging of a new well for Town water.

October 2nd found Tom Frost wanting to erect a filling station at Winchester and Alexandria Pike. At first the Council granted it, but October 11th, discussed the request again and refused it. A committee suggested making the road from the Courthouse past Fauquier National Bank one-way. There were to be changes along Main Street, too. Signs and awnings on stores are to be raised to allow a person six-foot tall to pass. There would be concrete pavements on Main Street between Culpeper and the Post Office corner, and the bad pavement in front of the Clerk's Office was to be repaired. One time, perhaps this was the year, some of the young lads of the community celebrated Halloween by hiding the benches from the Fountain. However, "they" found out who one of them was and made him return them.[154]

December 15th, 1923, someone wrote to The Fauquier Democrat asking if anyone remembered when "Reuben Rowzie rode his trained horse up and down the Courthouse steps on March Court Days?" This didn't just happen on those days. One Christmas someone, probably from the Free State "they" said, had a little too much of the bottle and rode his horse up the steps.[115] Then there was Dick Thompson who also did it. His horse was black as the Ace of Spades, a beautiful thing, and did tricks also. One day a man wanted to ride it, but Thompson bet him $5.00 he couldn't ride the horse to the corner of the next block. The man said anyone could ride a horse, got on him and started off. But halfway up the block Thompson gave a big whistle. The horse turned around and trotted back to his owner and no amount of persuasion could make it go to the end of the block.[116] At sometime a Buck Kendall, from the

Free State rode up the Courthouse steps, announced to a full court room that he was in Warrenton and if they wanted him, they would have to catch him. Then he rode down the steps.[182]

1924

A question was asked bright and early January 5th, 1924 in the paper. "Who remembers when Kitty Rose gave a week's show in the old Town Hall?" — the old building on No. 3rd and Main Streets. A man from Pennsylvania wrote January 20th, saying that 20 years ago he thought Main Street was like Broadway, and The Square was like New York's Times Square, and when the sun set over the Blue Ridge Mountains that the whole world was in darkness. February 16th the announcement was made that Warrenton would have a new Clerk's Office at the cost of $50,000. During the next couple months there were more questions. Who remembers, "when the street lights were about the only things 'lit' on the streets after dark" and "when we went to the movies night after night and did not know what picture we would see till the show began?" March 8th one wondered who remembers "when meetings for men, led by laymen were held in the Courthouse every Sunday afternoon" and "when Ian Montgomery and Anton Schwab were among the prize winners at a baby show held by the King's Daughters in the old Town Hall?" There was another in the April 5th paper, who remembers "when Martha Braddox sold pies and cakes in the Five Point Building which stood near the present Greek Restaurant?" That is the Warrenton Cafe they were talking about.

It was announced that the store formerly known as the Community Store on Court House Square will be in the future known as the "Fauquier Grocery" and will be conducted under the same efficient management as heretofore. Wonder if this was when Raymond Pearson had his grocery store in half of the building at the corner of Winchester and Alexandria Pike and a restaurant was in the other half. About this time "The Shenandoah" was in the Pattie Building, a double building with a curve in it.[117] Seems that this restaurant was run by a Greek person, and then, at sometime W. H. Kays, Kenneth's Dad, and Patties' Grocery were in the same building.[103] Kays had a restaurant in the Farmers' Hotel at the time of the fire.

The books of the Warrenton Library were transferred to the new building, but the formal opening had to be postponed until

WARRENTON LIBRARY, WARRENTON, VIRGINIA
Circa 1923
(From the collection of John K. Gott)

May because of the absence of Judge John Barton Payne, who had gone to Europe. When the former opening did occur on May 20th, 1924, there had been a rainy spell, the usual Blackberry Winter, and this day was 'passin', I heard it said. It wasn't bad, but neither was it good. The officers, friends and contributors packed themselves into the main room for the ceremonies, after which a luncheon was served in the basement of the building. The first entertainment in the assembly room was a success with the crowd lingering until late in the evening.[118] Among the Memorial Day Exercises, reported May 31st, Miss Louise Fox of Warrenton High School read "In Flanders Field".

Tuesday, June 17th, 1924, a Flower Show was held in the Library auditorium with an admission of 10¢. The room rented at $7.00 for an afternoon or $10.00 for an evening. The trees were being cut down in the Clerk's Office yard, June 28th, in preparation for the new building. July 7th the Town Council decided to post signs at each road entering Town, with the speed limit on it. They did that once before, but I guess the signs needed replacing by this time. Commencing July 14th the merchants of Warrenton will close their places of business at 6:30pm during the week days and at 10:30 on Saturday nights, to continue through the summer months and up to and including September 13th. Each merchant is to have the sidewalk in front of his place of business swept each Saturday night.

The Carnival this year, 1924, was held the first weekend in September for the benefit of the Fauquier County Hospital in a brightly lighted Square with lots of noise and gaiety, being one of the grandest and biggest yet. Betsy Bartenstein was among those who sat on the bench at the Fountain to watch the Carnival on the street between the Clerk's Office and the Courthouse. There was a fence on the side of the Clerk's Office next to Court Street. When her mother came on a shopping trip to town, she parked the pony cart along side the fence, looping the reins of the pony, Patsy, over the fence, who would stand quietly there for a couple of hours. This must be the same iron fence the Council talked about September 24, 1887, when they wanted to remove it.

A new heating plant was installed in the Courthouse during September, preparing for the winter. An interesting ad in the paper for September 27th, 1924, said,

The Warrenton Cafe

John Kreticos, Prop.

For Ladies and Gentlemen

Regular meals   Short Orders served Daily

Home made pies   Velvet Ice Cream   Clean and Refined

Polite and Promp Service

The Warrenton Cafe

Main Street   Opposite Court House

Warrenton, Va.

The Fauquier National Bank made an application October 7th, 1924, to build a new bank building. They have been in the present one since 1902. December 15th, the Warrenton Supply made application to build a modern gasoline station at the corner of their lot at Waterloo Street next to the Hospital. December 20th it was announced that the laying of the cornerstone of the new County Clerk's Office Building, which was supposed to have been Wednesday, was postponed because the builder thought the scaffolding that was necessary for the work at this time would interfere with the ceremonies. They'll announce another date later. The paper, December 27th, reported that Mr. Eppa S. Cox, Treasurer of Fauquier County, while on his way to his office on Wednesday morning, had quite an injury on the slippery street near the Municipal Building. An automobile passing Mr. Cox was carrying some wire in which he was caught, thrown to the ground and hit his head. It is said he is suffering very much and the extent of the injury is not known.

Two other things happened sometime during the year of 1924. First, the Warrenton Volunteer Fire Company organized by October with headquarters at 81 Main, which was the Municipal Building, where the other was. A steam whistle was installed on the electric company's boilers at the plant owned by M. J. O'Connell, that was used as the fire alarm. The signals were a short blast for a Town fire and a long one for a County fire. December 3rd, Mayor T. E. Frank presided over a meeting held by the organization.[81] Second, during 1924 or maybe it was 1925, a woman was jailed for a misdemeanor. At the trial, the Judge asked her if she had any visitors after her arrest. The woman said no one that she knew, but a small elderly man with a long white beard came to the cell every night. He never spoke, but did try to take away the bed clothes. Her description fitted a Mr. G., who is said to have died about 1899 in the cell in which she had been placed.[76]

1925

February 26, 1925 saw the formal opening of the Fauquier Hospital on Waterloo Street. March 3rd, the Town Council gave their permission to lay concrete from the W. C. Marshall Building to W. E. Bishop's Store on Main Street. It's not sure just when Ernest Bishop's Store went in, but it was located at the corner of South 5th and Main Streets in a tall building (now site of National Variety). People said he had a large stomach which sometimes got against the scales when he weighed an item. Many items the ladies had to say, "Step back a bit, Mr. Bishop".[144]

April 7th The Council agreed for concrete pavement to be placed in front of the Hospital. It was reported April 25th that a small fire which started Wednesday afternoon on the roof of the house next to the Municipal Building, occupied by Mr. Basil Fletcher, was soon put out by the Fire Company. A good thing they were close by and the Municipal Building—Fire house— didn't burn. The first fund raising for the Volunteer Fire Department was a ministerial show held May 20th on the stage of the movie theater operated by Mrs. Washington on Court House Square, or the "Opera House".[81] It was just before this that M. J. O'Connell went to work in New York and sold his holdings to Mrs. Washington. Services for the Confederate dead were held Memorial Day, Saturday, May 30th in the Town Hall. There was a luncheon for the Veterans, Sons of Veterans, and the American Legion: then the Memorial services. As usual, all places of business were closed from 3:00 to 4:30pm.

A Bond issue election was held Tuesday, July 14th, 1925 as to Warrenton's proposed Water and Sewer System. I'm not sure what it all meant, but there was something about a connection in front of the Courthouse and the sewer main on Alexandria Road, so it did concern The Square. Agusut 15th, the first in a series of dances for the benefit of the Warrenton Library was held in the lower room of the building. The new floor and other improvements recently completed make the room idea for dancing and other entertainments. The dance was successful in every way.

September 1st, 1925 saw a new Mayor—Thomas E. Frank— who had been acting Mayor for sometime. A large crowd, all happy and good spenders, attended the Street Carnival, September 12th, which was a Hospital benefit. A real fun time to end the summer. The Fauquier National Bank moved into their new building at the corner of Court and Hotel Streets - #10 Court Street. September 23rd. The dance given at the Library auditorium Christmas night was for the benefit of the Cripple Children's Hospital in Richmond. During this year Dr. J. O. Hodgkin had a fire in his second floor office (now Grayson Building) after which he retired and turned the practice over to his sons J. O., Jr. - "Biggie" - and Bill. A large party of French and Russians traveling in trucks passed through Warrenton the last of December as they went to Florida.

The Town and Public Stable was off "Cow Alley", back of Carter's, or was it behind Peoples National Bank (now their parking lot)? Anyway, Dr. Carter, who used to wear a derby hat all the time, kept beautiful saddle horses in it as did the Fire Department who had big draft horses like Clydesdales. Other horses were probably there, too. It was either 1924 or 1925 that it burned with at least four horses belonging to the Town and Dr. Carter being lost. The horses, they said, came out of the stable, but in the confusion went back inside. A youth, Jimmy Austin, who came to Warrenton in 1924, watched the carcasses placed onto sleds and then pulled to the burying place down Academy Hill below the school, and for a long time, Robert Anderson and others could smell the odor not only of the burned building but of the flesh, too, that lingered over that part of town.

1926

The new Clerk's Office Building was ready January 1, 1926, costing about $75,000.00. The brick and marble building is one of the most handsome in this part of the state as it stands bright and shiny new behind the old Clerk's Office. The dance held New Year's night in the Library auditorium was for the benefit for the Library itself. By January 23rd everything had been moved to the new building and the empty old Clerk's Office Building, the "Little Building" as some called it, was being torn down as fast as the solid work of over 100 years ago will permit - probably it was authorized to be built in 1795.

During March 1926 the Bon Ton Millinery Company opened for business on Main Street[119] next door to Carter's. Miss Kitty Phillips owned it.[154] A few ladies did not consider they had a "new" hat unless it came from here. Sometimes an old hat would be carried in and re-done with ribbon or flowers and it came out a "new" hat.[182] March 6th the Warrenton Flower Club was asked to supervise the planting of the grounds around the new County Building. As of April 14, The Fauquier Democrat began publishing twice a week.[120] Sometime in the night of April 24th, three boys broke into several houses after which they went into a freight car at the railroad station, lit a bonfire and sat down to divide their loot. The car began to burn. The police and firemen came. Needless to say, at 4am, the boys were caught. That is the way justice should work.

Robert Lunceford had paid $444 for his first car in 1923. Now, May 3rd, 1926, he bought one from Warrenton Supply for $420.50. They had to put the hood, wheels, and windshield onto the chassis. May 6th, the Town Council voted that the expense of paving on Main Street in front of the Clerk's Office and at the side of that building, on Culpeper Street would be on shares, half and half between the County and the Town. A month long drought has caused a hardship to the farmers by May 15th. The outside brick work for the County Office Building is now finished. The concrete walks have been laid, the ground is level and the added top soil ready for the planting of grass. The old brick walk has been taken up and a new pavement is to be laid soon from the corner of Main Street to the corner of the Woman's Realty Building on Culpeper. The large flagstones, which were taken up from the front of the old Clerk's Office were sold Saturday in five lots, bring in $143.00. Some purchasers were Colonel J. D. Richards, Mrs. John Webb Tyler, and Mr. Winmill. Betsy Bartenstein's father, who was Clerk of the Court, took home a flagstone step and guttering guards, as well as some other stepping stones and curb pieces, which he made into benches for their yard. He said General LaFayette stepped on the old stones, so Betsy was quite proud to have them. There are depressions worn in them from their long use. The stone slab vault floor from the office was placed as their front porch step.

Memorial Day, 1926, was observed with the usual order of events. A large crowd and an unusual profusion of flowers were on hand, many being those exhibited at the flower show and then given for the occasion. The basement of the Courthouse was used this time for the dinner, after which was the ceremony and then all went to the Cemetery. Warrenton was all dressed up, June 1st, to welcome some foreign visitors. Even the weather cooperated. There was a good shower the night before that laid the dust and made things shine. The pilot car and four large buses came up Alexandria Pike at 1pm, to assemble at the Courthouse for the formal welcome. The town really presented a gala appearance as it received the distinguished guests of the Red Cross delegates and the diplomatic representatives of our sister countries of the two Americas. The Courthouse and other public buildings were decorated with flags of the United States, the Red Cross and the South American countries.

An advertisement in the paper said Laborers were wanted "At Once", being needed for the Warrenton Sewerage and Water Works, for a Ten Hour Day at Steady Work For Balance of the Year, and

METHODIST CHURCH, WARRENTON, VIRGINIA
Circa 1926
(From the collection of Marguerite Peil)

**FAUQUIER COUNTY CLERKS OFFICE
WARRENTON, VIRGINIA**

**WARRENTON GREEN HOTEL
WARRENTON, VIRGINIA**

are to inquire at the Office of the Town Manager in the old Town Hall Building. The Town Council planned to buy a motorcycle June 8th, 1926, at a cost of $399.65, and decided to leave three trees in front of the Clerk's Office. After June 26th, one needed a license to carry a gun.[122]   The AAA was denying they were warning tourist to avoid Warrenton because of the strict traffic regulations. The 150th Anniversary of American independence was celebrated this year as the Sesqui-centennial Exposition was staged in Philadelphia.

The Ku Klux Klan formed on East Main Street at 8pm, November 17th, 1926 to march along Main Street to the Courthouse and down Alexandria Pike to Benner's Field for a meeting. Some people who watched it were able to look at the shoes under the robes and know who it was that marched. Even though the weather was cold and there had been heavy rains, about 200 Knights with their red torches and banners took part in it. Perhaps it was at this that Irvin Garrett and Wayman Carter watched the cross burn on the vacant lot at the corner of Winchester and Alexandria Pike. Robert Lunceford overheard someone in the watching crowd say, "If I have to cover my face to belong to an organization, I'll not join it."

The Community Christmas service was held in spite of a cold wind blowing. A crowd assembled by 7:30 that Sunday night on the Courthouse steps, in cars, and on foot in The Square, as well as around the Christmas tree with its beautiful lights in many colors, which this year was placed at The Fountain. The chorus sang carols and at 8:00 they had an indoor service in The Hall, which was crowded, too. This Christmas was almost noiseless. Fireworks were banned in the town limits except for harmless torpedoes and sparklers. Mable Riber (Martin) began living with the John Benner family in 1924. She went with Mrs. Benner to shop, especially at Christmas time, to Andersons on the corner of Culpeper and Main Streets.

It was during 1926 that Anne Brook (Smith) lived at "Suffield". Alexandria Pike between Warrenton and New Baltimore was being improved. Although one of the first paved, it was narrow with a high crown and sharply sloping shoulders. The work was being done by prisoners who lived at a camp near New Baltimore. Mules pulled the heavy scoops or pans as they leveled off the roadway. About now a building was built on the vacant lot between Hurst's Jewelry Store and the Carter Building on Main Street for Matthew and Fewell's Clothing Store.[154]   At least it seems it was now a vacant lot. Once there was a two story frame building where Miss Julia French had her home and shop. Most clothes and hats were made at home, but Elizabeth I. Hutton bought a hat with blue trim and her sister had one with pink trim from Miss French.[152]

January 8th, 1927 found the Warrenton Supply Company's Filling Station advertising Standard Gas at 26¢ and Esso at 28¢ per gallon. Rev. Mr. J. A. Frazier announced March 5th that he had bought "The Shenandoah", a restaurant located in the building next to the Town Hall, planning to reopen as a restaurant within a few days. About now Harder Brothers Electrical Contractors opened a shop in the Town Hall. Did Mrs. Frank Hodgkins have a millinery shop here before this or did that come a little later?[179]

The Town Council decided May 3rd, 1927, that restaurants and entertainment places were now to close NOT later than 12 midnight. May 20th Charles Lindbergh left New York and arrived in France the next day after the first solo flight across the Atlantic. May 28th the Confederate Memorial Day exercises were held in the Opera House, with the usual program, after which the children of the community, as is their custom, led the march to the Cemetery for the program around the Monument. A flower show was held June 4th in the Library auditorium.

Willard Kirby's family moved to Warrenton June 15, 1927 from Charlottesville. He thought Warrenton was so small after all the buildings Charlottesville had. Saturday night, June 25th, his Dad took the family—his mother, sister, and two baby brothers—to the movies. They didn't know where the movie hall was, so asked someone in front of the Courthouse. The man pointed to the building across The Square. There was no name on the building, but over the door was a goose-necked light with a naked bulb. At the ticket office, just inside the door, his Dad asked if the children needed tickets. He was told "No", not if they could be held on the lap, for they sold seats, not tickets, for 10¢. There were 150 or 200 seats and folding chairs with Piedmont Cigarettes written on them, and there was still the same problem with them that M. J. O'Connell had. The only person, maybe, to smoke during the movie was Charlie Jeffries. Even with ceiling fans running in the room on second floor, if the night was hot, it would be quite warm. At least it seems the room was upstairs.[133]

Sometimes when Mrs. Washington, a large portly woman, was running the projector she would have to leave it to tell some of the boys, such as Jimmy O. Hodgkin III, to quiet down. He and Blanche O'Connell were impressed with Lon Channey in The Phantom At The Opera, and laughed at Laurel and Hardy. Whenever

Tom Mix was shown, M. J. O'Connell had called his mother, whose home was between The Plains and Middleburg, so she could see "her boy". Hunter Bowman, a Mr. Allen or Sam Appleton played the piano for the movies. These people were suppose to play music to correspond with what was happening on the screen. But, at times the person would become so fascinated with what was going on that they just banged and banged without a tune.[164] As the Indians or the badmen were slipping up behind the good cowboys, someone would usually yell, "lookout!". The audience talked to the movie characters as if they were real. Along beside this building there was a dirt path leading from The Square to an alley way behind the Library. Here, where adults usually didn't walk, children played marbles. Some liked to play for keeps and they were told this was dishonest, getting something for nothing without paying for it, so they hid.[163]

Harry O'Brien who worked for the EPO, continued as projectionist but could not always get back to the theater in time for the matinees so he broke in W. Kenny Kays, (who eventually took over. "Kenny took my job", Harry would jokingly say). Bessie Woodzel (Whitmore) watched the silent movies as well as the woman in front of the audience who played the piano, and sometimes would sing. This may have been Mrs. Mary Richards, who lived on Winchester Street. Irvin Garrett continued as usher. Robert Lunceford went to see a movie one day that had a man asleep along a road. He woke up to see a lion jumping over him, which frightened him so much, even his socks rolled up in a little ball. The movie that impressed Albert Robinson was a comic, as most of them were, that he went to see in the Town Hall about a man who was in the way of a steam roller. It went over him, mashing him flat. A friend pulled him off the road while another used a sledge hammer to beat him back into the proper shape. Arrabelle Laws' (Arrington) grandfather wanted to see a movie about a prize fight. He took both she and her mother, who held Arrabelle on her lap during the whole silent picture. (When the talking pictures came, in Oct., the sound was on a record and at times it was hard to get the film and sound together.) Hunter Bowman also played for the minstrels that were held in the same theater.

During September 1927, the children of Fauquier County began to receive their first inoculations against diphtheria. Although by October 12th, the Red Cross had moved to the Fauquier National Bank Building, contributions of clothes could still be taken to their old room at the Fire House.

This year a wing was added to the Warren Green Hotel.26 Wallis Warfield was a guest at the hotel during the year, being among many other honored persons.123 A map made by G. Herbert Massie this year and perhaps also worked on by Town Manager Sidney Shumate and Mayor Richard H. Marriott, shows some new locations and names of the streets,16 although nothing changed around The Square. They probably needed revision with the installation of the sewer lines.

November 21st, 1927 was a Big Time in Warrenton to celebrate the opening of Lee Highway connecting it with Washington. An automobile procession of cars from the years 1907 through 1927 left Washington and arrived here about noon to be greeted by an awaiting crowd. After a parade through the streets, much noise by people and horns, cheers and waving, there were speeches made from the steps of the Courthouse. Lots of fun and excitement! It was in 1927 that Dr. Hiden bought the Town Hall Building on Court House Square from Lucian Moss. Guess the Town didn't buy it in 1920 when The Council discussed it. Mrs. Ethel Bishop bought and occupied the T. E. Pattie house on Winchester Street, while the house next door, owned by Dr. Frank C. Hodgkin, was bought by Dr. John L. Thornton. All buildings located almost in a row.

Well, wouldn't you know it. The pretty Christmas tree placed at the Fountain again this year got into trouble! It seems two fellows went out to the moutains for a little bootleg. When they returned, they were trying to go around the Fountain, but ran into the tree. One got out of the car, looked at the tree and said, "What do you know—We're still in the mountains!"

1928

The Warrenton Volunteer Fire Company had its annual banquet at the Municipal-Fire House Building, January 4th, 1928. A couple weeks later, January 21st, they presented the Town with a siren that was located on the Municipal Building which will be used as an alarm for fires, and also as a signal for drills at 7:30 on Tuesday evenings. I think the electric alarm at the door had to be turned off by a member when they left. The Company paid for this alarm out of its own treasury at a total cost of $734.23.

The basement of the Courthouse was used February 1st, 1928 for the tuberculosis clinic, when 16 people were examined. March

21st the Chamber of Commerce proposed a "White Way" for Warrenton's Main Street going from the Courthouse to the Post Office, and on Culpeper Street going from Main to Lee Streets. They would have to install a number of lights on attractive lamp posts along these streets with all wires of the light and phone companies being placed underground. That means more digging and tearing up of the streets. According to the crowd in Warrenton Monday of March Court day, it has not lost any of its attraction. It was a beautiful spring day which added to the holiday atmosphere. But, quiet and good order was had and the crowd left early. Not like the "good old days". During March Court there used to be three Civil War Veterans who put on their uniforms and came to town. Then there was only one - and one year, there were none.

Also in the 1920's, earlier than now, there was a clubfooted Black Man called, "The Town Crier". He wore a sandwich-board type of sign over his shoulders and carried a hand bell. As he rang it, he cried something like, "Hear ye, hear ye". He was paid, of course, to call out interesting news, announcements, sales, deaths, and so forth.[145] His name was Charlie Chancellor.[108] The last Friday and Saturday of March the colored school children of the county had an exhibition of their work in the Courthouse. It was well worth seeing in itself, people said, and as showing the training the children are receiving, it was given careful inspection. The large room and corridor was crowded with specimens of work such as sewing, both plain and fancy, basketwork and chair seating, useful and ornamental articles, and home crafts.

Memorial Day services were held in the Town Hall on May 26th, 1928 at 11am, having their speakers and program before the parade to the cemetery, after which was a lunch for the Veterans. June 6th the Blue Parrot was advertised as being on Culpeper Street, being run by Lucy Evans who had it on Winchester Street in 1920. Plans were being made June 13th, by the Library Association to place an iron fence around the Library grounds for its protection. The grounds will be just as pretty outside as it is on the inside, for shrubbery and flowers will be planted.

In July, 1928, Willard Kirby's father took him and two friends to a matinee, first stopping by the Lucky Strike Miniature Golf Course which was owned by Mrs. Isabel Hilleary. It was entered by an alleyway between Cornblatt's and Peoples National Bank. The man who ran the golf course said they could have a free game. The other boys were hitting their balls as if they were really playing golf instead of putting it, therefore tore up the course so badly, it had to be closed for a short time until it was put right again. Bill Gaines was a lawyer in town now with the nickname, "the poor man's lawyer" as he would help those with a problem even when they could not pay him.[133] August 10th found the Town Council making plans to repair the street between Warrenton Supply Company and the Warren Green so water will not flow into the street from the Hotel's outlets.

September 12th, 1928 there was a proposal for some streets to become one-way. They would be Culpeper Street from The Fauquier Democrat office to Main Street and from Main Street down Court Street between The Fauquier National Bank and the Courthouse on the one side and the Clerk's Office and California House on the other side. Workers from Washington held a preaching service on the Courthouse steps Sunday evening, September 16th at 7:30. Another Flower Show, September 28th, in the auditorium of the Library.

Religious services were held again, Sunday, October 21st, 1928 at 7:30 at the Courthouse steps. The Union Christmas service was Sunday evening, December 23rd around the Community Tree that this year was placed on the Courthouse porch and people in The Square sang carols in the open air, followed by a religious service in the Warrenton Theater at the Town Hall. Rev. Mr. Chinn made the address. The King's Daughters were collecting Christmas baskets which were to go out from the Fire Engine Room of the Municipal Building.

Frazier's Restaurant continued at The Square, being more of an ice cream parlor than a restaurant, for more of it and cakes sold than anything else. His two daughters, Julia and Ruth worked there. Apartments were rented above the place. Tom Hutchison was one who had a room there after he came from Leesburg in 1927. He stayed a short time before moving next door to Mrs. Ethel Bishop's place, as she took renters. Several of them liked to stay up late playing bridge.

Hallie Thorp moved to Warrenton in September 1928, found it pleasant to sit and relax at the Fountain. Welton Hansbrough liked to see the water come from the lion's mouth and fall into the basin below. There were three or four heads resembling a lion. But, when Edith Davenport (Lunceford) moved to Warrenton in November, she found the Fountain gone. It wasn't kept in good repair and was in the way of the increasing automobile traffic as cars would chip pieces off going around the turn. When it was removed, Pete Shirley took it to his home on Falmouth Street, placing the benches in the front yard and the fountain part in the garden back of the house (now belonging to Skip Harris).

At this time, the Garrett Garage of Gene Garrett, Sr. on the corner of Alexandria Pike and Horner Street, was the third largest Buick Agency in the United States. Upstairs of that building there was an entrance off the parking lot at the top of the hill as it went up Horner. The space in the garage was used as a storage area. Many wealthy people of the county had cars such as Stuts, Bearcats, or Rolls Royce, but did not want to drive them on the dirt roads, so stored them here, especially over the winter. In 1928 a Bowling Alley was put in this place. The former Methodist Church at Culpeper and Lee Streets was sold to Richard Wallach this year and remodeled into apartments on the top floors with the street floor having shops. Now the building was called The Wallach Building.

1929

Around January 3rd, 1929, the Community Christmas tree which brightened the evenings during the holidays, was stripped of its beautiful lights and taken down. Really a sad sight to see, but hopefully next year—that's this year already—will come, and they will be enjoyed again.

Hurray for the Ladies! There was a meeting February 20th, 1929, in the Library auditorium for the purpose of organizing a Fire Auxiliary to the local Fire Company. About a week later several members of the Salvation Army were in Warrenton with their musical instruments conducting street services. When thinking of the Salvation Army, the jingle of the tambourine is thought of more than other instruments.

March 2nd, 1929, people were asking for contributions for the "White Way" on Main Street. Tom Hutchison and Eddie Risdon were two of those collecting money from the store keepers. It was to replace the wooden light poles, and they said the street would be so bright, you could pick up a dime at midnight. Eddie Risdon had a hardware store (now Thrift Shop) on Main Street. Tom Hutchison bought the Fletcher Building across from Ullman's on Lee Street, to operate a Chevrolet Garage in it. After Prohibition both Ullman's and Fletcher's gave up their bar-rooms and were grocery stores. When the state went dry, a person was allowed one gallon of whiskey at a time. Someone, it is said, bought a baby carriage at Fletcher's, and a gallon of whiskey. He put the whiskey in the carriage and went rolling it down the street, the easiest way to carry it. Can't you just see the expression on people's faces when they looked to see the baby?[144] Another story tells that one day an elderly man came into Fletcher's store and wanted 1½ fish. His wife was a skinny little thing who didn't eat much. When Mr. Fletcher asked the man why he wanted only ½ a fish, he said his wife wouldn't eat but half a fish and there was no point in wasting it.[68]

Friday, March 8th, 1929, there was a public meeting in the Courthouse for the purpose of organizing a local chapter of Isaak Walton League of America. March 25th—Dear Ole March Court Day. People no longer look forward to it as they used to. They were like a child looking for and counting the days until Christmas. This used to be the first visit to the County Seat after a winter of hibernation. With the automobiles and improved roads, people are not confined as they once were, so reunions of friends - and fights with whomever, are not as great today. Things are more orderly and business-like. There was the horse parade on Main Street and Latham Shumate telling how wonderful they were as he cried the sales. Now he is selling confiscated automobiles.

Dr. M. B. Hiden applied, May 7th, 1929, to the Town Council to have a filling station on his Theater property but there were objections. He and, I think, Major McIntyre, as representatives of the Chamber of Commerce, asked that the rental of the hitching lot for the town be borne by the Town. This was agreed upon. I'm not sure just where the lot was, but there was a vacant lot on Main Street across from the Post Office and another one farther up. Don't think it was the first on, but could have been the second.

The usual Confederate Memorial Day was held in the Town Hall, with the parade to the cemetery. But, on June 1st, 1929, a letter appeared in the paper saying Memorial Day was dying from lack of interest. Once the program was opened by a Veteran known to everyone as Old Zoo, firing his cannon in The Public Square. The Flower Show was missed, as it was held June 19th in the Spilman Memorial Parish House of the Episcopal Church. The completion and dedication of the General Baldwin Day Spilman Parish House had been this year, connecting with the one built in 1912.[98]

Miss Mary Smith who inherited the California House in 1856, lived there until the property went to her brothers, Fred Waugh and

Thomas Smith. It was held by the Smiths until it was sold July 3rd, 1929 to E. W. Winmill for over $10,000. He bought from the estate of Mrs. Elizabeth Fairfax Gaines Smith Jones. Plans are to remodel it into offices and a stockbroker's office. The basement entries are to be left intact, but the front entrance facing the Warren Green Hotel, on the second floor, was removed. The entrance on the second floor of the Courthouse side was left.[21] The lower floor of the Courthouse is also being remodeled into five office rooms for lawyers or county officers. July 27th a clinic was held at the Courthouse with Dr. C. W. Scott as examiner, Mrs. Scott as the clerk, and several nurses assisting.

President Herbert Hoover is building an area for fishing on the upper waters of the Rapidan at his Summer Camp. The road and bridge builders for this with 12 trucks, passed through town Wednesday, August 6th, 1929. Although the President's party going through Warrenton doesn't really cause much excitement any more since it happens so often, many did gather at the street corners on August 10th in the hope of seeing Colonel Lindbergh and his bride. But, there was disappointment for they were either not in the group or they were not recognized. August 31st there was plenty of excitement, though, with fun and gaiety, at the bigger and better than ever Carnival benefiting the hospital.

An announcement, September 7th, 1929, said that Warrenton was not affected by the present drought as there was now plenty of water due to the new water system. October 1st the Town Council decided to sell two horses, a wagon and some equipment. I suppose the town is going to be mechanized pretty soon. The "White Way" work was begun October 5th and it's hoped to be an accomplished fact soon. October 24th was a terrible day for many people. The bottom fell out of the Stock Market. Two days later, Saturday the 26th, a large party of Shriners and Acca Temple Legion of Honor from Richmond passed through Warrenton on their way home from Winchester. They had dinner at the Warren Green Hotel and gave a colorful parade around The Square in their uniforms, with drum and fife accompaniment. That raised the spirits somewhat.

Friday, November 1st, 1929, one of the regular Tuberculosis clinics of the State Board of Health and Red Cross was held in the Courthouse. An Art Exhibit was put on by the American Federation of Arts, in the lower room of the Library. It was opened with a tea and teachers brought their pupils to see it. The Town Council, November 12th, said they would not allow slot machines in the town. At that meeting the Fire Company told them they wanted all of their building. November 16th, had a meeting of citizens and the Directors of the Chamber of Commerce to discuss the location of Lee Highway. It had been reported the survey would route the highway by leaving Alexandria Pike one mile or more north of Warrenton, and cutting across the athletic field to intersect with the old highway about one mile west of town. Also there was a discussion as to installing "Stop" and "Go" or "Red" and "Green" lights at the Court House Square where the four streets and two highways come together. The Town will no doubt install these lights IF the highway comes this way as the "traffic will be abnormally great at this point". In November, Peoples National Bank opened their remodeled and renovated building.

The Community Christmas tree was lighted on Sunday evening, December 23rd, 1929, being placed again on the Courthouse portico, a safe place for it. Because of bad weather carols were sung indoors with the usual union Christmas service in the Parish Hall of St. James Church.

During the year, a building was constructed on the corner of Alexandria Pike and Winchester Street, which was the largest building in Fauquier County. Because "Uncle" Lloyd Anderson owned the land, he was given shares in the business. Then, he and E. M. "Gene" Garrett, Sr. operated the Garrett Motor Company there. Besides Buick, Graham-Paige cars were sold. The three Graham brothers and "Cannonball" Baker, the fastest driver in the world, were there for the grand opening. Gene, Jr. had his picture taken with them, the Town Sergeant, Sam Hall and Tom Frank, the Mayor. There were also clowns, entertainment, and refreshments. But, it was a bad start, for it was not only the year of the Stock Market crash, but Buick came out with a car that looked like a box and no one wanted it.[124] During 1929 Fauquier County had 41 inches of precipitation, which was 7 inches below normal.

1930

The first Chest Clinic of the year was held Friday, January 31st, 1930 at the Courthouse. February 5th, the painters were busy at work on the Anderson Building at the corner of Main and Culpeper Streets, which will soon be turned out in the gay 'uniform' of an A&P Store. I don't remember when he closed his store, but by the time he did, Ford Anderson knew everyone in town; so, it was -

they said - expected that he would attend all the funerals. Many people working along Main Street are related, such as John McIntosh, who worked in the store, too, and was the husband of City Risdon's (Garrett) Aunt Lucy L. Risdon. When Anderson's closed, McIntosh opened a men's shop next door (now Jimmy's Market).[124] Mr. G. A. Vose was uncle of Wayman Carter.

Once again lovely flowers were going into the auditorium of the Library, but, they are an exhibition of flower paintings given by the Flower Club of Warrenton, to be from March 5th through 11th, 1930. A tea opened the show. They are working on the new Lee Highway west of town, and a lot of road machinery is coming through town. Wrestling Matches were held at The People's Pleasure Palace, March 26th, in the old Garrett Motor Company Building, on its lower floor. Other matches and activities are planned to be held there.

It was announced April 5th, 1930 that plans were being made to build a modern theater on the James Walden Jeffries lot near Main and 4th Streets. A beautiful sight was seen the other day. Mrs. Robert C. Winmill was driving a four-in-hand coach that had the name "Happy Thought". This rare sight attracted a lot of attention. The quarterly Chest Clinic was held at the Courthouse Thursday, April 17th. White patients were there from 9am to 12 and at 1pm until 4pm, the colored patients came. Four large excursion buses

MAIN STREET, WARRENTON, VIRGINIA

from a high school in New England passed through here Tuesday, April 29th, on their way to the Luray Caverns via Culpeper. No amount of unseasonable weather, late frosts, or drought can do away with the beauty of May in Fauquier County... and the tulips in the yard of the County Office Building are a sight to behold, too. Main Street had a new Spring Dress of tar and gravel on May 7th. An old house along Main Street was torn down May 10th. Miss Cowles of New York was in Warrenton to have a meeting at Carter Hall of the committees to arrange for the entertainment of the Fresh Air Children for this summer. Major McIntyre has consented to act again as head of the committee. May 24th the Memorial Day Services were held at the High School on High Street or Academy Hill, but the parade formed and marched to the cemetery as usual. More digging! May 31st they are to lay the Gas Lines.

ON A SUMMER DAY, Mr. and Mrs. Hotchkiss Hall (left), an unidentified lady and Tom Stafford have their picture taken at the dummy policeman-signpost that used to stand in front of the Court House.

The date that a Dummy Policeman went in at Court House Square is unknown, but one replaced the Fountain. During the summer of 1930 a picture was taken of some young people, including Tom Stafford, standing around it. Robert Anderson thought the mounting stone from the corner of The Pike and Main Street might have been used as its base. (However, in pictures taken later, the stone was still in front of The Warrenton Cafe.) But, the way traffic was directed around the "Dummy" was a bit odd. To go from Main down Waterloo Street, one goes down Alexandria Pike and swings back up, keeping to the right going around it.[166]

A Big Day Sunday, June 15th, 1930. A number of people, including Mayor Thomas E. Frank, and motorcycle men went outside town to meet Admiral Byrd as he came from Richmond by Fredericksburg. In town a large group welcomed him as he stopped about 15 minutes around 12:30pm. When you hear about someone for such a long time, it is exciting to see them in the flesh. In and around Court Street and the Courthouse, the Carnival turned the place into a fairyland with the colored lights Friday and Saturday nights, July 11th and 12th. The proceeds go towards a new fire truck. July 30th was the hottest night on record since 1876. Nights are dewless and the use of water has been limited.

August 7th, 1930, the State told the Town Council they needed 40 feet for the width of Alexandria Pike through the corporate limits. A small shower had fallen August 1st around Warrenton, but it only made us realize how much more we need, so on the 11th the drought was so bad that some business closed their shops and went to Winchester with the farmers for a prayer service. A large body of regular soldiers passed through here Tuesday, August 26th, as they marched down Winchester and Alexandria Pike without stopping. The troops from Quantico are being sent to camp out at various places in Virginia because of the shortage of water. Sometimes during this period the water pipes would "give out". People of the town, including Mrs. Nellie Downs went or would send the children to the Cistern beside the Hiden Building on The Square. At the time she lived back of the Post Office on North 4th Street in a house that belonged to Miss Lilly Thompson (now parking lot). By August 30th the water shortage was over here in town—at least for the time being.

Early in September, 1930, a Drought Relief Committee was formed in the county. Farmers were given a loan but it did not meet their needs. Songs reflect the country's mood, such as, "Brother Can You Spare A Dime", or "In A Shanty In Old Shanty Town". Again all Warrenton rushed out to get a glimpse of Admiral Byrd as he passed through town September 6th. They will have a chance to see and hear him Monday and Tuesday, the 8th and 9th, as he speaks at the Warrenton Theater in the Hiden Building. He'll talk of his thrilling adventures, one of the most dramatic stories in all history. Mr. Frey of Culpeper says he hopes to have his new theater in Warrenton opened by the first of November. September 20th, and the work is on the last lap of the Lee Highway between here and Washington with the surfacing of the hill leading directly into Warrenton from the west. During September, the miniature Golf Course was behind the Peoples National Bank as it had been in 1928. The popular entertainment was the enterprise of the two young people, Newton "Newtie" Brooke and "Buster" Brittle.

By October 11th, 1930, the work on paving Waterloo Street was nearly completed. The sidewalk at the corner of the Library has to be removed to widen the highway—and maybe the Cistern now had to be covered over since it is between the Library and Hiden Building, the work beginning October 25th. A coping was built around the newly rounded corner of the yard, the popular tree at the corner was taken away and the two box bushes were moved. When this is completed by the removal of the old telephone pole and the replacing of the sidewalk, a considerable width will be added to the road and the view cleared, besides eliminating a sharp turn.

During 1930 one of the cars Garrett Motors was selling had a name change. Graham bought out Paige, so the car was then called by that name. D. D. Sanford opened a grocery store in Warrenton (now Mémēré's Bakery). He had been in the merchantile business— feed, fertilizer, groceries, nick-nacks, etc., since 1919 at Auburn and Midland. Talk says we should have a municipal parking lot.

1931

The new moving picture house on Main Street, "The Fauquier Theater" did not open when planned, but announced that it would open Wednesday, January 7th, 1931. The prices of tickets went up to 25¢ for children and 35¢ for adults. February 3rd the Town Council decided that Warrenton would join the League of Municipalities.

Thursday, March 4th, 1931 was reminiscent of that dreadful night in November 1909, when once again the cry of "FIRE" sounded in the middle of Town! How I cringed shortly before midnight as flames poured from the roof and windows of the old Warrenton Theater. Surrounding buildings were threatened—the home of Mrs. Ethel Bishop, Raymond Pearson's store on the corner where he had been since 1924, and of course the Warrenton Library. It was two hours before it was safe to leave the place. The fire seems to have started at the stage end of the room. Decorations and some windows were destroyed by the fire and other windows were broken. In fact, Tom Hutchinson broke one of the windows. He was with the Fire Company and climbed a ladder to the second story to knock out a window so some of the smoke could get out. This was the first window he ever broke and it really made him feel odd. But the smoke was terrible inside. Damage to the building was several thousands of dollars. The curtain, screen, amplifiers and other equipment were a complete loss, but the picture machines in the front of the building were not harmed. The floor and seats were unhurt except from heat and water. The building has belonged to Dr. M. Hiden since 1927, and the picture equipment was Mrs. W. H. Washington's. Both were insured. The upper rooms were now used for storing furniture, all more or less damaged, and W. H. Kays lost paint and oils that were stored there as the building was being painted. The theater has been closed for the past two months so was neither heated nor lighted.

Trucks have been constantly passing through town the past weeks as they carry the hugh iron pipes to be laid for the gas main, which will pass about a mile southeast of Warrenton. The parking conditions were bad by May 9th, 1931, although the "Silent Policeman" has helped the driving considerably. One can not see down Alexandria Pike when coming around the corner, nor when one comes up from the hill because of the way the cars are parked. Somewhere around the "Pattie Building" area was D'Anglo's Cleaning Shop. George Woodzel (father of the now Mrs. Sam Harder) once drove the delivery truck. May 27th, President Theodore Roosevelt and party passed through town as they returned from the camp in Madison County.

A new schedule to light the town in its' "White Way" was presented to the Town Council June 8th, 1931, and June 26th, R. E. Foley made an application for a permit to conduct a Poolroom and Bowling Alley in the basement of the Garrett Motor Company at the corner of Winchester and Lee Highway, or Alexandria Pike. The Fireman's Carnival had good weather the first night, but what a downpour on the second night!

July 23rd, 1931, an exhibition of art by County artist was in the reading room of the Warrenton Library, to which the public was invited. A street preacher with flowing hair and beard and dressed in white robes delivered a discourse in front of the Clerk's Office

Tuesday morning as he predicted the end of the world and the closing of the Gates of Mercy on mankind forever within the next three years. His messages were received as coolly as those of Noah and other prophets were. He also claimed to succeed them. Kathleen Thoma, daughter of John Thoma, who has had the bakery on Main Street since 1905, had married J. E. Barnhart in May. Now in July, they renovated the bakery and opened The Coffee Shop.[43] Or was that in 1930?[125] Anyway, it had been done by opening the next section of that building. Barnhart was the one who came up with the name of Coffee Shoppe and they feature a large sugar cookie that children love to eat.[146] Lawrence Craig who lived at Shadow Lawn, also liked their coconut macaroons which he ate as he peeled potatoes for them. Since the main highway went through town, many customers from all states stopped to eat while admiring the collection of beer steins on a shelf all the way around the walls. John Thoma, from Germany originally, always had something good to say about a person, and if he couldn't, he didn't say anything. This was the meeting place of the Rotary Club, too.[126] The Barnharts lived in the apartment above the shop at this time.

By August 26th, 1931, Bowling fans were getting their teams together to play in the new alleys on Alexandria Pike and Horner Street in the old Garrett Garage Building. Guess they remodeled since they were denied their request of June 26th to move. Before Eva Pearson had the bowling alleys, and I can't remember just when, Robert Lunceford tried his hand at the game. It was the one and only time he ever did. At the time his occupation was chauffeur, but it made him so sore he could hardly get in or out of the station wagon. Tom Hutchison liked this place. Sometimes after a match-game was over, they'd still bowl until 2 or 3am, playing duck pins mostly, but there was an alley or two of ten pins. An interesting advertisement showing meat prices for the week appeared in the August 29th paper for Coons Market—

"Leg Lamb	25¢	Stew Lamb	15¢
Lamb Chops	35¢	Chuck Roast	17¢
Pork Chops	28¢	Stew Beef	10¢
Veal Cutlet	30¢	Baking Beef	10¢
Round Steak	25¢	Beef Liver	20¢
Sirloin Steak	30¢	Spare Ribs	20¢
Tea-Bone Steak	35¢		

You will find the above prices as low as it is possible to see them—

W. E. Coons-Proprietor." They were probably located on Culpeper Street. Wonder if it was now or earlier that the elder Mr. Coons, father of W. E., worked for Sudduth Funeral Home? He wasn't there long.[126] At this time Bishop's store was on one side of the Funeral Home and Willis' Drugstore on the other side. W. E. Sudduth would buy candy in the drugstore to take to his wife, Mildred. Perhaps it was at this time that Polly Sudduth ran it.[144] Also, Shirley and "Blinky" Maxheimer helped Thurston Willis, the pharmacist, run the store.[164] Next in line of stores, of course, was Anderson & Allison's Fancy Market.

By September, 1931, people could water their flowers and the town garages could now wash four cars a day. One good thing about all this drought, they say it was the healthiest summer the Health Department had ever seen because the flies were scarce. As usual the banks, Post Office, The Fauquier Democrat and all principal business closed for Armistice Day, November 11th. The 11:00am Memorial Service was held in the Courthouse. Another fire close by, and in November, too. This time the fire damaged the Bishop Building as the old Garrett Garage is now called. The ground floor, rented by Robert E. Foley had four Bowling Alleys and six Pool Tables. It is planned to have new alleys by next week. December 23rd the Rotary Club had the Community Christmas tree on the Courthouse portico as usual. There is not to be any caroling this year, which will be missed.

1932

January 13th, 1932 the Library opened the New Year social season with a silver tea held by General and Lady Washington in wonderful costumes, receiving friends. The Library will have a George Washington memorial exhibit of historical and biographical material already in the Library and some other things on loan for the occasion. Saturday, February 6th, an ad for Fewell & Company, "The Shop That's Different". At some time, Mr. Matthew left the business, selling to Mrs. Fewell, aunt of City Risdon (Garrett). It was announced February 17th that the work of laying the natural gas pipes on Main Street is nearly finished. However, Tuesday morning the workers accidentally tapped the water main near the Clerk's Office, which ran like a river down Culpeper Street causing much inconvenience to the users of the water. Imagine being all soaped up in the shower and the water going off. The Clerk's Office and corridors were crowded, the February 20th report in the paper said of the past Thursday, because of a Supervisors meeting in their room and the School Board meeting in theirs.

March 3rd, 1932, the Town Council decided to hard surface Winchester Street from its intersection with Alexandria Pike to the Methodist Church. March 5th reported that the truck parked all day Wednesday near Main Street did a lively business selling Georgia pecans at ten cents a pound, every street in town having a trail of shells. March 9th it was found that the one by-product of the blizzard on Sunday was the stopping of the Town Clock. People were stranded on Saturday and Sunday in the Fire House and a few other places that were kept open for them. March 23rd it was said the Saturday before, quite a crowd had gathered around the Courthouse all day waiting for the sale of the Gold Vein property. Reminded one of old March Court Day. And, on the Monday that was Court Day, the town was again crowded, looking a little like the old days when everyone came out of their winter holes and saw their fellow County-men for the first time since Fall set in. Now they might come from force of habit, more than anything else. There was one lone horse on the street. But, for the first time in history the March Court crowd was "downed by bad weather". Even with all the cars in town, at no time were the usual groups of men around the Courthouse or on the streets. It didn't rain after the early morning, but it was one of the most disagreeable days of the season with a very high cold wind. Good Old March Wind—needed to dry things out for the planting before the April showers begin. Nature is Wonderful.

April 2nd, 1932 and another couple of questions to test your memory. "Who remembers when Hilleary and Company had a store at the corner of Main and Culpeper Streets" and "when the Warrenton Town Hall was located where the Fire House is now, and moving pictures were shown there twice a week"? In 1929 the Fire Company wanted all of the building. Today, April 13th Main Street looks like "No Man's Land" with man-holes—or shell-holes—or some kind of holes, and ditches here and there. Everyone has to watch their step and their car, too, as they travel when the rain came down as it did on Saturday and Sunday, things were worse. All this from the unfinished gas lines being put in and not repaired—also telephone wires are being put underground. Finally! April 20th, the streets are being repaired and they will be hard surfaced from curb to curb.

May 11th, 1932 the paper told of the heavy traffic on Saturday along Main and Culpeper Steets immediately after the Gold Cup races. The officers directing traffic did a good job of keeping it moving and there were no tie ups. May 21st there were more memory teasers. "Who remembers when Carroll Curtis and Mosby Campbell worked in the Post Office where the Warrenton Cafe is now" and "when Ennis Coons was working for the late Richard Schwab in the store on Culpeper Street, now occupied by the Atlantic and Pacific?" This was the "little A&P" store since the new one opened in the Anderson Building in 1930. Although the High School was located on High Street, graduation exercises were held in the Fauquier Theater because the school was not large enough to accommodate 32 pupils. During May Graysons had a sale. They bought out Roadhouse & Bunch, who would move across Main Street (now Mēmērēs Bakery). The elder Grayson, John, was postmaster, being appointed during two or three different administrations. It was his nephew who ran the store, taking out the partition in the building, to enlarge into the men's and ladies' departments.

A Mr. Tyson had lived on Alexandria Pike at Nordix Farm (where Warrenton Motel was). When he sold the farm he bought the brick house on Main Street across from the Warrenton Baptist Church and operated a small store behind the house. It was a straight shot from High Street School down the hill to the store. The children, including J. O. Hodgkin III, thought it was a big thrill to make the mad dash to the store, buy a couple pennies' worth of candy and rush back before recess ended. One of the girls didn't wait for recess as one day she slipped out a ground floor window of the chemistry lab and ran down the hill to buy chewing gum. Sometimes Bessie Woodzel (Whitmore) and others thought the candy tasted like coal oil because the man had it on his hands from the stove that was in front of the store, when he reached into the candy container or showcase to get it. But the children liked to go there because Mr. Tyson might give them a free popsicle when one was bought.

July 9th, 1932 the Firemen's Carnival reported taking in $4000.00, clearing around $3000. "Even in the valley of despair, destruction, and depression", Ex-Senator Jim Reed said, "You cannot keep people of Fauquier down." David Doggette Sanford opened his store at the corner of Main and South 4th Streets, opposite the Post Office during August, it being the first of its type in town. The sign over the door said, "Sanford's Five Cent—One Dollar Store". People said, "If you can't find it, go to Sanfords".

The basement of the store was a Toyland and also had the men's work clothes. Its hours were from 8am to 6pm, except Saturday when they were open from 9am to 12 midnight. This was a town custom, not just for farmers or at Christmas for shopping. Everyone did it, and if there were customers in the store, they kept open after midnight. Wages were probably $1.50 a day and a work-day would have an hour off for lunch, and of course for supper on Saturday night. During high school two sisters, Margaret and Nina Minter, had worked part time for Cornblatts' store. The older, Nina, after graduating a couple years before, went to work for Roadhouse and Bunch. But, Margaret, who graduated this May stayed at Cornblatts' until Sanford's new store opened. Then she went there. When Mr. Sanford came to the County in 1919, the first person he becamed acquainted with was Margaret's grandfather, Randolph T. Minter, who was a wheelright, then restoring the old Auburn or Neavil's Mill, but living at Minter's Mill on the Springs Road.[127] Robert "Bob" Foley's family lived in the apartments over his restaurant, and other businesses have been in this building,[179] including a Mrs. Patterson whose name is approximately at this place, on an 1878 map. Shortly after opening the new store, was probably when Sanford closed his nearby grocery store and almost immediately Roadhouse & Bunch reopened in that building.

October 8th, 1932 there was an enthusiastic meeting held in the Courthouse under the auspices of the Women's Organization and the Democratic Committee. Election Day, November 5th, while the election returns came in, large crowds stood in the rain outside The Fauquier Democrat office and the Democratic Headquarters with three of its rooms also being packed. Everyone was anxious to hear the news. Finally the cry went up—Roosevelt wins! Warrenton was a deserted town on Thursday, Thanksgiving Day. The stores were closed and lots of people were traveling far and wide to various football stadiums in the state, such as Charlottesville, Roanoke, Richmond, or Washington, to see the big games. Many others took their guns and hounds or bird dogs and "lit out for the wilds". Others just hung around and waited for dinner, then took some bread soda and hung around some more, or dozed throughout the afternoon.

December 21st, 1932 the Firemen's new Assembly Room atop the Fire House had a dance in it even though there had been 15 inches of snow. The 'Old Town' is filling up with young men and young ladies who are returning from their different schools and colleges for the holidays. They are getting back just in time for what looks like a real old fashion Christmas. Stores do not decorate much for the holiday, but the Town Tree looks nice.

1933

Among the wishes for the New Year of 1933, The Fauquier Democrat wished the Warrenton Cafe to serve plenty of good food to the hungry and to sell it cheap, but at the same time to allow themselves a margin of profit. January 4th there was a Square Dance in the Firemen's Hall. The lower room of the Library was rented to the Red Cross who met there January 11th. On the 14th, someone said, the other day they saw four citizens talking together. They knew them fairly well and for a long time, so it was without fear of contradiction that they knew the total age of the four was 300 years as each man was 75 or thereabouts. They were all hale and hearty, which speaks well for the health of the community and the longevity of its citizens. They were Major McIntyre, E. J. Sudduth, A. S. Hamilton and William H. Risdon. Wellllll, they didn't say who, but Warrenton has a lady who would like to be a candidate for an elective office, that of a member of the Town Council. The duck hunters are unhappy. The season for shooting Canvas backs and their cousins ends on the 15th, but the weather is not "duck weather". They have been flying too high. The Warren Green Hotel Barber Shop was advertising on January 21st, they gave haircuts for 35¢ and a shave for 15¢. J. M. Baucum is the proprietor. January Court opened on the 23rd with Judge Alexander. Maybe things will pick up a little now, as its been slow. A man by the name of Adolf Hitler came to power in Germany during this month.

February 1st, 1933 two fires were reported, one in the ceiling of the kitchen in the Travers Building on Main Street with damage of $75.00 and one in The Village Inn, also a kitchen fire between floors. The first sign of Spring is seed catalogues, and they are about the area now. Cornblatts' Department Store is having a sale of women's and misses' coats at $3.98, all wool sweaters for $1.00, men's silk neckties at 25¢, women's silk hosiery at 64¢, and blouse dresses at 59¢. Herman and Edith Cornblatt have had the store for sometime. I don't know too much about them. They have a boy and girl and relatives who live in Baltimore, Maryland. Ruth Hart Perdum, a clerk there, used to live several miles west of town and rode the bus to work. That was the way she met the bus driver, Aubrey,[182] whom she married.

February 2nd, the Groundhog did see his shadow so everyone knows what that means. Thursday was one of those real good days with the sun shining on rich and poor alike. However, the gas and coal men were glad for more cold weather. It was reported that the rumor of Tom Stafford, State Officer, was to be transferred is a false one. He is a good officer and the people of Warrenton did not want to loose him. Yesterday, the 3rd, reminded people of old time March Court Day, although it was still the January term. The court was filled to overflowing with people and many officers, too, as a murder trial going on. By February 11th, the weather had been so bad since the 2nd, people were wondering if Spring would ever come. But, only a couple more months and a few days until baseball time. This winter the local American Legion Post has started a popular plan of having a monthly supper at the Coffee Shoppe. Judge Alexander, together with the Clerk of the Court and most of the local bar, talked matters over in the Courthouse this week trying to see how more seating room could be in the Temple of Justice for the spectators. The conclusion was to move the lawyers closer to the 'Bench' therefore putting seats where they were. The Firemen had a "masquerade round" at their hall on Valentine's Night, for their benefit. A lot of 'flu' is floating around, and also 'flue' type, too, with the cold weather. There has been good coasting around the various hills. Kirson's Department Store at the corner of Main and South 5th Streets had an ad in the paper. With natural gas in Warrenton, an ad for a Gas Cooking School being held at the Warrenton High School, said gas is the quicker, cleaner, and cheaper way.

February 22nd, Mr. McKee had taken over the management of the Warren Green, planning to have both American and European plan with a business men's lunch. Two signs will be placed in the hotel yard, one given by the State Historical Association which tells the history of the old building. The interior is being done over also. There were many stray dogs around town, February 25th and John Benner found one asleep in his car the other morning. The singing quartet of Warrenton are getting good reports. Chamberlain and Hamilton's Men's Clothing Store, established September 1919, at So. 4th and Main Streets are having a sale. There was a pool-room in the basement of that building which was entered through a side door from the alley-way off Main Street, between it and the Chinese Laundry in the frame building next door. Alex Hamilton, Jr. also ran this, but Mr. Chamberlain didn't have anything to do with it.[128] Remember when the elder Alex Hamilton was postmaster and the Post Office was at the corner of Alexandria Pike and Main Street?

He was also sheriff for a while. And, about the Chinese Laundry—remember there was one during the early 1900's? Seems as though it burned, so it is unknown when the business went into this building. Anyway, some people call that section of town, "Chinatown" and because the Orientals are not seen often and of course are different looking, some small children are afraid of them. Robert Anderson was one who felt that way and even some clerks in the stores don't want to serve them. Across from the Laundry was Mrs. Vizzi's Italian Restaurant with the 'old country style' cooking. It was reported during February that 30% of the U.S. work force was unemployed.

March 1st, 1933 Anderson Clothing Company was having a closing out sale. Don't remember where that was. March 4th, and Roosevelt is now the 31st President. People say, "Maybe it won't be long before everything will be adjusted and we are turning the corner". By March 11th, the Banking Holiday has created a lot of funny situations. You heard said, "I invite you to a duck dinner, you bring the ducks", and many people have a lot of money in the bank with "nary a nickle in their 'jeans' ". Banks will let you inside to pay a note, but what do you use for money? George Tongue says he wants to plant potatoes, but everytime he gets a hoe handy, along comes another rain or a cold snap. Mrs. T. N. Fletcher's car was stolen March 1st from where it was parked on Main Street as she was visiting at the home of Miss Ida Evans. It has been found in North Carolina. A funny thing happened March 15th. Trash cans had been placed around Warrenton and the Remington Mayor came to town, parked his car, opened the door and almost fell into one. You should have seen how he had to leap over it when he got out of the car. The Fauquier Theater manager, T. I. Martin announced that during the present bank crisis he would gladly accept checks or I.O.U.'s for all entertainment anyone wanted to have. That sounds fair enough. Bartering is going on which is good during these times.

A slight touch of Spring was seen with a few boys playing baseball. The banks are still closed and not a soul has been reported around here as starving or even approaching it. This community takes care of itself pretty good. By March 18th it was reported that the Marshall National Bank and Trust Company and two local banks had opened their doors. Congress has passed a New Deal social and economic legislation that will benefit everyone. A typical March day with a thunderstorm, a rainbow, a shower, and then beautiful warm sunshine. But, next came a high wind and cold weather. George

Tongue finally got his potatoes, peas, and onions in the ground. March 22nd, and all banks are open wide. Happy days are here again. A baseball game at the High School this week and at midday yesterday Spring arrived.

It was felt on April 5th, 1933 that one of these days somebody's perfectly good car is going to get 'bumped-off'. They park diagonally to Alexandria Pike just below the Court House Square and obscure the vision of cars coming up the Pike and are a menace. The line of The Square makes it rather wide as it curves around there. People from the country come into town on Saturday night, so stores may stay open until 2am, and cars park three deep in front of the Hiden Building.[124] Sometimes things moved slowly and that makes people relax a bit, or sit and think. The only place to go is into town and once there they enjoy each other. Remember when Aaron Nusbaum was where the A&P is now? That used to be a gathering place, too. Fewell's is having a Spring Sale.

Warrenton had a distinguished visitor a few days ago when General Glassford, the one time superintendent of the Washington Police stopped at the Coffee Shoppe with a party for supper. He made a name for himself with his approach to the Bonus Army last summer, but was finally railroaded out of his job. He will be remembered by the American people for the manner in which he handled a very delicate situation in the Capitol. Easter Sunday, April 14th, was a rainy day for raincoats, umbrellas and overshoes so the new hats and dresses had to stay home. Lots of things happened this weekend. Friday, a group of citizens stood on the Courthouse steps during the supper hour, thereby missing it, to see the Honorable John N. Garner, Vice President, pass through but it was all in vain. They had heard that he would be going to the Camp on the Rapidan and have with him others including Speaker Rainey. If he came through he must have disguised himself for no one saw him.

Saturday many cars went along the streets of town as they were going to the Middleburg races. The Bethel road had a string of cars ranging from the aristocratic eight cylinders of 1933 to the common Fords of other years. It was a fair day then, but on the following Saturday, people were wishing it would stop raining so the farmers could finish their plowing. It is a good hay year, but looks like anything put in the ground and expected to grow is going to be late. It's no use fussing with the weather for it "just don't get you anywhere". By Wednesday, April 26th, there are just a little more than three weeks until the schools of the county will close for the season. April 29th, Chaffraix Long and Isham Keith were planning a novelty dance in the dining room of the Warren Green Hotel. The big room will be made and decorated into a night club with all the trimming. This is the first dance of the "Club Tallyho", a newly formed organization that will have dances through the summer season. Chauncey Brown's orchestra will play for them. There will be a charge of $3 a couple. Mr. White, father of Georgia, Chauncey's wife, had a blacksmith shop in the one story brick building one block off Culpeper Street at the corner of Lee and 5th Streets.[144]

The traffic was well taken care of, May 6th, 1933, during the Gold Cup Races. May 10th, people were asking Officer Tom Stafford where his cap was. He says he ran "clean out from under it". He is offering free air to any car owner finding the cap and returning it to him with no questions asked. Mr. W. E. Rector, Jr. shot one of the largest hawks ever found around here, May 13th. It measured 4½ feet from wing tip to wing tip and 23 inches from the end of its beak to its talons. After the opening of May Court there will be no more regular term until September. Someone said that the term "dog days" meant hard days for the lawyers. Graduation day used to be a big day, especially for the boys. Not only did they get their diplomas but it was time to take off their shoes and stockings. It was 'barefoot day' for all the youngsters, and how tender those feet were the first day out.

George Tongue is like a weather-vane, with his new straw hat. If he wears it going to work, the weather will be fair. If he wears the old "fedora"—look out for rain. Wednesday, May 24th was not so hot according to the thermometer, but summer came suddenly bringing out shirt sleeves and perspiration. The fishermen are back from the lower Rappahannock, some buying more fish than catching.

A bob-white or partridge in one of the tall trees at the Warren Green yard had a crowd gathered around the area to hear and see it. The bird acted as though he enjoyed the people as much as they did him. By the next Wednesday, May 31st, it seems to be just one rain after another. The mornings start fairly cool; later turns warm and about the time one wants to quit work for the day, along comes a shower. The National Memorial Day was marred by rain, but the colored people had their usual services in the afternoon, and the annual Confederate Memorial Day was held in the cemetery Sunday, June 4th, 1933 at 5pm.

A warning was announced Wednesday, June 21st, that some boys are shooting rifles in certain parts of town at dogs, cats, and birds. In some cases people have been narrowly missed. Mayor Thomas E. Frank feels parents should take matters into their hands and see that it is stopped. A sign for the Warren Green Hotel has been placed so it points to the "Hotel de Shirley", supposedly the coolest place in town during this hot weather and yet a lot of guests want to leave. These involuntary boarders are keeping cool and being well fed with everything on the American plan, but they are not satisfied and use all kinds of methods and schemes to get out. On the night of Tuesday, June 27th, was a special meeting of the Town Council to see about having a Sanitary Survey of Warrenton. Something else in the financial world that will effect the town—the U. S. went off the gold standard this month.

Winter's hit! It is cold, but that didn't keep people home over the July 4th, 1933 weekend. So many Washington cars went through here, there may not have been anyone left in the city unless they were either bed-ridden or did not own a car. A lot of Maryland tags were headed for the mountains, too. The Sanitary Survey was begun July 8th. In the paper on the 12th was an ad for the "Warrenton Restaurant, Where eating costs less, Carr's Restaurant, Warrenton's Most Modern Eating Place." John Kreticos had the Warrenton Cafe, now Fred Carr owns it.

July 19th paper reported a kiddies' party during the Fireman's Carnival was held on the grass plot in the rear of the Clerk's Office and the adjoining street between that building and the Virginia Public Service, with the children wearing costumes. The Carnival grossed $2000. According to tradition, rain on St. Swithins' Day, which was July 15th, rain for 40 days. So far, there has been a shower each day since then.

August 23rd, 1933, it was so hot an egg could fry on the sidewalk, however, a couple days later, a storm of rain and wind damaged the farmers so much the cost will run into thousands of dollars. The corn was ripped and torn, the fruit knocked from the trees, and for the first time in history the Horse Show was limited to one day. It was the heaviest damage in 25 years. Of course, the town streets were littered with tree limbs.

The sign at the Warrenton Supply Filling Station, on Saturday, September 2nd, 1933, still says "Warren Green" and still points to Hotel de Shirley, a beautiful vine covered stone building. Just to have had one Indian Head or Lincoln Head penny for every car that passed the Courthouse from Saturday through Monday night, Labor Day weekend, would have been a fortune and one could have laughed at depression for months to come. Rainy weather hampered the activities Monday morning, but the rest of the time was nice. Wednesday, September 6th was a musical day on the streets. Two radio cars traveled along the main streets, one broadcasting the news that the Fairfax Horse Show would be held, and the other advocating a certain brand of beer now that it is legal to sell. The Fauquier National Bank, Saturday, September 23rd, was having improvements made by painting and gas being installed for heating. Monday, September Court Day is the official opening of autumn around here. Wednesday, September 27th, the Coffee Shoppe had a new front as the doorway was changed and is most attractive looking.

Friday, October 6th, 1933, completed 51 years in business for E. J. Sudduth. He was 78 in July, being 27 when he established his business. A surprise on Saturday, October 14th. George Tongue finally told how he grows macaroni. It is easy to raise, but the hard part is getting the 'hole' just right. The wires must be put carefully into the ground so the macaroni will grow around it. After the plant matures, pull out the wires and use them for another crop.

November 8th, 1933, they are knocking down the duckpins on the Arcade Alleys above the Carpenter Motors, on Alexandria Pike and Horner Street. There were snow flurries Tuesday, the 7th, election day. Banks were closed for it and Armistice Day, November 11th. The Town Council approved five lights to be used in the "White Way" around the Court House Square and that the ditch which has the underground wiring in The Square should be resurfaced.

December 9th, 1933, the Firemen are hard at work remodeling, and utilizing some of the wasted space that has been on the 2nd floor of the Municipal Building, and preparing a meeting room. The town must have kept part of the building. All the town merchants are making their windows attractive and have in lots of things for Christmas. The unemployed are filing their names with Alfred Austin at the office he has on the 1st floor of the Courthouse. So far 831 have registered. December 16th, a mighty hunter was bragging about town of how he killed three partridges with one barrel or the contents of one. That's better than "killing two birds with one stone". The December 23rd paper said it was noted that Dr. Martin Barbour "Saw Bones" Hiden was having a lot of work done on his building on Court House Square. Rumors say a bowling alley, a big dance floor, or that it will be equipped for a gymnasium and basketball court. Prohibition ended this month with the 21st Amendment. Will that be a good or a bad way to end the year?

1934

Someone said the definition of a "Mudwamp" was a bird that flies backwards and that reminded them of the streamlined look of some 1934 cars. They are built so you can't tell the front from the rear end, or if they are coming or going. The January term of the Circuit Court opened Monday, January 22nd, 1934.

Dr. Hiden's newly remodeled building is called The Fauquier Recreation Center. Bessie Woodzel (Whitmore) did love to rollerskate at the new rink there. A small hallway just inside the front door had the skating area beyond, which was a rather large room with seats on the right as one entered the door where people sat to watch or skaters could rest. Others stood outside the skating area, which had a rail around it. Pillars went from ceiling to floor so people could weave in and out of them. When people left, their hair might be white from the chalk put on the floor to make skating easier. Afternoons are filled with mostly ladies and children while at night there are men and women. Mary Lee Beach (Robinson) and Arabelle Laws (Arrington) were others who liked to skate, especially Arabelle, who went every Saturday night. Mabel Rider Martin had married in 1928, and went with her husband just to watch, as they didn't skate. Boxing matches were here, too. For them a rope was set up in the middle of the skating rink. About this time Stuyvesant School had an almost unbeatable boxing team. Warrenton decided to get a team up, too. It was not a school connected activity. On it were two brothers, George, about 185 lbs., and Cecil, about 175 lbs., Dickerson. As each of them fought their Stuyvesant opponent, they knocked them out with one blow. Warrenton made boxing history that night. Johnny Gaines was the boxing instructor for the Town team. Jimmy Hodgkin III and Lawrence Craig were both on the team, but before they joined, Lawrence used to "beat up" Jimmy at school nearly every day. Once Jimmy got a lucky punch in and made Lawrence's nose bleed. But, Jimmy was the one the Principal, P. B. Smith, corrected.[129] The Hiden Building was about the only place in town for entertainment[130] with Dr. Hiden's office and others on the 2nd floor, as well as an athletic club.

February 2nd, 1934 and Groundhog Day began with sunshine, but before noon it was overcast. Now what can we expect from the prophet? Austin McDonnell on Culpeper Street had an advertisement in the February 3rd paper for freshly killed native Jumbo Squabs at 60¢ each. Dr. Hiden and Mr. Keith asked the Town Council February 6th, for a license for "certain activities at the building on Main Street". It was granted at a cost of $17.10. By February 7th, the hills around Warrenton were popular with the good fall of snow and coasting parties or sleighriding, but the trouble with that is you have to walk back up the hill. Ice and snow on Academy Hill, or Mrs. Ford Anderson's Hill near the school, Horner's Hill down through "Haytti", Alexandria Pike or Courthouse Hill, the hill back of Conway Grove, and Culpeper Street were all good, with streets sometimes blocked off for sleding. Saturday, February 10th, found people still slipping and sliding and falling, and a map in the paper of "The Broadway of America" from New York City to San Diego, California, showing the highway going through Warrenton. More snow for Valentine's Day. It is being proposed that a flying field be built at Meadowville, 4 ot 5 miles north of Warrenton.

There was a Hockey Game at the Rec. Center, as some call it, Wednesday, March 7th, 1934, between the Warrenton Indians and the Silver Spring Flashers, and also a skating exhibition. The Hockey was played with a wooden ball. Harold Timberlake was Captain for the Red Wings Hockey Team. Can't remember the name of the other team, but maybe it was the Indians, with Jack Weeks as captain. One winter night Harold was very hot when he went outside to cool off. It was about zero, so he caught a good case of pneumonia.[163] The Courthouse steeple has scaffolding around it while it is being painted, as if it is all crated up to be shipped away. The base of the building will be all grey with walls of bluff. Columns, cornices and window frames will be white and the roof dark. After the warm weather, another snow on Wednesday, March 14th, and again the 19th so no potatoes out yet. The scaffolding was removed from the Court - Saturday, March 24th, and now it is all ready for March Court next Monday. And, when it came, the 26th, lots of people were on the streets and in the Courthouse. One of the still familiar sounds was the voice of Latham Shumate selling everything from land on down. Wallace N. Tiffany who moved to Warrenton this year watched some horses walk along Main Street. He was told it was the Stallion Parade, but with so few horses now, it might be the last one. On March 31st, the junior partner, a well known dog, "Rex" of "Shirley & Company" performed at the Rec. Hall.

April 1st, 1934 was Easter Sunday. The male population

enjoyed the sun rays while the females enjoyed wearing their "glad rags" to walk in the sunshine. Because of painting the Courthouse and Spring coming, on the 3rd, the merchants along Main Street asked the Town Council to have the Highway Department resurface it. A "Gay Nineties" dance was held at the Rec. Hall this date. Part of the proceeds went to the Warrenton Bed of the Cripple Children's Hospital in Richmond. Admission was $1.50, and women alone were charged 75¢. It was decided, April 7th, to have the 8 month school instead of going on until June 25th for the 9 month term. An ad Saturday, April 14th, said the Virginia Stage Lines bus fare one way to Washington was $1.00 and the round trip is $1.80. Lots of things happened on the 18th.

A new statue in the Town ordinance which referred to cursing or swearing. Someone stated that the dictionary says that to swear is to blaspheme, to curse . . . As the late Scott Carter used to say: "Any difference is about the same". Mrs. F. W. Sharp, who has a quail hatchery near The Plains sold 30 pair of birds to Woodmont Gun Club of Maryland. There was a subscription dance for the benefit of the Hospital on the same date. At the Town Council meeting Mrs. Ethel Bishop complained of the noise at the Recreational Building, which is almost next door to her house. And, last but not least, on this date, the Circus came to Town. The newspaper had the Anniversary Edition of the Lee Highway after 14 years—April 21, 1920 to April 21, 1934. The Courthouse was given a bath by the Fire Department Monday the 23rd, to take the dust off the ledges so its fresh coat would look its best for the Garden Visiting Week.

Stuyvesant School had a horse show Friday, May 4th, 1934 on its grounds opposite the school. That night, before the Gold Cup Race, was a subscription dance at the Warren Green Grill Room with music by Myer Davis. The cars, big Packards, Pierce Arrows and the like went rolling by for the Gold Cup on Saturday, the 5th, and the streets presented a busy appearance with the handsome limousines. It was like a 3-ring circus at Stuyvesant School Sunday with polo, baseball and tennis being played. The Seminole Trail was busy for the weekend. Wednesday, May 9th, was a drive to raise funds for the Fauquier County Tuberculosis Association. "Straws" and "Panamas" are on the streets now that the weather has warmed up. Some people are saying that all the crows should be killed because they damage the wildlife by hunting the eggs of the ground nesting birds. Maybe they just help balance things out, and the hunters think they are taking the birds away from them. Nelson's Auto Accessories & Parts was established May 10, 1934.[125] May 16th Dr.

S. M. Johnson wrote an article predicting the Lee Highway of 107 miles from Luray to Washington would be two strips of pavement with planting between. The modern cars then would go 100 miles an hour, and when Skyline Drive is completed from the Great Smokies to Front Royal, there will be many days when 100,000 cars will be using Lee Boulevard between Washington and Sperryville. Tuesday the 22nd, the High School graduated 17 people.

Sunday, June 3rd, 1934, was the Memorial Day in memory of the Confederate dead and the anniversary of Jefferson Davis' birthday. As usual there was the custom of strewing cut flowers at the base of the Monument by the small children. Long ago the 'Bethelites' always fired a volley over these unknown dead and then returned to Town where they drilled in front of the Warren Green Hotel. The poppy continues to be sold by the American Legion to aid disabled veterans and their families and the families of the dead.

The unusual sight of seeing a "lady lawyer", the first to argue in the Court of this County was one of the happenings Monday, June 4th in Judge Alexander's Court. She was Miss Goldie S. Paregal of Washington, D.C., for she practiced under her maiden name. Her partner was Walter Robinson. The suit was Mitchell vs Payne for an automobile accident damage which had happened in October 1933.

According to Sam Lewis, the proprietor of the Hotel DeShirley, he is accustomed to taking his afternoon siesta in the shade of one of the trees in front of his mansion or the shadow of Colonel John S. Mosby's Monument. Just about the time he really is enjoying his nap a tourist comes along and wants to know all about things in town. It is hard on a man that wants a little sleep. The Lee Highway Association met at the Courthouse Thursday, June 14th, in the evening. People were enthusiastic about the announcement that a bill just signed by President Roosevelt for the new 200 foot boulevard is practically assured to come by the way of Warrenton. Wednesday, June 27th, 36 beetle traps were placed in Warrenton in an effort to determine if, and how many Japanese beetles are around. The traps are painted aluminum in color. Saturday, June 30th, the Federal Emergency Relief in Fauquier County is moving along nicely. Cases on direct relief are being transferred as fast as possible to work projects such as the airport, road and street, sidewalks, schools, sanitation, installing water meters, and there is some housework for women, too.

As of July 3rd, 1934, the hot spell has been here for two weeks, with a little thunderstorm Saturday night. The Honorable Pete

Shirley continues to sit under the shade of a tree. Mr. Shirley had a large "ugly" dog of unknown mixtures, more like a boxer, named Rex. He knew everyone in town and everyone knew him. You might say he was the 'Town Dog'. He would go to Anderson & Allison's Grocery Store where they wrapped a bone and gave him. He carried it back to the Jail before unwrapping it. Even people could go to the store and get a free soup bone with meat on it. Once Rex and a small boy were looking at each other. The boy made an ugly face at Rex and when asked why—the boy said, "He did it to me first."[165] They have resurfaced Hotel Street. July 4th was celebrated with ball games. The Mighty Haag Show, complete with elephant, paraded along Main Street at noon, July 12th. That day the Town Council moved that the Virginia State Highway Department be requested to re-route the proposed road, Route No. 15 as suggested by tentative survey in its possession so as to leave Rt. 15 at or about the Blackwell Gate and intersect with Rt. 211 on said route at the Creamery thereon, provided this is feasible. The Fireman's Carnival for July 13th and 14th on Main Street had the usual booths, bands, food and games. July 14th the Bug Trap on the Clerk's Office lawn caught an odd looking bug that sort of looked like a cross between an old time locust and one of those young airships that fly around these warm nights and hit your screen door like a rock.

The Sheriff is disguised! He has a new "Chevy" and has discarded the ancient looking Pontiac. One could always recognize Stanley Wolfe by his car, but now he can creep up on the lawbreakers. A large Navy plane flew close to the trees and performed a number of stunts as he circled over them and over the housetops. It was a local boy making a 'flying visit' home. It is hardly an exaggeration to state that for several hours Sunday, July 15th, from dusk until about 9pm, there was a stream of cars on the Lee Highway all headed towards Washington. The highway isn't much good for the locals at times like this. July 18th it was suggested that at the next Carnival - No more confetti. Noise making is OK, but there should be no confetti thrown into people's faces as some have been scooping if off the street and there was dirt in it.

July 25th the Courthouse is still intact and Honorable J. W. Shirley is a hero. About 2am one morning last week he had his Chevrolet from the 1920's, parked at his accustomed place. Two gentlemen came up Lee Highway and apparently couldn't straighten out their car so hit the Chevy, demolishing it. Mr. Shirley said if his car had not been parked there, the Mosby Monument would have been taken down or the Courthouse would have been hit. Bids are being taken for a new Warrenton High School.

Saturday, August 11, 1934, there were two storms, the first having heavy hail. One stone falling at Bethel's Warrenton Orchard, covered the palm of a man's hand, and measured 2½ inches by 4 inches, but there wasn't much rain. Thursday night there was a good rain that helped the farmer and his corn. During the summer several plays were given at the Fauquier Rec. Center. Well! This time, August 22nd, the Temple of Justice was HIT! A number of bricks were jarred loose by the impact of someone's car being driven into it. Too bad the Manager of Hotel DeShirley didn't have his car there this time. Another law involving everyone. The Social Security Act has become a reality. The first ABC Liquor Store opened in Warrenton during August.

Wednesday, September 5th, 1934, the paper reported 6000 attending the Warrenton Horse Show, a good crowd both days, even though the first day was misty and rainy. Saturday, September 15th, had heavy rains and that night motorists had to stay here waiting for the water to go down. There is a problem with buses parking in front of the Hotel and not letting cars pass.

Saturday, October 6th, 1934, the work is to begin soon on the "White Way" to extend from the Fire House westward on Main Street to the Court House Square. The Warren Green Hotel wall along Culpeper Street is a favorite place for fans to gather and discuss the plays of the World Series and to hear the games through loudspeakers installed by George Poehlman. Wednesday, October 10th, the Fauquier Skating Rink is to be reopened, after being closed for the summer. On Columbus Day both banks were closed. Finally, Wednesday, October 24th, the work on the "White Way" began.

Hundreds of people were on hand the night of Friday, November 2nd, at the vacant lot of Main Street between the Fire House and the Western Union to see the "burying alive" of L. C. Flynn. He was to remain four days and nights in a waterproof cement burial vault filled with a wooden casket. Periscopes were at each end of the vault in order to have circulation of air, and one opening large enough to see and speak with him. He will accept voluntary contributions. But, on Saturday night, the authorities, on complaints, dug up Mr. Flynn and sent him on his way.

Armistice Day Memorial Services on November 11th were held

at the Warrenton Methodist Church. The Bowling Alleys on Alexandria Pike were open by November 14th, as the new season comes. The room in the rear of the Fire House was being used for storage of the "White Way" equipment, when, November 20th, it was gutted at 12:30, by a cigarette being thrown into a box of loose excelsior. Fire in the Firemen's home! Something new. November 21st, someone said that one of the sad night sights of the town is the darkened dial of the Town Clock atop the Courthouse. When the four dials, north, south, east, and west are illuminated, it looks hospitable and home-like. The town has been paying for the electricity used and the county pays for the bulbs used. The Council is ready to pay the electric bill, but not the "Bulb" bill. It took a week, but the town and county worked out the problem.

The "White Way" is lit up by Saturday, December 8th, 1934. It's memory testing time. "Remember Uncle Ned Sheppard and old kerosene lamps that were mounted on standards about ten feet high, and he would climb up on his little ladder and light them for the night?" Some think these 15 foot standards are too tall to cast the proper rays and we should go back to the old ones again. Monday, December 10th, was the first snow of the year and chains were popular. Frank Moffett resigned his position with Coon's Market on Culpeper Street and accepted one with Fauquier Cleaners, because Coons was planning to move into the Hiden Building.

Sometime during 1934 Ernest Pappas took over the Warrenton Cafe.[125] He was born in Dervizana, Greece, coming to New York City in 1920, at the age of 26. Eventually he moved to Charlottesville, Va., and after 18 years of restaurant experience, came to Warrenton, buying out Fred Carr and his first cousin, William Pappas, as the business was bankrupt. Charles Doumas was Ernest's partner. They remodeled, putting in a restroom where the small window was located on the Alexandria Pike side and had a contest for a name. Lee Turner, a former officer at The Plains, won the $15.00 for calling it The New Warrenton Restaurant. Ernest did not want his clientele to become too rowdy either, as he wants this to be a family-type place.[148] About now Harold Timberlake liked going to the movies that had Rudy Vallee because he enjoyed listening to songs such as "My Time Is Your Time", and "I Found A Million Dollar Baby In A 5 and Dime Store".

1935

The Chest Clinic was held at the Courthouse January 23rd, 1935. Every Wednesday night is a broadcast over the radio from Admiral Byrd and his companions at Little America. The last news said it was melting down there. If he wants to be in the Arctic or Antarctic he should return to Fauquier County. Even though a warm rain Monday, January 18th, took away the snow, it changed to hail and sleet Tuesday. It snowed Wednesday and Thursday the temperature dropped to zero. The eaves of buildings looked like Luray Cave. Some of the best "stalactites" were on The Fauquier Democrat office. One of them was a foot wide at the top and eight feet long. All this reminds one of the "Blizzard of March '32". Monday, January 28th, was the first time in history, I think, that a Judge sat on the bench and the lawyers shivered, all in their overcoats. It was zero that day. Horse drawn sleds have been about town. A group of young people with a 3-sled tandem went by being pulled by a horse. Shouts and laughter can be heard from favorite hills late at night. But, everyone will be glad to see January end.

There was a funny sight on the street the other day. Dr. Jimmy Sinclair and Cashier Turner Day stood and talked in the middle of Main Street while the traffic detoured around them. People are talking about the Lindbergh kidnapping and the trial going on in New Jersey during January. Also a little excitement down the street where a group of hunters were gaily shouting about their catch. They brought a big grey fox back with them to prove they didn't come from the chase empty handed. The joke going around town said, "Biggie" Hodgkin was telling Thurston Willis about a fishing trip. They go fishing at the drop of a hat. "Biggie" said, "I never saw such a fish!" Thurston replied, "I believe you". "Biggie" won the Liar's Contest one time. Seems he was after a big old Bass that eluded everyone. One day "Biggie" said he was going to get it and he took a good strong pole with line to use—and he did! When asked how he did it, he said the fish hid from him in a hollow log, which made him so angry that he built a fire at one end and smoked him out!

February 2nd, 1935, Thurston B. Willis' interest in Edward C. Thornton's and Willis' Drugstore was bought by W. B. Gates, Jr. I don't remember when Thurston Willis and Maxheimer dissolved their drugstore business and Willis moved across the street to Thornton's store. Wednesday, February 13th, people were discussing the Hauptman trial trying to guess the verdict. It's odd, on February

20th, not to see the Town Clock lit. Wednesday the 22nd, people were becoming a little frightened about spreading colds and tuberculosis, so rules on good and poor manners of coughing, sneezing and using the handkerchief were given, many times you see someone use one, put it into their pocket, and next time they get it out, they give it a good shake.

Only Sunday, March 3rd, but it must be Spring for the highway is filled with Washington cars, and Saturday the 9th, a robin appeared. But - boy! rain and more rain. By Wednesday, March 13th, people are wondering if we'd sink through to China. How quickly weather can change. Saturday, March 16th, a testimonial dinner was held for Warrenton's Grand Old Man, Hon. J. W. "Pete" Shirley, who began his official duties as Sergeant of the Town on March 8th, 1887. Not a green cravat or socks were seen Sunday, March 17th. What IS this world coming to? A pair of stone lions had been given by Mr. and Mrs. John R. Buchanan to Fauquier County and were being installed Wednesday, March 20th, in front of the Clerk's Office Building, one on each side of the main front entrance. The statues were originally imported from Italy and used by the Buchanans at their country home, Leny Manor. They do add a touch of dignity to the building. Monday, March 25th, brings back memories of the "Olden Days" for it's March Court.

Again a sign of Spring! Painting fever. The Coffee Shoppe and the Village Inn are getting a new coat. Or, did I speak too soon? Sunday and Monday, April 7th and 8th, 1935 wasn't spring. Rain, sleet and snow, but that didn't deter the Easter Sales. April 13th Cornblatt's Department Store advertised "new Easter dresses for $2.98, spring hats were $1.98, and chiffon silk hose for 69¢." Wednesday, April 24th a new route for #15 or the James Madison Road. Now it is along Main Street, then by Winchester Street, and the new one will leave at or about Turkey Run on the Bealton Road; then through the Nesbit property and left toward the Horse Show ground; on down Carlton Avenue to Culpeper, crossing that street which is Rt. 29 or the Seminole Trail. Then, across Mrs. Skinker's property and intersect with the Lee Highway or Rt. 211, at about Thompson's Filling Station; from there, northerly near C. N. Sullivan's land to E. B. King's property, crossing the Athletic Field, across the present Rt. 15 and down the Valley until it intersects with the Lee Highway north of Warrenton about a mile.

Mr. H. R. Nichol of the Post Office Department at Washington, as of April 27th, has been in Warrenton for the past three days making a survey regarding the establishment of delivery service for the patrons of the town's Post Office, with two deliveries a day. In the 1920's it was tried, but was not popular. The Post Office was a social gathering place and people didn't want to give up their boxes.[132]

The Town Council announced a mosquito control notice on May 7th, 1935. Friday, May 17th, had May Day celebrations at the High School. A free cooking school was given at the Fauquier Skating Rink, sponsored by The Fauquier Democrat for all the women of Warrenton and vicinity. An advertisement for the New Warrenton Restaurant on the 15th, had said it was just across from the school. Wonder if they thought people wouldn't be able to eat their own cooking and would have to eat there? The last several days of May were hot with clear skies, which have done more good than doctors or nurses combined to cut down on Scarlet Fever. "The Lord Almighty has stepped in with His sunshine and killed the germs." Also, a secretary of the National League of Women Voters spoke to a meeting of women in the Warren Green Hotel parlor regarding the league and its work. The skating rink closed the last of May for the season.

Sunday afternoon, June 2nd, was beautiful and with all sorts of things growing, so many flowers, and flags, were carried for the Confederate Memorial Day service. At the cemetery, the singing of the "Bivouac of the Dead" was among other presentations of the program. Monday evening a dinner was at the Coffee Shoppe for members of the Black Horse Camp, Sons of Confederate Veterans, and others. Commencement exercises for 26 high school graduates were held at 11am, Friday, June 7th, in the Fauquier Theater. June 12th, plans were made for a new high school with gymnasium and auditorium. The 16th Annual Junior Hunt Show was held June 22nd, being called the Warrenton Pony Show when first begun. By the 29th, the weather had really become hot. Arthur Godfrey was in town as he was buying property near The Plains.

Around July 13th, 1935, things are getting a little warm overseas, too. People talk daily about Mussolini adding to his armies, troops being mobilized, and how it effects us. Maybe that is a reason why so many marriage licenses are being issued. June had the record so far this year with 21 licenses. The street Carnival on Friday and Saturday, the 12th and 13th of July, had good crowds both nights. Proceeds this year are to go to the Warrenton Volunteer Fire Department and the Fauquier County Hospital. The Culpeper Municipal

Band was here for the first night and there was, as usual, the "Carnival Restaurant" featuring a fried chicken supper. The Town Council is concerned about parking conditions and the regulations not being enforced. The next week people were being cautioned about flies and are being told to stay away from crowds, because as of Wednesday, July 24th, there have been two cases of infantile paralysis.

They were kidding the Sheriff, Saturday, August 3rd, 1935, as he went "still-hunting" and also caught chiggers. August 7th, T. N. Fletcher bought from Mr. and Mrs. Lloyd C. Anderson the property on the corner of Winchester Street and Lee Highway, known as Garretts' Garage, built in 1929. Garretts sold Austins, and Thad Fletcher will sell Durant Star, Hudson, and Terraplanes. The basement was used as a garage with the shop in the rear upstairs.[171] They also sold Packards, for Mr. Risdon bought one.[124]

Tuesday, August 6th, was election day and it poured, but the rain was needed for it was beginning to get dry. In cooperation with the Health Department, the Horse Show was postponed until October 11th. Some years the Health Department determined when school opened, depending upon the number of polio cases. This year it has been announced that the Fauquier County schools will open Thursday, September 12th, unless delayed further. An announcement Friday, the 16th, said Will Rogers and Wiley Post were killed in an airplane crash near Point Barrow, Alaska. Aaron Nusbaum was 75 years old August 27th. Although now living in Washington, he returns here each year to vote. Fauquier Theater was crowded Friday night of the 30th, when there was a world premiere of the 3-act comedy, "Horse Play". It was an excellent amateur performance.

Labor Day, September 2nd, 1935 was wet and cold. The squirrels must have had a hard time Saturday, the 7th, judging from the number of hunters who went into the woods. Most of them came out with only red bugs and chiggers. September 12th, the Sheriff caught something the night before besides chiggers. One of the largest moonshine outfits ever taken in Virginia was found in Fauquier County's mountains. The operators escaped though. Saturday, September 14th, was quite a day for the news. The Queen of Belgium died, Huey Long was killed, and the Italian-Ethiopian War made the front page. September 18th, Edward Risdon had a demonstration of electric and radio supplies at his new store on Main Street, next to the Fauquier Theater. Sunday, the 22nd, a big day for flying as they said there were three planes at the airport on the Marshall Road. Monday morning, September 23rd, the Courthouse Bell rang, ushering in the September Court, which is the first since last May. Years ago the summer terms were abandoned. Indian Summer had set in by Wednesday, the 25th, and people were wishing Court was still abandoned.

Tuesday morning, October 1st, 1935, the Court House Square Garage opened for business with Thad Fletcher as owner and manager. They called Mrs. Kirby to tell her to send her son, Willard, as there was a horse van with a flat tire and he might like to see it. When he arrived, he found the movie star, Ken Maynard and his white horse, Tarzan. Willard was really excited to see the celebrities, but it was a toss-up if it was Ken or Tarzan that thrilled him the most. Maynard was on his way to a horse show around Upperville.[133] Gene Garrett's new garage on Waterloo Street is coming along fine.

October 4th the Town Council granted Newton Brooke permission to have a private garage at Waterloo and Diagonal Streets, which is just down the hill from The Square. Monday, October 7th had snow in the mountains and 25 degrees here. Two dances at the Fauquier Recreational Center on the 11th and 12th were for the Horse Show. Twenty percent of the proceeds will go to the Warrenton Bed at the Cripple Children's Hospital in Richmond. Wednesday, October 16th the Federal Housing Administration says Fauquier County is suffering labor shortages in carpenters, farm workers and other trades. Why are people on relief, someone asked, if we need workers? A memory tester, "What old timers remember Polk Miller and his famous quartet of colored singers? Back around 1895-1900 this famous banjoist and storyteller of Negro stories always paid Warrenton an annual visit and the Old Town Hall, now Fire House, was always packed." Sunday, October 20th, was so pretty many cars were on the highway for Skyline Drive. Next day, the 21st, the contract for the new high school building on Waterloo Street was awarded so work will begin soon. The 26th, Main Street is getting a new coat of smelly tar. If it holds and binds as strongly as it smells, it will out last the Appian Way. Wednesday, October 30th, Eddie Risdon was in his new place of business by the Fire House and repairing the other half of the building for Thurston Willis who will open a drugstore there about November 15th.

Tom Stafford was out again Saturday, November 2nd, 1935, after the accident October 27th, when he was struck by a hit-and-run

Washington Taxi on Lee Highway. The Courthouse Bell will be rung on Armistice Day in Commemoration of the World War Armistice. Work is being rushed on the Hiden Building to remodel it into two stores as it is planned to be ready by the 15th. However, it was the 23rd that the Ben Franklin Bargain Store, or as the Big Gold and Red sign went up, it was also called The Red Front Store. Winter hit here with a bang the past week and every garage was busy filling radiators with cold preventives. By Saturday, November 30th, the Willis Drugstore was open, with fountain service. Phil & Alex, the theater, barber shop, and Old Man Mussolini, Western Union, Branch Smith and his Restaurant and furniture business, Eddie Risdon, Thurston, and the Fire House are businesses along Main Street on that block.

There was no November Court and now Judge William Woods is taking J. R. H. Alexander's place as he is ill, opening Court Monday, December 9th, 1935. The Arcade Bowling Alleys are now open, one block from the Courthouse on Alexandria Pike. Last year they were advertised as Foley's over Carpenter Motors.

There are attractively dressed store windows about town and Tom Stafford's Christmas present is a new white car with a black top. The busiest place in town during Christmas is the Post Office. Monday, the 23rd, The Northern Virginia Club of the Virginia Military Institute held its annual holiday dance at the Grill room of the Warren Green Hotel. Speaking of dances—in Pappas' New Warrenton Restaurant was probably the only juke-box in town, called Panarama Sound with 10 songs playing at 10¢ a single song or for a dollar, all without stopping, and about a 3 minute movie on a tiny screen to be watched while the song played. Many times the machine was borrowed to be used at dances. Young people liked to go to Pappas' after a basketball game for a milkshake.[163] Fewell & Company had closed the store at Carter's Building around 1933 and two sisters went to work at Graysons for a couple years. Mrs. Kate Fewell married Mr. Burke who worked at Thurston Willis' Drugstore before both of them went to Thornton's. The other sisters were Ruth Green, Mrs. L. L. McIntosh and Alice Woodzel. Around 1935, they got together again and reopened the store as The Fashion Shop in the old Willis Drugstore Building. City Risdon (Garrett) went to work for her aunts, working part-time and Saturdays. That made four people in the store, so when no customers were there, they played cards. City wondered what people thought when they came in and saw them sitting in the back at their game.[110]

1936

January 1st, 1936 came in after a Christmas week of the coldest temperatures for years. There was 8-10 inches of snow with it 15 degrees below normal, being only 8 above zero Saturday and Sunday, December 28th and 29th. The inside of the Warren Green is being improved, such as new carpeting and showers installed, by Ullman Bros., and will be under the management of Ralph McKee. A sheet of ice covered the town Thursday, January 2nd, making a wonderful time for coasting and skiing on the nearby hills. Someone said they would just as soon ride in an airplane as to get on a pair of treacheous looking skiis. Even though a few places were sanded, had sawdust or ashes, the safest place to walk was in the snow between the sidewalk and the car tracks. When Courthouse Hill was too icy for cars or trucks to get to the top, the Power Company had a White Line Truck with a wrench. A line was anchored to the Dummy Policeman and the vehicle pulled to the hilltop. The driver of the truck was Henry Butler and Pres Ruffner was line foreman. W. H. "Peanut" Gouldthorpe also worked for the company.130 The new Garrett Garage Building was finished by now, for Hunter Richie built it in record time, probably about three months. They sell Chrysler, Plymouth, and Hudson. The Town Clock was put in order Wednesday, January 8th and the strike restored after a long silence. C. C. Gill & Sons from Culpeper are to open a hardware in town and on the 11th, Mr. Emsweller is manager of the Sanitary Meat Market on Main Street at the Carter Building.

A different type of car is being driven by Phil Marsteller about Saturday, January 18th, 1936. It was called a "Terraplane" but Col. Appleton called it a "Terrapin". Phil says it is not that slow but it is just as sure to get you there as the terrapin. Garrett's Garage sells them, too. Tom Stafford's official car is suppose to be white, but he has trouble keeping it so. Most of the time it looks red or brown depending on the mud he goes through. Sunday, January 19th, there was a small-sized blizzard, if there is such a thing, with snow and sleet. Monday night, the 20th, was the annual banquet of the Black Horse Camp, SCV, the Black Horse Chapter, and the UDC at the Coffee Shoppe. Another meeting that night was of the Fauquier County Hospital Association held in the Fauquier National Bank. It's a good thing they weren't Wednesday as we were on the edge of a real blizzard then. The temperature dropped from 40 to zero in a few hours with a strong wind. Next day, the 23rd, there were 5 fire alarms. One was on Culpeper Street at Shadow Lawn apartments, where a man was using a blow torch to thaw the pipes. Wednesday, January 29th, the portrait of Lord Fairfax that was presented to the County some time ago by the Fauquier Historical Society, was hung in the Courthouse. A State Seed Show was held Thursday and Friday, January 30th and 31st at the St. James Parish House. Things such as this used to be held on The Square. Speaking of portraits. Those left by the will of Judge John Barton Payne to the Warrenton Library of his wife and her mother, have been received. Also Dr. Buckner Magill, who lives in Warrenton, presented a copy of his book, "Ten Years And Under", to the Library.

It was reported Saturday, February 15th that $5,000 was paid to the County for Dog Tags. They cost $1.00 for a male or unsexed dog and for kennels a cover of $25. That was a lot of dogs to collect that much money. Wednesday, February 19th, there was another sleet storm which knocked out the telephone and electric. Those with some age will recall the severe winters of 1918, 1899 and 1887, but our grandchildren will be saying "the winter of '36". The streets are muddy and dirty because of all the mud brought to town by the automobile wheels.

March 5th and 6th, 1936, because of the increased interest in better cattle breeding, a school was held in the Fauquier Bank Assembly Room. The Fire Department did a good job Tuesday night, the 10th, of washing off the streets. All day Wednesday people were saying, "Thank you, Firemen", for the street really looked clean and pretty. They are always ready and on the job whether it was fighting fires, holding carnivals, eating up everything in sight at banquets, or washing streets. John L. Thornton, young son of Mrs. John L. Thornton and the late Dr. Thornton, had lots of congratulations this day. He won a "Ten Gallon Hat" in a Tom Mix radio contest. Tuesday, March 17th, and not a single green tie or dress seen on St. Patrick's Day. Where are all the Irishmen, real or imaginary? Perhaps the rain washed them away. Anyway it was "no fittin' " day for potato planting. Ullman's store on Lee Street is advertising a big anniversary sale—from 1836 to 1936. By Saturday, March 21st, it has rained so much, many people have gone to Washington to see the floods. Again it's good to live in Warrenton where it is high and dry.

In the afternoon of Sunday, March 22nd, there was a strange sight to see in the sky, called Sun Dogs. There were two very bright spots on opposite sides of the sun, at equal distance from it and directly in line with it. Part of the time there was a halo of rainbow colors around the sun. People were stopping, pointing and staring at it. Some spoke in hushed voices, for they remembered what had happened before. The phenomenon, they said, has to do with weather—and war. A very brilliant display of one was seen here the year before the outbreak of the World War in 1917. With the things that are happening now in Europe, this makes one wonder. Judge J. R. H. Alexander accepted on behalf of the county, the portrait of Thomas, Sixth Lord Fairfax, Tuesday, March 24th, at the beginning of Circuit Court. It was formally presented to the county by H. C. Groome. That old March wind came, with trees damaged and limbs everywhere. But it did help dry up the ground.

Wednesday, April 1st. April Fool's Day. Some people got caught. The yellow forsythia is beautiful in its full bloom and flower beds have their Spring flowers. Other shrubs, Maple, Popular and Elm trees are budding, and of course, the Willows are very green. The only tree in town that is in full leaf may be the Horse-chestnut behind the County Office Building. Maybe it is warmer in its location between the two tall buildings. Warrenton Supply has a special on garden tools. For example, a 33-tooth bamboo lawn rake costs 19¢. Ullman Brothers are having electrical attachments installed in the halls and rooms throughout the Warren Green Hotel so everything can be vacuumed clean. Easter Sunday, April 12th, was showery, but it was said that "Solomon in all his glory was not arrayed like the Warrenton ladies in their Easter bonnets." By April 29th Dr. Hiden was having his large lot below Fauquier Hospital fixed up as a free playground with seats, swings and so forth.

May Day, but Saturday, May 2nd was more important as that was the 15th annual running of the Virginia-Gold Cup. The weather was good and the crowd was large. The Town Council, May 5th, decided an extra policeman was needed for all night on Saturdays. Sad to say an employee in A. S. Hamilton's Poolroom was assaulted and robbed on Lee Street, Saturday night, the 9th. Richard Thorpe was on his way home and did not know what happened after being knocked unconscious, until he awoke to find himself on the pavement and his money gone. Wednesday, the 13th, Johnson's Photographic Studio went in above Cornblatt's Store. By the 16th, Thad Fletcher had moved some of his gas tanks and now there is room at the Court House Square to "gas-up" several cars at a time and a truck can turn around between the tanks. An airport might be near if talk is correct. May 19th the Town of Warrenton entered into an agreement with the Dept. of Highways regarding the maintenance of the airport on the property of Clifford P. Zieger located about 3½ miles from town. The Chest Clinic was held at the Courthouse May 20th. Saturday the 23rd, was called "Poppy Day", as Sunday, May 31st was Memorial Day, "The South's Sabbath Day of Remembrance." Something new in the county this month—the first Rural Electric Cooperatives.

June 3rd, 1936, two people were holding a conversation in or partly in the street. Along Court Street, Town Manager, Sid Shumate had one foot on a running board of a car with the other pointed out in the street. A car came along, struck the foot, knocking down the owner and almost overturned in the excitement. Everyone was talking, too, about the behavior of Postmaster Frank, our Mayor, and the publisher of The Fauquier Democrat, who is a passionate Democrat. A stranger from Texas came riding a donkey into town, which he hitched at the Post Office. Mr. Frank seeing it, ran down the steps and gave it a big kiss right in the middle of the forehead. He said it looked so much like the Democratic emblem, he couldn't help it. Saturday, June 13th, the cornerstone of the new High School on Waterloo Street was laid. Saturday and Sunday Warrenton's First Air Meet was held at Meadowville, having stunt exhibitions by civilian and army planes, a parachute jumper, and passenger rides.

The stores were closed all day July 4th, but a crowd was on hand at the Courthouse to watch President Franklin Delano Roosevelt go through town at 10:45am on his way to dedicate Shenandoah National Park and Skyland Drive. The people were really rather patient as the motorcade was over an hour late. He stopped about 5 minutes to greet those at The Square's intersection. Miss Dolly Hiden, the Doctor's daughter, took pictures of it. The day was hot and some wished for those snowballs they had last winter. Ernest Pappas was among those who escorted the President to his destination. After the President spoke at the ceremonies opening the Drive, a woman began to rush towards him—wanting to shake his hand. Ernest was surprised at how quickly the Secret Service men surrounded her as they thought she might harm the President.

The Firemen's Carnival was to be Friday and Saturday, July 10th and 11th, but a heavy rain storm broke it up Friday night. They tried again Saturday and the same thing happened, so plans were made to have it Saturday the 18th. "Warrenton Day" or "Warrenton Baseball Day" at the ballpark in Washington was Wednesday, July 15th, as it is every year. Half of Warrenton must have gone, Tuesday, July 21st, to see the Bull Run Sham Battle. Next day, Peoples National Bank installed a Night Depository and Deakin's, Inc., a clothing store, was the first business concern to use it. Someone said it was like shoveling money in a "hole in the wall". During July, Warrenton had a new telephone system installed.

August 4th, 1936, the Town Council directed the Sergeant to trade in his present car for a new Oldsmobile. A storm, Wednesday night, August 5th, put the town in darkness for several hours, so people at the movie didn't see the end. They had to go to bed as they used to—by candlelight. To test your memory again. "Who remembers Ernest L. McLearen who worked for Ed Pattie in the store on Winchester, which was across from where Thad Fletcher's Garage is now?" Thursday, the 8th, Hansbrough's harness shop is to reopen next door to Coon's Grocery on Culpeper Street. About the last of August, some people were suggesting a traffic light at Court House Square.

September 8th, 1936, the Town Council asked the Sergeant to cooperate with the Sheriff in preventing loafing on the Courthouse steps. There isn't any place else to sit downtown now that the Fountain is gone. The public schools opened their doors Friday, the 11th, for another 9 month term. It will be a little quiet around here. Well, what do you know. The wooden steps at the Post Office finally came off. They had been put up in January as storm steps. In a couple more months they may again be needed. We do want for precipitation for there has been no rain since the first of August and people are asked to conserve water. The Coffee Shoppe, that can seat 110 guests, is installing an air conditioner. Think of all those cool people.

Mr. Thoma was "the old country-type of person" in manners, a most gracious and grand old man. He and several others of that age liked to chew tobacco. Sometimes when they met on the street, especially in front of Sanford's, they talked for a while and naturally had to spit. Now, it was against the law to spit on the street, and a young man asked the police to do something about it. . . even to arresting them. The policeman said he just couldn't do such a thing to those nice old gentlemen, so he just warned them. Mr. Thoma called the complainer a "young whipper-snapper with nothing else to do but to watch them".[134] Oh, yes, Johnny Kreticos has a restaurant called "The Mayflower" on the south corner of Winchester and Alexandria Pike where Rev. J. A. Frazier was in 1927. Jimmy Kreticos was in the restaurant with Johnny for a while,[149] and, Johnny went back to Washington to run a place, returning here,[145] perhaps between the time he sold The Warrenton Cafe and established The Mayflower.

Franklin D. Roosevelt won the election by a landslide as President over Landon. November 10, 1936, the Town Council wanted donations for a sidewalk on Waterloo Street to the new High School Building that opened last month. On the 12th, Dr. Hiden was remodeling half of the building next to the Ben Franklin Store. They knock holes in a building and then repair it. Memorial Services were held at the cemetery, but Armistice Day seems to have gone by without a single flag visible in Warrenton except the one at the Post Office, and when the Courthouse Bell tolled for 15 minutes at 11am, someone thought it was the hour striking.

Tuesday, December 1st, 1936, was the coldest day of the season at 12 degrees. Saturday, the 5th, the Warrenton Jail was said to be a menace as it was a fire hazard. That will have to be remedied. On the 9th there was an ad using the Dionne "Quints". An unusual event for that many babies to be born and to live. Saturday, December 12th, The Warrenton Garrett Garage Bus Center on Waterloo Street has been opened for the Virginia Stage Line Buses. Dr. Hiden bought the Western Union Telegraph Company on Main Street (now Charlottes), December 16th, which he will lease. Routes 29, 129, and 41 are to be called the Seminole Trail. Part of 29 already was named that, once being the old Hunting Path.

1937

1937 and lots of people living around, but bobcats are heard howling in the mountains at night. Gives a weird feeling on the dark still nights. A new feature in The Fauquier Democrat is called "Wings Over Warrenton" and the drawing with it has airplanes flying over the Courthouse. It tells the air news and of flyers in the county, as flying is becoming "the thing". Wednesday, January 20th, a popular movie, "Little Miss Marker", with Shirley Temple was in town. Other stars are Hoot Gibson, Tom Brown, William Boyd, Jane Withers. President Roosevelt was reinaugurated with John N. Garner as his Vice President. Saturday, January 23rd, Ernest Pappas, who bought the Virginia Inn Restaurant last October from Austin Barnes, has sold it. It is in what some call the Travois (Travers?) Building (next to present Risdon's) because Lee Travois had owned the restaurant first, then Austin Barnes. Frank Moffett liked their cream puffs, which cost 5¢. Arthur Anderson owned the building.[117] Pappas had several places at the same time, and with good dependable workers one could do that. Ernest Pappas gave a day's receipts to the Fauquier County Hospital Association recently.

Wednesday, the 27th, there was a terrible flood in the Mississippi, Ohio, and Kentucky Rivers area, said to be the greatest in history. The Ben Franklin Store is having a 9¢ sale with hundreds of items at that price. The Honorable J. S. Battle spoke to the Young Democratic Club the night of Thursday, January 28th, at the Courthouse. Tom Stafford, Jr. had been born January 8th, 1937 and Miss Kitty Phillips, "a nice old lady", had baby gifts at the Bon Ton Shop. Someone bought a gift there and Miss Phillips included a pink calendar for Tom Jr's room. She always did little things like that. Miss Phillips was the aunt of Mrs. Arthur (Virginia) Anderson.[165]

About 7am Tuesday, February 2nd, 1937, Kemper Hawkins was found unconscious, lying on the bank across the street from the New Warrenton Restaurant and Campbell Kearnes' place. He was in a badly beaten condition having been robbed of $20.00. Friday, the 4th, there was a bad accident at the Post Office. Two small girls, Adle Lunceford and Jeannette Barnes, were crossing over to the Silver Tower, located behind Sanford's Store, when a green Ford V-8 came very fast around the corner. Adle's book bag strap caught in the bumper and she was thrown to the ground. The driver did not stop, but our trusty policemen, Sam Hall and Tom Stafford, apprehended him. They also found the two men who were involved with Kemper Hawkins. It is said that things happen in threes. Guess the other is that someone took the Confederate State Great Seal from an exhibition cabinet in the Library, Saturday the 13th. There is also a flu epidemic in Warrenton—and, it was reported relief cases were increasing. One good thing at least did happen in February. The Mayflower Inn gave a day's receipts to the Red Cross for the flood victims.

There was a meeting Saturday, March 6th, 1937, regarding Bang's disease. The Courthouse was packed with farmers as the county produces one-tenth of all the milk sold in Warrenton. At an auction Monday, March 8th, Mrs. Mildred Kretico's bid of $18,800 bought the property on the corner of Winchester Street and Alexandria Pike, known as the "Pattie" property. Johnny K's Mayflower Inn and R. L. Pearson's store will continue on the lower floor. Pearson's have been there a number of years. Plans are for the second floor to be a rooming house. The Chest Clinic was at the

Courthouse March 15th, 9am to noon for white patients and 1pm to 4 for colored patients.

April 6th, 1937, the Town Council decided that trucks and trailers are not to park on the public streets of town for more than two hours. Saturday, April 17th, was the Warrenton Gymkhana, a meeting for sports, especially concerning horses, with contests, and an old fashion barbecue, held at Stuyvesant Field on new Route 15. That is always a fun day. Wednesday, April 28th and a 36-hour downpour resulting in county flooding, washing away livestock, "small fry", and some people, blocking traffic and cutting off electricity for a time. The Fashion Shop improved and enlarged so had an official shop-opening this month.

Gold Cup weekend of May 1st, 1937, had about 20,000 people attending. May 4th, the Town Council ordered that people cannot use mechanical means to collect kitchen and cooking odors, fumes or other offensive odors, and discharge it into streets of town so it would be offensive to citizens. It can only be through pipes and flues to the top of the buildings. People walking past some restaurants had the odors and smoke blown out into their face. They are discussing the explosion of the German Airliner Hindenburg and King George VI's cornation, both which happened by May 15th. Monday night, the 17th, J. W. Shirley, age 80, fell down the Jail steps while he was making inspections and broke some ribs. He had succeeded the late C. M. Pattie as jailor, remember. Memorial Day celebration Sunday, May 31st was at the cemetery as usual.

June 30th, 1937, the Third Cavalry went past Court House Square as they came from Front Royal on their way of a week's hike. They camped this night on the Country Club grounds. The Town Council decided July 5th, that in the future all municipal elections are to be held in the Courthouse. The Firemen's Carnival held at the Fletcher Lot off Waterloo Street, had their color theme as grey and white, representing their uniforms and the nurses' uniforms, showing where the proceeds would go this year. Even with a heat wave, lots of people attended. Zieger Field was licensed, July 27th, as the Warrenton Municipal Airport. A large air show was there July 31st and August 1st. A little far from the center of town, but still to have a major effect.

Big excitement on August 7th, 1937 at the intersection of Culpeper Street and Route 15. A truck from North Carolina with 18,000 cantaloupes overturned. Children from all over town ran to the site like so many flies to a honey dish. They first sold at $1.00

a crate and then went up to $1.50 for 36 melons. Wednesday, the 11th, Arthur Godfrey gave the jail a new name—"Rowdy Tank". Someone else came up with "Hoosegow". Fauquier National Bank is having a coat of paint inside and they say there is enough scaffolding to build the Tower of Babel. The second case of Infantile Paralysis was reported Saturday, August 21st. Always a dreaded summer disease.

By Saturday, September 4th, 1937, people were talking about the war between Japan and China and wishing for China to win. On Wednesday, September 20th, the wild geese were honking their way south. The Sheriff was busy Wednesday, December 15th, capturing a big Still. Improvements are being made on Pitt's Theater. The Community Christmas Tree, sponsored by the Public Welfare, was held December 22nd in the Warrenton High School instead of the Courthouse as originally planned. 215 county children both white and colored, received gifts. There is also a pretty giant Christmas tree at the Courthouse. The nation's Welfare Program began this year, and the County Office opened in the basement of the Courthouse. There is a movement to boycott Japanese goods, hopefully to help make them lose their war with China. During 1937, the frame house on the corner of North 4th Street across from the Post Office was remodeled. Alternate highways 211 and 15 are planned to by-pass Warrenton. What will that do to The Square?

1938

Saturday, January 15, 1938, found the old California House, or as it is also called, "The Stock Exchange Building", sold once again. The home offices for Gude, Winmill & Company closed and Allen Townsend Winmill bought the place. Among other offices in the building are the Virginia Gold Cup Race Association during its season, the Warrenton Production Credit Association, D. H. Lees & Company, L. R. Bartenstein and the Warrenton Hunt.

February 9th, 1938 Lerner Bros. Department Store leased the Sauer Building on Main Street and plan to open for business by the 17th. Mr. Sauer had bought the Kirson Department Store property on South 5th and Main Streets, at auction. By Saturday, March 26th, 1938, Thornton's Drugstore has seeds advertised. A good sign! Monday, March 28th—March Court Day, but not like it used to be. Lately the crowd and stallion parade is usually small with one or two draft animals. However, this year there were 5 stallions! Someone came up with the idea to give a ribbon to the best one, which was given a disinterested person to pin on the horse he thought was best.

Easter Sunday, April 17th, 1938, and all the ladies were out in their finer dresses and bonnets. An advertisement in the paper with two women had one saying, "The Reason that I Dine in the Mayflower Inn, is because there I get Real Home Cooked Foods and Because it is the only Restaurant in Warrenton that Cooperates with the Virginia Garden Clubs." The Newton Bros. Circus came to town April 30th.

It was a big weekend, Friday and Saturday, May 6th and 7th, 1938. The Good Year Blimp, "Enterprise" was here as guest of the Warrenton Supply and moored at the athletic field of the new High School. It is in conjunction with the demonstration of the new Good Year life guard tube, staged at 1pm on Lee Street between the corner of South 4th and East Main. Saturday was the Gold Cup Races and their dance at the Firemen's Hall. There's a feeling that things are gradually moving away from The Square. I used to have so much activity—now the carnivals are on Waterloo near 10th Street (now Chestnut), the music festival at the High School, Gymkhana at Stuyvesant School Field, flower shows and other exhibits at St. James. Sometimes it is lonely. Too bad for the Gymkhana on May 14, for it was postponed because of rain. The National Air Mail Week is from May 15-21st. John Drake from Warrenton will accept the mail pouch from the postmaster and fly it to Richmond. Poppies were on sale Saturday, May 21st, in preparation for Memorial Day, the annual Memorial Day services being held Sunday, June 5th. "Bivouac Of The Dead" was sung as part of the program.

June 5th, the 3rd Cavalry and a machine gun troop from the 10th Cavalry are now on a 100 mile march. 225 men started Thursday from Fort Belvoir and are stopping in town for the night.

Our "Pete" Shirley is 81 on July 3rd, 1938. Beginning Wednesday, the 6th, 21 firms will give that day and all other Wednesday afternoons off. It's a movement begun locally about a month ago. There will be nine weeks in July and August so people can have a summer afternoon to swim, fish, or whatever. Rumor on Wednesday, July 20th, says White Sulphur Springs may be restored, as fire had destroyed the hotels. The Firemen's Carnival had a time this year. It was to have been July 22nd and 23rd, but rain Friday was so bad it was postponed to the following weekend. That Friday was alright, but Saturday was rained out. Arthur Godfrey said that if it rained any more, he was going to have to jack up his cows to milk them.

Saturday night, August 6th, 1938, the Little A&P closed its doors on Culpeper Street, because the A&P Corporation has a policy of only one store in any one town. The "Little Store" was opened before the big one which is on Main Street. Jimmy di Zerega was the first manager, followed by Forest Williams. Poor "Pete" Shirley. Look at what happened now. Monday night, September 5th, 1938, someone hit him on the head, took his keys and five prisoners escaped. By the 10th, four were returned and the last one by Wednesday the 21st.

Saturday, October 1st, 1938, Edward E. Risdon, owner of the building on Main Street near the Theater, and J. W. Rhodes, the tenant, will unite to improve Rhodes Drugstore. Once, here was a small brick house with steps to the side of it that led to the pavement as it had no yard.[152] The present place may have been built in the late 1920's.[156] October 1935 Eddie Risdon was in the new place and preparing the other half for Thurston Willis' Drugstore, now Rhodes. Seems that Willis went to Fredericksburg at sometime.[110] A Marine Show on a railroad train was on display at the Southern Railroad Depot, Monday, October 3rd. Among the exhibits was a real-live mermaid. Stuyvesant School had a new bell installed Saturday, October 29th. It once pealed out for the Academy at Bethel to summon their students. A report in October said that for the first time the value of automobiles and trucks in Fauquier County was greater than the value of horses.

The Jeffries' window display, Wednesday, November 2nd, 1938, was showing old pharmacist's appliances and prescriptions, some probably as old as Charlie. The Indian Summer feels good. November 4th, Thomas E. Frank resigned as Mayor after 15 years. Wallace N. Tiffany was elected by the Town Council to fill the term until September 1st. Wednesday, November 20th, Virginia Gas Distribution announced they were going in the building of the old A&P.

One of the places people were to leave gifts for the children's party was at the Courthouse. Ernest Pappas again helped make Christmas pleasant for some families. Last year he donated 44 pair of shoes to the Welfare Office and now he bought 250 pounds of candy for them. In the restaurant he had a small Christmas tree inside the door and one in front of the window. They, like most people, did the Christmas shopping in the downstairs of Sanford's Variety Store. Saturday, December 10th, 1938, the Community Christmas tree and party was at the St. James Parish House at 1pm for the white children and at 4pm for the colored children. 200 children received gifts.

1939

1939 begins with trouble for the Elm trees. February 7th the Town Council agreed to purchase a sufficient number of gum strips to be placed on the Elm trees about town as an aid in the preservation of them against beetles and the like. A new building is going up across Main Street from the Post Office. This may have been a vacant lot, but for a while Billy Moore and his son, Billy, Jr., ran a live poultry market on the site, and when people walked past—they surely did smell it!

Wednesday, March 8th, 1939, was a beautiful Spring day. Makes one believe in better things to come. Around the 24th, Lerner Bros. moved from the Sauer Building into the new one that had been built on Main Street. The Town Council laid down the rules on parking at their March 31st meeting. The parking on all streets with the exception of the West Side of Court House Square is to be parallel to the curb and within six inches of it, except where provided. Parking on the West Side of The Square-and other streets,-

MAIN STREET BUSINESS SECTION
SHOWING NEW WARRENTON RESTAURANT
WARRENTON, VIRGINIA
Circa 1939

is to be at right angles to the curb and within six inches of it. Court Street from Main to Hotel on the east side only, at the corner on the intersection of Hotel and Culpeper Streets is prohibited. There can be parking on the south side of Hotel from Culpeper to a point 22 feet west for physicians' cars only.

April 4th, 1939, plans are to purchase and place a number of two hour parking signs at various places. By Saturday, April 15th, people were talking of how fast cars drove along the street now that curb parking gave more room. If you need an officer, you can call the New Warrenton Restaurant or the Silver Tower as they usually know where one is. The Silver Tower is a small lunch room with 5 or 7 stools and space behind them to stand. Hot dogs were 5¢ while a hamburger and a ham sandwich were each 10¢. Some thought that was a little high for hamburger.[133] It was owned by either Johnny Kreticos[148] or Tom Frost. There was talk about a fellow who had a "little too much", shall it be said, and he was told to leave the place. When he didn't, he was told he'd be arrested. The fellow said they couldn't do that and began tearing up the seats, actually throwing a couple out the door before he was subdued.[166]

Saturday, May 27th, 1939, is "Poppy Day" when World War Veterans of Fauquier are paid tribute by people wearing a poppy. Monday, the 29th is the last Court to convene until September. A contest, Wednesday, May 31st, was being given by the Fauquier Electric Supply Company, the winning of which will be a free trip to the New York's World Fair.

June 1st, 1939–RAIN and many, many thanks for it. Friday, June 23rd, a silver-haired, distinguished looking man, with a Southern drawl sat on the porch of the Warren Green Hotel. It was Colonel Bob Dalton, the last member of the Jesse James Gang. After serving 30 years in the penitentiary and being pardoned by Theodore Roosevelt, he is now president of Dalton Oil Company, Texas, and on a motor trip through the United States. The night of the 24th, there was a tar and feather party involving a Washington columnist and local boys which ended up on Culpeper Street.

People are debating if we should fight another war. England has a united front, but we fought one war and that didn't bring peace. Some ask, do we want another that will sacrifice the American family's happiness? Or do we help those in trouble? Or do we wait until something happens to us? Warrenton is gaining fame as the place to marry. The average marriage licenses bought is 150, but this year the Clerk of the Court has had more than 500 since January

1st. Also, in the last three years, hunting, resident trapping and fishing licenses have gone up, too. The Firemen had a good Carnival this year, Friday and Saturday, July 14th and 15th, with even St. Swithin's Day good to them. The Town Clock is having a face lift. It is missed by many, even though it was seldom just exactly right.

By Wednesday, August 2nd, 1939, the Clock is back and people can go to bed by its striking. August 5th, the Town Council approved payment of $640.36 for its overhaul and the refinishing of worn parts. Tree limbs that came down in last Thursday's high winds and rain are still being cleaned up. Another memory tester. "Who remembers Braddock's Well, also called Mitenger's Pump opposite the Post Office",[135] and "Who remembers Mr. Ferdinand Bartenstein wandering home along Alexandria Pike with his left hand on the horses' bridle and his violin tucked under his other arm? Sometimes when he played St. James' organ, it would be heard a block or so." Someone said, "God has given us memories that we can have a bit of summer in the dull winter time. Memories are like some sweet song that lingers to soothe you." But, memory does play tricks, too.

Now that they are in such constant use by Saturday, August 12th, 1939, the huge Army sweep-lights are causing Warrenton to stay up a little later to watch these modern war implements. Officers and enlisted men from camp in Manassas are in and out of town daily. Many from around here have motored down to inspect the tent city just across the Prince William line. There have been several local downpours lately. One caused flooding and Colonel Apperson was stranded on his own bridge. On this night there were two dances given here in honor of the officers and privates. It looked like an armed town so many uniforms were parading the streets. Ignoring a downpour, high winds and various other samples of stormy weather, Friday night, the 18th, the District National Guard Band presented their concert from the steps of the Courthouse. A large crowd came out to hear, applaude, or toot their auto horns, for people were parked as thick as traffic officers would permit and all surrounding windows were filled with music lovers. The Silent Policeman is gone, replaced by a bare white monument with "KEEP RIGHT" on all four sides. All the many road signs with names and miles that was on the "Policeman" have been placed at the Courthouse curb facing Alexandria Pike. We can be proud of two local girls. Josephine Wood and Virginia Ann Pearson received the Golden Eaglet Badge, the highest award which can be given any Girl Scout.

Warrenton's 40th annual Hunter Show of America closed Monday, September 6th, 1939, and County Schools began the next day. A petition circulated through the county is urging true neutrality in an effort to maintain peace. Saturday, the 9th, brought a foreign visitor into town. The Fire Chief from Chihuahua, Mexico left Mexico City on June 6th. He has accepted four rides but walked most of the way, averaging 30 miles a day, visiting the Fire Department of towns he passes through and asking for a letter from the Chiefs he visits, as he calls himself a "Good-Will Ambassador". The destination is the New York's World's Fair.

A notice in The Fauquier Democrat, September 9th, said, the world war is a week old—"Wanted! for murder, kidnapping, arson, highway robbery, burglary and all other crimes on the calendar, one Adolf Hitler, Madman of Europe. Reward for him dead or alive, preferably the former". March 1938 Germany annexed Austria. September 1938 Germany took Czechoslovakia. Last month Germany and USSR signed a non-aggression pact and Germany invaded Poland. They have been on the move.

Shrubs from the Fletcher lot on Main Street across from the Presbyterian Church, which recently was purchased by the Sanitary Grocery Company from George H. Hickman, were removed Thursday to the Rosenwald High School for the colored children, which is located on the highway east of town. Behind the Fletcher lot used to be the best apple orchard (now Farmer's Market). Among the school children who stopped to pick one was Irvin Garrett. Allied ships are attached to British and French now for fighting. The Town Council September 12th decided upon 'No Parking' signs to be on Main Street in front of the Clerk's Office so the bus lines would have a suitable place to park their buses, thus eliminating the present traffic congestion when the bus stops. Wednesday, the 13th, the season opened on squirrels and doves. Hope this is all the gunfire we ever hear.

Eddie Risdon, whose hardware store was across from the Post Office (now Thrift Shop) moved about 1934 and opened The Blue Ridge Hardware, but Carroll Risdon, who worked for him stayed on in half of the old building with a Paint and Hardware Store.[103] The Mayflower Inn moved into the other half (now 48 Main). September 13th, E. L. Timberlake moved his business from the Hiden Building to this, the Anderson Building to share Carroll's location (now 46 Main). Mr. Timberlake owned a Hupmobile, a streamlined new style of car. There was a small trailor with one wheel that he attached to the car in order to carry his Maytag washers. Once he went around a curve too fast and the washer fell off. Don't guess it was hurt for they said he put it back on the trailor and went on his way.[163] Forrest Gill's Furniture and Appliance Store may have replaced Timberlake at the Hiden Building.[137] He also had Gill's Implement Company on Franklin Street, opening there in 1936.[173]

Ennis Coons requested the Town Council October 3rd, 1939 for a parking sign for his own trucks in front of his store on Court House Square. It was denied as the Council felt it would be a dangerous precedence to grant. During the Indian Summer, October 11th, the Yankees won the Series over the Cincinnati Reds. Saturday, the 14th, some now say the people of America should face the fact that our country is in grave danger of war. The Lions roared mightly Monday night, October 30th, when 50 Lions and guests acclaimed Dr. Byrnal M. Haley King Lion of the newly organized Lion's Club of Warrenton, at an organizational dinner in the Warren Green Hotel. The next night, the ghosts and gobblins roared, but quieter than they had last year. One of the entertainments in town for them was given by the Business Girl's Circle at Fireman's Hall. Show windows on Main and Culpeper Streets were marked with soap and people had to wash them the following morning.

Wednesday night, November 8th, 1939, had lots of activity on The Square until the wee hours of the morning. For a while, people were moving pretty fast around here. The A&P at Culpeper and Main Streets stayed open until 6pm as usual. Then, they moved "bag and baggage", as Manager Bob Williams said, to their new location, which is where the Mayflower Inn had been in the old Pattie Building. Mrs. A. M. Randolph is the hostess for the three big opening days, Thursday through Saturday, the 9th-11th. They even decorated with balloons before opening on time Thursday morning. The John D. Sudduth Post, American Legion of Warrenton requested the merchants to display flags each holiday. The Town Manager bought two American flags with standards to be used on Main Street when occasions demand it. But, which Thanksgiving does one celebrate, the Presidential or the non-Presidential? Way down, or is it up, Main Street across from the Presbyterian Church, the Fletcher House is now being torn down for the new Sanitary Grocery Store Building.

As December 1939 comes, people in the Red Cross Work Room are busy rolling dressings and surgical bandages for War Relief. December 5th, the Town Council contributed $35 to the local Lion's

Club for use in decorating of Main Street for Christmas. December 13th, Lerner's had something to see! The world's tallest man was there. Robert Wadlow is 8 feet 9½ inches tall, weighs 491 pounds and wears size 37 double A shoe. The Coffee Shoppe donated the refreshments for the community Christmas Tree this year at St. James. The party was held the 22nd for the white children and the 23rd for the colored children. Mickey Rooney, they say, is the #1 Box Office Star.

1940

The Town Council met January 2nd, 1940. They were asked for permission to replace the Esso gasoline storage tank in front of the Warrenton Supply Service Station, which was granted, if the road is not disturbed. James Kidwell opened Kidwell's Market, Saturday, January 6th on Main Street in the McIntosh Clothing Store Building. Jimmy was formerly in charge of the A&P meat department and may have run the store on Culpeper Street.[174] Around 1900 there was a restaurant in this building and in 1920, Embry's Flower Shop.[156] Perhaps Albert Fletcher had a radio shop here, when radios had the large horn-like design for listening. Sunday night, January 7th, snow began and by Monday morning there was 7 inches of the white stuff. It hadn't gone away Saturday, the 13th, which was so cold that sleds, skates and even some skis were brought out. Again Tuesday, January 23rd, about 1pm, snow began with 9 inches falling before it ended, and children had an unexpected holiday. How about this—It is so cold that two people who were talking on the sidewalk had to go into the nearby drugstore to thaw out their conversation so they could understand what they were saying to each other. The Fire Department is getting a workout in this cold weather, too. The Fauquier County's President's Birthday Ball was held Tuesday, January 30th in the room over Lerner's Department Store, which is a large dance hall. President F. D. Roosevelt, born in 1882, was not stricken with infantile paralysis until 1921. He fought the disease for three years until he was finally able to walk with the support of steel braces and crutches.[10] Proceeds from the dance will go to the County Infantile Paralysis Fund, the theme of the dance being, "Dance that others may walk".

Friday, February 2nd, 1940, Groundhog Day and more snow. Monday, February 5th, Mayor Wallace Tiffany was out after his flu attack. They said he might be later than the groundhog, but at least he made it. A card party series, being held in the main room of the Warrenton Library, was opened Tuesday afternoon, the 6th, with a tea. Proceeds went toward purchasing new books. The sun came out for about four hours Wednesday the 7th, feeling good on the back and joints. Wednesday, February 28th, Ullmans on Lee and So. 5th Streets were having an anniversary sale. Mrs. Ullmans' father, A. Rindsberg, began in 1840 on Main Street and moved here in 1852.

The Warrenton Rotary Club had a Tall Story Contest, having had one annually since 1936. Saturday, March 2nd, 1940, Dan P. Wood won this year's contest with one of his "true experiences". He said he went fishing when a skim of ice was on the river. The ice was broken into small pieces and used for "bobbers" on the fishing line. That way when the fish was caught, the ice "floater" would slide down the line and lodge in the fish's mouth, freezing it so additional refrigeration wasn't necessary. The Town Council's regular meeting was March 5th at the Fire House. "Gone With The Wind" played in town, Wednesday the 6th. A real classic, people say. We have our own history, too.

It's unsure as to how the story went, but in the late 1890's the shutters on the lower part of Mrs. Jenning's house still had holes in them made by bullets during an exchange between some of Mosby's men who dashed out of the lane between the homes of Mr. Myer and Mrs. Bispham. They were attempting to capture General McPherson, it seems, as he went along Alexandria Pike and Culpeper Streets. BUT, the General had gone straight down Main Street to see Mrs. Newby and Mrs. Jenning, who had been ill. Mrs. Newby lived at that time across from the Presbyterian Church.

The New Warrenton Restaurant was being improved March 27th, 1940, both inside and outside. The waitresses and tablecloths will match in blue and white checked material. Virginia Painter, who worked there, loved to sew and usually made the uniforms for the employees. They might be like these or wine with little caps to match, and sometimes the all white ones were bought. The parking lot behind the restaurant has a new surface of gravel. Ernest Pappas wants residents to feel free to use the lot whenever they wish as it is convenient to the main part of Town and is accessible from Courthouse Hill. Saturday night, March 30th, a dance with a 12 piece orchestra from Winchester, was held in Mrs. Anderson's building, over Lerner's Store.

Monday, April 1st, April Fool's Day! And, it opened with the beginning of the census taking. The Gold Cup on Saturday, May 4th,

1940, used 7000 cedar trees for their jumps. Retail milk prices went up 1¢ and now it is 13¢ per quart on cash and carry bottles with a deposit of 3¢ on a bottle. Saturday, May 25th was "Poppy Day" with Thursday, May 30th, as Memorial Day. The celebration sponsored by the American Legion whose Post-Commander was Nelson Moffett. The parade began 10:30am at the Fire House and they marched in a body to the cemetery where Taps was played at 11:00. At noon they were to return to the front steps of the Clerk's Office Building with chairs provided on its lawn by Gold Star Mothers and ex-service men. A Memorial Table containing the names of 26 heroes who gave their lives in 1917 and 1918 was to be presented by the Post to the County for custody. But, the best laid plans of mice and men go astray. It rained. The ceremony was moved to the Fire House, so The Square was left out of the activities. The program consisted of roll call, the singing of "God Bless America", McPherson Gaines played Taps and the Tablet was unveiled, which will be placed permanently on the wall in the corridor of the Clerk's Office Building. Rev. Allen recited "In Flander's Fields" and the "Star Spangled Banner" was sung. The flags along Main Street, the two flags in front of the Clerk's Office and the Legion flags and colors made a colorful scene.

June 1st, 1940, the Gymkhama to be held at Maddox's Paddock on Culpeper Street May 25th, was postponed until this day because of bad weather. Even that is going farther from The Square. June 4th the Town Council advised the operators of the Mayflower Restaurant, the Warrenton Fruit Market Grocery Store, next to the Theater (now C&S Florist) and the Pool Room of the importance of closing at 11pm as well as maintaining order or they will have their beer licenses revoked. On the other side of the Theater was a shoe shop run by an Italian called Joe (now Creel's Jewelry).[134] By Saturday, June 8th, the "new View Tree" could be seen as it began to stand out against the sunset. The mountain, named for the huge chestnut tree at the top which died in the blight, changed hands many times during the Civil War as it was a signal post. One can see from there almost to Washington, D.C. Now the Government has it for an installation. The Edward R. Fletcher family was living there, and continues to do so as he is employed as grounds-keeper.[109] School children are doing without desserts and giving the money to the Red Cross Relief work. It is being said the Allies need airplanes and we should do something to help. Wednesday, June 19th, the stores begin their closings at noon on Wednesdays for the months of June, July and August.

The Town Council on July 2nd, 1940, felt the trees on Winchester Street needed protecting. They are too close together to put posts near them, so another means must be found. The Fire Department Carnival was July 12th and 13th at the Fletcher Lot on Waterloo Street. They grossed $4,000 and had a net profit of $2,500. Mrs. Grace Travers won the 1940 Chevrolet Town Sedan. The Sanitary Grocery Company opened their new store July 25th on the site of the old Tyler-Fletcher house at 418 Main Street, under the management of Louis B. Payne.

Charles M. Sauer, owner of the Ben Franklin Store, said Wednesday, August 7th, 1940, that the new building on the corner of So. 5th and Main Streets, would be ready to open this month. Painting is going on inside the Courthouse and there will be new chairs in the Courtroom. A gang that assembles each night about 7:30 on Main Street, has one or two people standing and three or four at two "sitting places". One place is at Cornblatt's door and the other is at the step of Charlie Jeffries' door, as he lives above the drugstore. In front of Ed Thornton's or Peoples Bank they stand. Usually the men are Tom Frank, Ray Larcombe, Albert Maxheimer, Bob "King Fish" Charland and Sprat Luke. There also may be Biggie Hodgkin, Sam Hall or Tom Stafford - whoever is doing duty -, Tom Hutchison, Dan Wood, and of course Charlie. It would be interesting to listen to all they have to say, as they may talk from about 4pm until dinner time some days. Biggie has thrown cigarettes out his open window during the summer several times which landed on Grayson's awning below causing a fire.[126] He was called the "poorman's dentist" as he had a habit of stopping children and telling them to come on in the office to have their teeth fixed. If the child said their mother couldn't pay, Dr. Biggie said that's OK, no charge on it.[133]

On Saturday, September 14th, 1940, over the tops of the buildings, it can be seen that two big trees on Culpeper Street are gone. The new Fauquier Democrat office building will take their place. Sidewalk superintendents line up along the old iron fence by the Fauquier Club to make sure things are going right.

Patriotic Americans registered for service in the Armed Forces Wednesday, October 16th, 1940. There were a total of 2,493 from the county to do so. Thursday night, October 24th, the colored citizens of Warrenton gave their annual dance for the benefit of the Fire Company. It was held in the colored Masonic Lodge with Chauncy Brown and his Society Orchestra. The first serial number in the National Draft Lottery was drawn Thursday, October 29th at 12:15pm by Secretary of War, Stimson. Number 158 went to Alfred Francis Deats in Morrisville of Fauquier County. The County Red Cross Motor Corps was organized October 1940 under the direction of Miss Dorothy Neyhart.[138] Oh, My! What some people do! Halloween night some very grown-up boys brought someone's "outhouse" to the front of the Atlantic & Pacific Store on the corner of Winchester and The Square. On the "little house" a sign was placed that read, "Come to the A&P".

F. D. Roosevelt had his third term victory on election day. Someone asked if we had Thanksgiving Day on November 28th, 1940 or Franksgiving Day on the 21st. Warrenton's Benefit Fun Fair was held at the Sanitary Grocery Store sponsored by the Lion's Club and the Children's House at The Plains. They grossed $1,358.

There is an essay contest sponsored by the merchants, businesses, and Lion's Club with a $10.00 prize for a school child who writes the best theme on "Why I Think The Christmas Lights Are A Benefit To Warrenton Merchants And Businessmen". Because of this, many children are walking around town to see the lights and get ideas. Here's a Memory Tester. "Who cut the picture from the frame when the Courthouse burnt in 1889? Charlie Jeffries says it was the late John W. Carter, a former merchant. Newton Brooke says he always heard it was his 'Uncle Dick' ". Wallace Brown and Cecil Dickerson, though, were responsible for the loudspeakers installed in the belfry of the Courthouse and carols pealing from the high tower on Christmas night. They were mostly chime records and were heard all over town. The Post Office was robbed of stamps and cash between midnight and 6am Wednesday, December 28th. The Lion's Club announced the Essay was won by Pauline Evelyn Gray, a sophomore at Warrenton High School. To end the year there was a party at the Warren Green Hotel Grill Room.

When Powell Thayer came to town in the 1930's he worked for a while at the Health Department. He said he "put together the best 'two-seaters' ever made."[164] Around 1940 he had an Appliance or Paint Shop, perhaps called the Fauquier Furniture & Electric Company. At least that was a store several doors away from the corner of North 6th and Main Streets where Carters is. Speaking of Carters, one thinks of Wayman who once accidently kicked a pickle under the back seat of Powell's car and forgot it. It was there so long that it began to smell, but Powell couldn't figure out what caused the odor. One day he stopped to talk to Wayman who realized the cause and retrieved the pickle. When Powell discovered who was responsible for the unpleasant odor, he chased Wayman down Main Street.[164]

1941

January 7th, 1941, the Town Council gave $25 to the Lion's Club to help pay for the Christmas Lights. Wednesday, the 15th, Tom Frost, Chairman of Fight Infantile Paralysis campaign, announced the President's Birthday Ball for the fund would be at Swanee Tavern on Thursday, January 30th. The first big snow of the winter was Sunday, the 26th. An advertisement, January 29th, was for the Safeway which is the new name for the Sanitary Store.

February 4th, 1940, the Town Council was again concerned with trees around town. They gave instructions to inspect some and see how to put them in a healthy condition and to put a guard around the Elm on Main Street in front of the Clerk's Office, which if satisfactory, might be used around scarred trees in need of such protection and that trees on Main Street from the 100 block through the 700 block, a total of 35 trees, should be prunned and fed. People are talking about Colonel Lindbergh testifying in Congress and how his sympathies are with Germany. A few years ago they felt sorry for him. Now they are tired of hearing him.

Wednesday night, March 12th, 1941, men met at the Courthouse to continue plans for a Fauquier Company of the Virginia Protective Force and a State Guard. The old Warrenton High School Building on High Street is to be used as the Armory. Monday, March 17th, St. Patrick's Day, but people were thinking more of the "Iron Duke". It is a scarred, shrapnel-torn Mobil Tea Kitchen from Britain that is visiting the country. On this date it was met outside of town and escorted with a loudspeaker truck, stopping at the schools and then finally displayed in front of the Clerk's Office. Addresses there were by Mayor W. Tiffany and Mrs. W. Murray Black, Chairman of Fauquier Branch, British War Relief Society and Mrs. Treherne-Thomas. Wednesday, the 19th, Lybrandt Barbee won the essay contest sponsored by the American Legion called, "What I Owe America and What America Gives Me". As a result of the meeting on March 12th, The Warrenton Rifles, Company 111, Virginia Protective Force, was mustered into the state organization on Thursday night, March 27th, at the Armory.

The British War Relief Society Thrift Shop opened Monday, April 21st, 1941 in the old Sanitary Building (now Carter's Furniture). Greek War Relief pins for men at $1 and for women at $2 are on sale at Johnnie Kreticos', Ernest Pappas', the Warren Green and the Robert E. Lee which is way down at the bottom of Waterloo Street. The theme is "Help Them Fight-Beat Hitler".

Saturday, May 3rd, 1941 - Gold Cup Day. A meeting Wednesday, May 7th, at the Warren Green was for the purpose of organizing the Warrenton Retail Merchants Association. Theodore Portnoy, Manager of Lerner Brothers' Department Store was elected president. Poppy Day was Saturday, the 24th. Charlie Jeffries brought a chair to the Club gathering a couple nights ago. They were kidding him saying that for 50 odd years he has sat and worn holes in his stone step. Now he brings out a chair! Tuesday morning, May 25th, there were 20 more boys leaving for camp. The Ladies' Aid Society of the Baptist Church had a Bake Sale Saturday, May 29th, in Mrs. Anderson's Building at the corner of Culpeper and Main Streets.

In June 1941, many people go to gasless Sundays to conserve under the National Emergency. It reminds one of 1917 and 1918 when gas could not be bought except for the most urgent emergencies. Guess people will be staying home more now, or strolling through town once again. A sad thing. Sunday, June 15th, the last engine whistle died away as the passenger service of the Warrenton branch of the Southern Railroad passed out of existence. The long wail of the distant steam whistle was lonesome enough on dark nights, but the sound today brought many a tear. Many people, including Sallie Sadler (Wood) reminisced about the old train and how in the olden days the only way to travel was by horse or railroad. The Depot used to be such a humming place, with the passenger train coming in at least a couple times a day. There might be only two or three cars, the caboose and engine with its little "toot-toot" almost like a man studdering. Captain Colvin, conductor in charge of the passengers, had an efficient air about him, or a feeling of a job to be done, as he entered the car saying, "Tickets, tickets". People would skurry around to find it and hold up for him to see. Since it was a small train, people felt it was "friendly", so they enjoyed the trip. The track ended at the Depot by having ties with dirt over the end and they turned on a Y-shaped track. Guess from now on the Post Office will have to have a truck meet the train at Calverton. Remember when a Black man with a push cart met the train for the mail? Also some of the entertainers coming to town will miss the train. Rudy Gill liked to see the Silas Green Ministral Show people come on a special train, march through town to the Courthouse steps and perform a small show, advertising themselves. Then they went to the vacant lot on Green Street, which was behind Rudy's Dad's place, the Gill Implement Company (now A Auto Sales).

Wednesday, June 18th, 1941, a year ago Hitler entered Paris. Warrenton is deserted after 1:00 on Wednesday afternoons now. Really quiet. Court is over for the summer, too. Rain Monday night, the 23rd, "busted" the heat wave and now everyone seems fresh as the daisies look. Some improvements on Main Street. The Coffee Shoppe has a new neon sign in front and there is a new sign outside Roadhouse & Bunch, across from the Coffee Shoppe. Probably around 1932, Roadhouse & Bunch had moved to this location (now Merĕmērēs Bakery), and after Mr. Roadhouse died, Mr. Bunch bought the business,[127] which became Bunch's Variety Store.[156] Lerner Bros. has installed 24 florescent lights, the third place in town to have them. Chamberlain & Hamilton cater-cornered from the Post Office, and The Fauquier Democrat being the other two. Saturday, June 28th, the Census results were given. The Town of Warrenton has 1,651 people, an increase by 201 since 1930 and a decrease of 103 from 1920. Lerners has a contest going on. In one of their show windows is a miniature treasure island. The contestant must guess the amount of money buried in the sand pile. Monday afternoon, June 30th, the United Service Organization Chapter for Fauquier was organized at a meeting in the Fauquier National Bank. The next planned meeting will be at the High School.

A drive was started Wednesday, July 9th, 1941, to collect aluminum. The Fireman's Carnival was July 11th and 12th. It seems the Aluminum Bin at the Courthouse was not large enough to hold the 1911 Pierce Arrow Coupe or the 1917 Rolls-Royce Phaeton that were donated to the drive, so the street was used to park them. The Warrenton Scout Troop was used to guard this defense material both day and night. Wednesday, the 30th, the Thrift Shop planned to move from Main Street to the Wallach Building on Culpeper Street.

The Town Council August 5th, 1941, adopted Daylight Savings Time with proclamations issued by the Governor of Virginia, beginning at 12 midnight August 10th and ending 12 midnight, September 28th. So, at the appropriate time, the Town Clock was set up one hour. Monday the 25th, the Mills Bros. Circus sponsored by the American Legion, came to town and set up on the Martin Grounds,

Route 15, back of the High School. That night, too, Warrenton looked like an Army camp. 5000 men and officers camped on Stuyvesant Field as they were on their way to Caroline County. Hardly a week goes by that some of the Armed Forces of Uncle Sam doesn't stay overnight in Warrenton. Churches and Townspeople welcome them with entertainment, newspapers, magazines, writing materials, washing facilities, games and so forth.

Saturday, September 13th, 1941, workmen put up STOP signs at some intersections with Main Street. Friday, the 20th, a Squadron of 375 men from Fort Myer Cavalry stayed at the Warrenton Horse Show Grounds. Midnight, Sunday, the 28th, the time went back to normal. Saturday, October 18th, the Duke and Duchess of Windsor were visiting at Oakwood outside of town. She is well known around here because of her stay at the Warren Green a while back.

A U. S. Destroyer was torpedoed and sunk west of Ireland, Saturday, November 1st, 1941. On the 5th, the Town Council discussed the Tongue Property at the corner of Main and South 3rd Streets as it is to be sold at auction. At the sale Wednesday, November 12th, the Town of Warrenton bought the house and lot of the late George Tongue for $9,400. At the present, the main house and two cottages will be rented. They are not sure what to do with it in the future. This is the first time the property has changed hands in 148 years. Johnzie Tongue bought it in 1793. His son, John Robert "Johnzie", and Johnzie himself, both had a tan yard on the place, operating it until after the Civil War. John Robert's son, "Johnzie", and the father of George, owned a store located where Carter's 5&10 is now. It is hoped that a lot of Red Cross pins are sold for 1942 during their drive. The Warren Green installed a Western Union Teletype Machine Saturday, November 15th, with a 24-hour service. Mr. Risque will still be the operator at the old Western Union stand in "China Town", at the corner beyond the Post Office. Barney Harris will be at the Warren Green.

Santa Claus arrived in Warrenton at 5pm Friday, December 5th, with his pack on his back. He turned on the Christmas lights to officially open the Christmas season of 1941, after which he traveled up and down Main Street giving lollypops from his pack to every child he met. Another Bake Sale, this time by the American Legion, the next day, the 6th, held in the Anderson Building. December 8th-12th there was the third and largest Army detachment passing through Warrenton this year. This one numbered 60,000 soldiers.

Sunday, December 7th, one half of Warrenton must have gone

to Griffith Stadium to see the Redskins' victory over Philadelphia. They said when announcements over the loudspeaker began calling for certain Admirals and Generals to report at once to headquarters, they had an inkling that something was wrong. George Sloane turned and said, "War has been declared". That was the day the U.S. possessions were invaded at Pearl Harbor, Hawaii, being hardest hit. Blanche O'Connell went to the Red Cross room on the lower floor of the Library during the afternoon to see her mother who was at a meeting. She found them sitting around the radio listening to the news. Monday, the 8th, War on Japan was declared by Congress. Saturday, December 13th, Lew Wood, Captain of the Warrenton Rifles in 1917 and a Captain of Infantry in France during the World War then, offered to head the County's Home Guard. Wednesday, the 17th, was the first session of an Air Raid Warden Course. They met at the Fire House, learning to prepare for home emergencies, blackouts, refuge rooms, water hoses, sand buckets, and fire extinguishers among other things. The Community Tree was had as usual. Christmas for the children anyway, but sad for the adults.

1942

Monday, January 5th, 1942, was the coldest night of the winter so far. The rationing of tires brings a new racket, crime wise, that is. Tires are being stolen and resold at a big price. Saturday, the 17th, Warrenton stores have the U. S. Defense Stamps and their albums so people can ask for them in place of change. A good way to sell them. The Town Council and T. I. Martin, Manager of Fauquier Theater, were requested, January 28th, not to have movies on Sunday, but probably more people want them than not.

The Fauquier Hospital, established in 1925, a losing proposition, was sold out in 1940. In 1941 several Warrenton physicians bought it, to reopen in the same building on February 13th, 1942.[121] It is now called Physician's Hospital. Once the building had been the home of John and Francis Gardner Grayson. Originally an actress, she attempted to follow Lindbergh hoping to become the first woman to fly the Atlantic. On her first trip she was forced to return to the States and on her second try, she disappeared. Not a trace was ever found of her or her plane, "Dawn".[121] Also it's unsure if she was flying by herself or if she had a pilot with her.[5] Once, too, there was a Carter who had a grocery store on Culpeper Street (now Hutton & Payne) and he lived in this house.[144]

THE PHYSICIAN'S HOSPITAL INC., WARRENTON, VIRGINIA
Circa 1942
(From the collection of John K. Gott)

Walter P. Chryster, Jr., of North Wales, contributed $1,250 on Thursday, March 12th, 1942, to Fauquier County for an Air Raid Patrol car. It will have fire fighting and first aid equipment, shovels, axes, stretchers, a water thief, pike poles as well as other things. There was a total Black-out in Warrenton Friday the 27th. The Fire Department sounded the Air Raid Siren at 8pm when all street lights, signs and home lights were turned off. It sure can be dark when the electricity goes off, but there is a different feeling about this way of doing it. Sort of "gives you the creeps". All-clear sounded at 9:00. It was said to be nearly 100% successful. All the restaurants, except the Warren Green, participated without a murmur. Air Raid Shelters were located in the basement of the Fauquier National Bank, the Courthouse and the Clerk's Office buildings.[145]

Thursday, April 2nd, 1942, there was a good sight—Pete Shirley, who hadn't been out all winter, was around shaking hands. Sunday, April 5th, a fair, warm spring day and Solomon in all his glory was not arrayed any better than the fair ladies on this Easter Day. Bad news Thursday the 9th, when fire that had begun Monday afternoon had burnt over 1000 acres in lower Fauquier County. Sugar rationing was being done at schools Thursday, April 30th.

Even though the crowd was not as many as usual, the Gold Cup got by alright Saturday, May 2nd, but Monday, the 4th, there was a "Gully-washer" shower. The Office of Price Administration announced Thursday, May 14th, that the basic rationing unit for gasoline was fixed at three gallons. It probably won't be as busy in town now. Trash trucks of the Town will be used to pick up scrap paper and metal if it is properly tied up. One of the old timers, James Walden Jeffries, died Tuesday night. He seemed in good health when he closed the store to go home for the night. Saturday, May 31st and Poppy Day.

June 2nd the Town Council appointed Mayor Tiffany, Town Manager Sidney Shumate, and Councilman Charles G. Stone, to act as a Civilian Defense Committee of the Council. Sunday, June 7th, was the usual Memorial Day exercise. Days are getting hot, but June is suppose to be. Thursday, the 11th, began the rubber drive. A lot of things are made of rubber that one doesn't think about until something like this comes along. The U.S.O. War Fund Campaign is on, too. Fauquier County's quota is $5,000. The Victory Gardens are growing to hear people talk about them. The Macaroni Garden is missed. Another Black-out Wednesday, June 17th, but this was the first all night test for the County. The Fire Siren or Air Raid Alarm sounded for 20 second blasts, punctuated by 20 second pauses, over a period of 2 minutes, which may be repeated. The all clear is a continuous blast for 2 minutes. The businesses with lights left on all night must have outside switches accessible to the Air Raid Wardens. The Black-out was a success.

MAIN STREET, WARRENTON, VIRGINIA
Circa 1942

From Thursday, July 9th to Saturday the 11th, 1942, the gasoline rationing was held at the schools. An "A" card is for passenger cars only and an "S" gas book is supplemental for trucks, taxis, buses, hearses, ambulances, and pickups, which can be obtained from the County Office Building on July 17, 18, 20, and 21st. The Fireman's Carnival was the 10th and 11th at the Fletcher Lot where they grossed $3200. Thursday, July 30th, two rooms at the Episcopal Parish Hall were open as reading rooms for soldiers from Vint Hill. The Methodists are trying to maintain an open church for the many soldiers and to help with entertaining them.[24] The stamp is due for people to get their two pounds of sugar. Friday night of the 31st, the Retail Merchant Association met in the Grill Room of the Warren Green to discuss reviving the railroad passenger service.

Beginning Monday, August 3rd, 1942, the Library is open at night to benefit the soldiers, and will be also on Wednesdays and Fridays between 7pm and 9pm. It was announced Thursday, August 6th, that Fauquier collected 290,000 pounds of rubber. A fire near The Square! and the Warrenton, Culpeper and Remington Fire Trucks were all working at the Warrenton Supply Garage to put out. The second state wide Black-out was Tuesday the 18th, from 8:30pm until 1am. The Service Men's Club began a campaign for funds Thursday, August 27th, in the former Grill Room of the Warren Green with dancing, games, and conversation.

The Town Council is still concerned about the trees. They felt September 1st, 1942 that certain five or six trees on Main and Winchester Streets, none around The Square, were dangerous and others were injuring trees next to them, so their removal was authorized. They were maples and aspen or cottonwoods. The town received an answer September 17th to the request for the railroad to be reopened. It was No.

Stores in Warrenton closed Wednesday afternoon, October 7th, 1942, so employees could take part in the scrap drive that day. Saturday, the 10th, a new place of business opened in the Ford Anderson Building at Main and Culpeper Streets. Johnnie Kreticos remodeled it for a restaurant called The Signal Corp Grill; featuring oysters, clams, and a beer license. He said his Mayflower Restaurant, across from the Post Office was not adequate. The new restaurant is planned to cater to the Vint Hill soldiers, for the town is filled with 2nd Lieutenants stationed there. Kreticos' helps make everyone feel good, as though they were at home. He doesn't mind people getting a little loud, and with so many crowded into his place, they couldn't help but be loud. Sometimes the people standing who are unable to get a booth, are so many one can hardly get through them. But, he managed to serve all. This was one of the places Luther Cox patrolled as a Military Policeman at the time.

Someone said Johnny moved down the street away from Ernest Pappas and now he's come back. When Virginia Painter came to Warrenton in 1935, she lived for two weeks with Martha Ellis and her husband on North Main Street. But, since she went to work at the New Warrenton Restaurant on the 28th of May that year, she wanted to be closer to work, so moved to the Riley home, a yellow house on Waterloo Street, behind the Library. She had long black hair and when she was suppose to be finished work, she would go home to wash her hair. Sometimes it wouldn't be dry yet, but Ernest would send word for her to come back because a bus load of people had arrived. They were quite busy most of the time and employed up to 16 people. This was a much quieter "family type" of place than others in town. If anyone became too loud, Pappas asked them to leave. When Johnny Kreticos had the Mayflower Inn on the opposite corner, he would go over to Pappas' and try to "steal" his customers.

People are saying, "The King is dead, long live the King". The St. Louis Cardinals took four straight from the Yankees. October 15th, 1942 saw 264,000 pounds of scrap iron collected. After two days of rain the Rappahannock River flooded going over into the streets of Remington. October 27th is Navy Day when flags were flying along the streets and at homes, with a patriotic display in a window of Lerners.

One cup per day coffee ration began November 28th, 1942. The County Rationing Board announced that each person over 15 is limited to 1 pound of coffee each five weeks. That's going to hurt a lot of people. Perhaps it was about this time that Mr. Sudduth was trying to run the Funeral Home by himself. At times he had trouble putting a body in the casket, so he would ask Gene Garrett, Jr., to hold the casket so it wouldn't slip. Then he'd pick up the body and put it in all by himself. City Risdon (Garrett), who worked next door at The Fashion Shop, sang for funerals. She felt the Parlor was a small crowded place.

The annual Fun Festival Friday and Saturday, December 4th-5th, 1942, was at the Hiden Building, sponsored by the Lion's Club with proceeds going for the Children's Home of Fauquier County in The Plains. It's a cold December. Nearly 600 men were sent to the Army in 1942 through the local draft. Perhaps now the H. B.

Carter Building at the corner of North 6th, or old "Cow Alley", and Main Streets was remodeled. The rear part of the building was an addition sometime ago, but the original building had a spiral staircase with a beautifully carved banister leading to the upper floor that was built like a balcony so one could look down from it to watch the people below. Some called the upper level the Christmas Shop and the store would stay open Christmas Eve until 3am when customers were there. Now the stairway is to be changed and the upper floor enclosed to help save on heat.[154]

1943

Another Black-out on the night of Thursday, March 4th, 1943, beginning at 8:50. Joseph A. Whitmore was one of the wardens who makes sure people have their blackout curtains in place. We had a daylight practice a couple weeks ago. There was an escape from jail, but after four days ended in Maryland Thursday, March 25th.

In a campaign to increase labor for farmers, Fauquier County authorities, at the request of farmers, are making a list of all able bodied non-workers in the county. If idlers do not work they will be jailed. Not only have they been losing farm laborers, but there is a need for more food supplies. The volunteers of 1917 and 18 doesn't seem to be happening now. April 16th, 1943, Fauquier exceeded the War Fund Goal by almost 25%, the total being $19,000. Ernest Pappas has finished redecorating his New Warrenton Restaurant April 22nd, and the new cook is Steve Chios. April 29th the U.S.O. was considering the Carter Furniture Exchange Building on Main Street as a possible meeting place. If this weather keeps up, people will be digging fishing worms. A surprise Air Raid made people scurry, but all went well.

May 4th, 1943, P. B. Smith is Mayor. Mother's Day Sunday, the 9th, was more recognized than ever before. Memorial Day's parade Monday, May 31st, began at the Fire House at 3pm, going to the cemetery for services. Tom Stafford went back to the farm, July 1st, and a good officer was lost. But Turner Grimsley is his successor, so people are sure he will be a good one, too. Fifteen Fresh Air Children arrived in Fauquier from New York slums July 15th, for a two week vacation.

August 5th, 1943. It is Dog Days and no rain, so there is drought damage, the worse since 1930. The Dairymen are using their winter feed. August 26th and the last Wednesday of the summer holiday of store closing. A bit of sad news when "John Stone" was killed. He was a familiar figure on Warrenton streets, the constant companion of J. W. Shirley. Yes, he was the Jailor's Cat, a large bobtailed yellow and white one, but to go the way he did—the victim of a hit and run near the cemetery. And, speaking of Mr. Shirley, sometimes he will want an item in a store, and if asked when he would like it, he'll say, "Yesterday". He often send prisoners in his car on errands for him or lets one drive him if he had some place to go.[46] The Red Cross, during this time, was busy rolling bandages in the basement of the Library. The Town Council discussed this date, Trailways Bus Lines' plan to pick up, discharge passengers, and so forth, in front of the Warren Green Hotel. D. H. Lees bought the building on Culpeper from A. Townsend Winmill, which is now occupied by Mme. Prikashikoff. It was built by Rice Payne in 1867 as a law office. He died in 1884 and his heirs sold to Warrenton Women's Realty Co. in 1903, which operated the Woman's Exchange for seven years. R. C. Winmill had bought in 1929.

Only one day this year for the combined Pony and Horse Show as a War effort. The weekend had showers, but with little effect on the show. September 16th, 1943, Johnny Kreticos is selling 10¢ tickets on a War Saving Bond. Saturday the 25th, at 8pm on the steps of the Courthouse all Warrenton packed the street for a Community Sing. Stage and radio talent now in the Army took part in the entertainment for the sale of War Bonds. Nice to hear everyone singing songs such as Swannee River, Dixie, and Oh! Susanna. Thursday, September 30th, Fauquier again went over the top of the 3rd War Loan Drive by more than $200,000. The quota was $600,000. People really come to town on Saturday night and just walk the streets, sometimes almost too crowded for one to move through. To entertain themselves several boys in town rode their bicycles up and down all the streets during their summer vacation. By the time school began, Rudy Gill thought they knew every nook and cranny in the place.

Armistice Day, Thursday the 11th, was a big day! A gala parade led by the Culpeper Boys Band and among others in it were the American Red Cross with its motor corps, the Office of Civilian Defense personnel, the Warrenton Rifles or the Virginia State Guard, the Minute Men or the Virginia Reserve Militia, the Warrenton, Remington and Marshall Volunteer Fire Departments, the Boy Scouts, Civil Clubs and Public Schools of the county. The celebration featured the dedication of Fauquier County's Honor Roll Board. The plaque stands beside the Courthouse on the Court or east side and has nearly 1500 names on it. The Mayor, P. B. Smith, Jr., is appealing for a larger collection of kitchen fats for the War effort.

The Scrap Paper Drive collected by December 9th, 1943, in the Warrenton area netted almost 6 tons. The people of Fauquier should be proud of themselves with all the successful drives for the war. Even The Fauquier Democrat cut down on the number of pages in the newspaper because of the war.

1944

The Bond Program Rally was held Sunday night, January 30th, 1944, in the Fauquier Theater. It was called "Heroes Night" with all the movie actors and war heroes appearing. Three new cases of rabies were found February 10th and the Supervisors ordered dogs to be confined so as to halt the disease.

The Risdon Paint & Hardware operated by Carroll Risdon, on the south side of Main Street between 4th and 5th, moved, March 9th, 1944, across the street to part of the Carter Furniture Exchange Building. The U.S.O. finally made plans for their move from the Warren Green Hotel to Main Street, going into the second floor of Mrs. Ford G. Anderson's building with Lerner Bros. Department Store on the ground floor. However, the Shamrock Dance for the U.S.O. on Thursday, March 16th, was held in the dining room of the Warren Green Hotel from 8-11pm.

Tuesday, May 31st, 1944, the Memorial Day colorful parade left from the Fauquier Theater going to the cemetery where they would honor the soldiers dead from the four wars. Dogs are being vaccinated to help stop the rabies. Spring means new dresses for buildings as well as people. Painting is going on up and down Main Street, including Madison's Barber Shop.

June 8th, 1944, about 400 Fauquier men were taking part in the invasion of occupied Europe. The country's prayers go with them as they fight the Nazis in France. The Firemen's Carnival was held as usual and was rather successful. A train wreck in Calverton August 3rd, with ten cars of gasoline burning was really a sight, I guess. Smoke could be seen for miles. Finally, August 10th, a soaking rain broke up the drought.

The 45th Annual Horse Show was held on Labor Day and despite the war effort there was a big crowd. Ernest Pappas and Virginia Painter were married September 28th. Neither of them could drive a car, but Ernest did own one that George Chichester chauffeurs. He drove them on their honeymoon to Luray where they spent the night. Virginia laughingly told that the next day they went to Front Royal to check on their Blue Ridge Restaurant there and she "spent her honeymoon folding napkins". Their apartment was the remodeled second floor of the New Warrenton Restaurant. It was used as a Tailor Shop and offices years ago. Ernest's brother, Gus, lives with them and he would open the place at 6am. Virginia's sister also worked the breakfast shift. Alan Poe stayed with them to work there (until he graduated June 1949, then went to The Fauquier Democrat). The restaurant was kept open until 3am each night and the only day it closed was Christmas.

October 12th, 1944 the World Series closed with the Cardinals as champions. It is good to have something else to think and talk about other than the war. Sunday the 15th, was remembered as the anniversary of the death of John D. Sudduth, though, since he was the first man from Fauquier killed in World War I. Tuesday morning, October 17th, a fire damaged the Warrenton Fruit Store in the Fauquier Theater, that has apartments above. It is owned by Dr. George H. Davis.

F. D. Roosevelt was elected President for a 4th term by a vote of 3-2 in Fauquier. Stores were closed Saturday, November 11th, 1944 for Armistice Day. The Post Office wants people to mail their packages before December 1st. The 6th War Loan Drive goal on November 23rd, was $800,000. November 30th— Thanksgiving Day.

December 7th, 1944, the U.S.O. dance was held in the newly decorated club room over Lerners. Mrs. W. E. - Mildred - Sudduth and Mrs. Coons helped supervise the youth group that met here. There could be a little trouble at times for they were not suppose to go outside, but they would try. About now, E. L. Timberlake and the Maytag washers moved to the Warrenton Supply.[163]

1945

Purple, Bronze and Silver Stars have been awarded many Fauquier people during the past year, and also there are many Gold Star Mothers beginning the new year. The winter of 1945 may not have been the most severest, but there was lots of snow, sleet and rain. On March 1st something different. The War Prisoner Farm Labor were housed in Front Royal, but it was required that they work within 25 miles of the camp. March 3rd, an old timer was gone. J. W. Shirley, Jailor, died at the age of 88. He had been a town officer for over 60 years and will truly be missed.

The first part of April there were three nice gentle rains, but as someone said, "We still need more from Heaven". April 12th, 1945, steeple-jack, H. M. Brummett, gave the Courthouse Steeple a new coat of paint - in fact three of them - the first since 1934, at the cost of $50. Also the weather vane was covered with gold leaf and its bronze staff was refurbished. A sad time for the nation. Saturday morning, April 14th, many people went to Calverton Station to see the funeral train of President Roosevelt who died Thursday afternoon. The train stopped at 8:45am to take on water. Memorial services to honor him was that afternoon at the Baptist Church. Harry S. Truman, who was Vice President, is now President.

April 28th, a peace report was flashed by radio at 7:55pm. Main Street was crowded with shoppers and people who come to town on a Saturday night, but they heard the news almost immediately. Two places selling beer closed their doors. Town officials prepared to ring the Courthouse Bell, and ministers went to open their churches. But disappointment sounded when President Truman announced the broadcast was false.

May 1st, 1945 the Town Council ordered 12 Elm trees sprayed at a cost of $48 in the hope of saving them. VE Day was proclaimed Tuesday, May 8th, when Germany surrendered. This time the celebration was on! The churches were open then as well as on Sunday, May 13th, which was declared a day of prayer. Dr. M. B. Hiden bought Mrs. Ethel Bishop's 16 room stucco building on Winchester Street, which has been an apartment and rooming house for years. Cpl. Grenville Jacobs of Warrenton and PFC Robert Canard of Marshall were among the first group of men to receive honorable discharge under the point system. People are happy about some of the boys coming home, even if it isn't quite finished. There was a high wind storm which uprooted some trees, broke limbs and wires, causing a power outage for a while, but nothing too serious. Wednesday, May 30th, the Memorial Day parade assembled at the Fire House before marching to the cemetery. Most stores were closed during the services.

It has been a cold spring but nothing like 1816, "The Year Without a Summer". May then had frosts, snow and ice and as late as July 4th, New York had 3 inches of snow while water froze on ponds in Virginia. It was reported June 7th, 1945 that the first of 100 or more, German prisoners are here to help on farms. The terms

ARMY INFANTRY PARADE – JULY 2, 1945
Soldiers on roof tops shoot blanks. Ernest picked up empty shells afterwards. Town Officer is Turner Grimsley.

(Courtesy of Ernest Pappas.)

of the contract signed Friday at the County Office Building said they will be paid 35¢ an hour while the government will pay 80¢ an hour in coupons that are good at the camp canteen. D. H. Lees & Co. Inc. and other occupants of the California Building moved to the adjoining Payne Building that he owns as Walter P. Chrysler, Jr. recently bought the California Building.

Monday, July 2nd, 1945, the largest crowd in Warrenton history was at the Warrenton High School on Waterloo Street for the Army Infantry Show on its grounds, even with rain in the afternoon and the temperature in the 60's. Although rain Saturday night the 14th caused the Carnival goers to retreat inside, the Firemen did gross $3000. July 12th, Postmaster Thomas E. Frank announced that the Warrenton Post Office now had first-class rating. They had hoped for home delivery but was turned down by the P. O. Department because it was not warranted at the present. W. H. Blythe, former photographer, was carrier in the early days when there was home delivery. When he died, Nelson Moffett took over until June 30, 1922 when it was discontinued. That was in the days when the Post Office was a fun place to get your mail because people went to wait and talk while the mail was being put into the boxes. The bulletin board in it was like a weekly newspaper.[139] On July 19th the War Loan quota was exceeded by 71%. The stores decided, July 26th, to have a "Paper Holiday" for the duration. The purchase will be taken home unwrapped unless something is brought with you in which to carry it. Something else to be wary about along with the rabies or polio. The second case of Rocky Mountain tick fever has been reported in the county.

People are talking about a new age beginning. July 16th, 1945 the first atomic bomb was exploded. August 6th the A-bomb was then used in war, as it was dropped on Hiroshima and August 9th was the bombing of Nagasaki. The American Legion's annual carnival was held Saturday night, the 11th, on the Fletcher lot. Hot dogs and hamburgers could be smelled for a couple blocks as they cooked. Tuesday, August 14th, word came that the Japanese surrendered, but it was the next day that the official notice of VJ Day was sent to President Truman. Most Americans couldn't think of enough ways to express their relief when it was all over. But, Warrenton was really rather calm. The Town Siren and church bells sounded for a few minutes and people cheered a while, and many attended their churches for prayer and thanksgiving.

September 2nd, 1945 the Japanese signed the surrender on the deck of the Battleship Missouri. The Town Council had complaints September 4th about congested traffic on Main Street caused by the buses. They asked Mr. S. A. Jessup to come in October to talk about ways to improve it. The apple orchards were having the best crop in five years until a tropical storm moved up the Atlantic coast on the 20th, to cause crop damage and some flooding.

The United Nations began October 24th as a peace keeping organization. October 25th, 1945, the work started on the new 12 room wing for the Physician's Hospital located on Waterloo Street. By December 6th, lots of "Vets" have returned home to civilian life. Schools closed Monday, December 17th, a little early for the Christmas holidays, but there is a flu outbreak. Beginning the 20th, the stores plan to stay open until 8pm during the Christmas season. During this year the Warrenton Supply Co. gave up their Ford dealership for the Nash cars.[143] —And, so "Goodbye" 1945.

1946

Monday, January 14th, 1946, opened the March of Dimes Fund for Fauquier to fight Infantile Paralysis. Old Man Flu is still going around. The snow Sunday, the 27th, was beautiful. It is wonderful how the layer of white is sent to cover all the brown when people tire of it and to cheer them up.

Stuyvesant School's main building burned February 21st, 1946, fanned by high winds. Reminiscence of '09. The Remington Fire Department also helped put it out. Sunday afternoon wasn't too quiet or peaceful around here for a while. February 28th, two white men were discovered in the Peoples National Bank when D. Turner Day, the president, entered it at 3:30. As the unknown thieves went out the back window, the way they had entered, Day called the police, who captured them near the High School and found to be from Tennessee. The many "Vets" around town lost no time getting into their "civies" not forgetting the little "duck" in the lapel of their coat, a sure sign they saw duty.

The Town Council on March 5th, 1946, had 128 people requesting a solution to the bus parking problem. It was decided first, to find a suitable site for the terminal; second, to have parking lots provided for all-day parking; and third, to order parking meters which will be installed on Main Street for short parking periods. It seems that the first parking meters were at Detroit, Michigan on July 16th, 1935, so they are not new.

Excitement at the foot of Courthouse Hill. Two Trailways Buses collided Thursday morning, April 18th, 1946, about 9:30 and one went through a fence, ending up in the field. It was determined that as they were both coming from Washington, D.C., one started to make a left turn into Haiti for the bus station located at its intersection there. It was followed too closely by the second bus, which almost bumped the rear of the first one. To avoid really hitting together, the second one went off the road, and four people were slightly hurt.

May 2nd, 1946, had a food collection for the starving in Europe. During January there had been a Victory Clothing Collection for their aid, too. The first post war Gold Cup was held Saturday, May 4th. The Parking Meters arrived by May 7th. They are to be located on both sides of Main Street from 2nd to Alexandria Pike, on Court House Square in front of the A&P and Hiden Building, the east side of Culpeper Street from Lee to Main, and the west side of Court Street. The schools of Fauquier County closed temporarily Thursday, May 9th, because of an epidemic of measles and Scarlet fever. Thursday, the 23rd, Peoples National Bank bought from the estate of C. H. Jeffries the lot immediately behind the bank building and the Sowers property where Thornton & Burke's Drug Store is. The people around here are pretty proud of our Free State Ramblers. They went to the National Folk Festival in Cleveland for the week of May 20-25th, and were one of the two bands chosen to make recordings.

The warm, quiet, peaceful afternoon of Friday, May 31st, 1946, was suddenly broken. A man boarded a bus in Washington, but on the way here, he became louder and louder in telling the driver what to do. By the time the bus reached about the middle of Main Street, the man was standing in the aisle demanding the driver to stop. As he did, the man hit the driver in the face, jumped off the bus, ran down the street and across the Clerk's Office lawn, shouting "Heil Hitler", while people tried to catch him. The man attempted to hide in the building, but was found, handcuffed, and put into Jail until it was decided what to do. He was suppose to be a shell-shocked veteran of WWI. By June 13th, he had been judged insane and committed to the Veteran's Hospital. July 4th, the War Department stated that the County Army deaths totaled 55. The Fireman's Carnival was 12th and 13th of July, after the parade to the Fletcher Lot.

The Parking Meters were set up August 1st, 1946, to be used

except on Sundays and legal holidays. 1¢ gives 12 minutes, and 5¢ gives an hour from 8am to 8pm. One of the offices in the Hiden Building now is the Law Office of Wallace N. Tiffany who, after being discharged from the Army, has resumed his practice. August 6th the Town Council wrote a letter concerning the bus still parking on Main Street, saying that unless the Virginia Stage Lines submitted a plan for a terminal, they will prevent them from using the streets for loading and unloading the passengers. Two couples came into Ernest Pappas' New Warrenton Restaurant about August 8th. He recognized one as being the French ambassador, Henri Bonnet, so he asked them how they enjoyed the meal. The lady with the other man surprised Ernest when she answered in Greek. Warrenton's U.S.O. Club celebrated its 3rd birthday August 15th, by having a formal dance in the club's room on Main Street. Sunday afternoon at 5:30, August 25th, on the lawn of the Warren Green Hotel, the new fire truck was dedicated. The King Bros. Circus was in town, Thursday afternoon and night of the 27th, at the Arrington Lot on Alexandria Pike. William "Billy" Harris went, about this time, to hear a Black touring music group who sang revival songs. They had a tent pitched at a vacant lot on Green Street.

In connection with Acca Temple's 60th annual celebration, Warrenton's Shriners paraded in the downtown area at 4:30 Friday afternoon, September 13th, 1946, and attended a concert on the lawn of the Warren Green Hotel. Later they had dinner at the Warrenton House, Fauquier Springs. The month's parking meter revenue was $840.00. They are being used a lot, although the streets are not as crowded since their installation.

A lovely Indian Summer suddenly ended, December 5th, 1946 with an 18 degree temperature, snow flurries and ice on the ponds. Because of the coal strike, they say there won't be lights put up for Christmas. The local Lion's Club has been sponsoring the festive decorations for the business section of Warrenton. But, the Virginia Electric & Power Company officials say that since they have been rationing the electric power, it would be impossible to allow power for this, even if the miners did return to work. Early Tuesday morning until 9:00, December 13th, the firemen were called out seven times in a series of fires, the largest number in any one day for months. Well! Downtown Warrenton IS going to be gaily lit with colored lights after all. President J. E. Barnhart announced, the 19th, that the Rotary Club had completed plans for a large tree on the Courthouse porch and President Winfee Hughes said the Lion's

Club will sponsor the lights. Don't know how they did it, but it's nice they worked something out. Once getting use to the lights, Christmas just isn't Christmas without them. There has been a "mystery boy" in the Jail for eight days. The 13 year old arrived on a stolen bicycle, saying he and his family had moved recently from Richmond to Washington. He went shopping with his parents, but "lost" them in a large store, so he doesn't know his new address. He seems contented and spends some of his time drawing pictures. Several people are making and collecting gifts for him so he'll have a Christmas, too.

1947

At the Town Council meeting, January 7th, 1947, Mr. Weston and Miss Gildersleeve from the Fauquier County Health Unit requested special permission to park automobiles owned by their personnel in front of the Hiden Building, without parking meter restrictions. The Council voted—No - but gave the Health Unit permission for one car, owned by the Health Nurse to be parked at the meter, provided it was marked or tagged with letters large enough that it could be plainly identified.

The Town Council was requested, February 4th, 1947, for a Town garbage collection and incinerator disposal. The parking meter collection was down a little last month. Only $764.18. The

FEBRUARY 1947

worse snow storm in a decade was Thursday, February 20th, with 12-15 inches. A picture taken for the newspaper showed how the snow was piled up along Main Street and in front of Gill Appliances & Furniture Store, alongside Coons' Market on the first floor of the Hiden Building with the A&P beside it on the corner, being shoveled over the tops of the parking meters. Although Forrest Gill could have opened this business about 1939, it seems that Powell Thayer managed it. But, Powell had a place on Main Street probably about 1940.

There was some question about the U.S.O. now that the war has ended, but March 27th, 1947, it was decided to keep it open until December 31st of this year. By proclamation of President Truman, Monday, April 7th, was officially designated Army Day. On Wednesday, the 9th, the public was invited to attend the Army Day dance at the U.S.O. A County Fire Control was organized because of the many field fires occurring by Thursday, April 10th.

Wednesday, May 14th, 1947, at noon, began the half-holidays for the summer Wednesdays. David Silvette built himself a platform inside the Courthouse, Thursday, May 15th, in order to copy W. D. Washington's portrait of John Marshall, which is to be hung in the Law School of the University of Virginia. The Memorial Day parade, Friday, May 30th, began from the Fire House, going to the cemetery as usual.

The Warrenton Rifles disbanded again, June 5th, 1947. This time they had been organized since 1941. Here's hoping they never have to be again in service. Friday, June 14th, at 7pm the Firemen's Parade opened their Carnival by coming down Main Street and then to Culpeper Street as they went to the Warrenton Horse Show Grounds. Heard someone ask another on Thursday, the 26th, if they were tired of paying 70 or 90¢ a pound for steak and pork chops. Said in 1886 - a long time ago - it was 14¢, pork was 12½¢, sausage was 13¢ and roast beef was 12¢.

The Warrenton Rotary erected a granite Monument with bronze plaque listing the names of service people who lost their lives. It was dedicated on the lawn of the County Office Building, Thursday, July 3rd, 1947, at 1:40pm, "In Honor of Those From Fauquier County Who Made The Full Sacrifice In WWII". The Town Council decided to forbid firecrackers in town. It was also agreed to remove the bus stop from Main Street.

**COUNTY OFFICE BUILDING WITH NEW MONUMENT
WARRENTON, VIRGINIA**
Circa 1947
(From the collection of John K. Gott)

FAUQUIER COUNTY PUBLIC LIBRARY
2 Court House Square, Warrenton, Virginia
Circa 1947

An electric storm broke the heat, but burned a couple barns around, just before September 1947 came in. On the 2nd of the month Mayor R. H. Marriott and the Council heard John R. Benner voice a complaint about the parking at the corner of Main and Alexandria Pike and in front of the New Warrenton Restaurant. It is hard to see around the corner with cars there. Labor Day, September 3rd, the stores in town were closed and all was quiet.

The Town Council recommended October 7th, 1947 that parking lines for a 45 degree angle be marked off on the Alexandria Pike adjacent to the New Warrenton Restaurant, hoping it would help people see around the corner. Before the meters parking in town was a big mess. Some double parked beside those at the curb so they couldn't get out. Now with the meters—they still do the same. The rain Tuesday, October 28th, diminished the threat of forest fires in the county.

Election Day, November 4th, 1947 was a holiday for banks and ABC stores. The Police requested that the town through the Council purchase three outside telephones, one to be installed at or near the Courthouse, so they could be used by the officers. The Courthouse Clock is acting up again, Friday, the 14th. It is keeping time, but not striking because one of the weights dropped off, falling with a loud crash, scaring the ladies of the Welfare Department in their office below. Thursday, November 27th, the traditional Thanksgiving holiday was observed.

December 2nd, 1947 the Council wanted the Board of Supervisors to pay half and the Town would pay half on an electric clock, which would cost $1,692. The present clock installed 1890, was last repaired 1939. They planned also, to raise the sidewalk and install a storm sewer and retainer wall along Alexandria Pike from Court House Square Garage on the corner of Winchester, on down the hill. When it rains the road and sidewalk at the foot of the hill is usually covered with water. The 100,000th service man to enter the U.S.O. Club was in August 1945. Two years later the 250,000th man was honored. Now, December 26th, it is ending its activities. A sign was displayed in Korea during this year that said, "Warrenton, Virginia-9,124 miles". Lucy Barbe who had moved to the County in 1937 moved into town this year. One place she stopped was Vose's Store which had Guinea pigs in its window.

1948

Thursday, January 8th, 1948, Chrysler sold the California Building to Alan Jenkins. The Courthouse Clock has had its chimes repaired at a cost of $465. Main Street was portrayed in a painting published in The American Druggist. How about that? Warrenton is becoming famous.

February 3rd, 1948 the Town Council authorized the removal of a tree on Main Street in front of the Bishop Apartments, saying its condition was dangerous to the public. February 12th was the grand opening of the Blue Ridge Hardware and Rhodes Drug Store. They are now across the street from each other.

At the March 2nd Council meeting, Mrs. Eva B. Hall who operates bowling alleys on Alexandria Pike, asked for permission to keep them open after midnight on Monday, Tuesday, Thursday and Friday so league bowlers and others could have longer time to play. It was denied as the ordinance requires such businesses to close at midnight. Mrs. M. J. O'Connell, Chairman of the Fauquier County Chapter of the American Red Cross asked for three parking spaces for the volunteers working on surgical dressings in the local chapter rooms, which are in the Library. Officer Luther Cox was requested to see if he could find space on the property adjoining the Red Cross Rooms. By March 4th, a television set was in Town! Almost overnight antennas seem to sprout from the rooftops. Monday, March 15th, the Jeffries' Drug business was sold to Robert H. Gardiner, Jr. who will continue to operate under the name of Jeffries' Drug Store and kept the old phone number - 6 -, too. Main Street had a bath. The Fire Department worked about two hours starting at 5am to get rid of the dirt and dust.

May 4th, the Town Council decided another tree had to come down. This one being on Diagonal Street opposite Carter Hall. The effort to save the Elms doesn't seem to be working. Hosts were wanted, May 6th, for the Fresh Air Fund Children. The war years interrupted the program in 1943, which was the last summer the children - 15 of them - were in the county. Court House Square Garage, 101 Winchester Street, is advertising the new Austin of England, Kaiser and Fraizer cars. At the New Warrenton Restaurant, on the opposite corner of the Pike, John L. Lewis had lunch, Saturday, May 8th. He let the newsmen take his picture, but didn't talk as he walked in the warm sunshine returning to his big black Packard he had parked on Lee Street behind the Warren Green Hotel. Then he drove off all by himself. Sunday, the 30th, the Memorial Day parade left the Fire House at 2:30pm and concluded with services at the cemetery. Jimmy's Market-Meats-Fancy Groceries advertised a one pound jar of Monarch preserves for 28¢. Their phone number is 53. The Warrenton Appliance Center, also furniture, was now at Court House Square. Probably belonging to Gill.

A fire broke out Thursday, June 3rd, 1948, over Jimmy's Market and Madison's Barber Shop, which did some damage, especially when it went through the walls. Everyone was glad there was no wind. Something new this year for the Warrenton Fireman's Carnival. It opened as usual Thursday night, and the parade was formed on Friday night, June 4th, going to the Courthouse where the 54 piece Osbourne High School Band from Manassas played at the coronation of the Queen of the Carnival, and the Court of Ladies in Waiting. Jean Kirby of Marshall was the Queen. Then, the parade went on to the Horse Show Grounds.

September 2nd, 1948, men were registering for the draft. They are those between 18 and 25 in age. Mrs. Lucille Scates is Clerk of the Fauquier Draft Board located in the County Building. About this time the passenger shed and part of the Southern rails were removed.[39] Shortly after that the Town Council received a complaint, September 7th, because livestock was being kept overnight in pens owned by the Southern Railroad. They were noisy and on a hot night might not be too pleasant. Also a loafing and drinking ordinance passed. The last of September, the new Warrenton High School on Waterloo had their Athletic Field named "Benner Field", dedicated to John Benner, a person who had excelled in school at anything he attempted, especially in the way of sports.[146] Years ago activities were at Benner's Field near where he lived on Alexandria Pike. Grayson's have remodeled the store on Main Street, with their "Grand Opening" September 30th.

When people went to bed Election night, they thought Thomas Dewey was winning the Presidency. One newspaper even had it published in big headlines. What a surprise when they awoke the next day to find Harry S. Truman was still President.

1949

February 1949, at the section of Main Street known as "China Town", the building of the old Chinese Laundry is being remodeled for the Women's Exchange which is now on Culpeper Street in the Kirby Building. According to J. A. Jeffries, the original building at the Laundry site, had been built before 1854 as that was the year E. N. Cologne, Town Sergeant and Saddler, had a shop there. Also in 1854 A. H. Spilman, Postmaster and Tailor, lived in the building next door that was remodeled for Chamberlain & Hamilton's Store. In the other direction, had been the home of the Misses English, the Tongue property, the Fletcher home and on the other corner that · of Colonel Gaines. Tom Willis, a slow talking man and Thurston's father, had a grocery store behind Gaines (now Fauquier Laundry).[144]

Snow the first of March, 1949 and now flurries on the 15th, but a flock of wild geese were seen overhead. There must have been 200 in their perfect formation and "making more noise than a pack of hound dogs". Snow or no snow, Spring is on its way.

A little excitement at the Warren Green the morning of April 14th, 1949. A man from West Virginia attempted suicide. He was taken to the hospital and then turned over to the Army Doctors. There is good news and bad news. The good news is that the Gold Cup this year is on television. The bad news is that there are 28 Japanese Beetle grubs being found in every square foot of earth. The weather was perfect for the Memorial Day Parade on Sunday, May 29th, which began at 3pm from between the Baptist Church and the Post Office. A crowd watched the Son's of Confederate Veterans and United Daughters of The Confederacy in cars - remember when they walked -, the American Legion Post No. 72 with the colors in formation, Boy and Girl Scouts, Cub Scouts and Brownies. A Warrenton Fire Truck was lost in the line, there was so much to see. At the cemetery services were held at the Confederate Monument, Capt. Marr's Grave, John D. Sudduth's Grave and the grave of Samuel Woodzell, a World War II person.

July 4th was on Monday, so stores stayed open the Wednesday following, however, after that they will have their half-day closing for the rest of the summer. The stores closed at 4pm Friday, July 15th, 1949 for the Firemen's Carnival. Everyone wanted to be ready when it opened with the U. S. Marine Corps Band playing on the Warren Green lawn. At 6pm the Queen of the Carnival, Nancy Martin, was crowned by Lt. Gov. L. Preston - Pat - Collins in a ceremony at the Judges' stand, also located on the lawn. The parade began at 6:30 going along Main & Culpeper Streets to the Horse Show Grounds. A 1904 Rambler was in it, which looked odd to see. The Japanese Beetles were so bad by the end of this month, they sprayed over the County for them from a helicopter.

WARREN GREEN MOTEL, WARRENTON, VIRGINIA
Circa 1949
(From the collection of John K. Gott)

Banks and stores closed Labor Day, Monday, September 5th, 1949. At the Town Council the next day Charles G. Stone and Mason Carter requested the installation of a public rest room to be located under the Courthouse steps. The proposal was referred to the Water Committee. At the following meeting on the 14th, the request was opposed. They did decide the trees on Winchester Street should be trimmed, but not to exceed $100. September 15th, shots could be heard in the surrounding woods, as squirrel season has opened, the limit being six a day or 75 a season.

October 4th, 1949 the Town Council voted to remove all parking meters on the Courthouse side of Main Street opposite the Library so the space could be reserved for officials around the Jail. The Town Police like to sit along the curb there where they can see that all is under control throughout the Town.[163] On the 14th, a former soldier walking from Putnam, Connecticut to Little Rock, Arkansas came through town, as he was making the 2000 mile trip to see his four year old daughter, whom he had not seen since she moved there with her mother three years ago. He travels with a camera and a diary, hoping some day to write a book of his experiences along the way. He averages 20 miles a day, but once he made 27 miles. This day he was Ernest Pappas' guest at the New Warrenton Restaurant and the Warren Green donated a room for the night. As usual, Warrentonians opened their hearts.

Something wicked comes this way! Monday night, October 31st, 1949, downtown Warrenton swarmed with ghosts and goblins and so-called critters from the spirit world. They appeared a bit terrifying but seemed to be harmless. That is until Tuesday morning when a trip down Main Street revealed not a window, except maybe the small ones on the front of the Peoples National Bank which must have been out of reach of tiny goblins or overlooked by a fast flying witch, had been missed being soaped, waxed, or some way marked. Police Chief Luther Cox said no serious damage was done, but many doorbells were rung for a treat or trick. A few years ago the black horse that was used by the Town to draw the trash wagon was given a good coat of whitewash and then turned back into the pasture. The horse was believed to have been lost or strayed and enjoyed a few days of rest with the other horses—until a heavy rain came.

1950

At the Town Council meeting, January 3rd, 1950, Officer Luther Cox was employed at a salary of $15 a month to keep the parking meters in repair, but he was to work on them in his spare time, not while on duty. Lerners' had an interesting Scout Exhibit in their display window that attracted a lot of attention.

Mr. P. B. Smith appeared before the Town Council, March 6th, 1950 to call attention to the school boys who were gambling in several of the mercantile stores in town, the matter being turned over to local Town Police officers. The first snowfall of the year was Thursday, the 16th. Although late, it was beautiful and made people remember what they were missing. Warrenton or Fauquier bred horses and cattle have been nationally known a long time. But - perhaps for the first time in history a pig bred by a Warrentonian has made its mark, and on television, too! Monday night, March 30th, on a show sponsored by the Tailwaggers Club, the small pink pig from the Rapparidge Farm of Mr. and Mrs. Ian S. Montgomery made its debut. The show plays a regular performance on TV Channel 7.

The Town Council decided April 4th, 1950 the tree across from D. H. Lees & Co. was too rotten to let stand, so it was ordered removed, and was gone by the 20th, soon there won't be an old tree left. The circus came to town April 26th at the Hitchock Lot. Sudduth Funeral Home continues on Main Street where it was founded in 1836. At one time the elder Sudduth owned the frame house across from the Post Office (now Thoromans) and W. E.

Sudduth was born in an apartment on second floor. He inherited the business from his father in 1948, but he really didn't care for it. (He sold to his sisters, one who was Mrs. Ethel Bishop who sold to Moser with the stipulation that it continue under the name of Sudduth-Moser Funeral Home, but after she died it became just Moser's).[149]

The Memorial Day Parade, Sunday afternoon, May 28th, 1950, was led by the U. S. Marine Corps Color Guard and Firing Squad from Quanito. Among the marchers were the American Legion and the Manassas High School Band.

Friday, June 2nd, 1950, opened the Fireman's Carnival with a Concert by the Metropolitan Police Band at 5:30pm on the Warren Green lawn. The Parade of 50 units consisting of floats, trucks, and bands lined the street from the Safeway Store on east Main to Culpeper and on to the Horse Show Ground. There Betty Clark was crowned the Firemen's Queen by Senator Harry F. Byrd. The Town Council on the 6th, discussed "no parking" on the left side of Winchester from the A&P Store to Diagonal Street, the matter being referred to the Street Committee. Mr. Bailey Arrington was interested in a bus terminal at the foot of Alexandria Pike. At one time Trailways was there and the Virginia Stage Line used Main Street. The stores began their Wednesday half-day closing on June 7th. Fifteen buses came into town the 17th, carrying 546 Boy Scouts from the Greater Cleveland Council. They will spend three days camping on the estate of Hubert B. Phipps adjacent to Neptune Lodge on Culpeper Street.

The Town Council July 4th, 1950, voted to move all idle taxi cabs off the town streets. They also wrote the Board of Supervisors asking they take action to prohibit the sale and or shooting of fireworks in the Center District. Fauquier had its first Polio case, July 6th, when it was discovered in a Bealton youth. The Japanese Beetle is still a menace, too. The New York Fresh Air Children are back for another two week visit, arriving Wednesday, July 19th. North Korea invaded South Korea in June and the United Nations asked for troops so Truman made the decision to send some from the U. S. Fauquier reservists were called to duty this month.

Lots of things happened at the Town Council meeting August 1st, 1950 with R. H. Marriott as Mayor. Mac's Cabs was given a permit to build a cinder block building with toilet facilities on the lot in the rear of the New Warrenton Restaurant. A parking lot behind the restaurant was also used by Graysons' customers. The stopping places to be used by the Virginia Stage Lines, Inc. for the north-bound bus was determined to be at the corner of Main Street and Alexandria Pike parallel to the curb adjoining the New Warrenton Restaurant. For the south-bound bus it is on Main Street directly in front of the Clerk's Office Building. The time for stopping to take on and or discharge passengers was set at a maximum of two minutes. The Tongue property, now owned by the town, is being painted.

Food for the New Warrenton Restaurant was ordered from big companies and delivered. One way to advertise when they had lobsters was to put them in a large tank in the Main Street window. They could leave them there only a few hours and then had to put the lobsters back in the refrigerator. The cooks, one who was Paul Carter, were all good and people ordered different things. Sometimes the cook made "fancy dishes" and they would have to ask him what it was, but there was lots of "plain food", too. Virginia Pappas did go across the street to the A&P Store for some items. It was a day in 1950 she had been there and was returning to the restaurant when a car backed out of its parking place, bumped her on the back, almost knocking her down. She began to run, but being pregnant, she could not go fast, though managed to stay ahead of the car. Two women on the restaurant corner started screaming at the driver who couldn't seem to hear or see what was happening. When Virginia reached the sidewalk, she was quite frightened to say the least. Besides the people who came into the restaurant, they also catered to picnics such as the Lions' Club would have.

September 12th, a building built in 1842 at South 5th and Lee Streets, across from Ullmans, was torn down because the street was being widened. This was once the "First Chance-Last Chance", so called because those traveling on the train could get their first drink or their last drink in town.

Rather an exciting time was had in Court House Square October 12th, 1950. The Gas Company was laying the lines along the street in front of the Courthouse and dug up, or opened, the Old Well, from the early 1800's at least. People gathered to see and take pictures of it. Heard said a map from 1850 had the wells circled and one was about where this one was discovered. The Woman's Exchange, after moving to Main Street last year, closed October 15th. The first Exchange was in 1909, the name being changed to the Woman's Reality Company in 1922.[141]

The Bloodmobile in the Soldiers' Lounge, or the old U.S.O., over Lerner Bros., November 7th, 1950, collected blood for the men in Korea. Friday evening, the 24th, began the worse storm since 1938. There was thunder, and freezing rain turning into snow, which tied up traffic in the north over the Thanksgiving weekend. But, thankfully, the roads here did stay open.

The first part of December the Christmas lights sponsored by the Lions' Club and the Rotary Club's tree on the Courthouse porch were put up and decorated beautifully. At 2pm, Saturday, December 7th, 1950, Santa arrived driving down Main Street in a 1951 Ford. He couldn't use reindeer because there was no snow. He spent the afternoon visiting the stores in town until 6:00. Sometime during 1950 Forrest Gill combined his two stores into one, moving to Shirley Ave., so part of the Hiden Building is again vacant. Powell Thayer went with him.[173]

1951

Prices on everything seems to be rising. Now, January 10th, 1951, the Fauquier Theater is charging 35¢ for adults and 16¢ for children. Another fire in town. This one Thursday morning, the 18th, destroyed the Soldiers' Lounge, doing $65,000 damage.

April 5th, 1951, a fox was seen trotting across a lot near the bus station headed up town. There was no evidence it was sick, although last month rabies was around. A few years ago all sorts of animals were getting it, such as dogs, cats, foxes, skunks, coons, cows, and horses.

May 2nd, 1951, the Town Council reported part of the parking meter fund went to Town wages and the Police Pensions Disability Fund. Memorial Day, May 30th, the parade was led by the Black Horse Chapter going to the cemetery. The Negro ceremonies were held first at Mt. Zion Church, after which their parade formed to march to the cemetery for ceremonies at the graves of their war dead. The parade was led by the Boy Scout Troop and Sunday School children dressed in white, who carried flags and flowers.

Friday, June 1st, 1951, the Warrenton Firemen's Carnival Queen was crowned on the Warrenton Green lawn at 6:30pm. At 7:00 the Parade began with the wail of a fire siren. Main and Culpeper Streets had the largest crowd yet seen. By June 14th, every week a fox bites or attacks someone. 1472 dogs and cats have been vaccinated free by the Hunt Clubs.

Seven of the Fresh Air Program children came by train from

New York, arriving at the Calverton Station July 5th, 1951. Monday morning the 30th, a large gasoline truck with a flat tire parked for several hours across from the Courthouse. Its gasoline was leaking into the gutter, and a careless smoker could have caused a bit of damage. The State Highway Department is working on a part of Alexandria Pike that was higher than the sidewalk as of August 2nd. A storm sewer is being put in from the top of the hill to the bus station. August 30th a number of county farmers met in the Court Room regarding loans and credit.

September 4th, 1951, the Town Council discussed the question of making Court Street one-way from Hotel Street, and Culpeper Street one-way from Hotel to Main Streets. No action was taken on it. By the 6th, the new Soldiers' Lounge was almost completed over Muntz Television on Main Street. The Association for Greater Warrenton is sponsoring it. The Town Council, September 20th, were thinking of adding Fluorine to the Town's drinking water. Some are for and some are against this new aid for healthy teeth. The first rain in three weeks, October 11th, settled the dust only. It has been 58 days since an inch or more rain has fallen. The dry summer has cost the county more than a million dollars. One good thing about this is at least it has retarted the growth of the beetle grubs. That night a committee for a Community Swimming Pool met at the Fauquier National Bank.

November 6th, 1951, the Town Council planned to plant a small Pin Oak tree on the south side of Winchester Street about half way between the two trees flanking the Shirley Carter property, next to the Methodist Church, and to provide a suitable guard for the tree. November 29th the Jaycees asked the public to donate toys for children. Santa's Workshop is at St. James Parish House, where the toys will be repaired if necessary. It sleeted Friday, December 14th and again the following Tuesday, helping to get people in the Holiday mood. During 1951, the Kreticos sold the Pattie Building which they bought in 1937, to Walter and Johanna Ostrow, thus it became known as the Ostrow Building.

1952

The old groundhog saw his shadow in a weak sun February 2nd, 1952. Charlie Jeffries has been ill, so when he can't leave his apartment above Gardiner's Drugs, he can be seen sitting by the front window to watch the town go by. Wednesday morning, February

27th, Warrenton got its first street signs. Mayor Richard H. Marriott put up the first marker at the corner of Main and Court Streets, in front of the Courthouse.

March 1952 came in Saturday the 1st, with blowing snow. The U.S.O. Art Exhibit for servicemen is in the Club Room Thursday through Saturday, March 6th-8th. Around the 31st, the old Methodist Parsonage of 1848 next to the Fauquier Democrat is being torn down, after being used for a number of things. The new building will be called The Phipps Business Building.

Many people said a "Thank you" on March 27th. A 250 pound practice bomb dug an 18 inch hole in the eastern end of the By-Pass and then bounded into the Rosenwald School playground, where the children had been a little while before. Gravels flew over the tops of homes, a gasoline station and the school. Planes fly back and forth over Town quite often and around 1:30pm five or six military plans had circled Warrenton. Three broke away from the formation and dived. The bomb fell from the wing of one plane. These were believed to have belonged to the Navy. Stanley Cockrill and others who lived near by watched the action. Marines from Quantico landed in a helicopter at the Horse Show Grounds to pick up the bomb.

Heard said the other day that a girdle is often the only difference between the facts and figures. April 1st, 1952 the Town Council asked the Recorder to write the Secretary of Defense regarding the low flying planes over Warrenton. April 3rd, Chief Luther Cox was directing traffic in the middle of Court House Square as the "Drive Right" marker was being painted and repaired. Someone came up with a plan for one-way streets. . . .

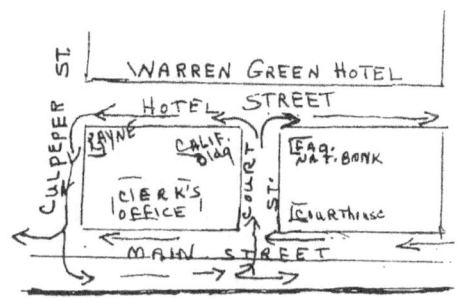

This was the plan the Council had talked about September 4th, 1951. Easter Sunday, April 13th, was a bad day for the ladies as there was rain most of the time. But, a sign of Spring was seen on the 17th. The curbs and hydrants were being painted. At noon Wednesday, April 30th, a meeting held at the Courthouse dedicated the Nations first "Cancermobile", being exhibited in front of the Courthouse. The late Mrs. Leo Rice left $6000, which paid half of the cost. It is restricted to educational activities and is not for treatment.

May 6th, 1952 the Town Council approved 'No Parking' signs for the south side of Winchester. Arrington Motors, located at the foot of Courthouse Hill, advised the Council they wanted to enlarge. May 17th the Air Force Ground Observer Corps' 24 hour Operation Sky-Watch began. It is part of America's Coastal Defense network to tract unidentified aircraft which may escape radar screening, having seven posts in Fauquier County. Friday, May 30th, the colored residents of Warrenton held their Memorial Day ceremonies in the First Baptist Church on Alexandria Pike, followed by the Parade to the cemetery for other services. The line of march was led by the Boy Scout Troop #530.

The Confederate Memorial service was held at 3pm Sunday,

OUT OF THE ATTIC

Heavy traffic is nothing new, as this 1952 photo by D. E. Saunders proves. The photograph, looking west on Warrenton's Main Street from the vicinity of the Third Street intersection, was taken to illustrate a *Fauquier Democrat* story on traffic congestion downtown.

June 1st, 1952, sponsored by the Black Horse Chapter and United Daughters of the Confederacy at the Monument in the cemetery, but without a parade this year. Frank Moffett, Legion Commander said that lack of cooperation from the Town organizations made it impossible to organize.

Another fire right here in the middle of things. It was raining June 5th, when the A&P on the corner of The Square and Winchester caught fire, doing $10,000 damage. The coronation of the Firemen's Carnival Queen took place at a stand on the lawn of the Warren Green. At 7pm the wail of the siren sounded for the hour long parade led by Vint Hill Farms Station Color Guard. It was so hot, until finally June 29th when a storm came up with a wind strong enough to break tree limbs.

One night about July 17th, 1952, Rhodes Drug Store was broken into and the safe was stolen. A Flying Saucer was seen Sunday, August 3rd, about 8:10pm in the vicinity of the Courthouse, heading west to disappear over View Tree Mountain. No one knew how high it was, but Dorothy Moore and her mother, Gladys Rowe, described the object as a long silver light with a head shaped like an egg. A similar object was reported in Washington, D.C. about the same time. Although a drought has hurt the crops, Fauquier seems to have escaped heavy damage. The first Polio case was reported in the county August 14th. The Courthouse is getting shabby, and August 21st, bids were taken to patch up the stucco, to paint and so forth. Over the weekend of the 30th, the welcome rain caused lots of mud, but did not mar the 53rd Warrenton Horse Show. When school began in September, the new Negro High School, William C. Taylor, was ready.

On October 1st, 1952, K. A. Thompson, Jr., with his shiny new mailbag, began Warrenton's home mail delivery. His father makes the truck delivery, and together they cover the entire town, as well as a lot of the adjacent territory. It was learned October 9th that Sheriff Hall's son, Samuel S. Hall, III, had been killed in Korea. The fall weather is brisk and wonderful, October 23rd, but the traffic is terrible! with everyone going to see the beautiful mountains. Since the By-Pass, traffic does not go through town as it once did. The trucks have been prohibited in the business district, too, so unless they are delivering they had better not come this way. The Lions' Club and the PTA sponsored the 4th annual Halloween Parade Friday, October 31st. Witches, goblins, harlequins and anything going, lined up at 7:30 in front of the Baptist Church to march down Main and Waterloo Streets to Benner Field. A fire engine escorted them to the bonfire and refreshments. There is a similar program for the colored children who met at Lee and Falmouth Streets and marched southward to Taylor High School.

November 1st, 1952, Luther Cox resigned as Warrenton Police Chief, which he had been since 1949. Turner Grimsley, former Town officer and Jailor is to replace him. The Town Council also employed Grimsley November 4th, to service the parking meters at the salary of $35 a month to be paid from the parking meter fund. That's more than twice what Cox was paid when he began keeping them repaired. Dwight D. Eisenhower was elected President of the U. S. in a landslide. Those "I Like Ike" buttons helped. A five inch rain soaked the county November 20th and the land of Fauquier did soak it up, too. Thanksgiving again!, that 300 year old tradition of hunting, feasting, and worship. There's not much hunting now—more feasting. A new type of bomb was exploded this month, called a hydrogen bomb.

Santa dropped in at Sears & Roebuck on Main Street (now Thrift Shop) Monday, December 1st, 1952. The Town Council decided on the 2nd that a two hour parking limit would be placed on Main Street between 1st and 2nd Streets. The first snow of the season fell, amounting to 2.9 inches. It is so quiet with it that you can hear the wind whisper. The Christmas week was busy with last minute shoppers, but things calmed down as "the Day" arrived.

During this year Luther Allison bought out Arthur R. Anderson, changed the name of Anderson & Allison Grocery Store to A&A Market and made his brother Alex Allison manager.

1953

January 9th, 1953, the Town Council rescinded the 2-hour parking limit on Main Street between 1st and 2nd Streets. That didn't last long. They are now going to research an area between Main, Alexandria Pike, Horner and 4th Streets for a parking lot.

February 3rd, 1953, the Council thought of erecting 'No Parking' signs where all curbs are painted red, but decided that stencils are to be used instead of the signs. The welcome mat is out at the Jail February 12th. Jailor Luther Cox painted his house and remodeled the kitchen, so as many as 22 prisoners can be fed at one time. Although the U.S.O. Lounge is a popular place, the U.S.O.

organization has withdrawn their funds from the local club. February 19th there was a drive going on to raise funds for it. And, speaking of popular places, another they say, is the ABC Store in the new Phipps Building on the corner of Lee and Culpeper Streets. At least a lot of people go by with little brown bags.

Monday, March 2nd, 1953, was the first real snow this winter, followed by rain mixed with sleet. Did things up right all at once. Fauquier National Bank is painting their building. Stalin died this month which caused some unrest in Russia. New lights were proposed April 3rd by the Town Council for Alexandria Pike and Winchester Street on the north end of Court House Square Garage. The parking lot in the Horner Street area must be out for now. The Town Council decided April 7th, to lease the parking area at the rear of the Warren Green Hotel at the cost of $1.00 a year. The Town is to light the area and will prohibit overnight parking except for the Hotel guests. Easter bonnets bloomed Sunday, the 5th, as did the fruit trees. So pretty—the woods are putting on their green dresses as Spring returns. The Red buds or Judas trees make a pink haze with blooms. By the end of the month Dogwoods are at their peak.

Sunday, May 31st, Memorial Day, there was a gentle rain as people gathered at the cemetery for the service. Sunday beer sales have been banned in the county.

At 7pm Friday, June 5th, 1953, the Firemen's Parade went along Main and Culpeper Streets to the Carnival grounds. Gold and silver trophies were awarded in 12 divisions. Saturday night it was rained out and then planned for the following Saturday. However, there were storms that night, but they didn't give up. They just moved everything - well almost everything - to the Fire House.

The Town Council passed an ordinance July 1st, 1953, to be effective immediately that no beer or wine is to be sold from midnight Saturday until 6am Monday. Guess that went along with the decision in May for the county. During July there was a Korean War truce. Four men from the County have been killed in its war. The middle of September if HOT! The Hobo King, Sam H. Cole, came to Warrenton Saturday the 26th, stopping by The Fauquier Democrat office. He is making his way south from Canada and Alaska, carrying his belongings in a newsboys' sack and a handbag.

October 15th, 1953, Culpeper Street became one-way from Lee to Main Streets. Finally, the first rain October 29th in nearly eight weeks, but too late to help the farmer. November 5th, the water ban is off so people are able to wash those dusty, dirty cars and go hunting. Friday, November 6th and now there is 7½ inches of snow with heavy drifts. From hot to winter in one giant step. Chief Turner Grimsley has a new souped-up Police car that he's driving around on November 26th. Christmas came early for him.

Turner's Taxi will pick up toys for Santa's Workshop December 10th, 1953 and afterwards. One of the collection points is the Warren Green Hotel. The Arthur Murray Dance Class meets at the Hotel, and people attending seem to have a terrific time. Christmas Eve Main Street was enlivened by carols broadcast from the Service Lounge, which continued all through the week. The Town heard the voices of young people singing carols throughout the streets, too, in the Baptist Church's Annual program. After the carols the young people went to the Service Lounge for refreshments and a social hour.

1954

Monday, January 4th, 1954, the drugstore and restaurants in town are selling coffee by the cup, the proceeds which will go to the March of Dimes Fund. The quota for Fauquier County is $7000 and a large thermometer on the lawn of the Clerk's Office will keep score as it is collected. A 4½ inch snow on the 14th helped fill the lakes and ponds that have been built in the county over the years. However, with the snow was ice that blocked roads and gave the schools a three day holiday. Several Korean missing casualties are now being declared dead. A six inch snow on Friday, the 22nd, was turned to slush on Sunday by a 60 degree temperature.

February 2nd, 1954 the Town Council hired a fourth policeman for this growing town. Again, February 4th, the 40 bed Physician's Hospital is up for sale. They say there are signs on the highways with, "In the event of Enemy Attack This Highway Will Be Closed To All Except Civil Defense & Military Vehicles". The Air Raid Shelters are still in the Courthouse and Fauquier National Bank basements. School children have been practicing a "Duck and Cover" air raid program for years.

By March 25th, 1954, the 11st case of Rabies for the year had been reported. April 22nd, Wayman Carter's Store had a big box of baby chicks in its show window, which was heated with an electric bulb suspended just above the box. They were painted every color in the rainbow. Wayman said his better half stayed up all night giving the babies their Easter dresses. Sunday, Daylight Savings Time began. Someone said, "Old Nuisance is back". Monday, April 26th, was Memorial Day for the Confederate Dead in several states, but Virginia will not celebrate until June 3rd, which is Jefferson Davis' birthday. Thursday, the 29th, a rabid dog bit a woman on Waterloo and a man near the Fire House on Lee Street.

May Day 1954! The first day of May and the town was crowded from 10am to 6 in the evening with people going to the Gold Cup. The Peoples National Bank purchased the Hilleary Building, that adjoins the bank on Main Street, now Cornblatt's Department Store. On the 6th Street side of the building is still to be seen a sign painted on the bricks saying,

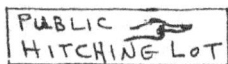

Many things were on the second floor over the years. Miss Minnie Fisher, the piano teacher there about 40 years ago and Mr. Sherman, a painter, had his home in an apartment for awhile.[172] May 20th people were in a quandary as to what would happen. The Supreme Court outlawed segregation in the schools. The county has an overflow of both Negro and white children, so needs more school rooms. Sunday, May 30th, the American Legion Parade left from the Fire House at 2:15pm going to the cemetery where services highlighted the day. After the Legion program, the colored Memorial Day observance had a parade to the cemetery led by the Boy Scout Troop. During the night someone stole the flags from both American and Confederate graves. May Court looked as though there were more lawyers than clients.

Wednesday, June 2nd, 1954, at noon the stores began their summer half-day closing time. The Firemen's Carnival, June 4-5th opened with a good parade. Warrenton's new Marching School Band, in their second Warrenton appearance won a prize. The first time they appeared was last week in the Memorial Day parade. There was a high wind and storm Saturday, the 27th. It did a little damage around town. It was about 1954 that "Biggie" stopped driving after he was in a car accident. His wife would bring him to town in the morning, come and get him for lunch, bring him back, and come to get him in the afternoon. He got in the habit of sitting on the Courthouse steps to wait for his ride, and while there, other men stopped to chat, so a group began to form.

A man about this same time, had his driving license taken away because he insisted on driving while "under the influence". Then he came to town on his tractor, but still driving it while having "a little too much". One day he went around the "Dummy Policeman" and tried to go around the second time, but went right up the Courthouse steps for 3 or 4 steps before the tractor stalled out and stopped. The tractor was taken away from him then, but he'd ride his horse into town to the liquor store.[129] A young man in town also liked to ride his motorcycle up the steps, doing it about three times.

A change in the skyline was proposed July 1st, 1954. Behind the Post Office is to be a Town Water Tank tall as a 12 story building. On the north side of the Silent Policeman and going across Main Street towards the Courthouse, new yellow tacks about the size of a silver dollar have been nailed down into the street. These plastic disks may replace paint to mark the safe walkways for pedestrians and parking spaces for cars. Nineteen New York Fresh Air children arrived at Catlett Railroad Station, July 8th at 3pm for their two week vacation. The town was almost deserted this day, so many people went to the Charles Town Races.

Wednesday, July 14th, about 5:40pm people in town thought the world was coming to an end. There was a dead humid calm under black skies and suddenly—the wind hit!, reaching 100 miles an hour with hail and everything else. The statue was blown off the top of the Confederate Monument at the cemetery and a big limb fell from the tree on the lawn of the California Building, coming down in the middle of Culpeper and Hotel Streets. The tree behind the building damaged a room of D. H. Lee's office. The wind could really whip around the corner of Main Street and Alexandria Pike at the New Warrenton Restaurant. The cook had been warned not to go out the back door for anything in the freezer on the porch if the wind was coming in that direction. One particular day - not sure when - the wind seemed alright to open the door. BUT - as the door opened, the front window on Main Street exploded in the draft and glass flew everywhere, a lot going into the street. The electric went off, too. Glad the lobsters weren't in the window. Fortunately no one was hurt either, but upstairs Virginia was feeding her daughter. When the lights came on, a wall plug sparked and the curtain above it almost caught fire, so Virginia pulled out the plug—and everything became dark again. What a night the Pappas had! The Atlantic & Pacific Tea Company announced July 22nd that they plan to build a new store on Waterloo just below the Physician's Hospital. People are glad all those neon signs and service stations are on the By-Pass instead of Main Street. What a mess it would be.

Good news. The Fauquier Hospital, formally Physician's Hospital, Fund Drive went over $110,000 goal on August 5th, 1954. There are 140 new parking meters to register two-hours of parking for 10¢. The total cost of the exchange of meters was $6,790. The proceeds are to go to the police retirement fund. Moses Hall on Waterloo, that escaped the fire in 1909, almost had it August 19th. An oil stove exploded in one of the apartments. The top floor has the rooms of the Lodge of the Sons and Daughters of Moses. In its earlier days dances and festivals were held there.

A 150 persons attended the new Community & Armed Forces Lounge last Friday evening over Lerner Brothers, it was reported September 2nd, 1954. The Town Council announced on the 7th that the parking meter collection was over $900 for August, and Fauquier County is to have a dog pound soon. Stuyvesant School decided not to open this term, the first time since 1912.

October 14th, 1954, the State Drought Committee asked that Virginia be declared a drought disaster area, Fauquier County being a part of it. Rivers and streams are beginning to run dry. But, would you believe it? On the 21st, Hurricane Hazel came along. Everyone was warned that the storm was coming so all the stores closed at 4pm and people went home before it hit. The Pappas family took sandwiches, nabs, and little things like that next door to the Graysons who were staying in their store basement because they were too frightened to go home. The radio told them that the eye was coming through Richmond and was headed for the Warrenton area, and as it came closer the wind would have a strange whistling sound. All of them were just about scared to death and thought they could hear the whistling getting louder and louder. The rain was pounding on the windows, a real gully washer! Even when things quieted down, they were still afraid to go out of the basement. Suddenly—there was a knock at the door! It was Mrs. Luther Cox, who worked at the ticket window of the theater, to tell them the storm veered off and was not coming here, so they could all go home. It did take down some of the oldest Oaks in the county. Friday, October 13th, had been in the 90's, but after the storm, it is just above freezing.

Tuesday, November 2nd, 1954, an early storm brought an inch of snow, beginning about 9am melting almost as fast as it fell. It is said that when the first snow falls on a certain date, that is the number of snows for the year. If true, this year there will only be two snows. Farmers and streams need more. Although dry, the newly built Lake Brittle is filling up. Early Friday morning, the

19th, a little lost duck landed on the roof of the County Office Building. There was fog that morning, so he must have been weather-bound. He stayed around until about 11:00, looking over the edge of the building watching the people on the street looking up to watch him. The funny part about it was that some of those watchers were hunters going to the building to buy hunting licenses. Camden TV Sales & Service had a fire also early Friday morning. It is on Main Street next door to Sears Roebuck & Co. The wall separating the two stores began to burn through before it was put out. Operation "Speed Watch" went in Wednesday the 24th, as the police use a new electrical speed check. Good thing they didn't have that when the sleds were going down Courthouse Hill. Santa Claus came to Sears Monday, November 29th, after a parade through town that was led by the Warrenton School Band.

The Town Council reported, December 7th, 1954, that the parking meter collection for November was $1034.02, so they are paying for themselves. Even with the meters, people complain that parking is a problem on Main Street due to so many trucks and cars double parking. Monday afternoon, the 13th, two Army trucks pulled up in front of the Community & Armed Forces Lounge, which is being used as a toy distribution center. The soldiers are helping the Jaycees this year. Warrenton's Main Street is gay and fragrant with Christmas trees, wreaths, holly and mistletoe as shoppers go about their last minute gift buying. The Methodist Church has been playing carols each evening at 5:30 over their amplifying system. At 10am Christmas Day, the Hallelujah Chorus sounded loud and clear. Probably during 1954, the Fashion Shop moved from Anderson & Allison's Building to one at the corner of South 3rd and Main Streets, across from the Presbyterian Church. When City Risdon Garrett had her own shop she often thought of the days she and her aunts played cards while keeping the shop and felt she really wouldn't want her employees to try that in her place for now they were too busy.[110]

1955

January 4th, 1955, the Town Council was doing a count and survey with the possibility of having "Stop" and "Go" lights on Main Street at Culpeper, 2nd, and 4th Streets. Would that help the traffic? Through the 1940's and continuing now, it seems that everyone from the country comes to town on Saturday nights when the stores are open until 9:00. Sometimes they just park along the street and sit for hours watching the other people. Some drive along Main Street, turn around the "Dummy" at The Square and go back up Main often causing a tie-up.[134] Warrenton Training Center now has View Tree Mountain. This January has been the driest, coldest and most miserable in 4 years.

The Virginia Museum's Artmobile visited Warrenton Tuesday and Wednesday, February 8th and 9th, 1955, being located at the Odd Fellows' lot on Main Street. It has paintings of the 16th and 17th Centuries. Work is progressing on Waterloo Street for the new wing at the rear of Fauquier Hospital. Ten trees of the town are to be removed, some on Winchester and Main Streets. It's near zero after the storm Wednesday the 9th, that began with sleet and now sleding is fun. The U. S. has decided to help the Vietnam Army.

The school children are to have Polio shots March 10th, 1955, which should cut down and stop the dreaded disease that comes each summer. By March 17th, the old Hilleary Building is being torn down with a walkway in front of Peoples National Bank to block off the construction, but it is so narrow, it would be terrible if two fat people met in it. The new bank will be a colonial-style building. Time to put in the onion sets, seed potatoes, peas and other cool weather vegetables. After a wonderful day, the very next one, the 18th, people woke up to—snow!

April 5th, 1955 the Hi-Y Club requested the Town Council for permission to rope off a street for a dance. It was referred to the Mayor and Police Chief for a decision. Didn't hear the results. The A&P moved from Court House Square and April 14th, is installed at the store on Waterloo Street, which is the old Garrett Motors Building site. Monday, April 18th, the Polio Vaccination began at the schools.

The Gold Cup descended from "The Best Steeplechase in America", being called The Warrenton Races in 1830 with the first organized steeplechase in 1844. Saturday morning, May 7th, 1955, the town was full of people. Then, no one was around until after 5pm when the Gold Cup was over, and once more people were everywhere. The State Highway Department decided May 12th that Warrenton did not meet requirements, so would not get traffic lights.

The Firemen's Parade Friday, June 3rd, 1955, had 60 units as it went along Main and Culpeper Streets to the American Legion Grounds on the By-Pass. There, after the parade, former Governor John Battle crowned the Queen. The Fauquier Democrat had its

50th anniversary. How time flies! Guess what "they" say now... Dinosaurs lived in Fauquier County when it was taking shape millions of years ago. Rocks here have been found to be of Precambrian age. That's a little too long ago to remember. By June 30th Lake Brittle opened and people were talking about how nice it is. Also the Water Tower is being built on North 3rd Street. The 43 foot column will have a 500,000 gallon tank on top. It will be 140 feet tall with an aircraft warning light on top of that, being tallest thing in town.

An era ended July 14th, 1955, as the stands built about 1903, at the Warrenton Horse Show Grounds are being torn down. A street sweeper was bought for the town at a cost of $2,315. It'll be a cleaner place now. Although Hurricane Connie hit over the edge of the county Friday, August 12th, causing some streams to flood there was no severe damage. Thursday, August 18th, Diane came along without any harm, too. Heard it said that in the 1880's and 90's, Juvenile Court was held in the woodshed.

Something very, very unusual for Sunday, October 2nd, 1955, or any other day for that matter. Not many lions take a casual walk around the Courthouse, BUT—Blondie, a magazine glamour girl did. She is an African lion, weighing 203 pounds, that appeared in Life Magazine for September 19th. She was at Vint Hill this weekend for a Welfare Fund Carnival and came to visit Warrenton, too. Halloween, the 31st, the Lions' Club had its annual parade and costume contest, leaving from the Baptist Church at 7pm. A school band and a fire truck with flashing lights and siren led the screaming warlocks, witches, ghosts, and cavorting weird creatures totaling about 150 maskers to Benner Field. Warrenton Wholesale Co., established 1946, had been in the old Garrett garage building on Horner & Alexandria Pike for a number of years, but moved across the street and in 1955 opened a gift shop.

The first snow fell Saturday, November 19th, 1955. Santa made the final part of his trip from the North Pole to Warrenton by Fire Truck, December 1st. A group met him, including the Mayor and Police at Sears. Carter's window display has dolls and doll furniture for the benefit of Christmas seals. At the Council meeting, the 6th, the Police Committee reported that the loading and unloading spaces provided on Main Street to eliminate commercial double parking has been put in effect and is doing a good job. Also during 1955, Ernest Pappas retired, giving up the New Warrenton Restaurant. Ernest was one of the "best citizens that ever existed".

No matter who needed help he was always ready to lend a hand whether it be money, free meals, or gifts. At the time of the Depression when the so-called tramps came through town asking the Sheriff to let them spend a night in Jail to keep from freezing in the winter, Ernest made sure they had a meal.[103]

About this time, C. H. Braun bought the building and store of Charles M. Sauer to remodel it for Braun's Variety Store. Sudduth-Moser Funeral Home moved to the By-Pass, becoming Moser's.[178] Was it now, too, that Nina Minter Thorpe, who worked at Roadhouse & Bunch's since 1932, bought the business and renamed it Nina's 5&10¢ Store? Then, she and her sister, Mrs. D. D. Sanford, were in competition a few doors from each other. Although they really didn't look alike, people might go from one store to the other and ask, "Weren't you just in the other place;"[127]

1956

January 3rd, 1956 the Council had parking meters put on the North side of Hotel Street and on the East side of Alexandria Pike from Main Street to the New Warrenton Restaurant's parking lot. The Council agreed to pay for the electric power used for the Christmas lights. Monday afternoon, January 9th, a sleet and snow storm closed schools and caused some minor accidents. It was followed Thursday, the 12th, with three more inches of snow. While the weather was bad in February for outside work, the interior of the Courthouse was painted.

Lots of people planted their "spuds" Saturday, March 17th, 1956 and went to bed with warm air and a glorious moon shining. Next morning they woke up with 2-6 inches of snow, depending on in which end of the county you were. Spring arrived the following Tuesday at 10:21am. April 19th Peoples National Bank has had Open House the past several afternoons to show off their remodeled building. The Garden Club Tour Tuesday, April 24th, had a cold drizzly day for it.

The frost about May 20th was the latest in 46 years when it was supposed to have been caused as the earth went through the tail of Halley's Comet in May 1910. This is really a Blackberry Winter with gardens suffering. "They" have figured out that Warrenton winters stay colder over a longer period than they did some 25 years ago. Wednesday, May 30th, the Memorial Day parade left the Fire House at 12:30pm going to the cemetery. Also included in the usual ceremony is a new flag pole given by the Legion Post and dedicated "To The Memory of Those Who Lost Their Lives In Their Country's Defense". Poppy Day is being observed, too.

The Firemen changed their parade route Friday, June 1st, 1956. It began at 6:30pm from near the Fire House, went along Main Street westward past the Courthouse to Waterloo Street, on down it to the Judge's Stand, at the intersection with Chestnut Street. Past the Stand, and on to Warrenton High School and its Athletic Field. The Queen was crowned at the grounds following the Parade, by Dick Evans, Line Coach of the Redskins. This was the biggest Parade yet and a hugh crowd watched. Saturday was a frizzle-out though, because of an all day drenching rain. It was planned for the next weekend.

September 4th, 1956, the Town Council wanted to investigate Diagonal Street being made one-way from Winchester to Waterloo Street, at least on Sundays. Dr. Robert Anderson requested this as it is a congested area during church hours. The Council will take bids on repairing the Municipal Building. Another building needing repairs is the Library, which is seeking funds. School began on the 6th.

Edward C. Thornton, age 71, died October 3rd, 1956. He went to work at the age of 14 for Dr. Hunton in his drugstore. Later Thornton was partner with W. S. Sowers and at his death, succeeded ownership to the store that became known as Thornton's Drugstore, which is the Downtown Store, since Willard Kirby bought out John Davis. Wednesday, October 31st, spooks, goblins and whatever, marched through the streets of Warrenton as the Lions' Club sponsored its 11th annual Halloween Parade and Costume Party, which began at the Baptist Church at 6:45pm. It was led by the Warrenton High School Band and featured floats from the school's Homecoming Parade, that had been cancelled by rain on Friday.

Tuesday, November 6th, 1956, Dwight D. Eisenhower was elected President of the U. S. again. Since a new hospital is being built on a hilltop along the By-Pass, Tom Frost announced that the old Fauquier Hospital has been sold to the District Nursing Home at Manassas for $112,500. Tuesday morning, the 20th, a large number of adults and high school students stood in line in front of the Courthouse to have X-rays made at a Mobile Laboratory. It will continue until the 28th, and is sponsored by the County Health Department and the County Tuberculosis Association. There is also a Mobile Lab to test milk samples for Bangs' Disease.

Monday, December 2nd, 1956, the Rotarians and friends put up a 24 foot white pine on the Courthouse porch. For over 20 years they have been furnishing the tree. The tree lights show off all night in all directions. The front door of the Clerk's Office Building is decorated with running pine and long leaf pine in the form of an arch sprayed with snow powder. The Jaycees took 15 children December 13th, to see the tree and on a gift buying trip. They were really bubbling and wide-eyed with excitement. A couple of the children said it was the first time they had seen a decorated tree. Evelyn B. Richardson and Joseph W. Elliott on December 20th, bought the Warren Green Hotel from the estate of Herman E. Ullman for $200,000. They plan to take over on January 1st, 1957. During the Holidays there was heavy fog causing many wrecks.

1957

The March of Dimes collected used Christmas trees for a donation and had a bonfire on January 4th, 1957, for people to dance around. Sounds as though there was lots of fun at "Operation Torch" held at the American Legion Grounds. The activity is in association with The Twelve Days after Christmas-January 6th-or Epiphany. The March of Dimes netted $124 for the Polio Fund. There was a two inch snow Monday, January 6th, 3½ inches the next week, the 13th, and 2½ inches the following day. People are going back to hibernation. By January 24th, the temperature was from zero to minus 20 degrees, so that even the Rappahannock River froze. After the A&P moved to Waterloo Street April 14th, 1955, Sears Roebuck & Co. went into its former location, the Ostrow Building. Agnes L. Kemper of Remington went to work there in the fall of 1955. Nothing really exciting happened until an icy day about this time, when a car turned from Main Street to go around the "Dummy Policeman". BUT, instead of going straight, it came slowly across the intersection, over the curb as no cars were parked there at the time, and on through the store window. It seemed, as one watched it, to have happened in slow motion. Western Auto, at this time, was occupying the whole ground floor of the Hiden Building, as it replaced the Gill Furniture & Appliance Store.

February 14th, 1957, there was a truck at the Fire House loaded with food, clothing, and bedding for flood victims in Southwest Virginia. People in Fauquier County are generous and sharing. It could not have been at a better time than today, as it stands for love. At a ceremony March 28th, Thomas E. Bartenstein, Clerk of the Circuit Court since 1918, was given a portrait of himself, painted by Wesley Dennis, at the Clerk's Office by the Board of Supervisors. It was hung in the Clerk's Office and will continue to be there in years to come. Although many activities are now held at the Warrenton High School, the Warrenton Teen Club meets at the Fire House for Saturday night dances. Some have been selected to dance on TV. A joke is going around about the Judge saying to a woman, "This trial is to show if you threw a crowbar at your husband or not". The Woman answered, "Judge, it will show that I hit him".

Saturday, May 4th, is Gold Cup Day and the warm sun has brought out the Dogwood blooms. This time of year is heaven in Fauquier. Centralized schools are here to stay as more and more school buses are seen, and the little 1-2-or 3 room schools are disappearing. The Memorial Day Parade was from the Fire House to the cemetery as usual.

J. W. Elliott of the Warren Green Hotel asked the Town Council on June 4th, 1957, to be allowed to use town water for his swimming pool. June 7th and 8th, Friday and Saturday, was the Firemen's Parade and Carnival, grossing $16,000. On the 14th, Charlie Madison celebrated his 50th anniversary as barber. Lee Madison had observed his 60th year in January. Thornton Lee established the shop in 1870. Thursday, June 20th, the Warrenton Volunteer Fire Department hosted representatives of 66 Volunteer Fire Companies of Northern Virginia Firemen's Association at a meeting in the Warren Green Hotel. The County is fighting rabies with fox bounties. Only grey fox tails are wanted, which bring $2.50 each. Wonder why no red fox?

Tuesday morning, July 2nd, 1957, 25 New York Fresh Air youngsters arrived at Calverton Station. Fauquier is seeking to be named in the Drought Disaster Section, as it is reaching 1953 problems. August 1st had a nice rain, but a GOOD rain is needed. Every little bit helps, and "Thank-yous" went up above. Sunday afternoon, the 4th, a helicopter landed at Lee and 10th Streets with the press aboard. They attended a party at the Warren Green Hotel, enjoying its pool and flights over the Town. The American Legion Carnival was Friday and Saturday, August 23rd and 24th, at the Firemen's Carnival lot. The joyful sounds could be heard around The Square. A 3-inch rain August 29th, cracked the drought.

The Soviet Union launched a satellite into space October 4th, 1957, called Sputnik I. Sunday, the 6th, was a good day to stay indoors and watch the World Series and football on TV as there was a gale with 3 inches of rain. The Warrenton Post Office announced that effective October 20th, there would be afternoon mail collection from letter boxes. The Lions' Club Halloween Parade on Tuesday, the 31st, was held as usual while others made "trick or treat" rounds for candy and goodies or for donations for UNICEF. During October, Fauquier County had royalty visiting when Britain's Queen Elizabeth came to the U. S., but she didn't get to Warrenton.

Not much observance for Armistice Day, 1957. The Post Office was closed. Since June until November 14th, there were 211 grey foxes killed for bounty collection. The first snow this year was November 23rd. Wednesday night, December 11th, the Jaycees took 31 youngsters on a shopping tour and to talk with Santa. The bug-eyed children were given bags of candy as they shared in the real spirit of Christmas. A special policeman was hired during the holidays this year. People are not sure that the reasons for this is good for the town. Is the year ending on a bad feeling instead of good-will?

1958

The first United States satellite, called Explorer I, went into outer space during January 1958. The groundhog saw his shadow February 2nd. Sunday, February 13th, 1900, had a blizzard which is still remembered, but, Saturday, 15th is going to be remembered as the "Blizzard of '58". There was 12 inches of snow and zero temperature. Helicopters were used to rescue the stranded and ill. Someone said it was so cold his chickens froze to their roosts and he had to use hot water to loosen their feet, after which he carried them into the house to thaw out.

Sunday, March 9th, 1958, had 5 or more inches of snow. The look at fuel bills will tell you the winter has been a "humdinger". Ten more inches of wet snow Wednesday night and Thursday the 19th and 20th. It is the worse storm since March 1932. The news would be if it were NOT snowing. During the night of March 31st, Warrenton Supply's safe was opened in what seems to have been a professional job. The thieves were probably hidden inside the store when Blair Moffett and his son closed it about 8:30 in the evening. The glass from a rear window through which they must have escaped, was found to have fallen outward.

The old stone step leading to Charlie Jeffries' apartment above the drugstore is in much use now, April 24th, 1958, a sure indication the weather is nice and warm for no one patronizes that old rock when the weather is cold. Some of the ones who meet here with Charlie are, Dr. Biggie Hodgkins, Dr. Jimmy Sinclair, and Harry O'Brien. Dr. Sinclair was called "the poor man's doctor" because he helped so many people.[133] From now on the old regulars will be here except during thunderstorms.

By May 1st, 1958, the rain has been well over the normal. People can't get their garden planted. Everyone was invited May 15th to see the new hospital on Hospital Hill. It was something to witness when a 70 foot crane came lumbering into town to stop on Court Street. It was better than a circus to watch the 50 foot boom lift the air conditioner units into the director's room and onto the roof of the Fauquier National Bank. Tuesday night, May 20th, the granddaddy of a grey fox was shot on Winchester Street near Stuyvesant School. It weighed 20 to 30 pounds. Memorial Day, Friday, May 30th, had no parade, but only services at the cemetery that began at 10:30am. Banks, stores, Post Office and so forth were closed.

June 3rd, 1958, the Town Council gave "Operation Flower Box" permission to continue putting up flower boxes as people along Main Street request them. A. L. Carroll from the Bowling Alley at Alexandria and Horner Streets wanted to know the cost of his license if he put in automatic pin setters. He was told it would stay the same. Plans are being made for the Bicentennial. Among them was a contract made June 5th for a $45,000 statue of Chief Justice John Marshall to be placed on the sidewalk in front of the County Office Building. It will be a 6 foot 3 inch high seated figure, placed on a base 4 feet 8 inches high and 5 feet by 3 feet 6 inches in area. Boxwood bushes along the entry walkway will need to be replanted closer to the building and a circular sidewalk will be laid around the front of the statue. The Volunteer Fire Department had a huge two hour Parade, the longest ever and fine weather for the Carnival. On June 11th a violent wind and electric storm went through the area. Warrenton has formed a Rescue Squad and will begin a drive for donations.

The United States sent Marines to Lebanon during July 1958. Things are not too good in the Middle East. Friday, August 1st, the postal rates jumped again and now a letter if 4¢ with post cards costing 3¢. The rain Sunday, August 3rd, stopped the Jaycees' National Championship Country Music Contest at Lake

Whippoorwill for the first time in eight years. It came down in torrents that afternoon and night. Sack dresses are being worn by women.

The Lions had to postpone their Carnival because of rain from July 18th to Friday and Saturday, August 8th and 9th. But, rain again washed out Friday night. At least they had a good time Saturday.

The Warrenton Horse Show and Labor Day 1958 was good weather. Some people are trying to change the location of the John Marshall Statue. A few want a platform built in the center of the Courthouse steps for it. Others suggest replacing the Dummy Policeman at the center of The Square with a tiny plot of grass around it. If they took out the Fountain because of there being no room, how will there be room for this?

March 8th, 1956, the Chamber of Commerce wrote to the Supervisors requesting improvements on the Town Clock. An Ohio Clock Firm said it would cost $885 to repair. But, as of October 2nd, 1958, the Clock still has no numerals on two of its sides. Warrenton pays for the Clock lighting and the man to hand wind it, so they would like to eliminate the weights, cables and pendulum by electrifying it. A movie crew is making a documentary film for one of the Armed Services and using, as a background, the Courthouse among other scenes of Town. October 7th, the Town Council was again approached by Arthur Carroll who requested, and was given, a license to operate a Bowling Alley and Pool Room on Alexandria and Horner Streets.

The annual Lions' Halloween Parade from the Fire House Friday, October 31st, began at 6:30 marching to the Firemen's Carnival Grounds where there was a party for the ghosts, goblins, and things that go bump in the night. Others were out with trick or treat and collecting for UNICEF.

The Coffee Shoppe, operated by Mr. and Mrs. J. E. Barnhart, closed November 1st, 1958, after 27 years of business. Two service clubs, the Rotary and Lions who met there will now be meeting at the Warren Green Hotel. Dan Rector once ran the bakery of the Coffee Shoppe,[174] probably taking over when Mr. Thoma retired. Sunday, the 16th, at 3pm, the new $1,456,000 Fauquier Hospital was dedicated, having been begun April 2nd, 1957. The day after Thanksgiving, the 28th, began with snow turning to sleet and snow on Saturday.

The Jr. Chamber of Commerce, December 2nd, 1958, requested the Town Council for permission to set up a dollhouse in the Alleyway between Gardiner's Drug Store and the Downtown Store, which was granted. The plans for the Fauquier Bicentennial Committee of Fauquier County were made. The celebration will be May 1st, 1959. They asked permission to block off Main Street from the Fire House to Court House Square for the parade, speeches, introduction of guests and the unveiling of the Statue of Chief Justice Marshall which will be in front of the Clerk's Office Building. It was granted for both the morning during the parade and the afternoon when the speeches and unveiling will take place. The Jaycees took 35 youngsters on their shopping tour December 10th, both young and old enjoying it. A man who was summoned into Court was late arriving, and when questioned by the Judge, said his tardiness was due to the fact that he couldn't find a parking place. Sounds familiar. On the 11th, the Jailor's wife, Kay Godfrey, has been busy sewing and making gifts for eight children whose father was sentenced to nine months for non-support of his family. A bright red airplane carrying Santa Claus landed on the Polo Field adjacent to the Gold Cup Race Course Saturday afternoon, December 6th. From there he rode the Fire Truck into town, being sponsored by Radio Station WEER. Things are pretty as the Christmas lights twinkle along the streets. The star is shining from the Courthouse Steeple and the lighted tree brightens its porch while there are all sorts of interesting window displays. Sunday, the 21st, the patients are moved to the new Fauquier Hospital on the hill.

1959

Saturday, January 3rd, 1959, the first of six patients were admitted to the old hospital building, now called the District Nursing Home. Thursday, the 8th, when work was in process making way for the John Marshall Statue to be put in front of the County Building, a petition was sent to Governor Almond and the State Art Commission to place it elsewhere. The boxwoods being removed on the County Building lawn with their dirt balls weighs 1½ to 2 tons. Buildings are beginning to be readied on the 15th, for the big celebration, too. The County Office Building is having a new roof and painting is planned for it, as is for the Courthouse.

February 5th, 1959, Thomas E. Bartenstein died at the age of 81. After retiring he would return to the office to help out a little. Will there be trouble? The Council approved the purchase of three tear gas grenades for its police following a near racial fight last week on Main Street in front of the Theater. Some dispute over a car blocking pedestrians. The seed potatoes were ready March 17th, St. Pat's Day. Easter's theme this year seems to be A Living Christ For A Dying World.

Now, April 2nd, 1959, "they" come up with a proposal for a Main Street Shopping Mall, five blocks long with parking along the back of the north and south sides of the Main Street buildings. Trees would be planted in the center of Main Street from Alexandria Pike to 2nd Street, at a cost of $1,000,000. April 7th, the Warrenton Professional and Business Association requested the Town Council for Main Street lights to be changed and a parking area be built between Main and Horner Streets. An inch of snow on the white blossoms of trees, Sunday, the 12th, did little damage. Parked at the Warrenton Depot was the replica of the first train to enter regular service on Christmas Day 1830 at Charleston, South Carolina. It traveled at 15 to 25 miles an hour. John Marshall came to town all wrapped up so no one could see him. The 2800 pound bronze Statue was placed on the pink marble pedestal shortly after 9am Wednesday, April 29th. The Fire Department was requested to wash down the streets in the business area on Main and Culpeper Streets in preparation for the Big Day.

Friday, May 1st, 1959, Main Street was blocked off from the Fire House to Court House Square as planned last December. The crowd was at least 10,000 for the 200th birthday celebration, the most ever that packed and jammed the flag-bedecked Town. The Parade beginning 10am at 2nd Street and going to Warrenton High School on Waterloo, was more fun than the Mardi Gras. The Welfare Office located in the basement of the Courthouse across from the office of Mayor Dick Marriott, had been given a coat of fresh paint for they had an important part to play on this day. Nancy Price was among those giving out Box Lunches through an open window to the VIP's who were attending the ceremonies. Tom Frost had a big laugh at all those Congressmen and so forth going to the Welfare Office to get their lunch. At 2:30pm was the introduction of guests, speeches, and the unveiling of the Statue of Chief Justice Marshall by the daughter of William Marshall who used to live in the house at the corner of Diagonal and Winchester Streets. Historical relics were shown Thursday and Friday at the Courthouse, and a formal party and ball were at St. John's or old Stuyvesant School's Gym. Twelve boxes of pretty flowers decorated the Courthouse at a cost of $115 and are tended by the Garden Club. A meeting at 7:30pm Monday, May 18th, in the Court Room was for the purpose of the Supervisors to find out the wishes of the people in the proposed annexed area. Quite a group attended. Memorial Day was Saturday, May 30th, with a brief service at 11am at the Confederate Monument. Warrenton's Colored citizens had their annual Parade in the afternoon from Mt. Zion Church to the cemetery where services were conducted.

Six inches of rain Monday and Tuesday, June 2nd and 3rd, 1959, was a relief to the gardens. Last year the blackbirds ate up the peas, but weren't so bad this year. At the Firemen's Parade and Carnival this weekend, Joyce Beach was crowned Queen by Bernie Mahoney immediately following the Parade. They grossed $14,000, less than last year which was $16,276. A fisherman says three-fourths of the earth's surface is water and one-fourth is land, showing the good Lord intended a man to spend 3 times as much time fishing as plowing.

July 2nd, 1959, a drive-in was being installed at the rear of Peoples National Bank. The ground breaking on July 23rd began the 15 acre shopping center on the By-Pass. What will a big shopping area do to the town—or to The Square?

Three people in town who carry umbrellas are Dr. Hiden, Charles Stone, and Willard Kirby. When Dr. Hiden was asked why he carried one on clear days, he said, "Any fool would carry it if he had one when the rain came down, but it takes a smart man to carry one when it isn't". Mary Ellen Hudson said Mr. Stone always forgets his umbrella and she has to take it to him.

October 29th, 1959, the center of Fauquier County's governmental activities changed from the County Office Building to the basement or ground level floor of the Courthouse. Those departments were the Board of Supervisors, the School Board, and the County Planning Commission, all meeting in the room used chiefly by the County Court Judge Richard H. Marriott. The foliage is offering an "unsurpassed view" from Warrenton's lofty position with miles and miles of color. A 48 mile wind blew down a wall at the new shopping center but only a few small limbs from the trees fell in town. The 31st, Halloween, and the annual Warrenton Lions' Club Parade began at 7pm from the Fire House under the supervision of Luther Cox and led by a Fire Truck. They marched down Main and Waterloo Streets to the High School Athletic Field for refreshments and costume judging.

Rabbit fever has been found in the county just as the season opens on Monday, November 9th, 1959. On the 26th, it was decided Warrenton would annex 1750 acres, which will double the population. Wednesday night was the time for the shopping trip to the dime store and a visit with Santa Claus for 27 youngsters sponsored by the Jaycees, as things were decorated the last of November. On every street lamp is a Santa Claus and his reindeer racing across Main Street. Strings of gaily colored lights are on the tree at the Courthouse porch, and the Jaycees are working in their toy shop located this year at the former Coffee Shoppe on Main Street.

After C. H. Braun bought the property adjoining the Variety Store which was the Sudduth-Moser Funeral Home Building in 1956, he remodeled the two buildings, making one large place. He took out. the elevator that carried the caskets up or down between the street level and the lower floor, putting in its place stairways, one at the front and one at the back of the building. Margaret Cornwell, who went to work for Mr. Sauer in 1947, continued on when he sold the store, and after the remodeling, was working the check out counter one day when a woman checked out. Instead of going through the doorway, she walked through the glass! They got her back inside the store, called Dr. Pretlow who examined her and said, "Hell, No!—nothing wrong with her." The 1950's were thought of as being a time for fun or Happy Days. The first McDonald's Hamburgers Store was being talked of as something new in the country, while Rock and Roll music played loud, and hula hoops wiggled.

1960

Less than half an inch of snow Sunday, January 10th, 1960, gave way to having the last four days being the calmest weather for January that people can remember. But, on the 28th, the Asian flu was sweeping the country and Fauquier was not left out. Valentine's Day was a Sunday of five inches of snow and high winds that caused big problems Monday. Since the merchants have to clean their own sidewalk, people were busy early that morning. "Uncle Ollie" Penny of Western Auto Store, in the Hiden Building, came to work to find his clerks had prepared an agreeable surprise. They cleared the walkway, but piled the snow into a monster snowman. Even on Tuesday many county dwellers were still marooned. Ollie Penny says, "They close the banks for my birthday." He was born

January 19th, 1904. That's General Robert E. Lee's birthday, too. Eleanor Johnson is one of the workers at Western Auto. When first they moved there, sometime after 1950, they shared the building with Coons' Market in the other half. The Health Department and other offices are on the second floor.

At a meeting March 1st, 1960, the Hog Committee reported to the Town Council and they passed an ordinance that after March 5th, people would have to obtain written permission before any pig pen could be within the corporate limits. Shortly afterwards three people, A. D. Schwab, James A. Pearson, William H. Lewis, were granted permits. Thursday the 3rd, had 9 inches of snow and a 24 mile per hour wind that piled drifts 10 to 12 feet high. Temperatures for the next six days was around 10 degrees, but Monday it dropped to 6 degrees. Then, a promise of Spring. The crocus blooming in the snow look colorful on the white background, but potatoes won't be planted this St. Patrick's Day. However, Grayson's windows are blooming with Spring hats for the ladies.

April 21st, 1960, a Warrenton real estate developer offered to donate 300 acres for a consolidated white central high school. It is a $120,000 site on Waterloo Road. The Fauquier Board of Supervisors, May 5th, announced a program that would be completed in three years to consolidate the county's three white high schools, one which is on Waterloo Road, and to build three consolidated colored grade schools to replace the one and two-room colored elementary schools. The Fauquier County Republicans are "gearing up". A mass meeting May 16th at the Warren Green Hotel. The Census Bureau announced May 19th that the population of the town has almost doubled since 1950, as was expected with the annexation. Warrenton's population for 1960 is 3,522 and the County is 24,066. Memorial Day poppies are being sold by the Boy Scouts for the John D. Sudduth Post. The annual ceremonies for Memorial Day was at the cemetery, while banks and some stores were closed. The first Memorial Day was observed 1868 underscoring the North's victory, therefore, Virginia and other states have their own Confederate Memorial Day. A U-2 Spy Plane was shot down over USSR during May which has upset everyone.

Thursday, June 2nd, 1960, was the first night of the Warrenton VFD three-day Carnival. There were more than 100 entries marching down Main and Waterloo Streets for the Parade Friday night. The weather smiled and they grossed $14,327. The Warren Green Hotel closed in July and was put up for sale after 141 years. The war,

FAUQUIER NATIONAL BANK
Circa 1960
(From the collection of John K. Gott)

motels, and By-Pass killed it. Fauquier County made an offer to buy it as they need more office space. Someone suggested putting an elevator in the Clerk's Office Building. The United States has a new flag. There are now 50 stars in it as it flies July 4th. The million-dollar Northern Virginia Shopping Center along Route 17 North had their grand opening this month.

Thursday, August 11th, 1960, the County did buy the Warren Green Hotel and all its contents for $110,000 from the co-executors of the Herman E. Ullman estate. The Democratic Committee met Tuesday, August 30th, at the Peoples National Bank Building to launch a campaign—Kennedy for President. Heard asked, "Is Willard Kirby's Downtown Store uptown or downtown?"

School began the day after Labor Day, Tuesday, September 6th, 1960. Because of the annexed area it has been decided to give names to all streets. This has to be done before a new official Town map can be made. The Supervisors have ordered a renewal of the County's dog inoculation to combat rabies. The Sheriff's Department seized equipment for making illegal whiskey in a Free State raid, Thursday, September 8th. It was then set up in the Jail Yard for display, there being eight stave barrels of mash and two barrels of peaches intended for peach brandy. Was this the time that some of the confiscated equipment was stored under the Courthouse steps and jars of "white lightning" were lined on the top step of the basement entry to the Clerk's Office Building on the Courthouse or Court Street side to be thrown over the guard rail to the bottom of the steps to break them and the liquid could run into the drain there. The odor was terrible.[129] Rumor has it that once, perhaps at this time, whiskey was poured down a drain, but it surfaced onto a Warrenton street where people were waiting so they could dip it up to use.[134]

Well, for once The Square is not going to be dug up. The Telephone Company is to place the first underground cable in Warrenton going from Waterloo up Diagonal, and across Winchester Streets to Alexandria Pike for the new dial center. October 20th, 1960, the County Supervisors offered to lease the Warren Green. October 29th, Supervisors discussed that and also the need for either more Jail space or a new Jail. Prisoners have been transferred to other places because this one doesn't have the room for all of them. The Fire Truck and School Band at 7pm led off the Lion's Club Halloween Parade from the Fire House to the High School Athletic Field.

John F. Kennedy won the presidency in the closest election in 44 years. They are almost like a royal family as they bring a new image to the government. November 10th, 1960, Fauquier County received sealed bids for 40 rooms of furniture in the Warren Green Hotel. Friday, the 11th was quiet and banks were closed. The Auxiliary of the John D. Sudduth Post No. 72 placed flags on veteran graves and Legionnaries placed flags along the main streets of town. The only formal observance to honor the men and women of the Armed Forces was by the Lt. Charles Anderson No. 360 in which the American Legion sponsored a service at the Mt. Zion Baptist Church at 8pm. The Town Council, November 15th, planned to put an ad in The Democrat for two women to do police work such as directing traffic, check parking meters and parking time limits.

By Thursday, December 1st, 1960, the Christmas lights, sponsored by the Chamber of Commerce and Merchants, glow along Main and Culpeper Streets, while Santa Claus and his reindeer prance across Main Street in the center of the business section. Christmas stars shine around the gay lights. The Rotary Club has the tree on the Courthouse porch beneath the star that beams from the steeple for travelers coming into town. Colored lights outline the columns. The front of the County Building has wreaths, lights, and greenery. Shop windows along the street trinkle with Christmas joy. The old Town couldn't be lovelier. Santa came by helicopter on Saturday, the 3rd, at 1pm to the Northern Virginia Shopping Center. There was a blizzard Sunday, December 11th causing drifts up to five feet. The primary highways were still risky in spots on Tuesday and schools were closed Monday through Thursday to the joy of sled riders. The Jaycees Thursday night, December 15th, took the children, each with $2.00 to spend, on the annual shopping trip.

1961

1961. One hundred years since the Civil War. The Town Council meeting January 3rd was held in the Town Manager's Office. The two women hired for the Police Force, January 12th, were Mrs. Virginia Bunchfield and Mrs. Thelma B. Leach, at $200 a month, to begin work the first of February. County officials met with architects in the School Board Conference room of the Warren Green Hotel to view the site plan and lay out of a proposed $2 million Fauquier High School. Main Street has three new trash cans. Hope it keeps the streets cleaner. A special committee for the County Supervisors and the town began to investigate the cost and procedures for establishing a central fire, rescue, and police alarm. Also, Thursday, the 19th, had a 6 inch snowfall and high winds that closed schools. The snow looked like whipped cream at the drifts, but of course there were the usual dented fenders and cars stuck or in the ditches. The Kennedys, who have moved to Fauquier, say they won't upset the county by living at Glen Ora, south of Middleburg. A County man, A. Woodrow Patton from Midland, won an award for being the owner of a cow that produced more milk than any other in the state last year. A Marine Corps Officer, Captain H. B. Jones, was appointed Warrenton Police Chief, after Chief Turner Grimsley retired on the 19th.

By February 2nd, 1961, the Southern Fauquier Hunt Club spread four tons of birdseed during this-called the coldest winter in 16 years. While others stay in the warmth, the police, public utility and municipal employees must be out in the cold and snow. Saturday, the 11th, was the sixth snowfall of the winter, then part of it departed in the mists of the early morning on Sunday. The Town Council approved $13,000 for Main Street lights February

16th. Work is to begin in the Spring for the 11 standards to be replaced and 12 new ones with a type of fixture having a long sweeping bracket extending over the street. The standards will be 25 feet tall and give 50% more light than the present ones. They say it will be lit up like 5th Avenue around here. The "Great White Way" will be no more. By Tuesday, the 21st, plans were for new Town office quarters in the old Hotel Building so they can meet in the Council Room. A few repairs, new paint, and a light to be installed in front of the building must be made first. A couple days later there was visibility zero in the fog. You'd think it was old London around here, but the winds Saturday afternoon and Sunday morning, the 25th and 26th, were so strong that trees came down, knocking out power.

By March 2nd, 1961, the roads of the county were a miserable mess after two months of deep freeze and heavy snow. This may be the worse winter since 1899 since it had 66 inches of snow. Statistics show that in 1850 the county population was 20,868 and in 1950 it was 21,248. But in 1960 the 24,066 population was an increase of 133% in the last 10 years. At the Board of Supervisors' meeting, it was reported that more than 30 people were there and very upset about the road conditions. The Council is meeting in their new rooms.

April 30th, 1961, the clocks were put ahead at 2am. Warrenton merchants would like uniform time for the county as some places do not go on Daylight Saving Time.

May 5th, 1961, Cmdr. Alan B. Shepherd, Jr., became America's first astronaut going faster than sound. Finally, May 11th, it is decided that the whole county should be on fast time. Maybe people will be on time or know what is what now. Memorial Day, Tuesday, May 30th, the Monument to the 600 Unknown Confederate War Dead was rededicated "to the glory of God and the enduring memory and fame of the Confederate Soldier".

The Warrenton Firemen's Parade Friday night, June 1st, was nearly over when it began to rain and everyone had to run. The Carnival was rained out and planned for the next weekend. The dial telephone system began Sunday, June 4th. Also Fauquier's central fire alarm system began at the same time. The central control board and radio to handle all the county's fire and rescue squad calls is located in the Warren Green Building. It used to be that one picked up the phone, gave a name and never had to look up a number. Particularly Ethel Lunceford knew everyone and could connect you right away. The Warrenton Baptist Church was #1, The Commissioner of Revenue - #2, and the Sheriff was #11.[134] Some trees on Winchester Street have both auto damage and disease so must be taken out. An Elm between the Courthouse and Fauquier National Bank is wasted with Dutch Elm disease and should come down immediately. Dr. Byrnal M. Haley won over Richard Marriott in the election for Mayor. Vandals overturned one of the flower boxes on the Courthouse steps, June 22nd. The soil and geraniums were replaced by the 50 year old Warrenton Garden Club.

In celebration of the year 1861, the First Battle of Manassas was enacted there Saturday and Sunday, July 15th and 16th, 1961. And, beginning the 15th, a Civil Defense Office to serve 19 counties, opened in the Warren Green Hotel. By August 17th some of the parents say they will be glad when school begins so they can't hear the bells of the Ice Cream truck. Three trees were bought for $20 each, one to be on the Culpeper side of the Warren Green Building and two for in front of the Clerk's Office Building. Heavy rains on August 26th caused the afternoon circus performance to be cancelled, but thanks to the elephants who pulled the truck out of the deep mud, they could show that night.

September 7th, 1961, Dr. William "Bill" Hodgkin, age 70, died. He was of the third generation of his family to practice dentistry in Warrenton. Glad the By-Pass is in now as they said Saturday night, October 28th, there were more than 6000 cars from Skyline Drive who had been sightseeing in the Indian Summer. Good weather for the annual Halloween Parade, too. But five youths were fined for damage in the county. Had some damage last year also.

Snow fences have been put up and suddenly people begin to notice its a little colder and, it snows Monday, November 20th, 1961 with two inches coming down, but school didn't have to be closed as it soon melted. Another old friend of Warrenton died on the 29th. As someone said, "Charlie Jeffries goes away". He was born in 1882 in the tall building on Main Street that housed Jeffries' Drug Store, now Gardiner's. The old stone step will be lonesome. Robert Lunceford remembers how many years ago there was a little fire and he helped Charlie roll out the two wheel cart with the hose reel on it. A 40 foot hand dug well on Hotel Street was found November 30th, which may have at one time provided water for the California House. Three trees were planted; a Magnolia at the Warren Green, a Willow at the Library, and a Willow Oak at the County Building.

The Warrenton-Fauquier Jaycees brought Santa at 9:30am

Saturday, December 2nd, 1961, to the Fauquier Theater where he talked to friends in the lobby. After that was a cartoon show, the admission to which was one toy that the Jaycees will use in their workshop program. The Fauquier Hospital Endowment Fund Chart was displayed on the lawn of the Clerk's Office Building before it was moved to the Hospital grounds. Saturday the 9th, the wet snow changed to fog and rain that lasted all weekend. It is cold and depressing so most people stayed inside taking it easy. Thursday night, December 14th was the shopping tour for 25 children by the Jaycees. They were given $3 to shop at the Ben Franklin Store. Much in the town is missed after the Northern Virginia Shopping Center came into being.

1962

Thursday, January 11th, 1962, the oldest house in Warrenton, on South 4th Street, called the Ross House, was torn down and a parking lot will be put in its place. That's progress? Mrs. Wesley Dennis of the Warrenton Garden Club went to the Town Council January 16th to request that the $1000 given to the town by Mrs. Louise Tompkin be used for planting trees. They had $235 for trees paid by the Town and Planning Commission to work with the Garden Club for other planting. Since part of the Town Clock fell down last summer and hit a man on the head, it has yet to be repaired. On the 25th, Farmer Benner asked the Town Council to see to the repair with the Supervisors for, he said, "It is a disgrace to have the face in the condition it is and anyone coming up Alexandria Pike at 50 miles an hour - which is a 35 mile zone -, does not have a chance to figure out the time before they turn the corner".

John Glenn orbited the earth in February 1962, being the first American to do so. There's a new dance going on with the youngsters called "The Twist". The snow Monday, March 5th, was the worse March storm since 1932. By the time it stopped 19 inches had fallen with wind blown drifts. About the only thing moving was Deputy Sheriff James L. Eicher who rode his 8-year old Colorado quarter horse, "Catum" into town. And, from all the moisture in changeable March weather, after the snow came the floods over the county by the 15th. The Lion's Club began collecting food, clothes and bedding for the gale victims of "Misty's home", Chincoteague and Manteo. As usual, when you think something bad has happened to you, you find out there is someone else in a worse shape. Big excitement early in the week of March 29th. Philip Eastham, the Dog Warden, had an extra special job to do when he came to the rescue of shoppers who couldn't get through the front door of Highlander's Radio and TV Sales and Service on Main Street because a skunk was in the doorway. Eastham was very brave when he grabbed it by the tail and holding it far away from him, carried it around the corner, down the hill of Alexandria Pike to a vacant lot. There the skunk was tossed about 20 feet into the air and when it came down, it landed on its feet, tail straight up, and looking angry. It was then that Police Chief H. B. Jones killed the skunk by putting a 22 rifle bullet through its head.

The Clock was finally repaired April 12th, 1962, with the Town and County sharing the cost of $895. The face of the clock is 5 feet across.

May 17th, 1962, plans for a $160,000 Jail were being studied, perhaps to be built on the site of the present one. Another parking lot is going in and the swimming area of the Warren Green is needed as plans are for that building to be used for offices instead of building a new place. The Warrenton Garden Club had a sale along the street for the benefit of the Beautification Committee. Sounds of the Memorial Day ceremonies at the Confederate Monument could be heard Wednesday, May 30th. The Colored community's procession began at 3pm from the First Baptist Church with the Sunday Schools, Boy Scouts, church organizations and Taylor High School Band marching to the cemetery for a service. The WVFD Carnival began Thursday, May 31st, and giant Parade of 130 units was Friday, June 1st, beginning at 7pm. A project of the Venture Club brought unaccustomed life at the Warren Green Saturday, June 9th when there was an art show on the lawn.

An odd sight to see on July 9th. The 110 foot high Courthouse steeple was getting three days of scraping and two coats of paint at the cost of $500. And, there were Howard Gill and Donald Crummett suspended from a crane as they did the job.

August 2nd, 1962, things were bustling around the Warren Green with its exterior and historical sign being painted. Besides cornices, steps, porch floors and banisters, there are 38 doorways and frames, 10 dormers, 40 columns, 5 pilasters, and 122 windows, not to mention screens. Three of the columns had deteriorated so much they were replaced. On Winchester, the old Stuyvesant School is being demolished with the ball and crane. St. John's Catholic Church, which owns the property, is planning to build a new stone church for their old one on Lee Street has become too crowded. Even on Waterloo Street, a change. August 9th, the Acme Market opened at 856 Waterloo, where the A&P used to be. Labor Day, September 3rd, the time was turned back one hour to Eastern Standard Time, but two Warrenton firms, the Northern Virginia Furniture Company and Radio Station WKCW will still remain on "fast time" until the end of October.

October or Autumn is one of the most beautiful seasons God has given us to enjoy. The mountains, October 11th, 1962, are flashing their bright colors in the sunshine, with so many types of trees around and it seems each is a different color of reds, oranges, yellows, or browns. A sad event on the 18th, for the ancient Courthouse Elm tree must come down. From the lawn behind the building, its branches had given shade to the Jail and Fauquier National Bank, but now there are too many dead limbs due to Dutch Elm disease that is killing it. Because of the lovely mountains Sunday night, the 14th, there were miles and miles of backed up traffic, sightseers from Skyline Drive. Police Chief Jones said that from 2pm until 8:45pm there were 7,920 cars on Route 211 and another 2100 traveling north and south on Route 29. Before the month was over the threat of war was again in the news. President Kennedy had made a speech about the Soviets and their missiles in Cuba. Khrushchev did back down so things once again were quiet.

Banks and the ABC Stores were closed for election day. An unopened 10 pound keg of Eagle Gun Powder, dated July 12, 1857 was found Tuesday, November 6th, 1962 in rafters of the Brittle residence on Winchester Street. The history of the place goes back to Colonel John Walden, an officer in the War of 1812, the year he bought the property. The house was built in 1825, but sold in 1850. Colonel Mosby's wife and family are said to have lived there for a time during the Civil War, and another story is that it was his daughter and her two sons. She was Mrs. May Mosby Campbell, Postmistress in Warrenton at one time. But, getting back to the present, the west wall of the 140 year old brick house was being rebuilt when Inman Curtis, a workman, found the keg between the 3rd and 4th floor. It is thought from the date, that the powder was stowed during the Civil War.

December 4th, 1962, the Federal Reserve Bank of Richmond began a regular armored car delivery and pick up service at the Fauquier National Bank that replaces the Post Office handling the banks coin and paper money exchanges. The Christmas tree and lights on the Courthouse porch send their greeting message of joy and peace into the night. This year the tree is a living Norwegian Spruce that will be planted on the Fauquier Hospital grounds when the holiday season is over. Six inches of snow fell on Tuesday, the 25th, making a nice Christmas gift for beauty and for those with sleds. But, at midnight Christmas Eve, the streets needed cleaning, so it was a workday for those men.

1963

After the snowy and cold holidays, it is a little better by Thursday, January 3rd, 1963. However, one person was traveling the old fashion way. People smiled when they saw a donkey and cart stopped at one of the parking meters. A flu epidemic was in town February 7th. Friday night, February 15th, fox hunters met at the Courthouse to discuss scoring the hounds. March 14th during another snow storm a wreck occurred one mile south of town on Route 29. A truck load of chickens, ducks and eggs were dumped. It wasn't funny, but imagine all those broken eggs with chickens, ducks, and feathers flying around in the snow.

There was a jam of last minute buyers of Fauquier County tags Saturday morning, April 13th, 1963, at the County Office Building. They were lined up along the sidewalk as they waited for entrance into the building. On the buildings' lawn, the Luther Lee Allison Sunday School Class took advantage of the situation as they held a bake sale. So while some ate, some read, some talked, and some just looked bored, the class did alright.

The WVFD made headlines with their largest Parade yet on May 31st. Marchers gathered at 6:30pm and by move-off time at 7:00, people were lined up on Main and Waterloo Streets to see the more than 150 entries. The Carnival grossed $16,000 as it closed on the night of June 1st. Three Negroes have applied at Fauquier High School, which the Richmond School Board began to consider. The last day of school this year was June 8th.

Another car went into another building July 11th, 1963. A truck was making a delivery at Braun's Department Store on the corner of Main and So. 5th Streets, when the brakes failed. It rolled on down the hill and into a house on 5th Street. Warrenton's first "City Directory" was delivered the 18th. It is a reference work listing 3,561 adults 18 years of age and over, business places and so forth. Saturday, July 20th, there was an eclipse of the sun. The Chinese used to shoot off firecrackers, beat on drums and shout during an eclipse to drive away the dragon that was eating the heavenly body, be it sun or moon. Everyone has to reorganize their memories July 25th. The streets from 1st through 10th and the By-Pass from Falmouth to Alexandria Pike are being renamed. Numbers on all the streets will start at the corners, even including Court House Square will be different. In the downtown area, the streets from 1st through 6th have been reversed. That means

    6th Street is now 1st Street
    5th   "   " "   2nd   "
    4th   "   " "   3rd   "
    3rd   "   " "   4th   "
    2nd   "   " "   5th   "
    1st   "   " "   6th   "
    7th   "   " "   Ashby Street
    8th   "   " "   Marshall "
    9th   "   " "   Pelham "
    10th   "   " "   Chestnut "

The By-Pass from Falmouth intersection to Waterloo Street is to be called Shirley Avenue. From Waterloo to Route 17 it is to be known as Broadview and from Route 17 to Alexandria Pike intersection, it will be Lee Highway. Is all that clear? In a few years everyone will think if has always been like that.

    By August 1st, 1963, this had become the worse dry spell since 1929 and the corn crop is withering. The children are combining fun with work as the Red Cross gives water safety lessons. Finally, August 15th, a four hour rain gave some relief, but drought emergency carloads of corn arrived on the 22nd.

    Confused time begins Monday, September 2nd, 1963, Labor Day, as some parts of the state go off Daylight Savings Time. School began the next day with the new Fauquier High School opening on Waterloo Road. There was a new era in Fauquier hospitality on the 12th. The Welcome Wagon began to visit the newcomers. Marchers of the Committee for Non-Violent Action, a pacifist organization, came through town September 13th. They were demonstrating against the Cold War with Cuba by displaying placards and handing out leaflets.

    Although no curfew for a time to be off the streets was in effect Halloween night, the police reminded people that Halloween was over at midnight. Remember Francis Gary Powers, Pilot of the U-2 plane that was shot down in 1960 over Russia? It was announced on the 31st that he just married Mrs. Claudia Edwards Downey in Catlett. There is a sign on the Clerk's Office Lawn about the Bloodmobile at St. James' Parish House. A Sad, Sad Day! November 22nd, President John F. Kennedy was assassinated in Dallas, Texas. His Vice-President, Lyndon B. Johnson has taken over as President. The day of Kennedy's funeral people who went into Braun's Variety Store would ask Margaret Cornwell if they were closing for it. Mr. Newton, Manager, said they couldn't until they heard from New York. They did receive the word and closed, along with most of the other stores in town.

1964

Thursday, January 9th, 1964, there was a large gathering at the Courthouse, being the Sunday beer ban crowd for the Supervisor's meeting. By January 16th there was a two day storm that dropped 14 inches of snow with wind to make 6 foot drifts. One dead and three decaying trees have been removed by VEPCO at the request of Town officials to make way for electric lines. It was a strange sight to see a worker in a skylift sawing limbs from the Elm of the Clerk's Office corner at Culpeper Street. They may be cut down to aid in the new lighting system, but they are not going without a fight. Saws are being ruined by concrete in the trunks as well as nails and even a horseshoe where they were used as hitching posts. Someone said that more light and less trees would make the town look like Coney Island.

Mrs. Frances Carter Ritter, February 4th, 1964, appeared before the Town Council because of the trees. She presented the following petition bearing 145 signatures, "We the undersigned feel that the time is overdue when we must unite to prevent the ruthless sacrifice of our heritage for gain in the name of 'progress'. By every lawful means we are determined to preserve those vistiges that remain of the rich history and beauty with which our town has been blessed. We do not agree that all change constitutes progress, and we refuse to allow our town to contribute to the growing pattern of an ugly America. Our immediate aims will be, 1-replanting trees that have been ruthlessly destroyed, 2-preservation of historic buildings, 3-removal of billboards within the town limits". Tuesday, the 11th, there was another 12 inches of snow with blustery blizzardly winds. Even so, 103 people donated blood to the Bloodmobile at St. James'

Parish House after it was two hours late arriving. Many of our boys are now stationed in Vietnam, such as Private Joseph C. Hackett, who went this week.

By March 12th, 1964, Air Raid Shelters here at home, have been marked in cooperation with the Fauquier Office of Civil Defense. The public shelters from fallout are identified by signs with three yellow triangles on a black circle. Two places, as were before, are in the basements of the Fauquier National Bank and the Courthouse. The Virginia Electric & Power Company erected the lights Thursday, the 12th, also, on Main Street. The older lights gave only one-fifth as much as the new 20,000 lumen Mercury vapor lamps will give. A far cry from what there was during the days of the "Little Old Lamplighter". About this time each year it seems rabies begins and because of the rabid fox situation, there is again a $2.50 bounty on grey fox tails.

Another fear of this time of year is Polio, but there is hope that it will soon be no more. At noon, Sunday, April 5th, 1964, the County wide Polio Prevention Clinic began to give a dose of Sabin Oral Vaccine to 14,000 people. The Town Council is to try an experiment. April 7th Norman Ellis on behalf of eight merchants on Main Street requested the hooding of parking meters in this area for a period of four months and to permit two hour parking. You know Spring is here when people begin "redoing" the buildings. Gardiner's Drug Store is being remodeled so it will be lighter and brighter. Those days of lovely sled rides have to be paid now. April 11th was one of at least four Saturdays to make up the snow days, with the children attending school until 2pm.

Poppies were sold for Memorial Day Saturday, May 30th, 1964. The usual 11am service was held at the cemetery and the Colored Parade left at 3pm from the First Baptist Church to march to the cemetery for their service. President Johnson set forth his ideas of The Great Society during May, which will include a Civil Rights Act, a Voting Act, and many social changes for the nation. We wait and see how all this effects Warrenton.

The Firemen's Carnival began Thursday, June 4th, 1964, with the biggest parade yet on Friday night led by the U. S. Army Band from the Fire House, down Waterloo to the Carnival Grounds. Sunday, June 21st, at 3pm, Company K 17th Virginia Infantry Regiment, CSA, held a service at the Confederate Monument in the cemetery. They were reactivated for the Centennial years and performed a military memorial service for 24 of the original company who were buried in the Warrenton Cemetery. The phrase, "long hot summer", has been used a lot lately. This is the second summer in a row that drought has burnt the fields.

Art Instructor, Mrs. Louis Jaeger, coached her weekly classes on methods using advantageous locations about town. One place was, July 4th, 1964, as the students sat on the porch of the Warren Green. The Town Council July 7th, received a letter from the Secretary of Commerce, Luther Hodges, suggesting that the Town of Warrenton set up a Bi-Racial Committee as a means of solving future racial problems. The Council will consider the matter when and if the need for such a committee arises. It was on the 16th, that a group of people went before the Board of Supervisors to sponsor "Save The Old Jail" and to have the new one on Lee Street.

The Town Council gave permission to Town Manager, Edward Brower, July 23rd, to order final plans for rechanneling traffic through Court House Square that calls for a system of through lanes on Waterloo and Main Streets and a yield system for entering traffic from Winchester Street and Alexandria Pike. There would also be a left turn onto Alexandria Pike from Waterloo Street. The work would require the raising and lowering of grades and new sidewalk construction. (*See diagram, page 247.*)

August 13th at 332 Main Street, the old frame building that used to have a saddle shop fell to make way for the brick store of Silco Cut Rate Store. Parking meter replacements was discussed at the Town Council meeting October 6th. More activity lost from Town that will go to another location. The National Guard Armory was dedicated Tuesday afternoon, October 15th. Sometimes it feels that if this keeps up, The Square will be the only thing left in Town. October 29th, the leaf watchers were out.

Good weather Election Day, November 3rd, 1964, brought out the voters. For 13 hours there was a continuous waiting line of people at the Courthouse. President Lyndon Baines Johnson was elected with Hubert Humphrey as Vice-President. There are no "sky-hooks" in town for the Christmas lights. Trees were used to support lead wires for them, but there are no trees now. It is hoped that new lights can be had by next year. VEPCO helped this year, but it did take a lot of thinking as how to do it. By Saturday, the 28th, their servicemen and the firemen had the holiday lights up. Santa came that day, riding on a Fire Truck with bells ringing and siren wailing as the Jaycees hosted a program of cartoons at the Fauquier Theater. The admission was one toy to help with their Christmas gift program.

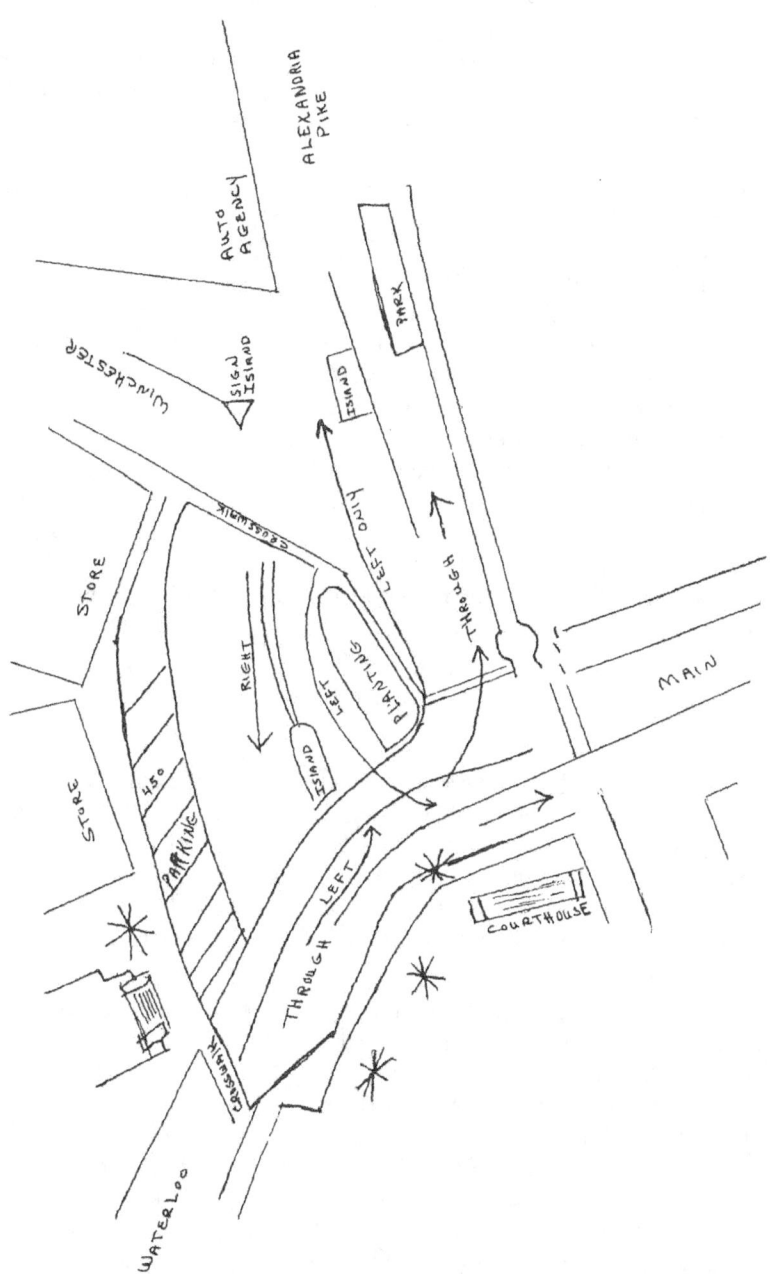

The Holiday Season began with a good start. Even Monday, December 1st, 1964, tried to get people in the mood with a light wet snow that later froze. They say the hornets have built their nests high off the ground this year and you know that means deep snow. The 13th, Robert E. Palmer bought The Saddle Shop at the corner of Court House Square and Winchester Street, from Miss Lee Hilts. Mrs. Robert McClanahan had been managing it as it was in one side of the Ostrow Building and Robert "Pooch" McClanahan's Photo Shop was on the other side, having moved there after Sears left, which was about 1962. One of the people at the Saddle Shop was Welton Hansbrough who is the 3rd generation to work with leather. His grandfather, John, had a harness shop or as it was called, Hansbrough's Tack Repair Shop on Culpeper Street. After he died in 1912, his son Josh continued until about 1943, when he was forced to give it up due to health reasons. Welton had a small shop at his home near Auburn, then went into service. Josh died in 1945, so when the war was over, Welton went to Washington in 1947. The McClanahan's asked Welton to teach them about the leather business. At first he came on his days off, then moved back again. Strange as it seems with it so dry, the rain fall for 1964 was about average. The Red Cross moved out of the Library Building during this year.[150]

1965

As the new year, 1965, came in, the "Save The Jail" work continued by the Fauquier Historical Foundation. Sunday, January 10th, the 10 inches of snow caused some accidents, but it wasn't over. A few days later three more inches fell on the unmelted previous snow. The Town Council determined, February 2nd, that there would be a two hour parking limit for Court House Square, Court and Hotel Streets.

The Firemen have been waiting for decent weather to take down the Christmas decorations, and after the snow, February 14th, were finally able to begin until by the 18th there was only one star remaining at Culpeper and Main Streets. On behalf of the Blue Ridge District Boy Scouts, Wayman Carter had an interesting display in his store window. Talk about Good Samaritans. Jimmy Kidwell noticed a mother shopping at his store with her 2½ year old. The child's eyes were quite bad, so Jimmy notified the Lions' Club who helped save his sight. Some of the highways are being put under a Federal System. Route 17 is now called US 17.

March roared its loudest Friday the 4th, 1965. There was flooding at one end of the County and snow at the other end, causing the schools to let out early. C&S Flowers had been located at 310 Main Street since 1949, which was where the Chinese Laundry used to be. March 11th, they moved across the street to reopen at 309. The 18th someone put a bag over a parking meter with the words, "15 min. sure isn't much time for nickles in the Town of Warrenton." Keeping the meters in a working condition is a continuous maintenance job, so some do get out of whack.

A Free Parking Trial began April 1st, 1965, and that was no April Fool when people saw the covered meters. The April skies have been filled with what seems to be millions of grackels that roost in the Cedars and Honeysuckle around the County. People do not like them for several reasons and make all sorts of noise—clapping hands or shooting, to try making them go away. So many birds flying at the same time, reminds one of how the Passenger Pigeon flying used to be. April 15th, the workers finished removing the heads from the parking meters in the business section of town for a 90 day trial of two-hour free parking. The officers of the Town are expanded now into all of the ground floor of the Warren Green Building's west wing. A model of an X-15A-Z stopped briefly in Warrenton Friday, April 16th, while the Air Force attendants found something to eat, and people flocked to see it. The gardens are blooming beautifully for the annual Open House Program on the 28th and 29th.

The Town planted 48 trees, May 13th, 1965, at a cost of $917.00. Among them were 12 flowering Crabapples and 6 Sugar maples for the cemetery. They will make it a pretty place in Spring and Fall. May 20th another plan was being considered to eliminate motorist confusion and occasional tie ups on Court House Square. The Marker at the center is to be removed and a stop sign put in. The other directions as shown in the diagram are to be painted. If this is successful, then the islands will be built.

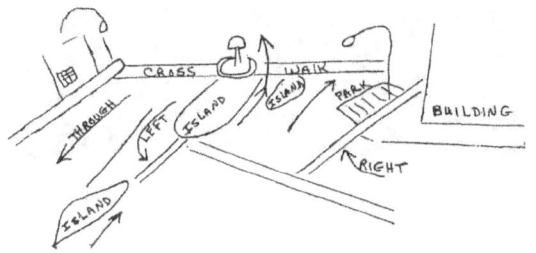

Sunday, May 30th, at 3pm, was the Memorial Day services in the cemetery.

The Firemen's Carnival began Thursday, June 10th, 1965, with the Parade on the 11th. The Fauquier Historical Foundation met June 28th at 8pm in the People's National Bank to discuss the preservation of the Jail as a County Museum. Robert Gardiner's Drug Store, being here since 1948, was sold to Donald Farnsworth. You know Charles Madison has been on Main Street a long time when he has cut hair of four generations. Young William S. "Billy" Stokes IV, of Upperville had that honor when he received his first haircut from the person everyone affectionately calls "Charlie".

Another familiar Fauquier face was lost, August 15th, 1965. Dick Mayhugh, 1929-1965. Although he weighed 800 pounds, he was a devoted and energetic worker in the sports of the County and will surely be missed by the young and old alike. Others are moving from The Square. August 25th, Gay Oldsmobile, Inc., Alexandria

COURT HOUSE
Circa 1965
(From the collection of John K. Gott)

Pike and Winchester Street, has bought seven acres of land from the Town along the By-Pass. And, next day, Graysons, who had been in their building more than 45 years, is planning a move to that enemy, the Shopping Center. After things cooled off the last of July, August had a HOT spell and a week of humid 90 degree temperatures.

Labor Day came September 6th, 1965. It was Wednesday the 22nd at 2pm when the BIG excitement came. People went running to see "The Elephant Hunt" on Moffett Avenue. A few years ago there was a lion walking around the Courthouse. Now an "elephant hunt". . . ! Sounds as if we are in the wilds of the African jungle. Von Bros. Circus gave a performance last night at the Firemen's Carnival Grounds on the By-Pass. While they were packing up today, 4½ ton Blanche and Dolly were staked out to await loading. But, the grass looked greener on the other side of the fence, so they pulled up stakes and wandered around the neighborhood for a while. Little Johnny Swain, who was playing in his yard, went into his house and when his mother asked him what he had been doing, he told her, "Hunting elephants." Finally she realized he was telling the truth. Not one, but two elephants were in their yard.

The first part of October, 1965, UFO's were seen again over the county. Their sightings began in the 1950's. Many have been seen during the years over the county, so maybe we are not alone. Sort of makes chills go up your spine. October 10th, another old timer died. Lee Madison was 82, and if you think Charlie had been a barber a long time, he's young in comparison. Lee Madison was barber to at least 5 generations of two Warrenton families.

Thomas Maddux's cellar door from October 25th, 1790, is the starting point for a survey report presented to the Fauquier Board of Supervisors Thursday the 14th. They want to determine if Court House Square is owned by the County after the Town banned parking in front of the Courthouse. Judge Snead felt The Square was County property and Warrenton officials couldn't regulate parking in that area. The survey presented by John Bartenstein shows that it is County property. An area of 1.1559 acres, including The Square and running east to the Peoples National Bank Building was all County. According to the survey, along the northern boundary the County property took in a portion of the present Grayson's Inc. Department Store. To find the cellar door, surveyors located the stakes of today's boundary and did an overlay with the original survey. Thus the area was determined. An inset at the place of the store building seems to make it safe. No action was taken by the Supervisors but they asked that it be presented to Judge Snead so he might decide what to do.

More excitement during October. Crowds were on hand Saturday and Sunday the 23rd and 24th, to see passenger trains come into Warrenton for the first time since June 14, 1941. The diesel-powered Special arrived at 12 noon EDT and returned to Washington at 2pm. It carried the Washington Chapter of National Historical Society taking its 14th annual Fall foliage trip. The Fauquier High School Band played as the train pulled into the station. Band Boosters served hot dogs, sandwiches, and drinks at the station. There was also time for the passengers to take a walking tour around Culpeper and Main Streets and naturally Court House Square. The Warrenton Fire Department put water in the train while it waited. Workers are working under lights at night in order to finish the addition to the Library before the cold weather sets in. The Lions' Club Halloween Parade Saturday, the 30th, formed at 6:30pm, leaving the Fire House and going to Benner Field. The Fire Truck led all the ghosts and goblins.

Wednesday, November 24th, 1965, gale force winds damaged a few trees and the weather made you know the Holiday Season was at hand. If it didn't, you knew it on Saturday, the 27th, at 10am. Santa Claus was welcomed to Warrenton with a Parade led by both Fauquier and William C. Taylor High School bands. His sleigh and reindeer were riding on a sparkling float, as it went from the Warrenton Primary School along Main Street to the Courthouse, where, Mayor Byrnal M. Haley gave him the keys to the Town. The float remained in front of the County Office Building until noon or so, and from it, Santa greeted children and their parents, or posed with the youngsters for photographs. He was swamped by young people when he pulled up at the Courthouse. During 1965 Martha Ellis opened The Knotty Pine Coffee Shop at 37 Main Street. Once again the old building that had the Coffee Shoppe for so long is in use. Someone said Martha Ellis' husband at sometime, had a small place across the street from her (near present Sweeney's) where he sold sandwiches and ice cream.

1966

Although 1965 was the dryest in 20 years, 1966 began with some dampness—Fog! Thursday afternoon, January 13th, a drizzle turned to ice, and 5 inches of snow January 22nd brought a little relief from the winter drought. Then—three storms gave enough snow to last all winter. The 23rd had 7 inches, the 26th and 27th had 8 inches and a blizzard on the 29th had 14 inches with 5 foot drifts. People had to be rescued by helicopter from farms and road sides. The new Jail on Lee Street is to be ready May 1st, costing over $365,000.

Although in March a 2% state wide sales tax went in, the Supervisors on April 21st, 1966, proposed a $3.8 million budget, which included a 1¢ local sales tax. Again the Garden Club Tour on the 27th and 28th, a Wednesday and Thursday, and the Warrenton Garden Club put red geraniums in the flower boxes at the Courthouse.

A week of soaking rain the first of May 1966, did help all things to come into its fullest. The old Grayson's opened May 5th at the Shopping Center as the Southern Department Store. What was once an unsightly old frame building at 61 Main Street has been attractively built from the ground up by its owner Mrs. Ford Anderson. Behind brick veneer walls, Thoroman's Radio & TV Service has more space than before, and apartments are above it. The roof line has been altered to conform with neighboring buildings and masonite replaces the old wood on the new building. The Furniture Interior in the Wallach Building at 40 Culpeper Street is redecorating, too. A crowd of over 100 people stopped traffic on Main Street at 10am Tuesday, May 31st for the opening of the Smith-Byrd-Robertson political campaign headquarters at #40 on the corner of Main and 2nd Streets.

Each year the Firemen's Parade gets bigger and bigger. The Carnival opened Thursday, June 2nd, 1966, with the parade beginning Friday night at 7pm. Besides the trophies that had filled a window at Carter's Store, others were also given. By August 18th, Lerners Bros. Inc. that has been in business here for 30 years, moved to their new location, the remodeled Grayson Building at 11 Main Street.

The first of September 1966, streams are going dry and the corn crop is half what it should be. This is the 5th successive summer of drought and is the worse yet. Mayor Haley asked the people again to save water. The Town Council on the 6th, discussed the severe water problem and also urged conservation. They had a request from the Hope School to be allowed to hang across Main Street advertising their Fair to be held at the Elementary School on Waterloo Street, formerly the High School, on October 1st. Another tree goes down.

This one in front of the Safeway on Main Street. Finally! an overnight downpour Tuesday, September 13th, which was a blessing, but not enough.

The new Jail was open to visitors October 20th, 1966. That's one way to be in jail, but not to be there. It is planned to move in the prisoners from the old one on November 7th. Remember the Sheriff and Town Police shared an office in the basement of the County Building, with an entrance from the Culpeper Street side. Then, the Town Police moved to the Fire House, but the Sheriff's Department continued on until the new building was built.[134] The Old Timer died October 24th. Miss Louise Evans, age 79, had written many articles giving her remembrances of the Town and of the many things that had happened in it. The annual Halloween Parade and Party sponsored by the Warrenton's Lions' Club, was Monday the 31st. The Fauquier High School band led off from the Fire House at 6:30pm, going to Benner Field, where all had hot dogs and marshmallows cooked over a bonfire.

Two thousand dollars worth of brand new illuminated Christmas decorations were put up November 19th, 1966 by the VEPCO linesmen. They replace the ones that were 15 years old. Saturday morning, November 26th, a crowd watched Santa come down Main Street with his dog sled on a float. He gave a bag of jelly beans to Mayor Haley at his official welcome.

People are asking, "Has a Blight come to Downtown Warrenton?" because there are about 14 empty stores. Gay Oldsmobile has temporarily been occupied by Charter Industries. But, the place may be dying a slow death since the Northern Virginia Shopping Center came to town. The rent is high and parking spaces are few, as well as the run-down places need sparkin' up. Is it getting so nothing is safe. Six out of state college students were arrested by the Warrenton police about 1:30am Friday, December 9th, 1966, after they took Christmas lights off the shrubbery on the lawn of the Clerk's Office Building. A resident in a parked car on Main Street saw the youths' actions and told the police, who caught them a short distance from the scene. As the holiday season passed this year, it seems that the stealing of Christmas lights was popular over all the states. Why would someone want to keep others from seeing something pretty? A slick, slushy snow, the first of the year, fell Tuesday, December 13th. The cover of snow on Christmas Eve made it a lovely day, even with sub-freezing cold. Saturday, the 31st, at 10am, there was a Children's Hour held in the lower room of the Library with film, stories and songs. A good way to end the year.

1967

A beautiful way to begin the New Year came Wednesday, January 4th, 1967, when a freezing rain covered everything. Then the sun came out to turn the trees into "glistening chandeliers" and sparkling diamonds. It has been determined that the population for Warrenton is almost 4,100. A semi-blizzard late Monday and Tuesday mornings, February 6th and 7th, gave 10 inches of snow with high winds. It's from one extreme to the other. Next, on the 16th, was a temperature of 76 degrees. The Fauquier Historical Foundation held open house at the old Jail on George Washington's Birthday from 11am to 8pm. The public was invited to view the Jail and exhibits of history since this is a future museum.

A new store in town to help the "dead" look. Ray McConchie opened Mack's Pastry Shop at 44 Main Street Wednesday, March 8th. That's where Nina's 5 and 10¢ Store was. A committee met at the Library Thursday, the 23rd to discuss a proposal to form a Chapter of the Virginia Museum of Fine Arts. They decided to have an organizational meeting next month.

Rates for the Taxi cabs were determined at 50¢ for the first mile; 30¢ for each additional mile; 25¢ for a waiting stop and waiting time is $3.00 an hour. Sixty interested people attended the new Virginia Museum organizational meeting on Sunday afternoon, April 23rd, at the Library. The last Saturday in each month, a Children's Hour is held at the Library. There may not be many stores in town, but the Library continues to have lots of use.

Hotel Street was a flutter with $20 bills during lunch hour Friday, the 19th. Clifton E. Penn went to the Fauquier National Bank for money, but when he returned home he was $90 less than when at the bank. Miss Barbara Bartenstein, who works for D. H. Lee & Co., found one twenty and took it to Mrs. Mary Matteo, secretary to Town Manager, Edward Brower. James Swain, bookkeeper of Warrenton Supply found two more and Mrs. Nancy Brady, a secretary in the Town office, found one. Then, Mrs. Matteo on her lunch hour picked up a $10 bill. She called the bank and learned who owned all the money. Needless to say Penn was greatly relieved. Thank Goodness there are still honest people around.

The Firemen's Carnival opened Thursday, June 1st, 1967, with the Parade on Friday at 7pm. Its 200 units included bands, fire and rescue equipment, majorettes, floats, and marchers as they went to the Carnival Grounds. June 6th the Town Council asked the To⁓

Manager and Chief of Police, Jones, to make a study of traffic conditions at the intersection of Winchester and Court House Square and recommendations of ways to increase safety. Tuesday, June 13th, was election day for the Town of Warrenton. Things might be looking up as Old Main Street takes on a sparkle. The formerly empty building owned by Mrs. Ford Anderson at 40 Main Street, on the corner of 2nd Street, has its exterior painted a mistletoe green, and the 22nd, Hutchison Travel Bureau moved into it. Years ago this was the jewelry store of L. T. Hout. Interesting sights on the streets as knees are showing due to skirts getting shorter and shorter.

What is all that talk on July 20th, 1967? The Supervisors have a plan to add a two story wing on the Courthouse? They will move the Mosby Monument a few feet? Well, they are to get the public reaction later, so we'll see. It was announced July 27th that the Fauquier National Bank had bought the business block with the Hiden and Ostrow Buildings which have been vacant for some time, and the three houses on the left side of Winchester to Diagonal Streets, an area of 50,000 square feet. Dr. Hiden bought the Bishop house in 1945, but he sold it to J. W. Rhodes and Mrs. Rhodes sold to the Bank. At one time it had been owned by Dr. Frank C. Hodgkin, who also owned the adjoining property where he built his home after "the fire". That house was bought by Dr. Thornton, whose widow, Pearl Thornton Smith lived on the ground floor and rented the upstairs. She sold to the Raymond McClanahans, and they also rented out the house. The one on the corner of Winchester and Diagonal is believed to have been built by the late William C. Marshall, a direct descendant from John Marshall and was owned by D. M. Warren. Rachel Mills and family was one of the occupants of the Marshall house. It had been rebuilt after "the fire" as were all the others. But in this house they had reused some of the old lumber that had not burned too much, so it was not as nice as it originally was. Although there were three fireplaces, a coal furnace was used for heating. The Mills children loved the place, but they didn't have to clean out the coal dust. Also a five acre tract on Alexandria Pike was given to Fauquier County Community Action Committee for development as a playground.

At the Town Council meeting August 1st, 1967, in reply to the June 6th request, it was recommended that Diagonal Street have parking on the west side only and a warning sign to be placed on Alexandria Pike east of the Winchester Street intersection. The addition to the Courthouse was very much opposed at the August 10th meeting. People felt that the present Courthouse is the kind of building which cannot be added to without destroying its beauty, its balanced appearance or detracting from its dignity, as well as cutting off the view of the Jail. It was suggested that the Court be moved to the Warren Green Building. "Gardiners' Store" has a new owner, the first time in 90 years. Mrs. Florence G. Kinski bought the building from Mrs. Richard Kinski, daughter of Charles Jeffries. Plans are to remodel the second floor for offices and renovate the third floor apartment. Another meeting for the Courthouse hearing August 17th, with people jammed into the Courtroom. At the close of the meeting, the Supervisors said they would make a decision later. Dr. Hiden at the age of 81 died Thursday, September 21st. He will be missed, for he had been around a long time. . . and delivered many babies.

Another bright spot in the Main Street Blight October 19th. Furniture Interiors, established by Shirley Groome, 1962, has moved from Culpeper Street into the empty building at 52 Main Street across from the Post Office where Lerners' used to be. People are discussing the action in Vietnam. Some wonder why we are there, and if it is worth it. The usual Halloween Parade, led by the Fauquier High School Band, left the Fire House at 6:30 the night of the 31st. Every shrieking ghoulie seemed at their very best.

November 7th, 1967, there was a proposal before the Town Council for the elimination of outdoor privies and frost-proof toilets which had been prepared in conjunction with the Health Department. This proposal followed a field survey by the Health Department of existing toilet facilities and the preparation of the necessary ordinances to require the removal of these privies and toilets and the installation of indoor toilet facilities and water service in all dwellings within the town. A boundary survey by R. M. Bartenstein and Associates dated November 14, 1967 shows the old curb, represented by the solid line, at Court House Square, and the new curb, represented by the dotted line. Near the Library is a mark resembling a partial square, ⌐ . Probably that was the Cistern. The Christmas lights went up November 22nd, the day before Thanksgiving. By the 28th, the Charters Industries had moved into their own plant leaving the Gay Oldsmobile building empty again.

In December 1967, the Town Council met in the Council Chambers of the Warren Green Building. The Rotarians set the tall Cedar up on the Courthouse porch, Friday, December 15th.

Christmas is a time to believe in something other than self. Sometime during this year, Montgomery Ward Catalogue Sales Agency opened at 20 Main Street, corner of Culpeper and Main Streets. The Presbyterian Church was enlarged by having an addition to its west side.

1968

The VEPCO linesmen took down the Christmas decorations January 7th, 1968, the day after Christmas on the old Julian calendar, which is the 12th day of Christmas on the Western calendar. Tuesday, the 9th, was the 13th recorded snow of the season. There is ice under it, making walking hard, but good for sleding. The children haven't had school since December 20th.

There seems to be a problem in town with one of its famous treasures. The portrait of Gov. Francis Fauquier, given to the County in 1924 and hanging in the Courthouse is not Francis Fauquier, but probably William Fauquier. According to a Williamsburg scholar on February 2nd, 1968, Francis was not in the Army and the person protrayed is wearing a uniform.

Some people will steal anything. By March 7th, 1968, 35 dogs have been reported stolen in the last two weeks, some taken from their own yard. One person said she looked out the window and someone was putting her dog in a strange car that was parked IN her driveway. The big thermometer showing the growth from gifts to the Fauquier Hospital Building Fund was placed on the lawn of the County Building the 28th.

Stores were closed Tuesday, April 9th, 1968, some all day and some from 10:00 to noon, in observance of the funeral of Rev. Dr. Martin Luther King, Jr. Schools and other buildings flew flags at half-staff through Tuesday. The visitors during Historical Garden Week, April 24th-25th, are in for a pleasant surprise. There will be an exhibit of silver, porcelain and pewter in the old Jail. The U. S. Government wants the home basements for the War Shelters to be inspected since they have been in service over the past five years. A dog tattoo service has been offered to help combat the dog-napping.

People with Gold Cup signs are walking the streets to advertise its running Saturday, May 4th, 1968. At 3pm Thursday, May 30th, the Colored community's Memorial Day procession left the First Baptist Church to march to the cemetery where they held services at 4:00. The month closed with merriment as the opening of the Firemen's Carnival was Thursday also. The next night was the big Parade. 150 brilliantly costumed Kena Temple Shriners from Alexandria were in the parade led by the 75th Army Band from Ft. Belvoir and a 32 man Color Guard from Vint Hill Station. The cool clear nights gave a good turnout and they grossed $21,777.

Sunday afternoon, June 2nd, 1968, the other Memorial Day service was held at 3:00 in the cemetery. Monday night, the 3rd, a mass meeting of the Fauquier Democratic Committee planned to meet at the Peoples National Bank. However, so many attended, they had to move inside the Courthouse to the Courtroom. Another black day with another assassination. This time it was Robert Kennedy.

Something unusual. It seems, on July 4th, 1968, that some Canadian geese are spending the summer on several ponds in the county. July 11th, the Sunday beer and wine ban was lifted. Pretty fireworks opened the Lions' Club Carnival Friday night, August 9th, at the Firemen's Carnival Grounds. The display and noise was enjoyed by people "uptown", too.

As if to confirm the postal patron's frequent suspicion that conditions are upside-down in the Post Office Department, even Old Glory flew that way in Warrenton early Thursday, September 3rd, 1968. Maybe it was just the aftermath of a hectic Labor Day weekend that caused it, but it was quickly corrected. Some improvements are being made on the Courthouse, with the renewal of the exterior masonry. Also the Warren Green is to be rewired. Every little bit makes one think the Old Town will eventually come around.

In November 1968 Richard M. Nixon was elected President over Hubert Humphrey. The first snow fell early Sunday, November 10th, with 4 inches. Two days later, Tuesday, was a heavy wet snow that fell on many trees still with leaves. Then winds knocked out the electric power and phones, which wasn't restored for four days. Many people thought it was an outrage to take so long. Two events to take place that will greatly affect the whole county. On the 21st, a VISTA team planned an attempt to improve housing, especially sanitation condition of baths and toilets, and the public schools are to undergo a total reorganization during the next year.

Christmas comes. After a foggy morning Monday, December 2nd, 1968, the decorations were put up along the streets by VEPCO linesmen. A few days later, a 22 foot evergreen went up at the Courthouse. During 1968, the Stable Door, at the corner of Main and Alexandria Pike was sold by Robert Palmer to Tim Nevill. This year McClanahan's Photo Shop moved out of the Ostrow Building since the Fauquier National Bank has bought it. The A&A Market on Main Street was sold by Alex Allison to Wayman Carter & Co., owner of H. B. Carter & Co. A Mr. Johnson from Gainesville has a grocery there now.[154] This was a year of unrest and many people were taking things into their own hands to cause changes. Thus, there were many protests throughout the Country. But, it was an exciting time December 21st-27th, when Apollo 8 orbited the moon and on Christmas Day, they had a large audience as they read passages from Genesis.

1969

One of the things causing some of the unrest in the Nation is the marijuana threat and it is coming to Warrenton. January 2nd, 1969, came in with a flu epidemic so the hospital had to forbid visitors. With the cold weather, ice skating is enjoyed on the ponds by young and not so young people.

The Boy Scouts, members of Troop 161, celebrated their 59th birthday by camping out in front of the Clerk's Office Building Friday night, February 7th, 1969. There were 8 or so tents set up, flags and a large scout symbol. They left on Saturday in time to escape the snow storm that day. The works of local artist were displayed in the Peoples National Bank and Carter's show window for the benefit of the Heart Fund Drive.

The question was raised a year or so ago as to the use of sidewalks for displays of flowers and vegetable plants. March 4th, 1969, the Town Council recommended the stores be permitted to use the public sidewalk for a distance of 18 inches from the building line for the display of seasonal flowers and vegetable plants and ornamental shrubbery. Dwight D. Eisenhower, who had been a well-liked President, died March 28th.

Daylight Saving Time began Sunday, April 20th, 1969 at 12:01am. Remember—Spring Ahead, Fall Back! A proposal was made to the Town Council May 6th to relocate Winchester Street to connect elsewhere with Alexandria Pike. A little excitement Tuesday, May 27th when the engine of a Warrenton Yellow Cab caught fire at the corner of Ashby and Waterloo Streets. The driver, James Nelson Payne, leaped out in time to escape injury. Although the Fire Truck arrived and tried to save the car, it was destroyed.

Banks and the ABC Store closed Friday, May 30th for Memorial Day. There were the usual two ceremonies, the first at 11am at the cemetery and the second at 3pm when the Parade left Mt. Zion Baptist Church going to the cemetery with cars, floats, the Sunday Schools, the Scouts and Cub Scouts led by the Taylor High School Band. Many people are complaining about the number, noise, and dirt of the Starlings, saying they must be controlled someway.

The Firemen's Carnival and Parade was June 5th-7th, 1969. After the discovery made in January 1968, the Honorable Francis Fauquier, Lieutenant Governor of Virginia 1758-1768 came Thursday, June 12th to the County to stay. A copy of the original that is in London was given to the Board of Supervisors by The Fauquier Democrat in order to correct the 45 year old error. On July 20th, the U.·S. landed their first men on the moon. "A small step for man and a giant step for mankind", Neil Armstrong said, as they stepped from the spaceship to the moon's surface.

As school began this year, integration in the County was completed. September 11th, 1969, the Fauquier National Bank presented plans for their new Court House Square Bank. Their parking lot would be between Winchester and Diagonal Streets. September 18th, the Courthouse was saved and is to be refurbished. Only it will cost $17,775 to do it, AND, the original cost of the building was $10,000. How's that for the rise in prices? It is to be stripped of the old stucco and wire reinforcing installed. Then, three coats of stucco put on with three coats of paint on it and two coats of paint on the woodwork and steeple. Anti-pigeon devises will be installed, too. A crane is rented to help with the work at $170 a day. The Jail is also being done with replacement of chimneys and gable ends and repair to roof, walls and cornices at a cost of $2778.

The Warrenton Library Board Voted October 2nd, 1969 to turn over all Library properties free of all debts to Fauquier County and the Town of Warrenton to operate. The name was changed to Fauquier County Public Library to be supported by tax dollars as well as private contributions. Sunday, the 26th, at 12:01am, the time was turned back, making you realize winter is close.

The Jaycee's Christmas Toy Workshop opened November 6th, 1969 in the basement of the County Office Building. Shortly before 9pm Friday, November 14th, relaxing after dinner, Fauquier residents were rudely awaken when two very loud noises were heard. They were sonic booms from an airplane going overhead. The Rotary Club put up a 22 foot tree on the Courthouse porch as plans continued for the building of the new Courthouse by tearing down the 1928 wing of the Warren Green Building for it. The wind turned the Christmas Day snow into a disaster and by Friday morning the 26th, there were 12 foot drifts. And so goes The Age of Aquarius as the 1960's were called, which was celebrated with buttons, bumper stickers, T-shirts and in song.

1970

January 8th, 1970, the Gemini 7, being carried on a truck, stopped on its way to the Smithsonian Institute from the National Space Agency Headquarters in Houston. In this machine Frank Borman and Jim Lovell, Jr. had the longest space flight to date with 206 revolutions of the earth in 14 days, during December 1965.

Fifteen Boy Scouts of Troop 161 again this year bivouacked amid campfires for two nights, Friday and Saturday, February 6th and 7th, 1970, on the lawn of the County Office Building. The Demonstration Camp was to promote their Fund Drive. The balmy Saturday turned into a bit of wet snow on Sunday night, but by then the boys were warm in their own beds.

The Postman, Robert Fox, has quite a following these March days, as he walks the streets of Town. In 1968 a gang on Moffett Avenue attacked him when he tried to deliver the mail. Then, Robert hit on the idea of food and he began to throw a biscuit to the culprits. Now, he's followed by his admirers, especially the leader of the pack, a Collie named Fluffy. The Courthouse steps and area around the building was the background for poses by Valerie Edwards as she had pictures taken to show her modeling ability. (She went off to New York shortly after this to become a fashion model.) March 26th, 1970, the police began to crack down on the parking violators along Main Street. There are lots of overtime and double parking, especially with loading and unloading. Late in March, Comet Bennett began to appear in the northeast direction during the predawn until the middle of April and then it will grow fainter and disappear to where comets go.

The census was taken during April 1970 that showed the population for Fauquier County was 26,375. It had been 24,066 in 1960. As the Gold Cup Race goes on, people are talking about the Stock Market being the lowest since President's Kennedy's assassination in 1963. Something a little different this year for Memorial

Day. The ceremony honoring all the Fauquier Dead was held at the Flag Pole in the cemetery at 10:30 Saturday, May 30th. After the Legion program, the Sunday Schools of the Mt. Zion and First Baptist Churches and others who wished, moved to the lower cemetery for their annual program.

The Firemen's Carnival began Thursday, June 4th, 1970, and as usual, the Friday night parade began at 7:00, going to the grounds behind the Warrenton Elementary School. The first elevator in Warrenton was installed June 25th, at Bain and Trundle's Office Building #9 Culpeper Street, which is the old Masonic Building. Once used to the noise of airplanes overhead you know someone mortal is looking down upon you. Now, you may hear a little whish, whish. Sometimes there may be nothing seen, but then again, you look up to see a pretty colored hot air balloon floating along—and someone is staring down at you.

The oldest Pony Show of America opened their 51st edition on Saturday, July 4th. By the 16th, four separate storms brought a record rainfall in the county. And, a couple of years ago, we were praying for rain. The demolition of the vacant G. A. Vose Grocery Store Building at 26 Main Street began Tuesday night, August 11th, 1970, when a 23 year old soldier drove into the building as he was making a U-turn at 11:45 pm. His 1966 Mercury had $1100 damage and the building had $500, with the police and firemen being called. A 'No Parking' sign was destroyed and a town trash can valued at $54.50. Ian Montgomery, who had a purchase bid on the property, saved a bit as the sign in the window said, "Bids wanted for demolition and removal of building."

The Town Manager reported to the Council, September 1st, 1970, that the proposed improvements in Court House Square had been presented to the County Planning Commission, and to the Board of Supervisors. On the recommendations of the Planning Commission it had been approved by the Board of Supervisors, with the stipulation that the Square be renamed "Mosby Square", and that Mrs. Pauline Blackwell be contracted before the statue of Col. Mosby is relocated. The Town Manager requested authorization to proceed with the preliminary studies and engineering and estimates on a storm sewer in Diagonal Street, curb and gutter and sidewalk on Winchester Street adjacent to the new Fauquier National Bank and a general estimate on the Mosby Square project. The plans for the proposed plaza of Court House Square, or Mosby Square, would be an area of walk ways, trees, benches, and the Monument moved to the west side of the present Square. As of the 1st, too, Warrenton has its own Municipal Court, being held in the downstairs Courtroom. The 81 year old Warrenton Horse Show was Labor Day, September 7th. It was after that date that the Library's first bookmobile went into service. Luther Cox was named Sheriff when Sam Hall retired on the 17th.

At 12:01am, Sunday, October 25th, 1970, that old clock was turned back, so everyone had an extra hour of sleep. There was Trick or Treating for UNICEF from 3-5pm on Friday, October 30th and Saturday morning from 10-12. Also on Friday, the Warrenton Lions' Club Parade began at 6:30pm led by the Fauquier High School Band from the Fire House to the Carnival Grounds for the bonfire and spoooooky scene.

The Supervisors bought the Wallach Building, November 9th, 1970 for $45,000 as part of the site for the new County Building and Circuit Courthouse. The three story Methodist Church Building, used by Federal troops as a hospital, was sold in 1919 to Paul C. Richards who, with Mason McCarty, operated an auto sales agency and car rental; then, sold in 1928 to Richard Wallach who remodeled it into shops on the street level and apartments above.[142] Amy Brown was one who lived there. She would hear strange noises, which could have been the creaking of old boards, but the one noise in particular that sounded as though someone was walking down the hallway was real enough—and they stopped at the bathroom door.

The Town Council December 1st, 1970, saw the estimate prepared by Meade Palmer Landscape Architect for the development of Mosby Square, which would cost $22,931.93. Approximately one-third of the work included in that cost, would be required for the replacement of sidewalk and curbs whether The Square is developed or not. This proposed development would improve the traffic control problem. It was suggested that the idea time to transfer the Monument would be as the new Bank building was built. (*See diagram on page 265 — not to scale.*)

December 10th, the Town Council voted for The Square. It would occupy a dozen parking places in front of the Bank site and will extend in what is now the street. This is suppose to afford better visibility down Alexandria Pike from Winchester Street. People are still asking who is going to pay for it. At least one tree in Town was saved. The old Walnut tree will stay at the Warren Green Building. It had been marked to go to the sawmill last week but someone at the Supervisors' meeting yanked it back. For the

PROPOSED DEVELOPMENT OF MOSBY SQUARE

last time the Jaycees' Workshop is held in the Warren Green wing that will be torn down for the new Courthouse. They took the children shopping on their annual outing to S. H. Kress & Co., 160 Main Street, with $10 to spend. Remember when they only had a dollar? They went to Gay Oldsmobile-Buick for help in wrapping their purchases as they were served ice cream and cookies. During this year C. H. Braun sold to S. H. Kress. Margaret Cornwell continued to work here, as she jokingly told people she had been "sold" and this was her third owner. What a New Year's Eve! Thirteen inches of snow put a stop to some of the parties to see in the New Year.

1971

The rain of January 4th and 5th, 1971 caused some of the New Year Eve's snow to melt down to about six inches. The soft fog made the Christmas lights glow. A permit was approved January 14th, for The Flying Circus, composed of World War I planes and a museum to see them, being located at Bealton. That means more people coming to town and old airplanes flying overhead. At least you can hear them and you don't feel as though you are being spied upon. Tuesday, the 19th, had 200 people jammed into the Warren Green for Warrenton's Master Plan Hearing. It seems the Mosby Square plan is injurious to old ancestral residents and would cause traffic congestion, especially since there is already a lack of parking spaces. High winds on January 26th, blew down some signs.

Twice weekly, Tuesday and Friday, Robert Franey climbs three sets of stairs above the Courtroom, that become narrower, darker and colder towards the top. At the top is the heart of the Clock with the words stamped on the frame—E. Howard & Co., Boston, Mass. Above that, a ladder leads to a trap door and in the rounded garret is the bell which tolls the hours. The words— McShane Bell Foundry, Baltimore, Md. 1889—are on it. The bell is said to have originally hung in a church in Philadelphia and was bought for $500. Cold weather doesn't agree with it but the Town of Warrenton coddles the aged hand-wound Clock. One frosty morning recently, three trips were made up the steps before the Clock continued to run. February 18th noise of the Wallach Building being knocked down could be heard.[24]

The Town Council was requested March 2nd, 1971, by the Virginia Historic Landmarks Commission to make a survey and study of "Old Town" buildings and points of interest in Town. Heard it said Downtown Warrenton is really uptown because from any point, one has to drive up to get to it. March 25th, they now say the Warren Green Walnut tree must fall for the new Courthouse and a wider street, probably not living to see Autumn and have pretty yellow leaves again. It may not be as old as previously thought for it could have been planted about the time the rear wing of the Warren Green was built, 1926-28, and the tree may have been 5 or 6 years old at that time. March 31st, right on Main Street in the daylight, two youths assaulted and attempted robbery of an employee of the Shade Shop as he walked along the street. Martha Ellis of the Knotty Pine Coffee Shop on Main Street was witness to the attack. Speaking of Martha, she is an artist and displays her pretty paintings in the windows of the shop.

Thursday night, April 22nd, 1971, fifteen young EARTH People lit candles at the Courthouse. They want Fauquier County a cleaner and more beautiful place to live. At a reading of a pessimistic view of present day ecology, all candles were extinguished except two. Again the candles were lighted as another member presented an optimistic view. Other parts of the program included a recitation of EARTH's beliefs, pledge and clean up projects, ending with the singing of "America, The Beautiful". EARTH Week is April 19-25th. Two women trying to obtain money from mostly elderly persons, were pulling the old "Flim Flam" on Main Street Friday afternoon, April 24th. The Garden Club planted the geraniums, the 29th, in the boxes at the Courthouse to go along with Garden Week.

Monday, May 3rd, 1971, was election day for the town. The Supervisors authorized the topping of the lofty Elm on the Culpeper side of the Warren Green Building. The 40 foot Elm is higher than anything else on the skyline now, with no barrier to protect it from wind as it stands on terraced ground. But, when the top was removed, May 6th, it was discovered that the tree had Dutch elm disease. The Post Office Department announced that Sunday, May 21st, the 6¢ stamp would be raised to 8¢. The old Town Cistern uncovered by workmen at the new Bank was found to still have water in it, being supplied by a downfall from the Courthouse roof. The Cistern was 20 feet wide and 25 feet deep. Although many people had obtained household water and horses drank from the trough beside it, no one can remember exactly when it was closed up. It had stone, concrete pieces and all sorts of things put in this time to fill it in. May 27th came the announcement that the Mosby Monument was to stay where it is, due to unexpectedly high costs and a certain amount of "resistance". The Plaza plans has now changed to having grass, walkways, two or three trees, Colonial-style lamps and some benches. Aggregate concrete would be used on some walkways for a different design. An article in the Washington Post's Potomac magazine designated the Warrenton-Culpeper area as one of seven best places to live in the U. S. and is just about the only place with really clean water, clean air, noise-free community east of the Ozarks. Will it stay that way?

On June 1st, 1971, The Warrenton Improvement League protested to the Town Council regarding the removal of trees from Winchester and Diagonal Streets adjacent to the new Fauquier Bank parking lot. The Council advised that the widing of Diagonal Street and the installation of entrances to the parking lot necessitates the removal of the trees. They have also become weakened by being run into by cars and could fall, especially in a storm. The Bank has plans for landscaping their site which will include the planting of trees on Winchester Street at the rear of the new sidewalk. Plans were made for curb and gutter extension for approximately 250 feet on Waterloo Street from the Library to Diagonal Street. This section of Waterloo had recently been excavated during installation of new gas lines. Thursday, June 3rd, began the three day Carnival Time. At 7pm Friday the Kena Temple participants were the highlight of the Parade. One Sweet Gum and two Pin Oaks were planted June 10th as part of the creation of the Plaza on the north side of Court House Square. Two men broke into a couple places on Shirley Avenue and made the mistake of walking along Main Street. There, they were recognized and arrested.

July 1st, 1971, Mark Hailey of the Shoe Center, 67 Main Street, took his first vacation in 14 years. On the 6th, the proposed comprehensive plan for the town was viewed. It was felt that the Historical District of Warrenton must be established and that new zoning ordinances give consideration to the special character and uniqueness of Warrenton. Each Thursday, beginning July 22nd through August 12th, the 18 year olds may register in the basement of the Courthouse so they can vote. Moving day begins Friday the 23rd, at 7am for the Fauquier National Bank from Hotel and Court Streets to their new building on Court House Square as Monday, July 26th, at 9am, they open for business.

The Grand Opening of The Fauquier National Bank was August

5th, 1971, with the sun shining and the band playing. People had a good time visiting the Bank or milling around the grounds while workmen continued laying brick and concrete or watering the newly placed sod. Rachel Mills felt the small park with benches was what the town needed for people to rest, especially when Court recesses and those attending want a breath of fresh air. Now there is some place besides the Courthouse steps to sit. She suggests there also be "handicap benches" or some place the elderly could sit and rest while they wait for those they are with to finish their shopping. Sometimes when walking, one likes to sit and relax a while or be able to meet friends and talk.

September 2nd, 1971, part of a wall at the train station collapsed and the rest of it had to be demolished. The Town Council was told on the 7th, that Airport Markings, Inc. of Alexandria, Va. were presently painting the pavement markings on the By-Pass and would complete the markings in The Square. The Jail Museum opened Saturday, October 2nd and will be open to the public through the month of October.

November 11th, 1971, G. A. Vose Grocery, 28 Main Street, is really coming down. After being there 65 years Vose died in 1969 and the store closed. Linwood Embrey now owns the building which will become a dress shop. The building had outside blinds which opened across the windows and folded up into niches on either side. He plans to incorporate them in his new building. Thanksgiving Eve brought several inches of snow north of town but the closer it came here, the less fell. Warrenton's sprinkle disappeared Thanksgiving Day and south Fauquier had no snow. The Bi-Centennial Group is planning to restore the Old Jail and "Hanging Yard" in time for the big celebration.

1972

January 4th, 1972, the Town Manager was authorized to buy from the Fauquier National Bank, a tract of land containing 1,412 square feet for the purpose of widing Diagonal Street. $2,118.00 was paid for the land. The old Walnut tree at the corner of Lee and Culpeper Streets was bulldozed down, lasting longer than thought. Gardiner's Drug Store, 15 Main Street, had their front glass door smashed Friday morning, the 14th, but a man who lived in an apartment above heard the noise. However, $35 was stolen.

The two hour parking on Court and Hotel Streets was reduced by the Town Council February 1st, 1972, to one hour as was the west side of Ashby Street. Beginning late Friday, the 18th, a gale came after a freezing rain and snow to maroon thousands without heat, and snow again Sunday. The lines were still being cleared on Tuesday. Newly established Risdon Home & Garden Center, Inc., a reorganization of Risdon Paint & Hardware, purchased the Knotty Pine Coffee Shop at 37 Main. Martha Ellis had been there seven years. This will be the first time in over 75 years the building has not been a bakery or restaurant. Willis Risdon retired from the Air Force in 1971. Carroll's old place of 1938, across the street, is now Department of Agriculture.

March 7th, 1972, the Town Council was requested by the Fauquier High School Chapter of Future Homemakers of America to put a banner across Main Street. March 19-25th is the week designated "Future Homemakers Week". It was decided non-controversial banners are alright. They also OK'ed the new County Courthouse which is already under construction. Robert Fox and Fluffy are still making their round of 12 miles a day. For four years Fluffy has arrived at the Post Office at 7am and goes home at 5pm.

A woman with "Peace Pilgrim" on her sweater came through town April 6th, 1972. She began walking 34 years ago from Los Angeles and has covered 25,000 miles in her mission. At times the "old fashion way" is the best way to do things. It was necessary to find an underground sewerage pipe at 2nd and Main Streets. Not knowing exactly where it was and not wanting to dig up the whole street, Waterwitch, Bob Farkas, was called in. With a divining rod made of two L-shaped copper wires he found the pipe without any trouble.

May 4th, 1972, Howard Sweeney bought the 2-part building at 32-34 Main Street, which once was Anderson & Allison and is now Johnson's Food Store, but has had many businesses in it. A circus was at the Firemen's Carnival Grounds May 7th. Memories of By Gone Days came May 25th, when a member of one of the Mennonite families from Catlett came to town in a horse and buggy. The clop, clop, clop, slap of leather and jingle of the harness sounds were nice to hear again.

The Firemen opened their three nights of Carnival fun Thursday, June 1st, 1972, with a good parade Friday night. They grossed the most yet—$30,000. Wednesday, June 21st, Tropical Storm Agnes became the worse natural disaster to hit Fauquier County in

30 years. Churches, businesses and residences opened their doors to hundreds who were stranded by high water that closed the roads that night. The Fire Company was open to serve coffee. One family in a trailer set up their camp in the parking lot by the Bank of Warrenton at the Northern Virginia Shopping Center. By noon Friday, all power had been restored.

The Town Council July 11th, 1972, approved the relocation of the fire hydrant and the replacement of the sidewalk on Main Street adjacent to the County Office Building. Seventeen year old Jill Mansfield had lots of stares Monday morning, July 10th. She was helping her father direct traffic at 28 Main Street during the new construction on the site of the Vose Building, as a summer job. Guess that is Women's Lib. The smog was bad July 12th. Hope it isn't here to stay.

August 13th, 1972, Mayor Haley and Town Manager Ed Brower attended the opening of the Warrenton Wholesale House at 60 Alexandria Pike. School opened Monday, August 28th. Even with new stores going in, people are still asking if Main Street is in a "state of demise". Gardiner's Drugs was renamed Fauquier Pharmacy that day, too, after being bought from Donald Farnsworth by Jerry Wood. He is remodeling for a Colonial look giving it a coat of Williamsburg green paint, a new door with coachman's lights on each side and a Colonial sign. The building is owned by Joseph Kinski of Washington.

The former single family two story brick residence at 19 Winchester Street began to be refurbished in February. Mr. and Mrs. Walter Arrington have owned it since 1947 and it has been rented. Walter's Dad and an aunt had bought the two houses Dorans rebuilt after the 1909 fire. The Dorans were living in Chicago so rented the houses. The Arringtons inherited the house next to Gay Oldsmobile (now Library) from an aunt and Walter's two brothers, the other house next door through the father. This brick house is called the "Double House". Now, September 7th, 1972, the old porch, that extended to the sidewalk, has been pulled off, a new roof and guttering put on, central air conditioner put in, a new bath added, and carpeting put down. Arabelle Arrington drove around Georgetown looking at homes to find a color she wanted. The house is painted yellow as the Georgetown houses are with green shutters. The new office building will have four tenants. The 14th, the streets have their marker lines brightened up with thermo-plastic paint that has glass reflector beads sprinkled on top. Next time you look at them, you'll see they are not plain old paint. It seems the destruction of living beauty to make way for brick and concrete has become a way of life in the United States. The 100 foot diseased Elm on the Culpeper side of the new Courthouse site finally came down September 28th.

The Main Thing opened Monday, October 9th, 1972, under the direction of Gina Farrar and Josine Hitchcock. October 12th, after 42 years as the Standard Oil Station at Waterloo and Ashby Streets, it is now a Texaco Station with Barnett Roberts as manager. Monday, the 23rd, will be Veterans Day, which replaces the former Armistice Day observance of November 11th. The wooly bear or orange and black catepillars are marching back and forth across the roads. Some weather prophets believe it is a true sign of winter. The width of rust colored band or black determines the severity and the earlier they are seen, the rougher the winter will be. 300,000 starlings roosting at night between Opal and Remington is a serious problem, but it does seem the proposed step to put out poison bait for them is not too good. Wouldn't the song birds also eat it, is the question asked. The Audubon Society is alarmed about it, and say starlings are necessary because they eat the Japanese beetle grub. Sail planes from Warrenton Air Park make interesting sights in the air. Another reason to be careful of who's watching from above. Children from the Jack & Jill Child Care Center and Tiny Tots Kindergarten paraded the streets in Halloween costumes Tuesday, the 31st.

Main Street was being brightened up for the holidays. November 2nd, 1972 H. B. Carter & Co. and other stores were getting a coat of paint. President Nixon was re-elected this year, beating out McGovern. The Town Council, November 7th, said the replacement of sidewalks, curbs, and street improvements on Ashby and Hotel Streets were part of the Courthouse improvements. The poison bait idea was voted down on the 16th. With some blowing snow, VEPCO put up the Christmas lights the 30th.

1973

January 11th, 1973, and no snow yet except for a few wet flakes and the wooly bears said it would be a hard winter. On the 25th, the Arrington Motor Sales at 156 Alexandria Pike requested rezoning for enlargement of their building. Our peaceful town has rumblings of bickering and corruption as of February 15th. On the far side of the Presbyterian Church is Carter's Gulf Station at the corner of Main and North 5th Streets. The neighbors around them are a little unhappy. Next, there were some purse snatching youths on North 1st Street and several stores reported shoplifting during the Holidays. One good bit of news, the military draft is over. The young men of the county had been drafted from the U. S. Service System Board No. 40, located at the Clerk's Office Building, at 14 Main Street.[157]

March 1st, 1973, the Fauquier National Bank had a currency exhibit showing the evolution of money from the Revolutionary War until 1900. To help combat dog-napping, a tattoo clinic is again available. April came in with Dogwoods, peaches and all sorts of blooming things. Tuesday, April 10th, the appraised value of the former main office of the Fauquier National Bank of Warrenton, on the corner of Court and Hotel Streets, was in excess of $150,000. After it was donated to the Town, the Town Council planned a permanent plaque to be affixed to the building, "The acquisition of this property in 1973 by the Town of Warrenton was made possible by the contribution of The Fauquier National Bank of Warrenton and Edward L. Stephenson." The Town was asked April 26th to set up a Parks and Recreation Board.

It was estimated May 24th, 1973, that out of 300,000 Starlings, Redwings, Grackles, etc., 20,000 were killed this winter. Still a lot around. Monday, May 28th, the Memorial Day observance, was sponsored by American Legion Posts 360 and 72 in a joint 11am service at the cemetery. The banks, ABC Store, Municipal offices and some businesses closed. The Safeway at 98 Main Street closed, which ended 32 years of their service in town. As of May 31st, people were talking about the strange weather. First there was a mist or drizzle that turned into 10 days of rain so by the 18th things began to mildew. There was frost in north Fauquier County that day, too, and now it is not only damp but still rather chilly. June 7th the Town Council approved the area generally conforming to the suggestion by Rossier Payne to be set aside as a "Historical Zone". The Post Office is being given a new coat of paint to make the summer days brighter.

Ahhhhhhh-music to the ears. An old steam whistle. The advertisement, July 5th, 1973, read, "Ride behind a real live steam powered passenger train. Thrill to the sight and sound of Southern Railroad's mighty Iron Horse as it journeys through the countryside." An NBC News television crew at Thoroman's TV Radio Service, 61 Main, were asking people what they thought of

FAUQUIER NATIONAL BANK
Circa 1973
(From the collection of John K. Gott)

Watergate. It was June last year that the robbers were arrested in the attempt to obtain information from offices there. The Thrift Shop, sponsored by the Women's Auxiliary of the Fauquier Hospital, has been on Culpeper for 15 years. Now they must move.

Jimmie's Market on Main Street and the IGA at 62 Waterloo Street, the old Garrett Motors site, as of August 9th, 1973, cannot get red meat for their stores. First a gas shortage and now a meat shortage. That means when the freeze goes off, the meat prices will go up 30-50¢.

Talk about the paperwork! September 6th, Fauquier Administrative Assistant, Dick Beach, stood at the John Marshall Statue and showed a 26 foot sheet of U. S. Government forms received by his office that had questions for all departments. The Hutton & Payne Insurance Co. moved from #7 to #33 Culpeper Street, Wednesday, September 26th.

October 18th, 1973, leaf burning is legal again between the hours of 9am and 5pm. The last of October the Committee for the Historic District was trying to decide where the boundaries should be. Because of the Arab-Israel War, the gasoline shortage continues. Cars are lined up along the streets when service stations have gas coming in.

One of the Cross Country Balloonist landed at Morrisville for a time, November 8th, 1973, and then took off so the race could be finished. The Old Timer, Louise Evans, notorized the log book of a racing balloonist in 1910 showing he landed nearby. Monday, the 19th, the new Municipal Building for Warrenton was dedicated. All the Town government offices are expected to be there in six months. The Police Department will move from their place in the Warren Green Building across the street, to the basement of the Municipal Building.

The Christmas lights were put up Monday, December 3rd, 1973, but not turned on. The Town merchants made the decision for the candles to be dark in response to the "energy crisis" to conserve electricity. The Town Council on the 4th, agreed with that. They also had a recommendation for improvement at Alexandria Pike, Main, Winchester and Waterloo Streets' intersection. 1-to be painted, delineation and a double yellow center line approximately 100 feet long on the Main Street west bound approach. 2-to remove two parking spaces in front of the Courthouse. 3-provide a stop for the Waterloo Street east bound left turn lane. 4-provide concrete channelizing island with Stop sign there. 6-and, provide stop bar with paint delineation adjacent to the channelizing island for the north bound Alexandria Street discharge lane.

Big Excitement in Town Monday, December 10th. Three deer frightened and chased by Warrenton Hunt Fox hounds raced up Culpeper Street from the Springs Road. This was the opening day for law offices of Robert de T. Lawrence at #7 Culpeper and it was opened with a CRASH! Two of the deer went through a front window, jumped over a couple desks and out a back window. The third ran along Main Street bumping against the glass in Willard Kirby's Downtown Store. Finally, all went into fields behind the Warrenton Elementary School on Waterloo Street. The hounds were rounded up by the Hunt, after they ran with nose to the ground up Hotel Street, past the Library, and around the new Courthouse. This isn't suppose to happen for the hounds are disciplined NOT to chase deer, but it is not the first time the hounds of the Warrenton Hunt Club, which was organized 1887, has met at Hotel and Culpeper Streets. They did so for a few years during the early 1900's on Tuesdays and Fridays at the Warren Green Hotel at 2pm, weather permitting. The members sat on the steps of the Fauquier Club and talked. The day following the excitement, someone placed a "Caution, Deer Xing", sign at the law office. December 13th had the first snow flurries of the year.

There is still confusion at The Square's intersection. The reason for the low number of collisions, which do happen, is that motorists approach with extreme caution due to the design. Maybe by next year things will be better understood. Friday, December 28th, at 4:30am, for those who were awake, there was a 45 minute display of flickering lights across the Fauquier sky. The UFO's were out in full force.

1974

At the Town Council meeting January 6th, 1974, they discussed the renovation of the recently acquired Municipal Building at #18 Court Street. Last year it was the gasoline and meat shortage. People are buying anything made of paper to stock up and have cleaned the stores out of—toilet paper. After 54 years Alex Hamilton announced January 17th that he is closing out Chamberlain & Hamilton Clothing Store at #64 Main Street, corner of South 3rd and Main. Mr. and Mrs. Eugene Brody plan to open a health food store about April 15th. Everyone was excited about seeing a comet this month, but Kohoutek was a frizzle.

The gas shortage is still on even in February 1974. About noon each day the pumps are usually empty and closed up. Around midnight February 22nd, one of the metal pillars in front of the Fire House fell onto 4th Street. Good it was at that time of night so no cars or people were in the way. March 1st the missing column at the Fire House was replaced with a wooden light pole. People are trying to decide what to do about the Greek style columns, which were not on the original building when it was used as a church, 1854-69, but no one knows when they were added. The Community Action Program, March 7th, is sponsoring rides for the elderly. They have a 15 seat van and are expecting, on April 1st, to have a meal program for them, which will be in the Presbyterian Church.

May 2nd, 1974, the fair Town of Warrenton had some criticism. Someone said the Town's sidewalks are for telephone poles and not people. There are too many wires, the water tower can be seen from a distance, the Town sprawls outward and lacks "ultimate charm". The buildings are too business-like with no relationship between them, their signs and nature. Sunday, May 12th, after 43 years the movie house at 71 Main Street closed. The final show was advertised on the marquee overhang as X-rated, "Last Tango In Paris", with Marlon Brando. May 18th there was the Homemaker's Club annual art show at the Warren Green Building. The sidewalk and porch were filled with all kinds of paintings and with many visitors in the lovely weather. The Courthouse offices were ready Friday, May 31st. That day, too, was the Firemen's Parade, that was 50 years old, had 150 units. The Carnival Friday and Saturday was rained out. It will be next week instead.

Sunday night, June 9th, 1974, a gas line explosion at Bealton was seen for miles. The flames shooting up into the dark sky made it seem as though everything was burning. As the people from the nearby trailer park were being evacuated they probably thought it truly was. The night of June 19th, someone spray painted VIVA LA on the front of the new Courthouse. On the 20th, the Warren Green Building was painted a warm gray and off-white. That's the same grey as the base of the old Courthouse. The Olde Towne Paint & Wallpaper Center opened on Main Street during July located at the corner of North 5th and Main Streets, where the service station was.

It was decided August 15th, 1974, to repair the Town Clock and wire it for electricity at the cost of $2,600. At the end of summer the Police Department finished their move to the new location into the Municipal Building. During August President Nixon resigned because of the Watergate affair. Gerald Ford assumed the office and Nelson Rockefeller became Vice-President.

September 2nd, 1974, the Welfare Department moved from the second floor of the Warren Green Building into Carter Hall where other office space is being advertised. The Downtown Store closed Saturday, the 21st, after 24 years, one month, and one day at 19 Main Street. The first frost was September 24th, that blackened vegetables and flowers alike.

The weedy lot on Main Street across from the Theater at 72 Main, is blooming with pretties October 3rd, 1974. Treese Nurseries, Inc. has an outlet in the space. Two White Oak trees were planted on the 17th, in front of the new Courthouse to replace the Elm that was removed September 1972. An 1838 business journal of Helm's Store was given to the Library, October 24th. May 1976 has been proclaimed Bicentennial Festival Month for Fauquier County. December 3rd, the Christmas lights were up and turned on this year.

1975

Monday, January 6th, 1975, was the first snow with four

inches. It's wonderful how the ugly brown can be turned into a fairyland white. The 16th, the Library is looking for a place to build a new home. Tuesday, January 21st, began the demolition of Kirby's Downtown Store at 19 Main Street. The workers built a fire in a barrel at the curb so they could keep warm as the 3-5 inches of snow from the day before lingered in the street. The county and bank employees had off that day as it was Lee-Jackson Day and the children were out of school for a two-day holiday thanks to the snow. After the building is gone, the plans are to fence off the lot and use it for a parking area until the bank is ready to build. Things went smoothly for a few days, until the workmen used a wire cable to drag down the building. Everything was to fall away from the street—but it didn't. The pedestrian catwalk was crushed.

Monday, February 17th, 1975, was celebrated as George Washington's Birthday with banks and other offices closed, and on the 22nd, there was work as usual, especially deep inside the old Courthouse where they were clearing basement rooms long hidden behind walls. It is being renovated for offices and a Courtroom of the General District Court, which is being held temporarily in the County Office Building.

OLD GAOL WITH MOSBY MONUMENT
1975

FAUQUIER COUNTY PUBLIC LIBRARY
1975

March 1st, 1975, a heroin seller was arrested and "Pot" is being sold on the streets. Warrenton is trying to keep up with the rest of the world. Fluffy Dog reports to the Post Office as usual in the mornings and has his run along the sidewalk as Larry Payne delivers mail from a truck. But, he then curls up and spends the afternoon asleep in the warm Post Office Building. Saturday, March 22nd, Bradley Elementary School sent up over 800 helium-filled tagged balloons into the sunshine. Last year one was mailed back from the South-North Carolina line. They can look almost like flowers floating overhead. Monday the 31st, a machine parked in the street across from Lerners' had the well digger wheeled through the door of the old Courthouse so the shaft to the elevator could be dug.

Tuesday, April 1st, 1975, the Town Council heard complaints that groups of young men on Main Street were using offensive language to women who might be walking past. There was a four day wind storm with gusts to 85 miles an hour that took down trees and blew off tin roofs among some of the damage. By April 10th, 650 claims had been reported. The Library Book Sale was at the Methodist Church Saturday, the 26th, bringing a lot of people out. Also that date Lt. Gov. John Dalton transferred to Fauquier County the deed to the John Marshall Birthplace which is located near

COURT HOUSE SQUARE
FROM FAUQUIER NATIONAL BANK LAWN
1975

Midland. The transfer ceremony was beside the Marshall Statue on the lawn of the Clerk's Office Building. The United States evacuated Saigon in April as it fell to the North Vietnamese.

Saturday, May 3rd, 1975, the course is ready and the Dogwoods make the countryside beautiful for the 50th running of the Virginia Gold Cup Races at the Broadview track. Renovation of the exterior of the Warrenton Volunteer Fire Department Fire House at 81 Main Street began May 6th, with the removal of the weathered and damaged facade. The cupola on the top houses the siren. Sunday, May 25th, the traditional Memorial Day program was held at the Confederate Monument. Poppies have been on sale as usual and Monday, the 26th, was the holiday.

The Firemen's Carnival began Thursday, June 5th, 1975, for three nights at the Carnival lot on Shirley Avenue. The Parade Friday stepped off at 7pm with over 150 entries. Tuesday, June 24th, at 3pm, Fauquier County was put under an air pollution alert, because of the Smog or stale air. A Fountain is behind the Warren Green Building, between it and the new Fauquier Court and Office Building, the official name of the new Courthouse. On hot afternoons children try to play in it and have to be shooed away. After the heat usually comes the storm and the one June 25th was a doozy, blowing down the Linden or English lime tree on Lee Street that was a state champ. In the yard next to that is the second largest Kentucky Coffee tree found in Virginia. There were 420 graduates from High School this year.

A public hearing July 3rd, 1975, by the Parks Board, was attended by about 60 people supporting a proposed Fauquier County community Recreation Center on the old High Street School site. The Fauquier Soroptomist Club would like to see a senior citizen's center in the community center, too. It was announced July 17th, that Warrenton and Fauquier are growing faster than the national average. In July 1974, Warrenton's population reached 4,300 and Fauquier's 28,100. Thursday, the 24th, the Parks & Recreation Board was still trying to obtain the use of old High Street School for the community center. By July 31st, the Fire House had a new look as the antique brick was painted beige with ivory trim. Some of the Martins left for their points south during July instead of in August. After all the gas shortage, now the prices are up to 64.9¢ a gallon. Many stations have gone out of business and others have opened as self-service.

August 21st, 1975 and the work goes on at the old Jail. They

MAIN STREET
LOOKING EAST FROM THE SQUARE
1975

hope to open January 1976 for the Bicentennial. A flag for the celebration is being designed also. School began Monday, August 25th in over 90 degree heat which was pretty rough for those trying to sit still in un-airconditioned classrooms. The new comet now and for the rest of August and part of September is Kobayashi-Berger. During the night of the 25th, the Fauquier Public Library was burglarized and an antique coin collection, valued at $800-$1000 was stolen.

A horse-drawn hearse took the body of Viola T. Winmill from St. James Episcopal Church up Culpeper and Lee Streets to the Cemetery, September 1st, 1975. W. E. Sudduth of the Sudduth Funeral Home gave the Winmills the hearse he had and it may have been that this was it. She was called "The First Lady of Fox Hunting". In 1953 she was in the Presidential Inaugural Parade for Dwight Eisenhower with an authentic Wells Fargo Stage Coach. One mile long Winchester Street could be called "Tree Street". On the 11th Mrs. W. L. Bond and Mrs. Wade Stinson walked its length and identified over 40 different types of trees along the way. Advertisements went out the 18th to find craftsmen with reproductive souvenirs that could be sold at the Gaol Museum for the Crafts Fair during next May's celebration. Schools were let out early Thursday, September 25th, as Tropical Storm Eloise gave heavy rains to Fauquier of over six inches causing much flooding.

October 2nd, 1975 a study was given by the Virginia Division of Highway Safety, which recommended the town widen streets, eliminate parking along Main Street and change the direction of traffic. It was suppose to reduce the congestion downtown, but when people saw the plan, they thought it was like the game they played as a child called, Round and Round We Go. It was one-way on Main Street going west to Chestnut, one-way up Lee Street going east to Falmouth, which brought you back to Main. Ashby and Culpeper Streets were one-way off Main to Lee Street; South 2nd from Lee onto Main Street; South 3rd from Main to Lee and South 4th from Lee to Main. On the North side of Main Street, 1st and 3rd Streets brought traffic into Main and 4th took it off. Did you understand all that?

Monday the 13th, was Columbus Day, a holiday by the town, state, and federal offices. October 20th also a Monday, a "Ladder" for goals of the Firemens' $150,000 drive was put up at Mosby Plaza. They would like to build a new Fire House on 5½ acres the department owns fronting West Shirley Avenue, adjoining the

Carnival Grounds. Ali and Karen Dorbayan are planning to open a restaurant in December at the old railroad Depot at 65 South 3rd Street, with Middle Eastern, Italian and Chinese dishes. Thursday, the 16th, through the rest of the month, there is an exhibit of classes in weaving and macrame at the old Gaol. At #9 Culpeper, October 23rd, a crane is being used to paint the old 1876 Masonic Building. That night around 45 people met to protest the traffic changes. They are upset because this is a peaceful country community on which they are trying to impose a city plan and other towns have "dried-up" when the one-way plans have been put into effect. Friday the 24th, was the Fauquier High School Homecoming Parade.

November 6th, 1975, the price of The Fauquier Democrat went up to 25¢ an issue. During the 11th, the original Veterans Day holiday, the banks, town and county offices and the ABC Store were closed. The Post Office was open though. The cost of the new Courthouse is given as $2,242,498.43.

Sunday evening, December 21st, 1975, Warrenton's Christmas lights illuminated a living Nativity scene on Court House Square. The Warrenton United Methodist Youth Fellowship staged the tableau from 6:30 until 8:30. Many people came to see it and were served hot coffee. Although there were freezing winds, it is hoped they were not discouraged, but will continue it through Christmas Eve.

1976

January 6th, 1976, the Town Council requested the 'No Left Turn' and 'Do Not Block Intersection' signs that were bought, to be placed by the Police Department. The Virginia Museum Chapter is showing a series of films at the Library.

March 4th, 1976, unlicensed solicitors hit Warrenton again as they tried to sell candy for an "interdenominational Christian group", as they call themselves. Albert Robinson saw an odd bird on Jefferson Street Friday, the 5th, with a flock of regular colored Robins. It was a white bird with a reddish breast, slate color on the shoulders and at the root of its tail. The first snow fell Tuesday, March 9th, giving 5-6 inches. Some buds and blossoms were already out since the temperature had been warm. March 14th the men of Company C, local National Guard Unit, led by Fire Engine #1, were on a 6-mile forced march going around and through Warrenton. Originally planned as part of the unit's weekend training the march turned into a "walk-a-thon" for the benefit of Warrenton Fire Company's building fund drive. March 20th the reliable herald of Spring checked in, when the Purple martins returned. Thursday, the 28th, Bradley School sent up balloons at 2:15pm to call attention to their Fun Fair on Saturday the 30th. The Library's annual Book Sale at #2 Court House Square was April 7-10th.

May 6th, 1976, the Old Gaol opened for the Bicentenntial and the Parade for it began 6:30pm on the 7th, with a concert at Mosby Plaza at 7:30. There were flags over town and suitable window displays. During the parade, Dr. J. O. Hodgkin, III, and about 15 or 20 others dressed as a Legion of Mosby's Rangers to ride horseback along Main Street. His father, "Biggie", and the rest of the "old gang", would have enjoyed this. Another fire right on The Square! Someway a fire began around 2:30am Sunday, May 23rd, in the Library's Virginia Room and part of the main floor, burning much of the Virginia and local history information. On the 25th of May the Town Council planned to close Alexandria Pike at the intersection of Eastern By-Pass of Route 29 and to open Blackwell Road so it will come through to town. That afternoon, John Marshall calmly gazed down on two cars that jumped across the curb, sidewalk and lawn of the County Office Building to rest at the base of his Statue.

The Firemen's Parade Friday night, June 4th, 1976, had some crowd pleasers. Among the marchers were animals from Pet-A-Pet-Farm in Reston such as an elephant, llama, zebu, and chimpanzee. With three beautiful nights, the Carnival grossed over $30,000. June 7th was a meeting of about 30 people at the Warren Green Building to organize the Parks & Recreation Department Puppet Theater with Betsy Hostrop heading it. The next planned meeting is for July 7th at the Library, since it had reopened for business on June 10th. June 13th, and also planned for July 4th, the Southern Railroad track had an antique train steaming into town bringing passengers to the old Depot building. June 17th there is still talk about a Warrenton Mall, but the merchants are opposing it.

Risdon's Hardware at 37 Main Street, said September 2nd, 1976, they would be catering to the demand for green growing things with some of the merchandise displayed on shelves in front of their store. The new Courthouse fountain seems to have been a problem ever since it was dedicated December 1974, and it was closed down last month. They say, not only is it dirty, but the pipes are ugly. Plans are to beautify it so when it plays again, it will have a morning-glory effect. A cocktail party and screening of "Somebody Moved My Mountain" were held in the Downtown Theater, September 17th, to benefit for the Warrenton Firemen's Building Fund. Jimmy Dean, country music star, was here on the 30th for the music festival on the Horse Show Grounds. He used to play for Saturday night dances at Rockwood Hall, which is now Clark's Building at 306 Lee Highway.

Fauquier County has many celebrities either looking for a place to live, such as Muhammad Ali, or living here, as Elizabeth Taylor will be doing at Atoka Farm when she marries John W. Warner next month. Friday night October 8th, 1976, a torrential four inches of rain causing much flooding. The second weekend in October is usually the most beautiful of the Fall season for colored leaves. There's a certain odor in the air, too, something about drying leaves giving Fall its own smell. It is good to have seasons that God made for us to enjoy. The Methodist bazaar with baked goods and homemade pretties was at their church Thursday, the 31st, and the next day, too. October this year was the wettest month on record with 11.7 inches of rain.

November's here and The Concorde cracks the eardrums when it flies overhead. Airplanes are going higher and faster all the time. There seems to be no slowing down or relaxation as "in the good ole days", when people sat at The Fountain and greeted travelers who passed. Jimmy Carter was elected the 39th President of the U. S. over Gerald Ford. A survey project of slides taken of paintings by American Artists from 1776 to 1921 for the Bicentennial, were shown at the Library November 11th. Wild turkeys last seen on Wild Cat Mountain in 1926, once again are beginning to live in Fauquier County. A small crowd was at the cemetery for Veterans Day. The gun salute, at least, still sounds over the countryside. November 18th, 1976, the Swine Flu Clinics are all set for the vaccinations. Moses Hall may have escaped the fire of 1909, but now people are wondering about doing something with it. December 12, 1883, ten black men, most who had been slaves, bought from James Brooke, the school house of S. C. Linsay for the start of a benevolent association. Brooke had bought the property located at the corner of Diagonal and Waterloo Streets from Ann E. Norris. The new association was designated as "Union Tabernacle Number 60 of the Ancient Independent Order of the Brothers And Sisters of the Sons And Daughters of Moses of the U. S. and the World At Large". Moses Hall prospered during the height of American Industrial growth. The top floor had dances and festivals. Today it has apartments and stands as a one-time organization that spread brotherhood throughout the county, and country. November 30th two young girls in their 20's and their two dogs came through Warrenton enroute to the Mardi Gras. They are rather brave as they ride their ponies from New York, traveling over the miles.

Jimmie Kidwell, of Jimmie's Market, 22 Main Street, retired December 23th, 1976. The new proprietors are Susan Feeley, Alice Pumilia and Pat Dingwall. Douglas Marshall, who continued on, has been cutting meat there for 24 years. The headlines in the newspaper said, "Miraculous Birth Revealed", an article written as though it was something that happened just yesterday. Rather an interesting presentation of the Christmas story. Christmas night and the 26th, some snow problems developed. During 1976 the Old Town Warrenton Merchants Association organized.

1977

Evening Grosbeaks are unpredictable. Usually they are at the feeders by mid-December, but they didn't arrive this winter until January 6th, 1977. It is 15 degrees below zero by the middle of January, the coldest since 1957. Monday, the 24th, was snow again, crusted with ice.

Anne Brooke Smith has many tales of the past. One she tells is about a gold watch during the Civil War. It seems that General Tolbert and the Union Army were encamped on Academy Hill. His headquarters was in the home of Mrs. Gookin's father on Main Street. A soldier took a watch, and the father told the General, who found and returned it. Later, a detachment of soldiers were around the Courthouse and the General, taking an orderly, left them to ride up Main Street to call on the father. A cousin at the father's house saw the General as he walked to the porch and started after him. The General jumped on his horse and took off with the cousin right behind, firing shots at him. The General made it back to the Courthouse safely.

February 10th, 1977, it was reported this has been the coldest Fall and Winter in 120 years. An executive order came for people to save fuel so stores and restaurants have cut operating hours and night meetings have been canceled. Even with this, four Robins have been seen. The Warrenton Volunteer Fire Department moved into their new house on West Shirley Avenue, after being at 81 Main

Street since organizing in 1924. Monday, the 21st was celebrated as George Washington's birthday.

Wednesday, March 16th, 1977, the Purple Martins began to appear. Can Spring be far behind? They were almost blown away Friday afternoon, the 18th, by the wind that destroyed the 90 foot light poles at Benner Field, along with other damage. The lights had been installed in 1949. Friday, March 25th, had 527 balloons floating in the sky from Bradley Elementary School. The one whose balloon returned from the farthest away will receive a $25 Saving Bond.

The Town Council was notified April 5th, 1977, Harrington "Skip" Harris planned to repair and renovate Moses Hall. However, there was a problem. Waterloo Street, or old Jail Street, has a 50 foot right of way, which means that for 125 years the building has encroached three feet on the town's street. The Council decided to let the building remain and everyone gave a sign of relief. After all these years what does it matter? Sunday, April 24th, and its Spring Ahead time. The First Baptist Church celebrated their 110th anniversary, April 28th.

June 2nd, 1977 the Fountain in the Pavillion of the Fauquier Court & Office Building was dancing merrily, after more than two years of silence. The Fire Department's Carnival began its three nights as usual with the Parade on Friday night. The Hotel Street Players formed June 9th, sponsored by the Parks & Rec Department. Jim Timberlake, Jr., opened The Paint Shop, June 23rd, at Alexandria Pike, across the street from the Warrenton Wholesale, Inc. Before that it had been The Olde Town Paint & Wallpaper Center on the corner of No. 5th and Main Streets, and for the past two years in the Northern Virginia Shopping Center as Sherwin-Williams. Bowling Alleys were in this old garage building and for a while the lower floor has been a telephone company storeroom. Campbell Kearnes had a body shop there, too. The Fauquier Hospital Auxiliary Thrift Shop is located on Main Street now. It's name was changed from Women's Auxiliary for men have joined the organization. Many things are being changed because of what is called "unisex". For example, you don't have Chairmen anymore. They are Chairpersons since it could be either male or female. At noon Thursday, June 30th, a street theater was at the Fauquier National Bank or Mosby Plaza, being the premiere performance by the Children's Do It Yourself Rainbow Theater and is a planned regular feature for each Thursday during the summer. The world of make-believe in which fairy tales will be portrayed, is sponsored by CETA to help the children with their reading.

Robert de T. Lawrence, owner of Carter Hall, presented to the Town Council July 5th, 1977, a renovation plan with additional off-street parking, the replacing of sidewalks and the removal of three trees which are in the right-of-way. A resident is suing to have the Fire Siren stopped. Since moving to the new location, it has been disturbing those living nearby. The Hotel Street Players opened at the Warrenton Junior High School, July 23rd, so they are on their way.

Monday, August 1st, 1977, was a good and needed rainstorm. Is the firefly or lightening bug vanishing? Its only function is to serve as a brief sparkling jewel adorning the balmy summer nights as it beams into the dark to find a mate. People are wondering, if with all the new building going on in the county, is it destroying their breeding grounds. August 11th, the Presbyterians are adding a wing to their church. The first church built 1813 on East Main Street, was used by both the Presbyterians and Episcopalians until they separated to build St. James in 1849. The next year the Presbyterian Church was destroyed by a tornado, so the present sanctuary was built 1855-56. Sunday, the 14th, a sudden storm hit Lee's Ridge with the destruction of about 200 trees. The large black storm cloud, wind and heavy rain came across Great Run Valley from the west. Even though Monday night, August 29th, had a brief shower, the water in the reservoir dropped another half-inch and they say the Town may have to ration their water.

By September 6th, 1977, water use was restricted as there is an estimated 24 days' supply left in the reservoir. The farmers are also having trouble with Army Worms, which are greater due to the dryness. The Town Council told "Skip" Harris he could definitely go ahead with all his plans for Moses Hall. To date the drug market report is--pot steady, LSD down, PCP up. Sad to say, the outside evils in the world eventually come to Warrenton. It was announced the 29th, that the Downtown Theater will be remodeled into office space, especially for the Welfare Department.

October 6th, 1977, the Town water supply was down to 15 days' supply. The sheriff asked October 20th, that a vote be taken on "festival ordinances", which may end field parties. There have been a number of them the past couple years throughout the county. A new shop opened at 35 Main Street called, "Olde Town Wood Chop", specializing in handcrafted wooden products and antiques.

The annual Halloween Patrol by the Fauquier Chapter of the Citizen's Radio Federation of Virginia or CRFV, was available on the night of October 31st, to give assistance for the Trick-or-Treaters. Radios in the cars are used to call the Rescue Squad.

November 3rd, 1977, the Old Town Gallery opened under new management of Pat Tucker who took Barbara Noland's place after she had it for so many years. That's in the old Sanford Store Building. Good news for the water supply. It has rained nine out of the first ten days of November. The use ban has been on since September 6th and at one time, it dropped to a 10 day supply being available. Now the Town has eased restricted use. The Town Council would like to sell the old Fire House at 81 Main Street, but the deed has been lost. Carroll Martin suggested they should find out what 'Title Ins. Cq.' requires. On the 17th, Robert Seidel had an exhibit of his paintings at the Peoples National Bank.

Mabel McClanahan of 99 Moffett Avenue told that where she lived when a child she, and other children, dressed in costume to go bell ringing on Christmas Eve. As they went from house to house, they visited awhile to talk and sing. It was so long ago, there was no Halloween at the time. December 15th, the Town's Christmas decorations were put up making everything gay for the Holiday. Some of the farmers in the county participated in a "march on Washington", for subsidy of their products.

1978

The Fountain of the new Courthouse has been removed for it didn't work right no matter what they did to it, and a Dogwood tree planted in its place. Mayor Lineweaver announced "Clean-Up Warrenton Week" to be April 10-22nd, 1978, with geraniums planted at the old Courthouse by the Warrenton Garden Club to coincide with Historical Garden Week in Virginia. Spring is here when that happens. All day Monday, April 10th, the Fire Siren Suit was heard in Court, continuing on the following Thursday. Also in April, the Senate voted to turn over the Canal to Panama in 1999. Some comments heard on that did not agree with them.

May 4th, 1978, Warrenton elected its first Council Woman, Henrietta Marriott, widow of former Mayor Richard H. Marriott. Peoples National Bank displayed an exhibit of counterfeit currency. Some so good it is hard to tell the difference, even for an expert. When May 18th came, there had been four inches of rain since May

Day. Monday, May 29th, was Memorial Day but services were on Sunday, the 28th, at 3pm, in the cemetery. The cicadas sound off with a steady sound of sawing coming from the woods. Any Oak, Hickory or fruit tree is a favorite place for the insect to lay its eggs.

A solution must have been found for the Fire House, because June 6th, the Town Council planned to sell.

Plans were made July 20th, 1978, to renovate Carter Hall, 31 Winchester, and to have it house attorneys again. August 10th, #44 Main Street is to be D&K Bakery with Jim Demetroulis and Minnie Kincade to be the owners. The ladder for the Fire House Fund Drive was put up on the Court House Square Plaza, August 17th, with hopes that they can pay off the loan by September 11th. Dr. Anderson proposed to the Town Council, that trees be planted on Main Street and some metal sign posts be replaced with other types of traffic and street name signs.

September 7th, 1978, Dr. Robert Anderson's Dental Office at 33 Main Street, once a cellar storage area, had been transformed into a bright and airy professional suite. He first began his practice over Lerner Bros., Inc. Plans were being made September 28th to renovate the 2nd Street area and have a parking lot put in. October 5th, the old Courthouse steeple was having a face lift and a plaster coat put on the columns, and it - #4 Court House Square - is now called The General District Court Building. Once a man was looking for the Circuit Court and he asked for the "circus" Court. Well, you have to admit they do sound alike. The County Office Building at 14 Main Street is also being spruced-up. The Senior Citizens are mobiling. October 18th, they met at the Warren Green Building to discuss a meeting place. The Presybterian Church has had the Area Agency on Aging's Nutrition Program there. October 19th, Stocks were installed at the Gaol, #2 Court House Square. Richard Beach designed them and County Maintenance Supervisor, Buddy Payne, built them. The redwood and Western cedar stocks cost $72. After being installed, the men proved they work, including the padlock.

The sign at 31 Winchester, telling that Carter Hall has lawyer offices is illegal, but the Zoning Board, November 9th, 1978, voted they may keep it as the sign is the only way to tell who is there. Saturday, the 11th, Veterans Day had ceremonies at 11am at the cemetery. The Dollar General Store has been at 78 Main Street for sometime.

December 5th, 1978, the Downtown Beautification Fund had $1,555 and the Town Council planned to proceed with the plantings.

A meeting was held, December 14th, to discuss a park at the end of Horner and Haiti Streets and running diagonally northwest to Alexandria Pike. Another meeting was at the Warren Green Building on the 18th at 7:30pm. A skateboard park was also proposed for the fad sweeping the country, but not approved because no one knew from where the money would come.

1979

January 4th, 1979, the Main Street tree plantings began. A London Plane tree was put in at 5th and Main Streets near the Inter-Technology Solar Corporation or the old Safeway Building. Two aristocratic Bradford Pear trees were planted at the Post Office, 53 Main Street. They will have flowers in the Spring but little fruit and are one of the last to lose their leaves, which turn a bright red. Monday, the 15th, was Lee-Jackson Day, celebrated because of General Robert E. and General Stonewall. Federal offices are opened, but state, county, town and bank offices were closed. Merēmērē's, The Quality Bakery opened Friday, January 19th at 44 Main Street. Merēmērē's is "My Mother" in French. On Route 29, the Farmers' Tractorcade to Washington, D. C., went through town January 25th. At last South 2nd Street is being cleaned up. The Shah, ruler of Iran, was forced to flee his country because of unrest there. People wonder how this will effect us.

A Robin was seen February 8th, 1979. It is said that not all Robins go South, some stay protected in the woods during the Winter and some that are around here are really from farther North and by the time they fly this far, it is 'South' to them, and those that stay eat seeds. The Children's Hour is held at the Library on Saturdays. This week mime artists are to perform for it. There were many objections to a suggestion for the new Library to be built at West Franklin and Culpeper Streets. It snowed again the 15th, and it began Sunday the 18th, to continue for 12 hours, becoming the worse storm since 1966. The snow was less, but the winds whipped up high drifts. It's good the next day was celebrated as George Washington's Birthday and many things were closed. Who remembers Tom Stafford, called "the Last of the First State Policemen" when he retired in 1945? He began work at $100 a month, but his salary was cut to $85 in 1932. He did get a white patrol car that year though. A saying is going around, "It's 10 O'Clock, Do You Know Where Your Children Are?" Remember when there was division of opinions as to dancing of any kind? What would those people think of the Beatlemania of the 1960's or Rock & Roll? Tuesday, February 27th, between 10:50am and 1:23pm a partial solar esclipse occurred as the moon passed the earth and the sun.

Sunday, March 11th, 1979, again reminiscent of by-gone days when a steam locomotive chug-chug-chugged into town at 12:30pm. The Southern Railroad excursion train's passengers had time to take a stroll over the historic district before pulling out at 2:30pm. The Martins arrived on the 14th this year. Last year it was April 5th before they came. March 22nd the town planned to buy Bekins Transfer Building with the $130,000 contribution given to the Library by Edward L. Stephenson. That was originally Court House Square Garage at 11 Winchester Street. The Parks and Recreation Board, unpaid advisory group to the Board of Supervisors, was formed 1974. It now runs more than 70 recreation courses among other activities. There was a nuclear accident at Three Mile Island, New York, which has many people asking questions about safety.

Friday, April 6th, 1979, was the 6th annual Ascension-day for the Bradley School balloons. The week of April 16th is "Clean-up Warrenton Week", but homeowners are being warned to watch out for gypsy home fix-up crews. They will put a pretty coat of paint on your house, but it will wash off with the first rain, and, they have already left town with your money by then. A meeting in the Municipal Building on the 17th, urged historical zones for Warrenton. Spring Ahead on Sunday, April 29th. Cherry blossoms are everywhere.

Saturday, May 19th, 1979, was Spring Festival Day sponsored by the Downtown Merchants Association. Main Street was closed to vehicles for 6:30am to 6pm, as hundreds of visitors wandered past 75 craftsmen and watched bands, the Village Square-dancers, the Rainbow Street Theater, puppet shows, special art for children display by the Fauquier Chapter of the Virginia Museum, and pony rides. A much needed Senior Citizens Center is planned at 70 Culpeper Street, Shadow Lawn, for fellowship and nutrition services. Another organization is the Piedmont Environmental Council, with the Main Street trees as one of their activities. Memorial Day was Monday, May 28th, with the usual closings and services at the cemetery. The Moving Arts Center opened at 9 East 3rd Street in the renovated movie theater.

Rain plagued the VFD Carnival that began the night of Thursday, May 31st, and went through the weekend, with Friday, June 1st, 1979, being good but the next day was rained out again. Even so they grossed $40,600. Will Gasohal replace gasoline? Some service stations ran out of gasoline on the 4th. There was talk for a while about a new Post Office, but it was decided to let this one that opened September 1918 stay.

A large crowd gathered in the evening of July 4th, 1979, at P. B. Smith School to celebrate with fireworks at 9:00. Sprays of light from the skyrockets were seen for several miles. The 5th, families are again asked to open their homes to exchange high school students in the Youth For Understanding program. Visitors last year were from Austria, Denmark, Germany, and Norway. The gas crunch has put a pinch on tourism for the summer. Sometime during August Merēmērē's was broken into, with baked goods and cash taken.

October 2nd, 1979, the Town Council accepted the Bekins Building for the Library. First Sgt. M. G. Millner of the Virginia State Police Office in Warrenton was chosen to direct traffic patrol efforts in Northern Virginia during the visit of The Pope in Washington Saturday and Sunday, the 6th and 7th. Monday, the 8th, was Columbus Day. And, October 10th was a surprise snow storm that really did things up right and left homes powerless for almost a week. The wet snow weighted down and broke tree limbs that were still full of leaves. However, the town was fortunate to lose their electric for only a few hours, and Shadow Lawn Senior Citizen Center officially opened the next day. The students at H. M. Pearson Elementary School set off balloons Friday, the 19th, that carried their names and so forth, in hopes to see how far they will travel. October 29-31st the Warrenton Fauquier Jaycees had a Haunted House at Shadow Lawn Center. The $1.00 admission fee proceeds will go to the Jaycee's Christmas Toy Workshop.

Election Day, November 6th, 1979, Luther Cox was elected Sheriff again. After 23 years, he had resigned in 1971, taking a little vacation. Although The Carousel opened November 1st, its grand opening was the 8th and 9th. The new clothing store at 35 Main Street is for infants and children. Ginger Anderson Van Wegen is very optimistic about downtown Warrenton as the walking traffic has increased a great deal over the last ten years. The Carousel replaces The Shade Shop that had been at #35 about 9 years. Before that Paul's Electric & Furniture went in around 1955. This is the same place where Lee Travers' Furniture was about 1920.[156] And, then, someone thought perhaps Travers was a restaurant, which became the Village Inn or the Virginia Inn, which went out of business around 1935 or 36. Sometime or other it was Thayer's Appliances, and Keith Fletcher and his mother may have had a furniture store and radio shop that also became a TV shop.154 So long ago, its hard to remember. Bad news for the U. S. Iranian militants took over the Embassy in Teheran and are holding the people there as hostage. Guess that's what the effect was of the Shah's leaving.

The light poles were decorated with fresh greens and red ribbons Monday, December 3rd, 1979. After 12 years, at 20 Main Street, on the corner of Culpeper, the Montgomery Ward Catalogue Sales Agency will move to Lee Highway. William F. Robinson of Falls Church bought the Kress Building from the owners Carl and Grace Braun of Warrenton, who had been there 15 years when they moved. The 13th, Scott Humphrey of Midland, owner of the old Fire House wanted to build an "island" extended from the sidewalk into Main Street where a tree could be placed. The idea was copied from the design for the Downtown Beautification Committee, but last May, the Town Council voted two tree islands be built in front of Carter's Department Store and the Dollar General Store as a tryout for the Palmer Plan. He wanted a brick sidewalk with a herringbone pattern such as in front of the Fauquier Bank, on Culpeper Street to Court Street, past the Wheat First Securities Office and 4th Street in front of the Presbyterian Church. The Humphrey plan was rejected. So, Bob and Ford Johnson employed Humphrey to design a renovation for shops and apartments in the building. There's a store called The Town Duck on Main Street. Friday evening, December 22nd, at 7:30, Students For Christ International left the high school to go on a caroling hayride around town. December 28th the Town bought Thaddeus N. Fletcher's building. His deed from Lloyd C. Anderson was dated 31 July 1935. So, the Town has the new Library building which now must be renovated. 1979 set a record rainfall of 63.08 inches. The previous record was set in 1972 with 57.53 inches. More upsetting news this month as Russia invaded Afghanistan.

1980

The first snow for 1980 was January 17th. On the 31st, someone came up with Warrenton having all types of architecture and proceeded with the following: at 7 Main Street, the Stable Door is Italianate Commercial; the old Fauquier National Bank or Municipal

Building is Neo-Classic; 182 Winchester is Georgian Revival; 12 Smith Street is Steam-boat Gothic; 197 Main Street is Gothic Revival; 139 Culpeper is Second Empire; Carter Hall is Federal; St. James Church has Jacobian chimneys; Warrenton Methodist Church, 44 Winchester, is Romanesque Revival; Ullman's old building at 53 Lee Street is Greek Revival, and Mecca, 194 Culpeper, is Italianate.

The Fauquier National Bank featured a display of Tombstone Rubbings, February 11th, 1980 through March 1st. The Warrenton Methodist Church began to make plans to move to a larger location. For a number of years they have had two Sunday services due to the growth of the county's population. Saturday, March 1st, from 8-10 inches of winter snow caught people unaware. March 4th the Town Council made plans for work to be done on the sidewalk from Alexandria Pike to Carter Hall. As the steam locomotive came chugging into town on the 30th, from 1 to 3pm, an enthusiastic crowd welcomed it and its load of passengers.

April 11th, 1980, was Good Friday and Spring had arrived. That day and the next was the Library Book Sale in the Methodist Church. Along with the arrival of Spring comes clean-up week, April 14-18th, and the Library and the old Gaol are getting new coats. Arches are being built for the new facade on the former Bekins or Fletcher Building. And, with Spring also comes the hatching of tent caterpillars.

People were wondering, about May 1st, 1980, where the theater was that had been promised two years ago. On the 15th, Silas O'Bannon found off Waterloo Road, a green balloon from an Ohio first grader, after it came 320 miles. Wonder where the ones from here travel? After midnight, Friday there was no parking on Main Street because Saturday May 17th, it bloomed with color, music, and gaiety as Old Town Warrenton saluted the Spring with the Second Annual Festival. One hundred craftsmen displayed their wares, merchants had special items on the street, there were dances, pony rides, children's theater by the Hotel Street Players and a good crowd enjoyed it all.

The Firemen's Carnival opened Thursday, June 5th, 1980, with six girls vying for Queen, the winner being crowned that night at 9:30. Friday at 7pm, the Parade marched down Main and Waterloo Streets with the Fauquier High Band leading. Fire engines sounded their sirens, clowns made people laugh and Kena Temple miniature cars made people hold their breath as they did their maneuvers. First it was balloons carrying people overhead, then gliders that look like an airplane, but silently floating over, and now people talk of "hang gliders". You never know who is up there looking down at you, be it mortal or immortal. June 21st, the Town Council gave the Women of Warrenton United Methodist Church permission to block Diagonal Street between 10am and 4pm from Winchester to just beyond the entrance of The Fauquier National Bank parking lot, in order that they could hold an auction.

The sweet perfume of blooming honeysuckle is on the warm July night air, smelling so good, it is possible to forgive the vine of its vices. It was 13 years ago when Robert Fox gave out dog biscuits to Fluffy and others in the Moffett Avenue Gang, resulting in a true friendship, although he was Shelby Kerns' dog. Fluffy had to go to the Vets several times, once with a sore foot and once when he was hit by a car on Frazier Road as he followed Billy Shackleford. But, the morning after that, Fluffy reported for work as usual. Now, he will not be there again, for Fluffy died July 5th, 1980. Although The Warrenton Fire House Craft Market opened a few days ago, this day was its grand opening. The temperature on the 17th was 103 degrees. July 24th, the Selective Service Registration was at the Post Office, with all men born in 1960 and 61 registering.

By August 14th the 1980 heat wave burned itself into the record books as being worse than the Dust Bowl weather of 1936. However, some say 1934 was the worse. It was announced on the 28th that due to construction, the schools will not be opened until September 8th. There is a "Fluffy Memorial Fund" at the Post Office, contributions which will go to the S.P.C.A. So far the Fauquier Animal Shelter has over $100.00.

September 4th, 1980, they say the population is up 35% in the county, now being 35,156. The Old Town Business Association held a Fall Sidewalk Sale on Main and Lee Streets Saturday, September 13th, their wares being placed on half of the sidewalk in front of their store. Sunday afternoon, the 28th, about 60 people attended a ceremony on the grounds of the Old Gaol Museum to dedicate a plaque honoring M. Louise Evans, the Old Timer of The Fauquier Democrat writings.

Sunday, October 26th, 1980, at 12:01am was Fall Back time. Again Shadow Lawn had the Jaycees' Horror House from the 24-31st. Warrenton planned a leaf pick-up November 3rd. On Tuesday, the 4th, Ronald Reagan became the 40th President, winning over Jimmy Carter. The Sculpture on the grounds of the new Library, was dedicated in the rain Monday, November 17th. It is "Young

Girl Reading At The Fountain", by Heath King. The next morning icicles were hanging from eaves caused by the freezing rain.

December 11th, 1980, the tall cedar tree was standing on the Courthouse porch decorated with strands of lights. People were complaining, on the 18th, about the Town parking lots being "Loiterer's Haven". They can't park their cars there for the people standing around. The Town Council set aside the decision about the Historical District for sixty days.

1981

January 15th, 1981, the Depot Restaurant is to be expanded so the enterior will be changed a little. Ronald Reagan was inaugurated one week, but the next week there was a better celebration. Yellow, red, white and blue ribbons were even here, tied to light posts on Main Street for a "Welcome Home" to the 52 American hostages after their 444 days of captivity in Iran. More people were glued to their television for that parade than the one of the previous week.

Tuesday night, February 3rd, 1981, the Town Council approved the boundaries for the historic district within the Town limit. It will be all of downtown Warrenton, High Street to North Street, Falmouth and Lee Streets, Culpeper Street to east Shirley Avenue, Waterloo to Chestnut, Winchester and Horner Streets. George Washington's Birthday celebrated Monday, the 16th, had the usual closings and stores open with their sales.

The business and laboratory equipment formerly belonging to Intertechnology-Solar offices at 100 Main Street were sold at auction Tuesday, March 3rd, 1981. The next week, Saturday the 14th, was an old-time auction on the steps of the new Courthouse, as people braved brisk winds to bid on a partially completed house. Friday, the 27th, people saw the gay balloons from Bradley School as they floated high into the sky. There is a $25 prize for the one that is returned from the farthest away. One from New York state was found here recently. Something not seen often around this area are seagulls. This week hundreds were visiting during spring plowing in Calverton. March 30th, the Town passed on anti-loitering ordinance.

April 9th, 1981, the Warrenton Rescue Co. 6, the Fauquier Hospital and the U. S. Army with their helicopter began a new service. A patient was transported into the city where there are different services from those available here. The first step was taken to have Cable TV installed. The 30th, a banner was put up at the Courthouse advertising the May 16th Spring Festival.

Over 100 craftsmen with food, music, and other entertainment were on hand Saturday, May 16th, 1981, for the big day. Main Street from Court House Square to 5th Street was closed for the Festival. Most of the stores were open Memorial Day, Monday, May 25th. The ceremony at the cemetery included the firing squad from the Virginia National Guard of Warrenton for "those who lie in comradeship of a common cause—the cause of freedom." At their meeting the next night, the Town Council approved the neighborhood park between Alexandria Pike and North Street.

The Firemen's Carnival opened their three nights of festivals Thursday, June 4th, 1981, when the Carnival Queen was crowned. She rode in the Parade that was led off at 7pm Friday, by the Fauquier High School Band. Even though there was rain Thursday and Saturday nights, they grossed $38,000. Mark Hailey, cobbler of The Shoe Center, 67 Main Street, has been there 23 years. The Methodist Church requested a permit, June 16th, for a new building on Church Street. Surles and Associates moved into the old Safeway or Solar Corporation Building Thursday, June 25th. A sudden summer storm that night about 7:45, struck Warrenton uprooting trees and knocking out the elctricity for a time. The third rabies case, a fox, has occurred in the county. Not long ago there was seen a skunk chasing a dog. Besides the rabies, the ticks are bad and there is fear of the Gypsy moths.

By July 9th, 1981, the rabies had become epidemic, especially among the dogs and raccoons. The wild flowers are out in force with Queen Ann's Lace heading the list. A campaign with signs requesting everyone to Give A Dollar for the Library fund. Friday, August 14th, the Review Board of Warrenton's Architectural Board denied the request of the Methodist Church to remove their beautiful windows so they could be placed in the new church. The drought continues although there was a torrential downpour of ten inches Saturday and Sunday, the 29th and 30th. Now the blooming white clematis is filling the air with perfume. People with air conditioners don't know what they miss.

September 1st, 1981, the Haiti Street Town Park was begun. Thieves hit the Post Office over Labor Day weekend, sometime between 7pm Saturday, the 5th, and 8am Monday, the 7th. Other than that, things were pretty normal for the month. Last year's sidewalk sales were repeated with good results.

Models posed at the Library Fountain October 22nd, 1981, to advertise the Fashion Show Benefit for the Library that will be held on the 31st. Twenty-one cases of rabies have been reported over the county to date. Cider Day was repeated again this year, as Boy Scouts, on October 24th, served free cups of cider from 10am-2pm at stands throughout Old Town Warrenton. A costume contest was judged on the Post Office steps for children ages 1-4, 5-8, and 9-12. The ages 8-12 had carved pumpkins at home and brought with them to the Post Office for judging at 1pm. Of course, store windows were decorated to fit the occasion.

Another move is being made in town. November 5th, 1981, Lerner Bros. Store announced they were going out of business in February, after being here 46 years. Ted and Mollie Portnoy set up shop in 1937, first at the Hiden Building and relocated several times. After they close, the Hayloft is planning to expand, using their store area. The leaf picking-up machine is busy three days. Once leaves were raked to the gutter of the street and burned. Choking smoke everywhere, but something nice about the odor, too. The American Legion, with combined Posts 72 and 360, began their parade in front of the Dollar General Store on Main Street at 10:30am, on Veterans' Day, November 11th, marching along Main and Waterloo Streets to the cemetery for ceremonies. The Jaycees set up the Toy Shop in the Kress Building at 36 Main Street on November 23rd, which has been closed for several months as their lease expired. The Toy Shop will be operating Monday through Thursday each week until December 20th.

Saturday, December 5th, 1981, at 1pm, there was big excitement in town. That great man, Santa Claus, arrived and handed out candy along Main Street. At 2:30 the Cedar Lee Jr. High Chorus sang carols at Eicher's Florist and Gift Shop at 103 Main Street on the corner of No. 5th Street, who have been there several months. The Christmas tree in their parking lot was lit at the same time as the twinkling white lights went on in all the Main Street store windows. The utility poles on Main are wound with living greenry and lights which is then trimmed with ribbons. Other poles wear garlands and bows. The Rotary Club tree on the old Courthouse steps welcomes travelers as they come up the hill of Alexandria Pike. Things looked pretty and Christmasy, but after the two inches of snow Tuesday, the 15th, it was even better. No tinsel was needed for the evergreens, and New Year's Eve was icy.

1982

Monday, January 12th, 1982, was especially freezing cold, which continued on into the next week with snow on Wednesday the 20th. A rider came into town on horseback, the old way for transportation that is still more dependable. Late at night with the trees shaking in the wind to make moving shadows on the empty streets, the imagination can play tricks to bring back ghostly figures from the past. Here and there they go, moving in and out of closed and locked doorways. So busy, they are—but gone by dawn.

Tuesday morning, February 9th, 1982, had icy roads. Typical winter-time. Ted Portnoy locked Lerner's door for the last time Saturday, March 20th. Something about that which makes one feel a little lonesome and sad. There are two new organizations around now, MADD—Mothers Against Drunk Driving— and Hospice of Fauquier to help people with long-time illness and death.

Spring finally came to Old Town Warrenton April 15th, 1982, as winter released its tight grip. The law office of George Mayhugh and Daniel O'Connell, on the corner of Main and 4th Streets is adding a third story to the old telephone building that was built around 1955. The Stable Door and The Hayloft will no longer be two separate units, as both plan to move into the Lerner Bros. Building. The new Fauquier Public Library Building was dedicated on the 24th. The Francis Fauquier Garden Club donated plants for its grounds. And, what happens? At 6:40pm, the 28th, someone reported hearing a window being broken and called the police. Two juveniles were caught vandalizing the new Library!

Number 20 Main Street, the Ford Anderson Building at the corner of Culpeper and Main Streets, became the home of the investment banking firm, Wheat, First Securities on May 1st, 1982. The original octagonal light shaft in the roof has been restored to become functional once more. Gene Garrett recalled that the enormous skylight had always been on the building. Phil Hyde thought it resembled a Signal Corp edifice and so had a good name when it was The Signal Corp Grill, that opened there in 1942. At that time Phil used to come to Warrenton to bowl at the alleys in the building at Homer Street and Alexandria Pike. May 2nd, Great Meadows was purchased for the Gold Cup races by Arthur W. Arundel of The Plains, a member of the Gold Cup Race Committee. Saturday, May 15th, the Spring Festival grew larger by having 163 booths. The National Variety Store opened for business also on that day, in the old Kress Building. Monday, May 31st, was Memorial Day.

NO. 20 MAIN STREET 1882, 1972, 1982

20 MAIN STREET, WARRENTON, VIRGINIA
Circa 1882

SOME OLD buildings still stand on the block. Montgomery Ward building is much the same. The building next door was remodeled but still houses Madison's Barber shop, as well as Jimmie's Market. Vose's grocery is replaced by The Main Thing. (1972)

AND IN 1982, RESTORED by Harold Spencer, left, branch manager of Wheat, First Securities, with staff members Dave Gerrish and Jane Hitt.

Thursday, June 3rd, 1982, the Carnival of the VFD opened its first of three nights and was washed out. Over 160 units were in the parade Friday. The 45 trophies, its prizes, were on display in the former Lerner Store windows. The longest lunar eclipse of the century occurred Tuesday morning, July 6th, beginning at 2:38 and lasting until 5:26 when the moon totally emerged once again to light up the countryside. Among the offices in the New Waterloo Court Condominium-Office Building, located below the District Nursing Home, is now Waterloo Coiffures of Old Towne.

At 9pm August 18th, 1982, 72 Girl Scouts from Virginia boarded a bus to go to Tennessee to visit the World's Fair for four days. Since the bus station moved away from the center of town as other Courthouse activities did, things around The Square area is quiet sometimes. At least the Library still has different meetings in it. School opened August 26th. The evening the firemen used their 100 foot ladder in a training exercise at the Courthouse. The biggest drug burst since 1978 also took place.

September 1982 had its annual Sidewalk Sale. Many cars going past The Square seem to have child restraints in them and people using seat belts. Things change with something new all the time. Labor Day was Monday, September 6th, so people relaxed a bit. October is the State Recycling Month, proclaimed by Governor Charles Robb. Its purpose is to draw attention to the need for conservation of Virginia's natural resources and to remove litter from the state. The Vision Quest Wagon Train with 11 Conestoga Wagons stopped at the Warrenton Horse Show Grounds on the By-Pass. That is a program formed in 1973 focusing on the positive aspects of rehabilitation. A handicap awareness campaign began a while back. One of the things that changed was to have curbs repaired with a ramp so wheel chairs may be moved on and off them. They are also good for the baby strollers. During October 21st, Robert Jacobs, the Chairman of Fauquier High School's Social Studies Department and teacher, led two walking tours for teachers to historical sites in Warrenton.

Thursday, November 11th, 1982, Veteran's Day, the American Legion and VFW Posts sponsored the parade through town to the cemetery where ceremonies were held at 11am. December 2nd was the Town of Warrenton's Family Christmas with special events on Main Street, lasting until 9:00 that night. The Rotary Club put the tree upon the Courthouse porch and afterwards a little snow fell. The Methodist Church moved to their new location during this month. The 23rd, the sign of The Stable Door was being painted at the newly renovated building. Beginning at 4:30am, December 30th, was a total lunar eclipse, from 5:58 until 8:07, a shorter one than before. This year the U. S. invaded Granada Island in response to too much Communism.

1983

Beginning January 18th, 1983, night time may not be too lonesome around The Square, at least on Tuesday and Wednesday, for the Library plans to be open until 8:00 those nights, but will be closed Sundays and Mondays. Redskin Mania was in town during January, especially the week before Sunday, the 30th, which was Super Bowl. The workers in the Clerk's Office were "hepped-up" as they showed up at work with signs, sweatshirts and all sorts of memorabilia. Early Thursday, January 27th, the old Warrenton High Street School on Academy Hill began to be razed, ending mid-day Friday. A number of people picked up a brick as they passed by it to have a memento of their school days.

Chief Herschel B. Jones retired February 10th, 1983, after 22 years of service with the town. He had been sworn in by Mayor Richard Marriott on March 2, 1961, at the Courthouse. The old Library or the Library Annex at 2 Court House Square, on the 10th, is now officially The John Barton Payne Building, in honor of the man whose gift to the Warrenton Library Association in 1923, made its construction possible. It is planned for it to become the focal point for all types of civic and social functions. The first snow of the new year was this day, which turned into a record fall of two feet by Friday the 11th. The old record was November 25th, 1971, that had 20 inches and the blizzard on February 15th, 1958, with more than a foot.

The Fauquier Hospital's helicopter pad now gives MEDEVAC aid. March 1st, 1983, the Town Council was requested by the Warrenton Hunt that they be allowed to have a banner across Main Street to advertise the Warrenton Hunt Point To Point on the 19th. They were refused because before, due to high winds, banners have posed a problem when hung.

During the weekend of April 9th, 1983, Fauquier County almost reached its saturation point with 4.65 inches of rain, so there was some flooding. Evelyn Krage made a survey of what people need to help in pre-retirement planning and came up with Warrenton being found to be a model town. But after the occurrence April 12th, on Culpeper Street, it seems like any other city over the nation. There is now a rapist being sought. Several schools in the area have launched their helium-filled colored balloons, making quite a display in the sky.

Someone was remembering when the brothers and Doctors W. N. "Bill" and J. O. "Biggie" Hodgkins, Jr., were in adjoining offices above the present location of The Stable Door. Together they had 50 years of practice. That's a lot of patients. "Biggie's" son, J. O. IIIrd was there, too. He still laughs when he remembers the day that office hours were over and as he came down the steps, he heard a loud racket and smelled burnt rubber. On the street, he found an elderly woman in her Ford V-8 convertible had backed into a parking meter, hooking the bumper around it. She had the motor wide open trying to pull loose, but only succeeded in spinning the tires, while police hit upon the closed windows, trying to attract her attention so she'd stop.

May 12th, 1983, Edgar Snowden Ltd., with Oriental Rugs, is the newest Old Town business on Main Street, in the former

Olde Town Art Gallery. The Warrenton Architectural Review Board showed little enthusiasm when they were presented with designs for a new three story office building planned for 70 Main Street. Heavy rains dampened the 5th annual Old Town Warrenton Spring Festival Saturday, May 21st. Most activities were cancelled but a few stands were on Main Street with umbrellas. The alleged Warrenton rapist was arrested May 21st and people felt a little freer about going out at night. Monday, the 30th, Memorial Day, was opened by the Legion and VFW's Parade which assembled at the Farmer's Market area on South 5th Street at 10:30am. As usual they marched through town to the cemetery for services. A small crowd was on hand to help honor those who died while in service for our country.

The Firemen's Carnival opened Thursday night, June 2nd, 1983, and their Parade with 125 entries, beginning at 7pm the following night brought out everyone for miles around. In the local primary election, Ashby W. Olinger ousted Luther Cox for Sheriff. A Photo-journalism Exhibition was displayed at the Fauquier National Bank for a couple weeks.

Sunday night, July 3rd, 1983, nature celebrated the 4th a day early with her own fireworks. Some trees and utility poles were taken down in the storm. Good news! Warrenton Town Police Chief H. Gary Heath reported burglaries were down in town during the first six months of 1983. The Washington Hospital Center provides the helicopter to transport Fauquier trauma victims. The services of the flying ambulance is now available around the clock, so when you see the white plane go over, you know something is very wrong. The Bluemont Concert Series sponsored by the Fauquier Parks & Rec Department is held each Saturday evening at 7:30 on the lawn of the Warren Green Building, with the audience bringing their own chairs. These concerts include bluegrass, jazz, blues, and classical artists from all over the nation. Once this would have been held on the Courthouse steps and people sat around the Fountain.

August 4th, 1983, Ali and Karen Dorbayon bought the old Methodist Church, planning for it to be used for several activities, one being art exhibits. Pots, pans, sticks, firecrackers and boxes of blank ammo or anything else, are being used to make a noise around the birds roosting nightly in Warrenton. The starlings, blackbirds, and grackles come from the west by the thousands at dusk to several places in town. Sad news this time. A rapist is again in town and women are not happy if they have to be out on the streets after dark.

Another new business on Main Street, at #68. Linda and Tom Roop, operators of J/R's Hair Cutters, renovated their building. Ron Pearson, Fauquier National Bank trustee researched the building's history to find it was erected 1880 and used as a residence until about 1900. Hats of a millinery shop decorated the interior for a while, to be replaced in the mid-1930's by a Chinese Laundry. In the late 1930's a floral shop came in, and from 1949-1964 there was C&S Florists. Then, it was used by Bill Nelson as a hair saloon but was empty from 1981 until April 1983. Sunday, August 28th, fire destroyed what was left of High Street School.

Another mall is planned below Waterloo Court. After several months without substantial rainfall, Monday night and Tuesday morning, September 12th and 13th, 1983, there was half an inch. In the basement of the old Methodist Church on the 22-24th, was a Jumble Sale for the benefit of FORE Workshop and World Vision.

October 20th, 1983, a new building mall planned at 158 Main Street, between the Dollar General Store and the hairdressers, which is a vacant lot. A children's clothing shop is at 34 Main Street next to Sweeneys, called "Little Folks". When Sweeney's bought the building May 1972, they went into the small store that was next to the A&A Grocery. After that closed, they used the original side as a men's shop and had the shoe store in the A&A side. Now, they have moved all of Sweeney into the A&A side and the smaller store is the "Little Folk".[170] Ghouls, witches, clowns, jailbirds, or anything horrible invaded Main Street Saturday, October 29th. The Old Town Warrenton Business and Professional Association sponsored the Halloween Parade and Costume Contest. Judging was in front of the John Barton Payne Building with prizes in cash, ribbons, and lollipops.

November 1st, 1983, the Town Council adopted the Proposed Historical District Boundary Map and Inventory of Historical Buildings as prepared by the Historical Landmarks Commission. On the 3rd, the building at Main and South 3rd Streets, #66 - where Chamberlain and Hamilton's Men's Store operated 50 years, was sold to Mrs. Roger O. DeMarco of Vienna for $68,500. It has been empty since the Natural Food Store closed. In 1887 Lawrence T. Hout bought the property from Albert Fletcher for $1,500, and M. Louisa, Cornelia and Kate Sinclair, who had sold it to Mr. Fletcher. The house was acquired by the Sinclairs in 1864 from Dempsey Padgett for $600. It was then home of Mrs. William B. Sinclair, being opposite the office and lot of B. H. Shackleford on Main Street and

Miss Anna Ward's brick store on the cross street. Streets were blocked off from 5th and Main to Chestnut and Waterloo for 30 minutes during the Veterans' Day Parade which began at 10:30 going to the cemetery for the 11:00 service.

Sunday, December 4th, 1983, wreaths were placed at the Mosby Monument during ceremonies that marked the 150th anniversary of the Gray Ghosts' birth. During this month, Mr. Arundel, the publisher of The Fauquier Democrat and four other newspapers in the Piedmont region, donated the land for the race course to the non-profit Meadow Outdoors Foundation which serves as the trustee and manager of the new race course.

1984

January 5th, 1984, was a day with an icy glaze on everything, and Wednesday, the 11th, was a 2-4 inch snow fall, that gave the school children the day off. It seems years and years ago, a day such as that, the shouts and laughter of children riding their sleds or just playing in the snow making snowmen and forts for a snowball battle, would have been heard over the town. Now they either live too far from the center of town or are probably inside where it is warm as they watch television. Over the weekend of January 21st the temperature went to minus 5 degrees F.

Many cars have the FISH symbol on them. It is a volunteer organization formed here about 14 months ago, to help people in emergencies. Chincoteague resident, Royce Cherrix, and his horse passed through Warrenton on the way to Arizona, Saturday, April 7th, 1984. This was a one million dollar ride for cerebral palsy research. The 12th, a garbage truck overturned on Waterloo Street near the Junior High School, and April 23-27th was Spring Clean-Up Week. April 26th, the police say they have the rapist. Another time, a long sign of relief was heard.

Wednesday, May 2nd, 1984, the Farmers' Market began its 10th season in the parking lot at South 5th and Lee Streets, being open every Wednesday and Saturday beginning at 7am. Saturday, the 5th, was the last Virginia Gold Cup at Broadview Farm, after 51 years. Next year the 60th renewal of the timber classic will be at Great Meadow, which is 8 miles away on North Route 17. Steven Wray of Scientific Skin Care Salon is now at 66 Main Street. The Olympic Flame was carried from Washington along Route 50 and on west Tuesday, May 15th. Many people were talking excitedly about being able to see such an occasion. Saturday, the 19th, over 180 artists, craftspeople, and exhibitors were at the Old Town Festival. A new one this year was the Art Show sponsored by the Fauquier Chapter of the Virginia Museum, shown in the John Barton Payne Building. That organization and others, have many functions in the building— too many to relate. Also, in it's basement was the Library's Book Sale at the same time, given for the Library's benefit. Sunday, May 27th, at 2pm, services were held at the Confederate Monument in the cemetery by the Black Horse Chapter of the United Daughters of the Confederate. The official Memorial Day holiday was Monday. The American Legion Posts 72 and 36 conducted their services at the flagpole in the cemetery then. May 30th, had a solar eclipse of the sun occurred and at 7:30pm a Substance Abuse Seminar was held in the John Barton Payne Building. The Firemen's Carnival opened Thursday, May 31st, with the biggest parade yet on Friday, June 1st, their 60th Anniversary.

It was also on June 1st, 1984, the Balmoral Gift Shop opened at 63 Main Street and the Warrenton Christian Bookstore, called The Living Branch, relocated to Moses Hall at Waterloo and Diagonal Streets. People are still fussing about the parking in town and getting tickets. The Warrenton Chamber Music Consort gave a concert at the Piedmont Cultural Arts Center or old Methodist Church, with another planned in July. The Bluemont Concert Series returned to the Warren Green Lawn beginning June 23rd through August 25th. On July 8th, an Eighteenth Century Bisque Doll Show with wardrobe and handmade furniture was on exhibit at the Old Gaol. Presidential Candidate Walter Mondale chose for his running mate the first woman, Geraldine Farraro, for the job of Vice President.

October 5th, 1984, Sam Hall, Jr., died. He retired in 1970 after being Sheriff for 25 years. Spittoons used to be in public buildings, and, of course, were in the Sheriff's Office when Mr. Hall took over, but he had them removed. They did have an odor and people could miss when aiming at them. Some who gathered socially in the office refused to go in again after he did that. These were tobacco chewers who felt they were not wanted. The week of October 15-19th is Fall Clean-Up Week. The first race at Great Meadows had 10,000 people attending it.

The Republicans swept the country and Ronald Reagan with George Bush won again. So, we don't have a first woman vice president yet. The kitchen of the Old Gaol has been restored to show life as it was 150 years ago. The Museum is closed from November until

May because of cold weather. November 15th, 1984, the 65 foot Baptist Church steeple was being refurbished with a crane parked on Main Street in front of the building, so the painter could be raised to the proper height.

December 13th, 1984, people were singing, "Deck The Poles". Sponsored by the Old Town Warrenton Business and Professional Association, the light poles near the Courthouse were wrapped with garlands. The Jaycees' Workshop this year was in the old IGA Store on Waterloo Street. Other activities during the year were: #20 Main Street's basement with entry at 5 Culpeper Street, became a sandwich shop called Caprice Cafe, and the old Methodist Church was a Country Cousin Craft & Gift Shop in the Annex. The Warrenton Bible Fellowship meets there on Sundays. The Cub Run Country Antiques went into 7 Court House Square at the corner of Main Street and Alexandria Pike.

1985

Janaury 1, 1985, Police Chief H. Gary Heath resigned. By the 31st, the SPR Building built by Stefano Parlagreco, at 70 Main Street had opened and Color Collections, a dress shop, was in it. This is the town's largest commercial building with 22,000 square feet of leasable space for offices and four shops. Although it is five stories tall, it is not overpowering of the other buildings on the street. There was snow again that day as there had been on the 10th, 17th, 18th, and 20th. Not much, but enough to let you know it was there.

And, again on February 1st, 1985, there was snow. Three of the five snow dates were on a Thursday. February 7th, another store opened at 70 Main Street called "What's Cooking", for gourmet cooks. After all the cold and snow, Tuesday, the 21st, was springlike and Sunday, the 24th, the temperature was in the 70's. It seems on February 28th, Warrenton is no longer "a sleepy little town, and if it is waking up from a long nap, Developer Phillip Green plans to help rub the sand out of its' eyes." Growth began in 1982 at Waterloo Court and now the Waterloo Center at Pelham and Lee Streets is planned for seven offices, ten shops and a restaurant.

March 7th, 1985, artist William Woodward opened a studio on Main Street on the second floor of the old Fire House. Sunday, March 10th, Martin J. O'Connell was 101 years old. Remember he came in 1911, purchased and operated the Warrenton Electric Light and Power Company, as well as making many other contributions to the Town.

The "Warrenton rapist" was sentenced to 70 years, March 14th, but is eligible for parole in 12 years. Sad to say, the Dognappers are out again. High Country Casuals and two other stores have had openings at the SPR Building. The 28th it was reported that Fauquier County's population is 40,365. Fauquier School Board wants to use the entire Warren Green Building, so the Warrenton-Fauquier Chamber of Commerce and General Registrar must find new homes. The old County Building at 14 Main Street, now called the John Marshall Building is being renovated and the General Registrar may move there on the bottom floor with a Culpeper Street entrance. The Parks and Rec Department is there now.

The old IGA Building had been for lease and on April 1st, 1985, the Waterloo Mini-Mart opened in the front of the building with the grand opening on the 4th. Montgomery Ward is in one of the new units in the rear and a swimming pool business is in the other part, with space for another shop. All these new businesses bring more traffic. You can't have one without the other. A "head-turner" on Main Street April 11th, made people gasp: "A rabbit" was driving an automobile through town as it had come to do some last minute shopping for Easter. Warrenton Supply's Service Station at the corner of Ashby and Waterloo Streets is now called Ronnie Poe's Olde Towne Texaco. April 15-19th, the Virginia Museum's Artmobile was at the Fauquier National Bank Plaza, as it has been during several other years. This April the Dogwoods are the most beautiful they have been in years.

While April the driest in history, May 1985 came in to the Bob White's call and the Goldfinches making bright spots in green pine trees. May 4th had a record attendance of 32,000 people for the Gold Cup Steeplechase at Great Meadows, the 60th running for it. May 9th the proposed town budget showed the Real Estate Tax rates remaining at 34¢ per $100 assessed value. Personal Property rates remained at $2.50 per $100 assessed value also. Fireflies were out when the locust trees began to bloom, May 8th, giving off the sweet smell of the flowers, making a lovely Spring night. The 7th annual Old Towne Warrenton Spring Festival on Main Street was held Saturday, May 18th, from 9am to 4pm. Live music featured the U. S. Navy Band, a children's petting zoo, pie eating contest, arts and crafts exhibits, sales, amusements, pony rides. An art show and Library Book Sale at the JBP Building and other activities. Temperature was in the 70's but a breeze kept the crowd cool. At 2pm, Sunday, May 26th, The Black Horse Chapter of the UDC had their

Memorial Day program at the cemetery. Monday, May 27th, more than 60 people attended the Memorial Day services sponsored by the American Legion Posts 72 and 360, which began with a parade along Main and Waterloo Streets. Merchants stood in their doorways while children were held on their father's shoulders. At the District Nursing Home, on Waterloo Street, several of the elderly were on the porch to watch, as the crowd marched along with the parade to the cemetery. Wellington's Restaurant opened at the new Waterloo Center.

The Warrenton Fire Department opened their Carnival May 31st, 1985, with the Parade on June 1st, grossing a record of $51,656.90. Friday, June 14th, people thought they were seeing ghosts as Confederate Soldiers and Southern belles wandered through town. Part of a TV show was being filmed with local residents participating. The third year for the Bluemont Series began Saturday, June 22nd, at 7:30 on the lawn of the Warren Green Building. A group of "old timers" as they call themselves, met on the old Courthouse steps June 27th to talk while shelling and eating peanuts, throwing the empty shells into a large cardboard box. Although they have been meeting for many years during the summer, "one of the younger ones", Wayman Carter, has been meeting with them only for about 30 years. Among others this day were Irvin Garrett, Jimmy Rankin, Tom and Rose Browning, Forest Persons, Willard Kirby, Stan Hayworth, Lawrence Sudduth, Bob Teats, J. E. Cox, L. B. and Edna Stephenson and Alice Jane Childs.

July 11th, 1985, plans were being made to improve Waterloo Street. This along with Blackwell Road, Winchester and Culpeper Streets lead from the By-Pass to the town, where some of the streets and sidewalks remind one of a previous time when traffic was slower and the vehicles smaller. "They" want Waterloo to have a sidewalk, a parking lane, new pavement, and better storm drainage. To have this some trees and hedges will have to be taken down. More business, more traffic, better roads, and to have all that, something must go. The Fauquier County Parks & Recreation Department moved from 14 Main Street to their new home at 62 Culpeper Street on Monday, the 15th. Bright green and white aluminum street signs are replacing the rusty, tin, black and white ones throughout Warrenton. The 374 new signs cost about $9,000. The second full moon for the month of July occurred on the 31st, and is called a "Blue Moon". The first one was July 3rd. This only happens every 3 or 3½ years, the next one to come in 1988. Because it is rare, the phrase "once in a blue moon" developed.

By August 1st, 1985, it was felt that Fauquier County would be declared a drought disaster area for the second time in three years. There had been a little rain from Hurricane Bob, but it brought mostly wind. Thursday, the 15th, was a day of record heat. In 1947 the temperature was 96 degrees. This day it was 98 degrees. Tuesday, August 20th, the Town Council and Supervisors met together in the Warren Green Building to consider the Warrenton-Fauquier Cable Television Committee's recommendation for a cable company to serve a portion of the county. Tuesday, the 20th, also, the American Civil Liberties Union, on behalf of several Warrenton citizens, said they planned to file a lawsuit challenging the Town's at-large election of Council members. School opened Monday, August 26th, for 7,085 students. Years ago it was after Labor Day, or when the Health Officer declared the Polio season over, that school began.

Monday, September 2nd, 1985, was Labor Day which is officially 104 years old, having begun in 1901, although the first Labor Day Parade was in New York City in 1882. By September 10th, it was the 8th straight day on record of being over 90 degrees. The 9th and 10th there were beautiful displays of lightning without rain. A two year old said this was God painting pictures in the sky. A full moon, the 28th, was called the Harvest Moon as it appears big and orange above the horizon. Peoples National Bank announced plans for a three-story addition between its present building at 21 Main Street and the Fauquier Pharmacy, the site being a vacant lot, but once was the Downtown Store. The front facade will be brick veneer, the same size and color to match those in the existing bank. Overhead telephone and power lines are to be replaced with underground ones. Also at the meeting of the Warrenton Architectural Review Board in the Municipal Building, James W. Timberlake, Jr., requested permission to build an addition of one story to the Paint Shop at 51 Alexandria Pike. There were two trucks parked for a while beside the Mosby Monument on the old Courthouse lawn, while the chimney of the Gaol Museum was being repaired and relined. The 26th, the rainfall for the year is almost 8 inches off norm. Cleora Pappas died September 29th. She had married William Pappas in 1929 when he had the Warrenton Restaurant.[148]

Twenty-five years ago, on October 1st, 1960, the Peace Corps was suggested. Many people have participated in the program. The Gaol Museum closed for the winter, and restoration work will be completed during that time. Saturday the 5th, was the annual bazaar for the Wesley Chapel United Methodist Church, held at the Presbyterian Church to raise funds for restoration to the 141 year old Methodist building. Monday, October 7th, a sewing class met in the Extension Service Office, which has been there at 14 Main Street a long time. Again, the Fire Department was using the new Courthouse to practice climbing up and down their tall ladder. Friday the 11th, the Fauquier High School Homecoming Parade moved along Main Street in preparation for their big game the next day. A long, soaking, welcome rain October 20th, brought out the worms for flocks of robins that were gathering before their southern flight.

Halloween is still a 'big thing', as the Warrenton-Fauquier Jaycees sponsored its seventh Haunted House at Shadow Lawn Center, 70 Culpeper Street, from October 24th to 31st. Friday morning, the 25th, the children and teachers from the Tiny Tot Day Care Center were walking around town in their Halloween costumes. This group was formed August 1984 and meet at the Baptist Church. Every Wednesday you can see them going to the Library and at Christmas time coming to see the decorations. Saturday, the 26th, the third annual Halloween Parade and Costume Contest was held, sponsored by The Fauquier National Bank and Old Towne Warrenton Business & Professional Association for children in preschool through sixth grade. They gathered at the parking lot of Surles & Associates at 11:15am, parading on the south sidewalk of Main Street to The Fauquier National Bank Plaza where they are judged. The killing frost in Fauquier was October 26th when the temperature was 30 degrees. 2am, Sunday, the next day—Time to 'Fall Back'. All this began in Germany during both World War I and II and was then called "War Time" to give factory workers more free time in the evening after work. Also it boosts the economy for people like to shop in the daylight. A proposal has been made to extend Daylight Saving's Time five weeks, from the first Sunday in April to the first Sunday in November.

Five days of rain - November 1-5th, 1985, brought the worse flooding in 40 years, from Tropical Storm Juan, but fortunately most of it was to the north and west of Fauquier County, but ponds and wells have been revived. The Red Cross began to collect funds for flood disaster aid. Tuesday, the 5th, Election Day, saw two firsts for Virginia. The first Black to win Lt. Governor was L. Douglas Wilder and the first woman to win a statewide office was Delegate Mary Sue Terry, who was elected Attorney General. Wednesday, the 6th, the American Civil Liberties Union filed a lawsuit in the U. S. District Court at Alexandria against Warrenton Town Council and Fauquier Electoral Board, contending that Warrenton uses "voting procedures which enhance the opportunity for discrimination against Blacks."

Veterans' Day, Monday November 11th, was a beautifully warm, almost summer-like day. The Parade began at 10:30am from the Farmer's Market on 5th Street, going down Main and Waterloo Streets to the cemetery for the 11:00 ceremony. Among the marchers were the Vint Hill Farms Station Color Guard and the Fauquier High School marching band. Some of the watchers were the students and teachers from the Jack & Jill School, who waved their miniature flags. After the ceremony, people were invited to the American Legion Building beside the Horse Show Grounds, to share in a lunch of soup, salad, coffee and cake. The U. S. Postal Service received permission from the Warrenton Architectural Review Board to double the size of the Warrenton Post Office at 53 Main Street by adding to the back of the building and the front entrance will be changed to have the steps going down the sides instead of leading directly to the sidewalk as they do now. Also a ramp for handicapped people will be built and new shrubbery will be planted. The Warrenton Architectural Review Board was formed several years ago to preserve the character of Warrenton's Historic District. The Black Horse Chapter, UDC, celebrated their 90th anniversary, since it began in 1895. Among their accomplishments over the years, the latest was this Spring when the Library was presented with a copy of the painting, Native Sons, The Black Horse Cavalry by Don Prechtel.

Monday, November 18th, The Fauquier Chapter of the Embroiderer's Guild of America held a Christmas workshop at the Warrenton Presbyterian Church. At the same place, Saturday the 23rd, a Christmas bazaar was sponsored by the Warrenton Rescue Squad Auxiliary. The Warrenton-Fauquier Jaycees opened their Christmas Toy Workshop in the former Warrenton Gift House on Alexandria Pike. Thursday, November 21st, was the day this year for The Great American Smokeout, which was begun in 1974 by a newspaper editor in Monticello, Minnesota. It was not observed nationwide until 1977, and now has spread to other countries. A card table on the sidewalk in front of the Post Office during the week had people from the National Democratic Policy Committee in Leesburg who were collecting money, as they said they are concerned about drug trafficking. Saturday, the 23rd, children were happily trying out the new basketball court in Haiti Street Park. It was perfect weather for the opening day and the nets were used from when they went in until sundown. November 28th was a foggy, rainy Thanksgiving Day, with a service for the community held at 10am at the First Church of Christ, Scientist Church at 50 Main Street. County offices and schools were also closed the next day. It was announced Saturday, the 30th, that if the one inch of rain in the last 24 hours were snow, it would have been 10 inches deep.

December 1st, 1985, came in on Sunday with the red and pink geraniums, yellow marigolds, many colored impatients, white asslyssm, and other flowers still blooming along Main Street and Mosby Square, while pine decoration for Christmas filled tubs in front of C&S Florist and Rhodes Drugstore. Roses are also blooming all over town. After over a week of clouds and rain, flocks of robins are eating the 'fishing worms' that have crawled to the top of the ground. That was on Sunday—but—Monday, everything froze! Friday the 6th, a ceremony commemorating the birthday of Col. Mosby was held at 10am by the monument on the old Courthouse lawn, sponsored by the Army of Northern Virginia and the Stuart-Mosby Historical Society, with a speech, music and wreath laying.

The green wreaths with bright red ribbon were put up at the utility poles along Main Street. Mosby Square's lights were wrapped with garlands and the tree was placed in front of the old Courthouse as usual. At night all the small white lights around the store windows, on the wreaths, and on the tree were very pretty. The 6th was called "Family Christmas Shopping Night" as all the stores remained open until 9pm with Santa Claus, music, carols, and prizes among other activity. The Town Council has decided to buy a lot along North First Street to be used for two-hour parking. It was needed for this time of year seems especially busy since Old Towne Warrenton will be open Thursday and Friday nights until 9pm for the Christmas shoppers. At 9:45 Tuesday morning, December 10th, a car was being backed into a parking space in front of Sweeney's Shoes and Men's Wear Store. It went out of control, jumped the curb and crashed through the store window. The bricks at that place had to be replaced but the frame of the old window was copper and could not be replaced. They will try to paint it so it will match the opposite window. At noon Friday, December 13th, a special concert of Mid-Winter English Carols was heard in the lobby of the Fauquier National Bank on the Square.

Halley's Comet is a subject of talk, although most people seem to be disappointed that it cannot be seen any clearer. It is a once in a lifetime thing so rather exciting for those who have waited for such a long while. Some people are fortunate to see it twice. Martin J. O'Connell and Sallie Wood Sadler are two who have. The year Mark Twain was born, 1835, Halley's Comet appeared, and he always said he'd die when it came again, 1910, and he did. All Fauquier County agencies, except the Public Library, will be closed from 4:30 Christmas Eve until Monday, the 30th. The Town of Warrenton offices will close December 25-27th. During December three buildings were torn down - two on Waterloo and one on Diagonal Street - leaving nothing behind the John Barton Payne Building except Moses Hall, as the Fauquier National Bank plans to enlarge their parking lot in the space. The buildings had been built after the 1909 fire and belonged to several owners over the years.

1986

Monday, January 20th, 1986, was Lee-Jackson-King Day, a holiday for county and town offices, banks, ABC store and Post Office among others. This year marks the 35th anniversary for the Warrenton-Fauquier Jaycees organization. Saturday, January 24th, had a little of this and a little of that, rain, sleet, freezing rain, but the Big Freeze came for a couple days with temperatures in the 20's with a wind-chill of 20 degrees below zero. January the 28th, the nation was shocked as they watched the launching of the shuttle Challenger, and it exploded, killing all seven of its crew.

What is happening in the rest of the world is getting to Warrenton too. About 8:00 Saturday morning, February morning, February 1st, 1986, someone called the Town Police Department to report a bomb was planted in the Courthouse, but didn't say new or old one. Both were evacuated as well as the old County Building. The streets on all four sides of the buildings were blocked off. Sirens sounded everywhere. Dogs were called in to sniff out the enemy, but none was found by 10 or 10:30, when things began to quiet down some. Remember Stanley Wolfe was Sheriff for 37 years but never carried a gun. James Timberlake was his deputy for $50 a month, but he didn't have to work much, only if something extra was needed. Times have changed.[144] Friday, February 14th, the Warrenton ARB gave Charlotte Sedan and Mary Ann Kinser permission to remodel the shop at 61 Main Street at the corner of No. 3rd Street. This was where James Thoroman, after he was discharged in

1946 from the Army, opened a radio repair shop over 40 years ago, going into the television sales and repair. The place closed in August 1985. It is planned that the new store will be an entertainment retail shop called Piccadilly, LTD. Monday night, the 24th, had a full moon on the white snow. Swain's House of Style Beauty Shop at 90 Main Street, closed on February 28th.

Monday, March 3rd, 1986, the Peoples National Bank began work on their addition to the main building, so a wooden covered sidewalk is along the gutter and a fence built with holes cut in it for old, young, short or tall "Sidewalk Superintendents" to watch the work. At the Council meeting March 4th, a letter was read from Carrie Madison who owns Madison Barbershop on Main Street. She wants the 20 year old loading zone moved from in front of her shop and rotated among all businesses so all could "share this inconvenience". They are still studying the parking situation in Old Town. Has there ever been a period of time when there wasn't a problem? Even in horse and buggy days, people complained. Dognappers are active again, even to going inside fenced yards for the pups. On the 5th, a banner announcing the Warrenton Hunt-Point To Point was hanging from the upper windows of Cub Run Country, 7 Main Street. Saturday, the 15th, people were driving and walking towards the Warrenton Junior High School on Waterloo Street to hear the U. S. Air Force Tactical Air Command Band give a concert that night. Different organizations or functions are held in the school auditoriums over the county during the year. The first Purple Martins were seen in Goldvein Sunday, March 16th as they return from the Amazon Basin in Brazil. Warm days have brought out the bugs for them. James Thoroman of the TV Sales and Repair Shop, died March 20th. Easter Sunday, the 30th, was a special day for Ernest Pappas who used to have the New Warrenton Restaurant. Because he was born in Greece, he celebrates his Christening Day as his birthday and it was on Easter when he was christened. This Easter he was 95 years old. Virginia, his wife, is 75, and jokingly says she has been working for him 51 of those years.

It's no April Fool on Monday, the 1st, 1986, since it has been so warm, things are bursting out all over. The white pear trees at the Post Office and Library, forsythia at the Courthouse and in tubs at Cub Run Country, the bulbs in front and Red bud on the side of The Fauquier National Bank, the saucer or star magnolia in front of the John Barton Payne Building and bits of green showing on other trees, makes ones' heart leap at all the beauty. The world is becoming alive as the trees and shrubs begin waking up from their winters' nap. The 3rd, Fauquier County Health Department reported five cases of rabies for the year. The 6th-12th was National Library Week, celebrated here on the 9th from 9:30am-2:30pm, by a Petting Zoo in cooperation with the Junior 4-H Livestock Club. Baby chicks, goslings, lambs, kids, and a calf on the Library lawn. A sign said, "books are friends". April 14-18th, Spring Clean-Up Week for Warrenton, and buildings, too, undergo clean-ups, as the old County Building shows. It is being remodeled on the inside and getting a new coat of paint outside. April 15th it is hoped that the income taxes all got in on time. The 17th, the Warrenton-Fauquier Chamber of Commerce sponsored a forum in the John Barton Payne Building, giving the Town Council candidates an opportunity to explain their platforms. Monday, April 21st, after a day in the U.S. District Court at Alexandria, the Warrenton Town Council decided to settle out-of-court and agree with the American Civil Liberties Union to have a Ward system in the town. Poor fruit trees in a windchill of 17 degrees on April 22nd. People are talking about the Red buds' blossoms being fuller this year than ever remembered. Monday, April 28th, it was detected that Russia had a nuclear accident when fallout showed up in the atmosphere. Since the U. S. had the Three-Mile Island episode, new measures of protection and safety have been found, in case we ever have another. The Duchess of Windsor was buried in England on the 29th. She lived at the Warren Green Hotel in the 1920's.

May 2nd, 1986, the pollen count was 238, a record level blown by a cool wind. This will probably be the worse season in five years. Sunday, May 4th, the Sweeney Building was being spruced up. That is a good day to have the ladder over the sidewalk for there are not many people to walk around it. No one wants to have bad luck by going under a ladder. This was the last good night to see Halley's Comet as it goes away from the earth. The stars were out big and bright and enjoyed by the watchers. It was 25 years on May 5th, since the U. S. sent their first man into space. "Farrar's At Harrington House" opened this day. The owner is Virginia Farrar who sold out at The Main Thing in 1982, and is in the old Moses Hall located at Diagonal and Waterloo Streets, which is owned by Harrington "Skippy" Harris. Ms. Farrar's husband is Jim Timberlake who owns and operates "The Paint Shop" at Horner Street and Alexandria Pike. Tuesday, May 6th, was election day for Warrenton and other Fauquier towns. Thursday, the 8th, the Town Council decided upon five Ward boundaries for next spring's special elections. The old sidewalk just beyond the Presbyterian Church, May 9th, was being replaced with a new concrete one. Sweet smelling locust blooms were filling the countryside this weekend. Saturday, May 17th, was a beautiful day, for the seventh annual Old Towne Warrenton Spring Festival. 184 craftspersons lined Main Street that was closed to traffic from 6am-6pm. Around 10,000 people came for their wares, food, and entertainment. One thing that was different this year, the Library's Book Sale was on their lawn. On this date Bill Anderson and Scott Leggat opened their Commercial Cabinetry and Millwork at 88 Main Street, where the Fashion Shop once was.

As of May 20th this has been the driest Spring on record. Thursday, May 22nd, at a meeting in Town Hall, Old Towne Business & Professional Association, town officials and a consultant, hired to help solve the parking problem, discussed the possibilities of a parking garage, parking meters, and increasing the parking fines for those who are repeatedly charged with violations. A meter maid was suggested, who wouldn't be a regular police officer, but who would write parking tickets only. Parking meters, which were used until the mid 1960's, it was felt, were not the thing to have again, for the merchants found they didn't work the way they expected. Others feel if people have to pay for parking, the shoppers will go to shopping centers. Poppy Day again when the red paper poppy is on sale during May 23rd and 24th, being used since 1960, by the American Legion Auxiliary. Volunteers from Post 72 in Warrenton offered them to the public for a contribution with proceeds going into rehabilitation and welfare work for children and youth as well as needy veterans and their families. Each poppy is handmade, petal by petal, by disabled and hospitalized veterans. Friday night, the 23rd, a full red moon rose in the sky, called the Corn Planting Moon. The Black Horse Chapter, UDC, had their usual Memorial Day service on Sunday, May 25th at 1pm, around the Confederate Monument. The next day was observed as the holiday, with the parade beginning at 10:30am from The Farmer's Market, going to the cemetery where a program was held at the flagpole, after which there was an open house at the Legion Hall. Sallie Fletcher said May 30th was really Memorial Day, no matter when it was celebrated. The candidates for the Fauquier Commonwealth's Attorney had a public forum Tuesday night, May 27th, at the JBP Building.

This was the driest May since 1945. At the Council meeting Tuesday night, June 3rd, 1986, they voted to grant The Fauquier National Bank's request that sidewalks adjacent to its temporary parking lot on Waterloo and Diagonal Streets be built when the planned expansion is completed or in ten years, whichever comes first. Thursday evening, June 5th, the Fireman's Carnival opened at their grounds on Shirley Avenue. The parade Friday had over 140 entries that marched the usual route with sidewalks filled by onlookers. The three balmy summer nights brought out a record breaking crowd for the Carnival. Friday, the 20th, enough rain fell to make the sidewalk steam so the drought is getting critical as it has been five weeks since the last good rainfall. Farmers are having to feed their livestock now what they should be saving for this winter. Saturday at 7:30pm, the Bluemonts' Warren Green concerts began and will continue throughout the summer. People will be dancing and singing in the street and on the lawn as they have their blankets, lawn chairs and picnic items while listening to the performers. June 26th a developer was planning office buildings on Blackwell Road. He said Warrenton was no longer a sleepy little farm community where people "didn't know where the heck it was". Wonder if he ever thought that maybe some people don't want to be discovered.

The Main Thing and Little Folks on Main Street, July 3rd, 1986, have been having a "Going Out Of Business Sale", and will close soon. However, Little Folks plans to reopen in September for the annual Sidewalk Sale. Their reason is the problem of customer parking and competition from the large malls. But, while some go—others come. For sometime a real estate agency has been where Swain's House of Style was. The Statue of Liberty celebrated its 100th Anniversary July 4th, and there were extra fireworks going off. On the 5th, Old Towne Handcrafts and Collectibles opened in a part of the Warrenton Supply. A heat wave has truly hit town by July 7th. Now, you'd never know there was some rain last week and night temperatures were in the 50's. July 18th it was being compared with the drought of the 1930's. At 10pm this night it was still 91 degrees. David D. Sanford was 100 years old July 23rd. He had Sanford's 5¢, 10¢, and $1.00 Variety Store on Main Street. Friday afternoon, the 25th, a painter was cleaning his brushes in the basement of the California Building, which they say is located on Wall Street instead of Hotel or Culpeper as it once was, when a fire began. Although there was more smoke damage than anything else, it caused great excitement with firemen there from three companies as well as the Warrenton Rescue Squad.

August 1st, 1986, Winchester Street was repaved to go along with the new sidewalk put in front of Britton Hall. Not yet officially declared a drought area, August 7th, the farmers can have emergency assistance. The new paint job on the Warrenton Supply brought out the old 'Wagons and Harness' sign. Glad they kept it for their "heritage". The Warrenton Surplus moved, August 29th, from the Northern Virginia Shopping Center to the former location of The Main Thing. That building didn't stay vacant long, and it's different —the shopping center coming to town for a change.

September 6th, 1986, a Saturday and the day for Sidewalk Sales in Old Towne. It's a hot fall month and September 26th was almost as warm as it was in 1930 when the record was 96 degrees. This year it was 93. And, the 30th did tie the record with 1954 when it was 90 degrees.

October 1st, 1986, A Get Acquainted Sale was underway at the Ivy Basket as it is under new management. Someone said they saw a boy on Lee Street talking to an electric meter and the nearby utility pole. Reminds one of the man who used to strike the pole there. The eighth confirmed case of rabies of the year was reported when a cat attacked its owner and his daughter. Because of the expansion of the Post Office, part of its operations has been moved to a building on Meetze Road, while some are continuing in the main building. It was announced on the 2nd, that J. Willard Lineweaver, Mayor of Warrenton for the past 14 years, was elected second Vice President of the Virginia Municipal League for 1986-87. A partial eclipse of the sun October 3rd, was not seen since it was cloudy.

The Wesley Chapel United Methodist Women had their Fall Bazaar on Saturday, October 4th, at the Presbyterian Church. Also that day was the grand opening of the Stitching Post at 34 Main Street, where Little Folks had been. October 7th, the Town Council is still discussing ways to ease the parking problem in town. One said "thousands" of people come to Old Towne daily for the Post Office. Sounds like the old days when people went there to visit and wait for the mail, but they don't do much visiting now. Also many large trucks have been shaking up Main Street as they go through town. They were only suppose to be here if delivering, but it seems they don't care for the new part of the By-Pass that is finished, so they cut through here. The rest of that By-Pass is to be opened at the end of the year. October 9th, was a report that since December 1985, rainfall has been almost 10 inches below normal. The building at 61 Main Street has been under renovation. The brick veneer and siding put on during its remodeling in May 1966, has been removed so some of the original old frame siding can be seen.

The banner for the Fauquier Hospital Auxiliary's Follies hung from the top floor windows of Cub Run Antiques as the show is the weekend of October 10th and 11th. Men are busy on scaffolding at the Old Gaol as they work on the stone walls. Monday, October 13th, Columbus Day, a holiday for some while others have big sales and work as usual. It was reported, the 16th, the man who allegedly scribbled with a ballpoint pen August 3rd, on the Old Fellows Lodge, Village Flowers, Eichers Flowers, Balmoral Gift Shop, Blue Ridge Hardware, H. B. Carter Funiture, Peoples National Bank, Risdon Paint & Hardware and The Stable Door - all on Main Street -, had been in court. By the 17th, J/R's Haircutters had moved out of their place on Main Street and Roop's Refrigeration from South 3rd Street was preparing the building for their use. The Fauquier High School parade marched down Main Street in celebration for their Homecoming game that night.

Again Shadow Lawn was the Halloween attraction, being called "Stephen King's House". Saturday, October 25th, the Old Towne Warrenton Business & Professional Association and the Fauquier National Bank sponsored the Children's Halloween parade at 11:30am from Surles & Associates, along Main Street to The Square. There, the Town Police helped the children cross the street to the bank plaza where the costume contest was held with prizes for the infants through sixth graders. The last of October found the painters working on the old Courthouse, as they rode up to high corners in a "cherry-picker" parked on the lawn.

Finally, Saturday night, November 1st, 1986, a wonderful rain, not just a short shower. Although more is needed everyone was grateful for this. An antique display room is now on the upper level of Furniture Interiors. That level was once the USO, which had an outside entry then. This Veteran's Day was the 68th anniversary of the signing of the Armistice to end World War I, and for 25 years it was called Armistice Day. But, by the 1950's there had been other wars, so Congress changed November 11th to Veterans' Day. This year the parade was rained on, so the Legionnaires met at the Legion Hall for services. By the 20th, things were beginning to look like Christmas along Main Street. The building housing C&S Florist, Hailey's Shoe Center and Wise Golden Buys was painted a "Christmas green" and a huge green wreath with red apples circles the entry to the florist. The pretty geranium decorating the Courthouse and the Fauquier National Bank lawn have all been nipped by Jack Frost and are lying limp. The Library is remodeling the lower floor of the John Barton Payne Building for offices, but they probably won't move into them until January. The public was invited again this year to join the Christian Scientists at #50 Main Street on Thursday, November 27th, for a Thanksgiving service. This has been the rainest November since 1972.

Although the Old Gaol closed for the winter, The Fauquier Chapter of the Virginia Museum had their Christmas party there Wednesday evening, December 3rd, 1986. By the 5th, the Peoples National Bank was removing the wooden wall around their new addition as the town prepared for the Holiday Season. Green wreaths with red bows are on the utility poles, bells and carolers celebrated the lighting of the Court House Christmas tree and Santa Claus came to Furniture Interiors to hear the children's wishes, while stores had refreshments as most of them stayed open until 9:00 that night. Warrenton's eastern by-pass for Routes 15 and 29 opened Monday, December 15. Charlotte Sedam opened her Piccadilly, Ltd. the 17th in the renovated store at the corner of Third and Main Streets.

During the afternoon of Tuesday, December 23rd, a single engine airplane was flying overhead with a banner trailing behind which said, "Merry Christmas". All day Christmas Eve and that night, too, it poured rain. Glad it wasn't snow for it would probably have been a couple feet or more deep. State, County and Town offices and departments were closed from Thursday the 25th until Monday the 29th. A good long holiday. There was some snow spitting over the area on December 30th, but the year 1986 went out under clear skies.

FAUQUIER COUNTY PUBLIC LIBRARY

REFERENCES

1. "Fauquier County 1759-1959", Fauquier County Bicentennial Committee, Warrenton, Va. 1959. Printed by Virginia Publishing, Inc. Warrenton, Va.
2. "A Virginia Scene or Life in Old Prince William", Alice Maude Ewell, J. P. Neil, Co. Inc., Lynchburg, Va. 1931
3. "Landmarks of Old Prince William", Fairfax Harrison, Chesapeak Book Co., Berryville, Va., 1964
4. "Fauquier During The Proprietorship", H. C. Groome, Old Dominion Press, Richmond 1927
5. The Fauquier Democrat - 2/12/53 - The Old Timer
6. The Fauquier Democrat - 12/18/52 - The Old Timer
7. Mary Fletcher
8. "Past, Present & Future - Historical & Industrial Fauquier County", John G. Claiborne-Fauquier Publishing Co., Inc. Warrenton, Va. 1927
9. The Fauquier Democrat - 10/12/50
10. The Collier's Encyclopedia
11. "Sketches And Illustrations of Warrenton and Fauquier County, Virginia", Annie G. Day, Dec. 1908
12. Fauquier County Va., Historical Notes, Published as a supplement to the map of Fauquier Co., 1914
13. The Fauquier Democrat - 8/25/49 - The Old Timer
14. "Fauquier County In The Revolution", T. T. Triplett Russell & John K. Gott, Warrenton, Va., Fauquier County, American Bicentennial Commission 1976, Printed by Warrenton Printing & Publishing Co.
15. True Index - April 6, 1878
16. The Fauquier Democrat - 3/13/52 - The Old Timer
17. The Fauquier Democrat - 10/12/38
18. The Fauquier Democrat - 3/7/36
19. The Fauquier Democrat - 8/25/85 - The Historical Society
20. The Fauquier Democrat - 5/4/72
21. The Fauquier Democrat - 1/15/38
22. The Fauquier Democrat - 1/6/55 - Charlie Jeffries
23. The Fauquier Democrat - 6/28/51 - The Old Timer
24. "Methodism In Warrenton", Jennings H. Flathers, Carr Publishing Co., Inc., Boyce, Va. 22620, 1980
25. The Fauquier Democrat - 3/3/49 - The Old Timer
26. The Fauquier Democrat - 6/16/49 - The Old Timer
27. Eastern Publications, Inc., Cincinnati, Ohio, Virginia Historical Chronicle
28. The Fauquier Democrat - 3/31/55 - Charlie Jeffries
29. The Fauquier Democrat - 7/17/80

30. The Fauquier Democrat - 8/17/50 - The Old Timer
31. The Fauquier Democrat - 6/10/82 - The Old Timer
32. The Fauquier Democrat - 10/24/74
33. The Fauquier Democrat - 2/28/40
34. The Fauquier Democrat - 4/26/51 - The Old Timer
35. The Fauquier Democrat - 6/8/50 - The Old Timer
36. Warrenton Baptist Church History Paper
37. The Fauquier Democrat - 4/5/51 - The Old Timer
38. The Fauquier Democrat - 9/30/82 - Mr. Parkinson
39. The Fauquier Democrat - 6/24/48 - The Old Timer
40. The Fauquier Democrat - 11/23/50 - The Old Timer
41. The Fauquier Democrat - 6/2/49 - The Old Timer
42. The Fauquier Democrat - 8/17/50 - The Old Timer
43. The Fauquier Democrat - 7/27/50 - The Old Timer
44. The Fauquier Democrat - 1/9/50 - The Old Timer
45. Joseph A. Jeffries - Directory of Warrenton, 1854
46. The Fauquier Democrat - 4/5/51 - The Old Timer
47. The Fauquier Democrat - 3/11/43
48. The Fauquier Democrat - 3/85
49. The Fauquier Democrat - 11/8/51 - The Old Timer
50. The Fauquier Democrat - 10/27/66
51. "Years Of Anguish - Fauquier County, Va. - 1861-1865" - Emily G. Ramey & John K. Gott, Fauquier Democrat, Warrenton, Va. 1965
52. The Fauquier Democrat - 8/24/50 - The Old Timer
53. The Fauquier Democrat - 5/29/52 - Charlie Jeffries
54. The Fauquier Democrat - 8/3/29 and 3/3/37
55. "Virginia Railroads In The Civil War", Angus James Johnston, II, Published for The Virginia Historical Society, The University of N. C. Press, Chapel Hill, 1961
56. The Fauquier Democrat - 3/28/68
57. The Fauquier Democrat - 3/30/49
58. The Fauquier Democrat - 6/10/82
59. The Fauquier Democrat - 7/21/49 - The Old Timer
60. The Fauquier Democrat - 8/1923 - D. P. Wood
61. The Fauquier Democrat - 5/19/49 - The Old Timer
62. True Index - January 26, 1878
63. The Fauquier Democrat - 5/26/77 - True Index 5/31/1879
64. Joseph A. Jeffries - Directory of Warrenton 1880
66. The Fauquier Democrat - 10/15/53 - The Old Timer
67. "Warrenton's Business District As It Looked in 1887-88", Charles E. Jeffries - The Fauquier Democrat - 10/31/51
68. Agnus Meyer
69. The Fauquier Democrat - 3/28/67
70. The Fauquier Democrat - 11/4/48 - The Old Timer

71. The Fauquier Democrat - 12/15/53
72. The Fauquier Democrat - 5/26/49 - The Old Timer
73. The Fauquier Democrat - 3/11/36
74. The Fauquier Democrat - 9/1/49 - The Old Timer
75. The Fauquier Democrat - 11/3/77
76. "Virginia Ghosts & Others", Mrs. Marguarite Du Pont Lee, The William Byrd Press, Inc., Richmond, Va. 1932
77. The Fauquier Democrat - 3/28/85
78. The Fauquier Democrat - 2/18/54
79. The Fauquier Democrat - 7/15/54
80. The Fauquier Democrat - 3/31/49 - The Old Timer
81. Town Council Minutes - 5/30/74
82. The Fauquier Democrat - 4/26/53 - The Old Timer
83. The Fauquier Democrat - 5/21/32
84. The Fauquier Democrat - 1/26/50 - The Old Timer
85. The Fauquier Democrat - 4/30/50
86. The Fauquier Democrat - 7/31/80
87. The Fauquier Democrat - 4/27/67
88. The Fauquier Democrat - 3/14/85
89. The Fauquier Democrat - 6/23/49 - The Old Timer
90. The Fauquier Democrat - 10/28/48 - The Old Timer
91. The Fauquier Democrat - 7/22/48 - The Old Timer
92. The Fauquier Democrat - 12/1/49 - The Old Timer
93. Susann (Mrs. Hugh) Moffett
94. The Fauquier Democrat - 11/10/55 - Charlie Jeffries
95. Marguarite (Mrs. Glenn) Piel
96. The Fauquier Democrat - 10/21/48 - The Old Timer
97. Dorothy Rust
98. "The 236th Anniversary of The Establishment of Hamilton Parish and The 50th Anniversary of the Consecration of St. James' Episcopal Church", May 1966, Anne Brooke Smith
99. "The Story of a Church - A History of the Warrenton Presbyterian Church - Warrenton, Va. 1771-1976", J. Richard Winter
100. Anne Brooke Smith
101. The Fauquier Democrat - 3/11/43
102. The Fauquier Democrat - 6/6/46
103. Irvin Garrett
104. "A Study of Roads in Virginia - Turnpike Era", Edited by Albert W. Coates, Jr.
105. The Fauquier Democrat - 12/23/48 - The Old Timer
106. The Fauquier Democrat - 9/6/48 - The Old Timer
107. The Fauquier Democrat - 2/13/58 - The Old Timer
108. The Fauquier Democrat - 1/4/43
109. Sallie Fletcher

110. City (Mrs. Gene) Garrett
111. The Fauquier Democrat - 5/14/81
112. The Fauquier Democrat - 7/8/48 - The Old Timer
113. The Fauquier Democrat - 4/10/85
114. The Fauquier Democrat - 3/10/49 - The Old Timer
115. Mary Ashby
116. Jo Lawler
117. Frank Moffett
118. The Fauquier Democrat - 11/18/48 - The Old Timer
119. The Fauquier Democrat - 3/15/51
120. The Fauquier Democrat - 4/12/51
121. The Fauquier Democrat - 2/14/54
122. The Fauquier Democrat - 6/28/51
123. The Fauquier Democrat - 9/4/50 - The Old Timer
124. E. M. Garrett, Jr.
125. The Fauquier Democrat - 9/30/36
126. Tom Hutchison
127. D. D. & Margaret Sanford
128. James Austin
129. Dr. J. O. Hodgkin III
130. Lawrence Craig
131. The Fauquier Democrat - 12/18/35
132. Charles Jefferies
133. Willard Kirby
134. Luther Cox
135. Chiton McDonnell
136. Lucy Barbe
137. Frost Jeffries
138. The Fauquier Democrat - 3/26/41
139. The Fauquier Democrat - 12/4/52 - The Old Timer
140. The Fauquier Democrat - 11/7/50 - The Old Timer
141. The Fauquier Democrat - 2/24/49 - The Old Timer
142. The Fauquier Democrat - 2/18/71
143. The Fauquier Democrat - 4/3/85
144. Robert & Edith Lunceford
145. Dr. Robert Anderson, Jr.
146. J. Albert Robinson
147. The Fauquier Democrat - 11/3/49
148. Ernest & Virginia Pappas
149. Mrs. W. E. Sudduth
150. Martin J. O'Connell
151. Jack Keith

152. Elizabeth I. Hutton
153. Sallie Wood Sadler
154. Wayman Carter
155. Nellie Downs
156. Kurt E. Schick - Dec. 1981 - "Study of Commerce On Main Street - Warrenton. From Blackwell Road to Sixth Street c1900-1981"
157. The Fauquier Democrat - 6/2/77
158. "The Civil War In Fauquier", Eugene M. Scheel, The Fauquier National Bank - Warrenton, Va. 1985
159. The Fauquier Democrat - 6/26/86
160. The Fauquier Democrat - 4/30/59
161. Deed Book 5, Page 469 - 1772-74
162. Mary Hartsell
163. Harold Timberlake
164. Florence Moffett Thayer
165. Tom & Virginia Stafford
166. Charles Beach
167. The Fauquier Democrat - 11/11/71
168. Bulletin Fauquier Historical Society - Warrenton, Va. Published June 1923 - Old Dominion Press, Inc. Printers, Richmond, Va. Article published True Index about 1875 and republished in Fauquier Democrat 4/15/16
169. Bulletin Fauquier Historical Society - Warrenton, Va. First Series 1921-1924 - Old Dominion Press, Inc. Printers - Richmond, Va. Bulletin published Aug. 1921
170. Ruby Sweeney
171. T. N. Fletcher, Jr.
172. Betsy Bartenstein
173. Rudy Gill
174. Mabel Martin
175. "On The Morning Side of The Blue Ridge - A Glimpse of Rappahannock County's Past", Daphane Hutchinson & Theresa Reynolds - 1982 - Warrenton Printing, Warrenton, Va.
176. Elizabeth Furr
177. Maxwell Harway
178. Mildred Moser
179. Mr. & Mrs. Sam Harder
180. Ralph Appleton
181. Scrapbook "Trees" by Mrs. Amos (Sarah Jane) Payne. 1871 Memories 1954. Owned by Ralph Appleton
182. John Gott
183. "The Silversmiths Of Virginia (Together with Watchmakers and Jewelers) from 1694 to 1850" by George Barton Cutten, The Dietz Press, Incorporated, Richmond, Va., 1952
184. "Historical Collections of Virginia", Henry Howe, Baltimore. Reprinted 1969, Regional Publishing Co., Originally published 1845
185. "Rebel The Life and Times of John Singleton Mosby", Kevin H. Siepel, St. Martin's Press, New York 1983
186. Nancy Chapelear Baird

187. The Fauquier Democrat - 5/4/72

For a particular month, day and year not given a reference number, information may have been from The Fauquier Democrat or The Town Council Minutes of their meetings.

PARTIAL LIST OF PROPERTIES AND THEIR USE OF COURT HOUSE SQUARE AREA AND MAIN STREET. SEE MAPS OF 1790, 1793, 1812, 1850, and two of 1878 FOR MORE INFORMATION.

NORTH SIDE MAIN STREET - West to East

#7 - vacant lot - corner Alexandria Pike or old Court Lane or Turnpike
    1889 - Building built by Charles B. Horner for Post Office until 1919
        2nd floor - 1896 A.M. Brodie, Merchant-tailor
            1/1899 G. W. Hurst, Jeweler's
                other offices over the years
    1920 - Kretico's Warrenton Cafe
        Carr's Restaurant
    1933 - Carr and Pappas' Warrenton Restaurant
    1934 - Ernest Pappas' New Warrenton Restaurant until 1955
    1968 - Stable Door - later Saddle Shop until 1982
        c1977 - The Hay Loft on 2nd floor until 1982
    1984 - Cub Run Antiques

#11 - 1854 - Elkon Lyon's General Store at rear of lot
    1880 - Jos. A. Jeffries bought vacant lot from R. W. Hilleary
    1887 - R. E. Foley's Bar Room in Lyon's building
    1888 - Ben F. Martyn's Tin Shop in Lyon's building
    1893 - Jos. A. Jeffries buy Lyon building - Build present building
    before 1920 - ½ of building - Roadhouse & Bunch Dime Store until c1940
            ½ of building - Hurst Jeweler until c1920
    c1920 - building bought by Grayson who had General Merchandise
        store in half after Hurst leave
    8/1965 - Graysons move - had remodeled to use both halves after 1940
    8/1966 - Lerner's Bros. Inc. - closed March 1982
    1982 - The Stable Door and The Hay Loft

#15 - 1847 - Building built
    1854 - S. M. Voss lived here - Voss & Beckham had store
    1873 - E. F. Kloman Drugstore for sale after burning
    1878 - Joseph A. Jeffries opened drugstore - called Jeffries Build.
    3/1948 - Jeffries sold business to Robert H. Gardiner, Jr.
    7/1965 - Donald Farnsworth's Drugs - buy Gardiner out
    1972 - Fauquier Pharmacy - owned by Jerry Wood
        Apartments always above

(next in line was)—1840 - Rindsberg Store?
    1846 - Erasmus Helm build a brick building
    1865 - Called The Stephen's Building - Stephen's & Jeffries Drugs
        1875 - Dr. J. O. Hodgkins on 2nd floor
    1878 - J. H. Stephens & Sons Drugstore (Jeffries had moved)
    1887 - Building divided into 2 parts - ½ Stephen's Drugs
        ½ had real estate and insurance
    1888 - Dr. G. W. Hunton (from across street) bought drugstore
    1897 - Hurst's Jeweler in ½ (established 1891)
    c1918 - Sowers Drugstore (Thornton work here)
    1934 or before - Thornton & Willis Drugs (Willis from across street)
        Burke work here
    2/2/1935 - W. B. Gates, Jr. buys Thurston Willis' interest,
        became Thornton & Gates Drug
    1946 - Peoples National Bank buys Sours property occupied by
        Thornton & Burke's Drugs
    1950 - until September 1974 - Downtown Store
    1/1975 - building torn down - became vacant lot
    1986 - Peoples National Bank building addition on it

(next in line was)—1887 - Vacant lot belonging to R. W. Hilleary
    1900 - Fletcher Brothers buy and build building for Fletcher Grocery Store &
        Hilleary's Variety Store
    1910 - Peoples National Bank buy and occupy until 1955

#21 Main Street - on corner
    1831 - Erasmus Helm bought lot from John Walden - built building and home
    7/1873 - Helm sell to William Perry Hilleary - R. W. Hilleary's Dry Goods & Notion's
        Store with Grocery Store - Hilleary's home until 1912
    c1920 - Cornblatt's Department Store - Offices and apartments above
    5/1954 - Peoples National Bank buy
    3/1955 - Building torn down - remodeled with bank building
    4/1956 - Open House for Peoples National Bank

Cow Alley
    1900 - Hilleary's Alley
        North 6th Street
    7/1963 - North 1st Street

#29 Main Street
    1887 or 89 - J. A. Spilman's Dry Goods & Grocery Store
    1889 - Johnzie Tongue III buy business and building. He and father, John Robert
        Tongue, had store
    1900 - Garner's Grocery
        Dick Schwab - Grocery Store
    1912 - H. B. Carter Butcher Shop in rear - Grocery Store in front
    1915 - H. B. Carter buy Roadhouse & Bunch's Variety Store here now
    1920 - H. B. Carter & Co. Clothing Store (Carter's General Store)

#31 Main Street
    1887 - A. W. Utterback's Dry Goods & Grocery Store
    1926-40 - The Bon Ton Millinary Shop
    1955 - The Bon Ton Ladies' & Children's Clothing
        - Stationary Store
    1981 - Town Duck
        Apartments above

#33 Main Street
    - Drs. Anderson & Sentz, DDS

#35 Main Street
    1887 - Aaron Nusbaum's Men's Clothing Store ?
    c1920 - Lee Travers Furniture - did he also have restaurant?
    1936 - Ernest Pappas buy Virginia Inn Restaurant from Austin Barnes
    1937 - Pappas sell restaurant
    c1940 - Thayer's Appliance - is this same as Fauquier Furniture & Electric Co?
        until c1947
    1955 - Paul's Electric & Furniture Co.
    1970 - The Shade Shop
    10/1977 - Olde Town Wood Chop
    1979 - The Carousel Infant's Clothes
    c1983 - The Ivy Basket
        Apartments above

#37 Main Street
    before 1887 - ½ of small frame building - John P. Wyer's Drug Store
        ½ had H. N. Graham's Merchant-tailor
    1887 - Theodore Kreisel's Bakery and Candy Store
    7/1905 - John Thoma take over bakery
    1930 - Coffee Shoppe added - Dan Rector ran bakery for a while
    11/1958 - Closed
    1965-72 - Martha Ellis' Knotty Pine Restaurant
    1972 - Risdon Paint & Hardware

#41 Main Street
    c1920 - Hurst Jewelry move here

#45 Main Street (first part -
        had a 2 story home and Millinery Shop of Julia French
    Vacant lot until
    1926 - Building built for Matthew & Fewell's Clothing Store
    c1932 - Became Fewell & Co. - close c1933
    c1934 - Carter's Furniture
        (J. W. Lineweaver, owner)
        (second part of building)
    Newton Brooke, Sr. Furniture Company
    1920 - H. B. Carter buys
    1939 - Sanitary Grocery until 1940
    1941 - War Relief Thrift Shop
    3/1944-72 - Risdon's Hardware
    1972 - Carter's Furniture included this side of building

Driveway for Post Office

#53 Main Street
    1887 - Small frame building had C. W. Smith's Marble Works
    1894 - Follen & Jolley buy Marble Works
    before 1899 - C. F. Galloway Livery & Sale Stable
    1895 - The City Drug Store - J. P. Wyer buy and remodel store above Galloway - formerly occupied by B. F. Martyn, Tinner
    1896 - Galloway's now behind Warren Green
    Vacant lot with entertainments and revival meetings
    1919 - U. S. Post Office built

North 4th Street
    7/1963 - North 3rd Street

#61 Main Street
    1836 - Boarding house
        - Warrenton Times Office
    1864 - Office and lot of B. H. Shackelford
    1937 - Building remodeled
    c1940 - Smith's Barbecue
    1946-85 - Thoroman's Radio & TV Service - 1966 Building remodeled
    1986 - Building remodeled for Piccadilly, Ltd.

#63 Main Street
    1920 - Kay Family Residence
    1940 - Vacant
    1955-70 - Barber
    c1974 - Tally-Ho Gallery (moved across street 1984)
    6/1984 - Balmoral Gift Shop

Alley

#65 Main Street
    Built about 1930
    c1933 - Vizzi's Italian Restaurant
    1940 - Vizzi's Produce - Warrenton Fruit Market & Grocery
    1955 - C&S Florists move from across the street

#67 Main Street
    Built around 1930
    1940 - Barber
    1955 - The Shoe Store
    1958 - The Shoe Center
    1967 - Hailey's Shoe Center

#71 Main Street
    James Walden Jeffries' lot
    Yates House
    1/1931-5/1974 - Movie Theater
    9/1977 - Remodeled for offices
    1978 - Kountry Key Boards
    c1984 - Wise Golden Buys

#73 Main Street
   1875 - House and lot of Joseph Mytinger for sale (next to Yates and Town Hall)
   1940 - Warrenton Fruit Market - Grocery Store - owned by Dr. George H. Davis -
       Apartments above
   c1970 - Creel's Jewelry

#75 Main Street
   c1920 - Western Union Telegraph - 1934 Dr. Hiden buy building
   c1940-1970 - Ellis' Frozen Custard
   1981 - Village Studio/Creative Photography
   1984 - Charlott's

#77 Main Street
   1924 - House occupied by Basil Fletcher - Building built in late 1920 on this part -
       rest a vacant lot
   1935 - Thurston Willis in ½ of building called Risdon Building
       as Edward E. Risdon owned
   1938 - Improve building and now called Rhodes' Drugstore in ½
       Blue Ridge (Risdon's) in other ½
   1948 - Blue Ridge move across street - Rhodes take all of building
       Gift shop above

Alley

#81 Main Street -
       Lot #2
   c1950 - The Red Store
   1848 - Methodist-Episcopal Church North buy lot
   1854 - Methodist build church
   1869 - Methodist Northern Church sell to Wm. H. Gaines
   1870 - Town buy for Town Hall
   1872 - Free School here - have entertainments
   1914 - Remodeled for Town Hall and Fire Department
   1915 - Named Municipal Building - have movies
   1920 - Red Cross Work Rooms close - Boy Scouts here
   1924 - Newly formed Fire Department given more space
   1929 - Fire Dept. wants all of building. Town offices move,
       but keep a room in the back?
   1977 - Fire Department move
   6/1978 - Town sell - buildling remodeled - ½ has Village Flowers
       ½ has Finance One
       Offices above

North 3rd Street
   7/1963 - North 4th Street

Main Street -
       Lot #3
       Owned by Wm. Horner
   1855 - Presbyterian Church built

#103 Main Street
> Lot #4
> 1790 - The Grenville Gaines property - originally owned by Dr. Gustavus Horner
> 1900 - Residence
> 1920-1940 - Butler Residence
> 1950 - owned by Vincent Jacobs - Occupied by Mrs. Berkley Ellis
> c1955 - Gas Station built
> 1973 - Carter's Gulf Station
> 7/1974 - Olde Towne Paint & Wallpaper Center
> 1981 - Eicher's Flowers & Gift Shop

North 2nd Street
> 7/1963 - North 5th Street

SOUTH SIDE MAIN STREET - West to East

#20 Main Street - corner Culpeper Street or old Culpeper Road
> 1830 - Part of Horner track sold to John MaCrae
> 1831 - MaCrae build house - sell to George Lemmon
> 1846 - Lemmon sell house to Samuel Chilton
> 1854 - Latham & Green Store?
> 1858 - Sold to Berkeley Ward as residence until 1860
> 1871 - Building leased to White & Smith for store
> 1882 - Latham & Green Store
> 1887 - R. W. Hilleary Store
> 1897 - Aaron Nusbaum buy building from Ward family -
>> Open clothing store
>
> 1907 - Nusbaum joined by F. G. Anderson -
>> renamed Nusbaum & Anderson's Clothing Store
>
> 1908 - F. G. Anderson buy buildling - called Ford Anderson Build.
> c1920 - Now Anderson's Clothing Store
> 1930 - A&P Store until 11/1939 they move on The Square
> 1941 - Bake Sales
> 10/1942 - Signal Corps Restaurant of Johnny Kreticos
> 1948 - Renamed Sportsman's Grill
> 1967-1979 - Montgomery Ward Catalog Sales
> 1982 - Wheat, First Securities
> 1984 - Caprice Cafe in basement - Culpeper Street entrance

#22 Main Street
> 1880 - B. F. McConchie Shoe Making & Repair Store
> c1900 - Restaurant
>> - Albert Fletcher's radio Shop?
>
> 1920 - Embry's Flower Shop
>> - John McIntosh's Clothing Store
>
> 1/1940 - Jimmie's (Kidwell) Market

#24 Main Street
> c1854 - Thornton Lee, Barber
> c1870 - Madison's Barber Shop - Charlie Madison, Sr. and brother, Allie
> 1897 - Lee Madison began working
> 1907 - Charlie Madison, Jr. began working

#26 Main Street
    1854 - Mr. Pipenbring's Bakery - Building built by John G. Beckham
    1871-1882 - A. M. Brodie, Merchant-Tailor
    1887 - William Shepherd's Butcher Shop
    1900 - Week's General Store
    1920-1969 - G. A. Vose's Store
    1970 - Vose's Building torn down
    10/1972 - The Main Thing closed 8/1986
    10/1986 - Warrenton Surplus

#32 - 34 Main Street (½ of building)
    6/1809 - Richard & Sally Thompson buy lot from Peter & Ann Glascock
    c1854 - Ruel H. Ross Bakery & Grocery Store
    1854 - Madison J. Follin General Store - lived above
    1887 - Dr. G. W. Hunton's Drugstore
    1888 or 89 - Hunton bought Stephen's Building and move across street
    1913 - Anderson & Allison Fancy Market
    12/1968 - A&A Market sold by Alex Allison to H. B. Carter & Co.
        became Johnson's Food Store
    5/1972 - Building bought by Howard Sweeney
    1973 - Sweeney's Shoes opened when grocery store left
    1983 - Sweeney's Shoes and Men's Wear

#34 Main Street (½ of building)
    - a frame house
    1867 - Shoe shop
    1887 - Thomas E. Saunders Boot & Shoe Making or Warrenton Shoe Store
        Henry Brewer Grocery Store with Restaurant above
        Schwabb's Grocery Store
    1905? - c1920 - The Fauquier Democrat Printing Office
    c1920 - Willis White Grocery, Movie Theater upstairs
        Willis & Maxheimer Drugstore and Soda Fountain
            Burke also worked here - Willis left before 1934 - then became
        Soda Fountain of Chester Maxheimer & Paul Sudduth
    c1935-1954 - The Fashion Shop
    1972 - Howard Sweeney buy building, opened as Sweeney's Shoes when they moved
        into #32, this became
    Sweeney's Men's Wear until 1983 and that moved into other part of building
    10/1983-9/1986 - Little Folks
    10/1986 - Stitching Post

#36 Main Street
    Large frame building
    1836 - John Saunder's Funeral Home
    1887 - ½ of building continue as Funeral Home
        ½ of building towards the corner - Joseph H. Nelson's Hardware & Furniture
            Store & Repair
    c1920 or 24 - ½ of building - Sudduth take over when Saunders died
        ½ of building - E. W. Bishop's General Merchandise
    1933 - Kirson's Department Store replace Bishop's side
        Sauer buy Kirson property

1938 - Lerner's Bros. Dept. Store lease ½ of Sauer Build.
1940 - New building built on corner and other ½ incorporated in it
1941 - Sauer's called Ben Franklin's Dime Store
1955 - Braun's Variety Store - Building remodeled to include both halves when Funera home moved out
1972 - Braun sold to S. H. Kress -
1/1979 - Kress close - Wm. F. Robinson buy building from Carl and Grace Braun
1981 - Jaycees' Headquarters
5/1982 - National Variety Store

South 5th Street
   7/1963 - South 2nd Street

#40 Main Street
   1887 - L. T. Hout's Jewelry Store
   c1920 - Moser's Grocery
   1940 - Western Auto
   1953 - Surplus Store
   1955 - Village Variety
   1967 - Hutchison Travel Bureau

#44 Main Street
   1887 - Brick building home of Henry Lee and his General Merchandise Store
   c1930 - Sanford's Groceries
   c1940 - Bunch's Variety
   1955 - Nina's 5&10¢ Store
   1967 - Mack's Pastry Shop
   1970 - a bakery
   8/1978 - D&K Bakery
   1/1979 - The Quality Bakery - Merēmērē's
   1/1987 - Cardinal Cake and Bake Shop

#46 Main Street
   1887 - Small 2-story frame house - Residence of Aunt Ellen
   1905 - The Fauquier Democrate opens office
   c1920 - Risdon's Hardware
   1938 (or before) Edward Risdon move - Carroll Risdon stay and share building until he moved 3/1944
   1939 - E. L. Timberlake's Utility Store share building
   1944 - 1955 - Sears' has all of the building
   1970-72 - Agricultural Loan Co.
   1980 - The Thrift Shop

#48 Main Street
   1887 - Cornelia St. Clair's Millinery Store -
      Dr. J. O. St. Clair, dentist in rear
   1894 - Dr. R. R. O. St.Clair, dentist on Main Street - here?
   c9/1939 - Kretico's Mayflower Restaurant
   1940 - Muntz TV Sales & Service
   1951 - New Soldier's Lounge over Muntz TV

c1953 or 54 - Camden TV Sales & Service
c1955 - Investor's Loan Co.
1970 - Outside-In Plant Store - until fall of 1982
1982 - A Plant & Gift Shop
1983 - Christian Science Reading Room

#50 Main Street
1983 - First Church of Christ - above the Reading Room

#52 Main Street
- Live Poultry Shop
- Silver Tower Restaurant
3/1939-8/1966 - Lerner's Bros. move into new building built
1944 - USO above Lerner's
10/1967 - Furniture Interiors
1986 - Antique shop above (in old USO Lounge)

#58 Main Street
1864 - Anne Ward's brick store
1887 - Captain Julian P. Lee's Toy Store
c1920 - Foley's Restaurant
1932-1955 - Sanford's 5¢, 10¢ & $1.00 Variety Store
1970-81 - Old Towne Art Gallery
5/1983 - Edgar Snowden Oriental Rugs, Ltd.

South 4th Street
7/1963 - South 3rd Street

#66 Main Street
6/3/1793 - Johnzie Tongue bought house from Martin and Ann Pickett
1854 - A. H. Spilman - postmaster & tailor lived here
1864 - Sinclairs bought from Dempsey Padgett
1887 - Lawrence T. Hout bought from Albert Fletcher and M. Louisa, Cornelia & Kate Sinclair who had sold to him
9/1919 - Building remodeled for Chamberlain & Hamilton Men's Store - until 1/1974. Had Pool Room in basement
4/1974 - Brody's Health Food Store
c1978 - Warrenton Natural Food Store
1981 - Briarclift Farms Natural Foods
11/1983 - Building sold to Mrs. Roger O. DeMarco
1984 - Steven Wray of Scientific Skin Care Salon
1984 - Tally-Ho Gallery (from across street)
also, Dove Cote Studio above

#68 Main Street
Prior to 1854 - home of E. N. Cologne, town sergeant and Saddle Shop
c1880 - Residence
1930's - Millinery Shop
1940 - Chinese Laundry (burn and torn down?)
- until 1949 - Woman's Exchange

1949-1964 - C&S Floral Shop
- Bill Nelson's Hair Salon
1981-83 - Vacant
1983 - J/R's Haircutters after renovation until 1985
1985 - Roop's Refrigeration moved from S. 3rd Street

#70 Main Street
1854 - Residence of the Misses English
Vacant lot
9/1972 - Treese Nurseries, Inc. Outlet on lot
10/1983 - Building planned
1/1985 - SPR Building open with shops & offices

#78 Main Street
Part of Tongue property (as is #82)
1909 - Library use cottage for a while after fire
11/8/1941 - Town buy 2 small cottages and tear down -
Was this where Drs. Pretlow & Chandler had offices?
8/1964 - New building - Silco Cut Rate Store opens
1977 or 1978 - Dollar General Store

#82 Main Street
1793 - Johnzie Tongue buy from Martin & Anne Pickett
Johnzie & son, John "Jonzie" had tan yard until after Civil War, probably on #78 part of porperty
c1900-1920 - All of property used for Tongue residence
1940 - Vacant
11/8/1941 - Town buy all of George Tongue's property
c1955 - C&P Telephone building built
1970 - Finance One
- O'Connell & Mayhugh remodel

South 3rd Street
7/1963 - South 4th Street

#88 Main Street
1914 - First Exchange - handmade blouses and tea
1920 - Dr. Mayphis' Office
1922 - Reality Co.
1954-1985 - Fashion Shop
5/1986 - Commercial Cabinetry & Millword - Meadow Oak

#90 Main Street
c1960 - building built
c1970-2/1986 - Swain's House of Style
1986 - Realty Company

#92 Main Street
1900-1940 - Fletcher Residence
1948 - Building built - Grand opening for Blue Ridge Hardware in February

#100 Main Street
- 1880's and 1890's - Thad Fletcher, Sr. home
- 1939 - Fletcher lot bought by Sanitary Grocery Co.
- 1940 - Sanitary Store open at site of Tyler House
- 1941 - Name changed to Safeway Store
- c1970 - Inter-Technology Solar Corporation
- 1981 - ITC's equipment sold
- 7/1981 - Surles & Associates, Ltd.

South 2nd Street
- 7/1963 - South 5th Street

THE COURT HOUSE SQUARE

#4 - The Courthouse
- 4/27/1790 - Present site deeded
- 10/28/1795 - Courthouse approved for use
- 1818 - Second Courthouse to be built
- 5/23/1853 - Courthouse burn
- 1854 - Rebuilt - Third one
- 1889 - Courthouse burn
- 1890 - Rebuilt - Fourth one
- 1978 - After new Courthouse built - This name changed to General District Court Building - New one called Fauquier County Court & Office Building

#3 or 2 Court House Square
- Was a part of the old Municipal Bldg. that burned 1909
- 7/8/1916 - Lucien Keith buy lot from Town?
- 7/16/1923 - Cornerstone of Warrenton Library Building laid, built through a gift from Mrs. Elizabeth S. Keith
- 10/2/1969 - Name changed to Fauquier County Public Library when the Warrenton Library Board turned over all properties to Fauquier County and the Town of Warrenton
- 3/22/1979 - Town planned to buy Bekins Transfer Building at #11 Winchester for Library's new building. Completed 12/28/1979
- 11/17/1980 - Sculpture on Library Grounds dedicated
- 4/24/1982 - New Library dedicated, leaving old building empty that is now called The Library Annex
- 3/10/1983 - Building now named The John Barton Payne Building because of his gift to make building possible

#3? - The Jail
- 10/28/1808 - Jail to be built next to Courthouse
- 1822 - Addition built to Jail
- 1964 - Jail moved
- 5/1976 - Old Gaol Museum open

#14 - The County Building
- 3/1795 - The Clerk's Office to be built
- 1/1926 - New County Building built - old one torn down
- 12/1974 - County Offices move into Warren Green Building
  - Renamed The John Marshall Building

#10 Fauquier National Bank property
    c1754 - Water's Tavern
    1818 - Turner's Tavern
    1852 - Town sell Water's Tavern to Ambrose Hord - tear down
    1853 - Five Point's Store - 1870 sold to H. C. Yates
              Waterman's Store on corner
    1880 - George Booth's 2-story brick house -
              On same lot, brick home of Mrs. Lulu Sowers Jennings
    1880 - Pattie's Store on corner of Winchester
              Behind this - Wm. Morgan's Eating House
              Next to Morgan - a vacant lot
    1894 - Municipal & Fire House built
    1909 - Everything burn
    1910 - Rebuilt: T. W. Pattie's "Busy Corner" store
              Fletcher Bros. Furniture Store Building
              Town buy Yates & Bartenstein property
              Booth house
    1913 - Fountain built
    1914 - Fletcher Building called Town Hall - Offices moved there
              Also called Opera House - movies and entertainments
    1919 - Movie Theater also called New Warrenton Theater
    1924 - T. E. Pattie Building - Store formerly known as "Community Store" now called "Fauquier Grocery"
    5/1924 - Warrenton Library built on vacant lot
       - Johnnie Kreticos have restaurant in ½ of Pattie Bldg.?
    1927 - J. A. Frazier buy "Shenandoah" and reopen restaurant
    1927 - Dr. Hiden buy Opera House - Town Hall
              Harder Brother Electrical Contractors (about now)
    1928 - Fountain removed
    1931 - Library corner rounded
    1931 - Cistern abandoned?
    1931 - Pearson's Grocery Store in corner part of Pattie Bld.
              Somewhere around here - D'Anglo's Cleaning Shop
    1931 - Silent Policeman Installed
    1/1931 - Movie Theater move out of Hiden Building
    3/1931 - Hiden Building burn
    1934 - Hiden Bldg. now called Fauquier Recreational with Skating Rink and Boxing
    11/1935 - Ben Franklin replaces skating rink in ½ of Hiden Bldg.
    11/1936 - Hiden Bldg. being remodeled in ½ next to Ben Franklin
              Is this when Coons went in?
    1937 - Johnny Kretico's Mayflower Restaurant in ½ of Pattie Bldg.
              Pearson's Store in other ½
    1937 - Lerner Bros. in Hiden - did it replace Ben Franklin?
    March 1937 - Kretico buy Pattie Bldg.
    1939 - E. L. Timberlake's Utility Store move from Hiden Bldg.
        Forrest Gill's Furniture & Appliance replace it
        Coons Market in other half
    11/1939 - A&P move into Mayflower Restaurant space - Kretico Bldg.
    1950 - Western Auto in ½ of Hiden with Coons in other ½
    1951 - Kreticos sell building to Walter & Johanna Ostrow

1952 - First street signs put up
4/1955 - A&P move
1957 - Western Auto in all of Hiden Bldg
  Sears on corner in Ostrow Bldg - Move 1962
1962 - McClanahan Photo Shop in ½ of Ostrow Bldg - Move 1968
  Saddle Shop owned by Lee Hilts in other ½
12/1964 - Robert E. Palmer buy Saddle Shop
7/1967 - The Fauquier National Bank buys Hiden, Ostrow, and other properties
10/1969 - Warrenton Library renamed Fauquier Public Library
8/1971 - FNB move in new building - Grounds called Mosby Plaza
4/1982 - Library move to Winchester Street
1983 - Old Library building renamed John Barton Payne Bldg.

#18 Court Street (behind old Courthouse)
1903 - Fauquier National Bank built at #10 Court Street
1925 - New FNB Building built
8/1971 - FNB move to The Square
1973 - Town has building for Municipal Building

Hotel Street
 California House -
 1813 - sold by Geo. B. Pickett to Wm. Lakeman
 1836 - sold to Ben R. Wallace
 1845 - sold to John Smith & Wm. H. Gaines - Daniel Warner had Barber Shop - They sold and larger building built
 1856 - Wm. & James C. Smith left to Mary Amelia Smith
 1878 - Fauquier Marble Works and Yard - in basement was Fisher Brothers Bar
 1929 - sold to E. W. Winmill from estate of Mrs. Elizabeth Fairfax Gaines Smith Jones
 1938 - sold to Allen Townsend Winmill, formerly office of Gude, Winmill & Co. To be called The Stock Exchange Building on Wall Street - Other offices
 7/1945 - D. H. Lees and others move to Payne Bldg., as California House sold to Walter P. Chrysler

Payne Building
 1867 - Built by Rice Payne as law office
 1891 - Gaines Bros. Bank - at corner of alley on Culpeper
 1903 - Payne heirs sold to Warrenton Women's Realty Co.
 1929 - R. C. Winmill buy
 8/1943 - D. H. Lees buy
 7/1945 - D. H. Lee and others move here

Warren Green Building
 1811 - Pickett's House
   School
 1817 - Thaddus Norris advertise for materials to build
 7/26/1819 - Norris Tavern open
 1843-1850 - Warren Green, a school by R. M. Smith
 1850 - Warren Green, a tavern with several owners and additions
 7/1960 - Hotel closed
 12/1974 - Town buy for County Offices in Warren Green Bldg.

Ashby & Waterloo Corner
- 1817 - Palladium Office at 7th and Jail Streets
- c1840 - Farmers Hotel - Had several owners or managers
- 1907 - Library rent a room in Farmers Hotel
- 1909 - Hotel burn
- 1921 - Warrenton Supply Service Station — Esso
- 1985 - Formerly known as Barney's Texaco, now called Olde Town Texaco

#11 Winchester - corner with old Court Street, now Alexandria Pike
- 1854 - Wm. S. Clark house and livery stable
- 1880 - Miss Jane Blackwell house, occupied by Miss Kemper
- 1896 - Miss Nannie Kemper's Ice Cream Saloon
- 1909 - Burn
- 1929 - Building built on vacant lot for Garrett Motor Co.
- 1933 - Hickman & Hutchinson take over business
- 1940 - T. N. Fletcher's Court House Square Garage
    - Sell to Smith Bros.
    - Sell to Gay Strawer
- 12/1966 - Charter Industries
- 10/1979 - Bekins Transfer Building bought for Library
- 4/1972 - Fauquier County Library in renovated building

MAPS AND ILLUSTRATIONS

Sketch of Courthouse,
by Lee Moffett — Front Cover
"Many Faces of Court House Square",
painting by Lee Moffett. Courtesy
Mrs. R. J. Hockensmith, Warrenton,
Virginia
Deed From Thomas Maddox, 1790,
1790 — page 7-8
Route Platt, 1790 — page 9
Prison Bounds, 1793 — page 10
Plan of Warrenton, 1790 & 1811 —
page 12A
Town, 1212 — page 13
Public Square Boundaries, 1818 —
page 15, 16, 17
Central view, Warrenton, c1819 — page 18
Town's New Boundaries, 1850 — page 25
Alexandria Pike, 1862 — page 33
Fauquier County Courthouse, 1863 —
page 33
McClellan's Farewell to His Officers at
Warrenton, Va., 1862 — page 34
Warrenton, Lately Occupied by The Army
of Va., 1862 — page 35
Gray's New Map of Warrenton, 1878 —
page 49
Gray's New Map of Warrenton, 1878 —
page 50
Main Street, c1900 — page 69
Yates or 5-Corner Building, c1908 —
page 71
Burnt District, Winchester St., 1909 —
page 78
After The Fire of 1909 — page 79
Ruins Of Carter Hall, 1909 — page 79
Warrenton c1910 — page 81
Courthouse, c1920 — page 101
Opera House, c1921 — page 103
Main Street, c1922 (#1) — page 105
Main Street, c1922 (#2) — page 105
Culpeper Street, c1922 — page 106
Warrenton Day, 1923 — page 107
Warrenton Library, c1923 — page 110
Methodist Church, c1926 — page 115
Clerk's Office, c1926 — page 116
Warren Green, c1926 — page 116

Warrenton's Main Street, c1930 —
page 127
Dummy Policeman, c1930 — page 128
Main Street, c1939 — page 168
Main Street, c1942 — page 184
Physician's Hospital, c1942 — page 183
Army Infantry Parade, 1945 — page 192
Storm, 1947 — page 197
Library, c1947 — page 199
County Office Building with New
Monument, 1947 — page 199
Warren Green, c1949 — page 204
Proposed Traffic system — page 210
Main Street, c1952 — page 211
Fauquier National Bank, c1960 —
page 234
Proposed Traffic System, 1964 —
page 247
Proposed Traffic System, 1965 —
page 249
Courthouse, c1965 — page 250
Sketch of Proposed Square Design, 1970
page 265
Fauquier National Bank, c1973 —
page 274
Sketch of Old Gaol With Mosby
Monument, by Lee Moffett, 1975 —
page 278
Sketch of Library, by Lee Moffett, 1975
page 279
Sketch of Court House Square From FNB
Lawn, by Lee Moffett, 1975 —
page 280
Sketch of Main Street Looking East From
The Square, by Lee Moffett, 1975 —
page 282
#20 Main Street, 1882, 1972, 1982 —
page 302, 303
Fauquier County Public Library, 1987 —
page 324

INDEX

A&A (see Anderson & Allison) – 213, 260, 270
ABC Store – 149, 200
A-Auto Sales – 180
Academy Hill – 77, 113, 128, 145
Acme Market – 241
Adams, John – 30
Agriculture, Dept. of – 270
Alexander, Judge J.R.H. – 137, 138, 156, 159
Alexandria – 5, 9, 20
" Gazett – 10, 20
Allen, Mr. – 119
" , Rev. – 175
Allison, Alex – 213, 260
" , Luther L. – 213
" , Luther Lee – 242
Almond, Gov. – 229
American Civil Liberties Union – 314, 319
American Legion – 193
Ancient Independent Order of The Brothers & Sisters of The Sons & Daughters of Moses of the U.S. & the world At Large – 402
Anderson & Allison – 93, 102, 133, 213, 219
Anderson –
, Arthur R. – 102, 163, 213
Building – 126, 135, 171, 301
Clothing Company – 139
Ford (and Store) – 74, 84, 97, 126
, Lloyd – 126, 154, 295
, Lt. Charles – 235
, Mrs. Arthur (Virginia) 163
, Mrs. Ford – 145, 253, 256
, Robert – 104, 113, 128, 139, 223, 291
Anderson's Dental Office 291

Appleton –
, Col. – 157, 170
, Sam – 92, 102, 119
Arcade Bowling Alleys – 143
Area Agency On Agings' Nutrition Program – 291
Armory – 178
Armstrong, Neil – 261
Arrington –
, Arabelle Laws – 119, 144, 271
, Bailey – 206
Motors – 272
, Walter – 271
Arthur Murray Dance Class 215
Arundel, Arthur W. – 301
Ashby –
, Charlie – 71
, John – 59
Ashby, Thompson – 19
Athletic Field – 152
Atlantic & Pacific (A&P) – 126, 135, 140, 167, 172, 177, 217, 220, 224, 241
Auburn – 1
Aunt Ellen – 55
Austin –
, Alfred – 143
, Jimmy – 113

Bain & Trundel's Office Building – 263
Baker –
, "Cannonball" – 126
, Richard – 12
Balch, Hezekiah James – 6
"Balloon White" – 81
Balmoral Gift Shop – 309, 323
Baptist – 24, 35, 36, 48, 58, 60
Barbee, Lybrandt – 178
Barbe, Lucy – 200
Barnes, Austin – 162
" , Jeannette – 163
Barnhart, J. E. – 132, 196, 228

Barnett, James – 11, 12
Barrow, Col. Edward – 1
Barry –
, Maj. John – 86
Monument (See Public Square Fountain)
Barten, Rev. O. S. – 31
Bartenstein –
, Barbara – 255
, Betsy – 111, 114
, Ferdinand – 170
, John – 251
, L. R. – 165
, R. M. & Associates – 257
, Thomas E. – 225, 229
, W. G. – 107
Baston, Dr. – 34
Bataille, Mr. – 93
Battle, J. S. – 163
" , John – 220
Baucum, J. M. – 137
Beach –
, Dick (Richard) – 274, 291
, Joyce – 231
, Mary Lee – 144
Becham & Payne – 24
Bechaur & Voss – 32
Beckham & Voss – 28
" , John G. – 40
Bekins' Transfer Building 294
Belgium, Queen of – 154
Bell, John – 5
" , William – 20
Ben Franklin Bargain Store 156, 162, 163, 176
Benner, John (and Mrs.) – 117, 138, 200, 202
Benner's Field – 117, 202
Berlin, Irvin – 95
Bethel Military Academy – 61, 70, 77
Beverley –
, J. Brad – 72
, William – 54
Bishop –
Building – 133
, Ethel – 120, 122, 130, 146, 191, 206

345

Bishop, W. E. (& Store) –
  62, 104, 112
Bispham, Mrs. – 174
Black & Gold Inn – 14
Black Horse –
  Troop – 31, 153
  , Mrs. W. Murray – 178
Blackwell –
  , Ann – 6
  , Jane – 52
  , Joseph – 5, 12
  , Pauline – 263
Bluemont Concert Series –
  306
Blue Ridge Hardware –
  171, 201
Blythe, W. H. – 193
Boland, Mary – 92
Bond, Mrs. W. L. – 283
Bonnet, Henri – 196
Bon Ton Millinery Shop –
  114, 163
Booth –
  , George G. – 34, 53,
    57, 68
  , Mrs. A. A. – 61
Bootwright, Wm. – 48
Borman, Frank – 262
Bowling Alley – 123, 133,
  143
Bowman, Hunter – 119
Boyd, Wm. – 162
Boy Scouts – 82, 100,
  260, 262
Bradburn & Clatterbuck
  Livery Stable – 75, 77
Braddock, Maj. Gen.
  Edward – 4
Braddock's Well – 4, 170
Braddox, Martha – 109
Brady, Matthew – 32
"   , Nancy – 255
Bragg, Charles – 30
Braggs – 51
Braun, C. H. (& Grace)
  (& Variety Store) –
  222, 232, 266, 295
Brawner, H. N. – 54
Bray, Tim – 71
Brent Town Block House
  1
Brewer, Henry – 93
British War Relief Society
  Thrift Shop – 179
Brittle, Buster – 130
Brodie, A. M. (Tailor) –
  40, 56, 63, 73
Brody, Eugene – 276
Brooke –
  , Anne – 117

Brooke –
  , James – 26, 37, 286
  , James V. Jr. – 52, 72
  , Newton – 130, 155,
    177
  , Newton Sr. – 102
  , Richard N. – 59, 63,
    68, 92, 177
Brooke's Furniture Store –
  104
Bronough & Fant's Hotel
  23
Brower, Edward – 246,
  255, 271
Brown –
  , Amy – 264
  , Chauncey (& Society
    Orchestra) – 141,
    176
  , Georgia – 141
  , Wallace – 117
Browning, Rose (& Tom)
  312
Brummett, H. M. – 191
Buchanan, John R. – 152
Bull Run –
  Battle – 32
  Mountain – 20
Bunchfield, Va. – 236
Burke –
  , Lester – 107
  , W. Henry – 80, 89
Burnside, Gen. Ambrose –
  34
Bush, George – 309
Butler, Henry – 157
Butts, Capt. Archie – 76
Byrd –
  , Admiral – 129, 151
  , Harry F. – 206

C&S Florist – 175, 307
California House – 13, 29,
  40, 54, 55, 124, 165,
  201
Caldwell –
  , James – 14, 21, 23,
    59
  , Lycurgus W. – 23
Calohan, O. B. – 84, 87
Camden T.V. Sales &
  Service – 219
Campbell –
  , B. M. – 38
  , May Mosby – 241
  , Mosby – 135
Canard, PFC Robert –
  191, 249
Caprice Cafe – 310
Carolina Road – 1, 2, 3

Carousel, The – 294
Carpenter Motors – 143
Carr, Fred – 142, 150
Carroll, A. L. – 227
Carr's Restaurant – 142
Carter –
  Building – 156, 157
  , Capt. & Mrs. Edward
    78, 85, 86, 99
  , Col. Robert S. – 2
  , Dr. C.S. – 67, 80, 113
  , George S. – 44, 46
  Hall – 67, 70, 78, 289
  , H.B. (and Dept. or
    5&10 Store) – 74,
    96, 99, 186, 295
  , Jimmy – 286, 297
  , John – 59
  , John W. – 177
  , Mason – 204
  , Molly – 92
  , Paul – 207
  , Scott – 146
  , Shirley – 209
  , Wayman – 85, 91, 96,
    102, 117, 127, 177,
    215, 248, 260
Carter's Exchange-
  Furniture Building –
  74, 179, 187, 189
Carter's –
  Gulf Station – 272
  Run – 3, 82
Cash, John A. – 21
Cassanova – 26, 77
Cathloic Church – 31,
  230, 240
Cattlett, Col. John – 1
CETA – 289
Challenger – 317
Chamberlain & Hamilton's
  138, 203, 276, 307
Chamberlain, Holcombe –
  92
Chancellar, Charlie – 121
Charity Lodge of The Odd
  Fellows (see Odd
  Fellows)
Charland, Bob "Kingfish"
  176
Charlottes' – 162
Charlottesville – 5
Charter Industries – 254,
  257
Chase, Lieut. – 38
Cherrix, Royce – 308
Chichester, George – 190
Children's House (of
  Fauquier) – 186

346

Children's Do It Yourself
  Rainbow Theater –
  (See Rainbow Theater)
Childs, Alice Jane – 312
Chilton, Samuel – 22, 23
China – 165
"Chinatown" – 139
Chinese Laundry – 138,
  139, 202, 307
Chinn, Rev. Mr. – 96, 122
Chios, Steve – 187
Christian Scientist – 324
Chryster, Walter P. – 183,
  193, 201
City Drug Store – 62
Clark, Betty – 206
"   , William – 28
Clarkson, D.H.M. – 66
"   , Mr. – 100
Clatterbusk, John – 94, 95
Clay, Henry – 22
Clerk's Office (see also
  County Building) – 10,
  19, 20, 56, 80, 111,
  113, 114, 152, 278,
  311
Cleveland, Grover – 59
Cochran, George B. – 46
Cockrill, Stanley – 210
Coffee Shoppe, The – 132,
  143, 161, 228
Cole, Sam – 214
Collins –
  , Capt. Newton – 78
  , Gov. L Preston – 203
Cologne, E.N. – 203
Color Collections – 310
Columbian Mirror – 10
Colvin, Capt. – 179
Commercial Cabinetry &
  Millwork – 320
Company K-17th Va.
  Infantry Regiment –
  245
Community Action
  Program – 276
Community And Armed
  Forces Lounge (see
  USO)
Community Store – 109
Confederate Dead
  Monument – 42, 47,
  217
Conway Grove – 145
Cooke, Edward E. – 22
Coolidge, Calvin – 108
Coons –
  Market (grocery) –
  132, 150, 161
  , Mrs. – 190

Coons, W. Ennis – 133,
  135, 172
Cornblatt, Edith & Herman
  137
Cornblatts' – 136, 137,
  216
Cornwell, Margaret – 232,
  244
Cordell, Wm. B. – 18
County Casuals – 311
County Club – 164
County Cousin Craft &
  Gift Shop – 310
County Building & Circuit
  Courthouse (see
  Courthouse)
County Office Building
  (see John Marshall
  Building & Clerk's
  Office)
Courthouse (see also
  General District
  Building & County
  Building and Circuit
  Courthouse) – 5, 6, 7,
  10, 18, 27, 28, 30, 59,
  60, 149, 278, 279
Courthouse Missions – 62,
  63
Court House Square (see
  Public Square)
Court House Square
  Garage – 155
Courtney, John D. – 82
Cowles –
  , Miss – 128
  , Wesley & William –
  12
Cox –
  , Eppa S. – 111
  , Luther – 186, 201,
  205, 210, 213, 231,
  294, 306
  , Mrs. Luther – 218
Craig, Lawrence – 132,
  144
Creamery – 55, 148
Creel's Jewelry – 175
Cripple Children's Hospital
  113, 146, 155
Cropp, Shelton – 70
Cross, Cyrus – 29
Crummett, Donald – 240
Cuba – 66, 67
Cub Run County Antiques
  310
Cunningham –
  , Alexander (& Co. of
  Glasgow) – 3, 5, 48
  , William & Co. – 5

Curtis, Carroll – 135
"   , Inman – 241

D&K Bakery – 291
Dalton, Col. Bob – 169
"   , John – 279
D'Anglo – 131
Davenport, Edith – 122
Davis –
  , Dr. George H. – 190
  , Jefferson – 216
  , John – 223
  , Myer – 146
Day, Turner – 151, 194
Deakin's, Inc. – 161
Dean, Jimmy – 286
Deats, Alfred Francis –
  177
Debtor's Oak – 78
Delaplane, D. – 53
De Marco, Mrs. Roger O. –
  307
Demetroulis, Jim – 291
Dennis –
  , Mrs. Wesley – 239
  , Wesley – 225
Depot – 179, 284
" Restaurant – 284
Dewey, Thomas – 202
D. H. Lee & Co. (See Lee,
  D.H.)
Dickerson –
  , Cecil – 144, 177
  , George – 146
Dingwall, Pat – 287
District Nursing Home –
  223
Dollar General Store – 295
Doram, (Dorum) James
  (and store) – 55, 56,
  69, 83, 271
Dorbayan, Ali & Karen –
  284, 306
Douglas, M. G. – 86
Doumas, Charles – 150
Downey, Claudia Edwards
  244
Downs –
  , Nellie Sudduth – 67,
  129
  , Wm. A. Sr. – 80
Downtown Store – 223,
  234, 277, 278
Downtown Theater – 289
Drake, John – 166
Drish, Dr. John – 14
Dummy Policeman – 128,
  129, 131, 157
Duncan, John – 4

347

Eastham, Philip – 240
Edgar Snowden, Ltd. – 305
Edmonds, Col. Wm. – 12
Edwards –
  , Andrew (and Tavern) 5, 9
  , Valerie – 262
Eicher, James L. – 239
Eichers', Florist & Gift Shop – 300, 323
Eisenhower, Dwight D. – 213, 223, 260, 283
Elliott, Joseph W. – 224, 225
Ellis –
  , Martha – 252, 270
  , Norman – 245
Embrey, Linwood – 269
Embrey's Flower Shop – 173
Emsweller, Mr. – 157
English –
  , John A. – 22
  , Misses – 203
Episcopal Church – 12, 13, 24, 27, 35, 40, 45, 74, 83, 84, 93, 124
Eustace, William – 5
Evans –
  , Dick – 223
  , Ida – 139
  , Louise – 81, 254, 275, 297
  , Lucy – 121
Explorer I – 226
Extension Service Office – 314

Fairfax –
  , Lady Catherine – 1, 2
  , Lord George William 2
  , Lt. Gov. Francis – 4, 258, 261
  , Sir Thomas – 1
  , Thomas the 6th – 2, 159
Falmouth – 5
Fants, Henry – 27
Farkas, Bob – 270
Farmers' Hotel – 21, 22, 30, 42, 53, 63, 75, 104
Farmers' Market – 306, 308
Farnsworth, Donald – 250, 271
Farrar, Gina (Virginia) – 272, 319
Farraro, Geraldine – 309

Farrar's at Harrington House – 319
Fashion Shop – 156, 164, 219
Fauquier –
  Chapter of Va. Museum 255
  Cleaners – 150
  Club – 275
  County – 4
  County Hospital – 111, 112, 218, 223, 227, 228, 229
  County Hospital Auxiliary Thrift Shop (see Thrift Shop)
  County Community Action Committee 256
  County Public Library (see Library)
  Court House – 5, 7, 10, 11, 261
  Court & Office Building (see County Build. & Circuit Court)
  Democrat Building – 74
  Female Institute – 29, 46, 70
  , Francis – 4, 258, 261
  Furniture & Electric Co. – 177
  Grocery – 109
  High School – 128, 160, 178, 280, 304
  Historical Foundation 248, 255
  Laundry – 203
  Marbleworks – 47
  Militia of Volunteers – 6
  National Bank – 72, 111, 113, 143, 260, 268, 273, 317
  Pharmacy – 271
  Recreation Center (& Skating Rink) – 146
  Springs (White Sulphur) 23, 46, 47, 166
  Theater – 130, 139
  William – 258
Feeley, Susan – 287
Fewell –
  & Co. – 133, 156
  , Lucy – 70
  , Mrs. Kate – 133, 156

Fire House (Dept. organization) – 41, 42, 57, 58, 60, 61, 72, 75, 104, 107, 112, 123, 134, 136, 143, 290, 295, 310
First Baptist Church – 38, 60
First Chance-Last Chance Bar – 207
First Church of Christ, Scientist Church – 316
FISH – 308
Fisher –
  Brothers' Bar – 55
  , Minnie – 216
"Fishtown" – 70
Fitzhugh, Dudley – 21
  ", Tho. L. – 21
Five Points Store or Corner 27, 28, 39, 44, 52, 71, 77, 109
Flag Factory – 87
"Flats, The" – 70
Fletcher –
  , Albert – 69, 88, 173, 307
  , Basil – 112
  Brothers – 70, 74, 81, 83
  Building – 81, 89, 100, 123
  , Edward R. – 175
  Furniture Store – 91
  , G. L. – 102
  , Judge – 96, 97
  , Keith – 295
  , Mrs. T. N. – 139
  , Thad N. – 88, 154, 155, 161, 295
Flynn, James – 53
  ", L. C. – 149
Foley, R. E. (Restaurant & Bowling Alley) – 54, 57, 86, 102, 131, 133, 136
Follen & Jeff Jolly – 62
Follin, Madison – 28
Forbes, Mrs. Murray – 67
Ford, Gerald – 277, 286
FORE Workshop – 307
Fort Belvoir – 166
Fort Duquesne – 4
Fort Myer Cavalry – 181
Fox, Louise – 110
  ", Robert – 262, 270, 297
Francis Fauquier Garden Club (see Garden Club)
Franey, Robert – 266

348

Franks – 48
Frank, Thomas E. – 74, 90, 112, 113, 126, 129, 142, 160, 167, 176, 193
Frazier –
, J. A. – 118, 122, 161
, Julia and Ruth – 122
French, Julia (store) – 55, 117
Free State Ramblers – 195
Frey, Mr. – 97, 130
Frost, Tom – 69, 223, 230
Furniture Interior – 253, 257

Gaines –
, Bill – 122
& Bros. Bank – 63, 64, 65
, Col. – 203
, Granville – 60
, Grenville – 7
, Johnny – 144
, J. S. – 63
Law Office – 56
, McPherson – 175
, Wm. H. – 23, 29, 39, 40, 61, 63
Galloway & Everhart Livery Stable – 48, 62, 64, 90
Galloway, C. F. – 54, 55
Gaol Museum (see Old Gaol or Old Jail)
Garden Club –
, Francis Fauquier – 301
, Warrenton – 83
Gardiner, Robert H. Jr. – 201
Gardiner's Drug Store – 250, 257, 271
Garner –
, John N. – 140, 162
, W. A. – 75, 76
Garrett –
, City Risdon – 127, 133, 156, 186, 219
, Gene Jr. – 126, 186, 301
, Gene Sr. – 98, 123, 126, 155
, Irvin – 77, 90, 93, 95, 101, 102, 117, 119, 171
Motor Co. (Garage) – 123, 126, 127, 130, 131, 133, 153, 157, 162, 220, 221

Gaskin, Wm. – 54
Gaskins –
& Digges – 48
, C. F. – 54, 70
, F. D. – 85, 86
Gates, W. B. Jr. – 151
Gay Oldsmobile – 254, 257, 266, 271
George VI, King – 164
Gemini – 262
General District Court Building (see also Courthouse) – 278, 291
Gibson, Hoot – 162
Gildersleeve, Miss – 197
Gill –
, CC & Sons – 157
, Forrest – 172, 198, 208
, Howard – 240
, Rudy – 180, 188
Gill's Furniture & Appliance Store – 127, 224
Gill's Implement Co. – 172, 180
Glascock, Ann – 11
" , Jennings – 12
" , Peter – 11
Glassell, Margaret – 20
Glassford, Gen. – 140
Glen Ora – 236
Glenn, John – 239
Godfrey –
, Arthur – 165, 166
, Kay – 229
Gold Cup Race – 105, 281, 301, 308
Golf Course, Lucky Strike Miniature – 121, 130
G., Mr. – 112
Gomez, Jose Miguel – 67, 68
Gookin, Mrs. – 287
Gospel Wagon – 63, 64, 72
Gouldthorpe, W. H. "Peanut" – 157
Graham, H. N. – 54
Granada Island – 304
Grant, Gen. Ulysses S. – 37
Gray Ghost – (see John Mosby)
Gray, Pauline Evelyn – 177
Grayson –
Building – 253
, Dr. Cary – 76
Family – 218

Grayson –
, Francis – 182
, John – 135, 182
Grayson's Department Store – 135, 202, 251, 253
Great American Smokeout 315
Great Meadows – 301, 309
Green –
, Charles T. – 29, 43
, Philip – 310
, Ruth – 156
Grimsley, Turner – 187, 213, 215, 236
Groome, H. C. – 159
" , Shirley – 257
Gude, Winmill & Co. – 165

Hackett, Joseph – 245
Hailey, Mark – 268, 299
Hailey's Shoe Center – 268, 299
Haley, Dr. Byrnal M. – 172, 238, 252, 253, 271
Hall –
, Eva B. – 201
, Hotchkiss – 128
, Sam – 126, 163, 176, 212, 309
, Sam III – 212
Hamilton –
, Alex Jr. – 138, 159, 276
, A. S. – 137, 138
Parish – 2
Haiti – 145
" Street Town Park – 299
Hampton, Gen. Wade – 47
Hansbrough –
, John – 248
, Josh – 248
, Welton – 122, 248
Hansbrough's Harness-Tack Repair Shop – 161, 248
Harder Brothers Electrical Contractors – 118
Harder, Mrs. Sam – 131
Harding, Warren G. – 108
Harris –
, Barney – 181
, Harrington "Skip" – 123, 288, 289
, Wm. – 196
Hauptman – 151
Havana – 66

349

Hawkins, Kemper — 163
Hayloft, The — 300, 301
"Hayti" or "Haytti" — (see Haiti)
Hayworth, Stan — 312
H. B. Carter & Co. — (see Carter, H. B.)
Health Dept. — 72
Heath, Gary — 306, 310
Helm, Erasmus — 21, 28, 42, 43
Helm's Store — 277
Hickman — 171
Hicks, Bill — 91
       ", Dr. R.I. — 58
Hiden Building (Theater) — 91, 129, 130, 144, 156, 162, 171, 172
Hiden —
   , Dolly — 160
   , Dr. M. B. — 120, 124, 131, 143, 145, 159, 162, 191, 231, 256, 257
Highlander's Radio & TV Sales & Service — 240
Hilbert, F. W. — 84, 87
Hilleary —
   Building (Store) — 43, 52, 54, 83, 134, 216, 220
   , Isabel — 121
   , P. W. — 52
   , R. W. — 55, 70, 80, 86
   , Wm. Perry — 43, 55
Hilter, Adolf — 137, 171, 180
Hilts, Miss Lee — 248
Hindenburg — 164
Hitchcock, Josine — 272
H. M. Pearson School — (see Pearson)
Hobo King — 214
Hockey Rink — 145
Hodges, Luther — 246
Hodgkin—
   "Biggie" — 102, 113, 151, 176, 227, 285
   , Bill — 102, 113, 238, 305
   , Dr. J. O. — 45, 62, 86, 113
   , Dr. J. O. Jr. — 305
   , Dr. J. O. III — 118, 135, 144, 285, 305
Hodgkins, Dr. & Mrs. Frank — 118, 120, 256
Holmes, Jack — 70
Hoover, Herbert — 125
Hord, Dr. Ambrose — 26

Horner —
   , Charles — 58
   , C. G. — 74
   , Dr. Brown — 14
   , Dr. Gustavus B. — 7, 12
   , Dr. G. R. B. — 38, 51
   , Inman — 14, 24, 28, 67
   , Joseph — 26, 27
   , Wm. — 6, 7, 10, 12, 18, 22, 48
Horner's Hill — 145
Hospice of Fauquier — 301
Hostrop, Betsy — 285
Hotel de Shirley — (see Jail) — 142, 149
Hotel Street Players — 288, 289
Hout, L. T. Jeweler — 55, 62, 256, 307
Howard, J. L. — 104
Hudson, Mary Ellen — 231
Hughes, Winfee — 196
Humphrey, Scott — 295
Humphry, Hubert — 246, 259
Hunton, Dr. G. W. (& Drugstore) — 55, 56, 59, 62
Hurst —
   , Clifton Jeweler — 100
   , G. W. Jeweler — 68, 99
Hutchinson —
   , Charles — 23
   , Tom — 122, 123, 131, 132, 176
   Travel Bureau — 256
Hutton — 42
   & Payne — 93, 274
   , Elizabeth I. — 75, 88, 117
   , Eppa Jr. — 59
   , Gen. Eppa — 61
   , H. O. or H. I. — 86, 87
Hyde, Phil — 301

I.G.A. — 311
Independent Register — 21
Inter-Technology Solar Corp — 292, 298, 299
Iran — (see Shah)
Ivy Basket — 322

Jack & Jill Child Care Center-School — 272
Jackson, Andrew — 20, 21, 76

Jacobs —
   , Cpl. Grenville — 191
   , John M. — 22, 23
   , Robert — 304
   , Vincent — 7
Jaeger, Mrs. Louis — 246
Jail (see also Hotel de Shirley, Old Gaol) — 19, 2, 54
Jail Museum — (see Old Gaol Museum)
James, Jessie — 169
Japan — 165
JBP Building — (see John Barton Payne)
Jefferson, The — 22
Jeffries —
   , C. H. — 195
   , Charles — 75, 104, 118, 167, 176, 177, 179, 209, 226, 238, 257
   Drugstore or building — 54, 62, 201
   , I. W. — 75
   , James Walden — 127, 184
   , Joseph Arthur — 42, 46, 47, 52, 55, 62, 68, 72, 202
   , J. P. — 54
   , Smith A. — 30
Jenkin, Alan — 201
Jenkins' Corner — 48
Jennings —
   , Lula Sowers — 53
   , Mrs. — 174
Jessup, S. A. — 194
Jimmy's (Jimmie's) Market 127, 173, 202
John Barton Payne and Building — 92, 108, 110, 158, 305
John Marshall Building — (see County Building) 311
Johnson —
   , Bob and Ford — 295
   , Dr. S. M. — 147
   , Eleanor — 233
   , J. C. — 53
   , Lyndon — 244, 245, 246
Johnson's Food Store — 260, 270
Johnson's Photographic Studio — 159
Jolley —
   & Kirby — 65, 68
   , Jeff — 62

Jones —
, Elizabeth Fairfax Gaines Smith — 125
, H. B. — 236, 240, 241, 305
, Wm. — 4
J/R's Hair Cutters — 307
Kays —
, Kenny — 75, 109, 119
, W. H. — 75, 109, 131
Kearnes, Campbell — 163, 288
Keith —
, Betsy — 95
, Elizabeth Sharpless — 108
, Isham — 141
, J. A. C. — 63
, Judge James — 52, 55
, Lucien — 5, 80, 86, 89, 92
, Mr. — 145
, Mrs. Julian C. — 186, 95
Kelly, Dennis — 61
Kemper —
, Agnes L. — 224
, Eliza — 24
, Mariah A. — 24
, Mrs. — 52
, Nannie E. — 64
Kendall, Buck — 108
Kennedy —
, John — 235, 236, 241, 244
, Robert — 259
Kerns, Shelby — 297
Khrushchev — 241
Kidwell, James — 173, 248, 287
Kidwell's Market — (see also Jimmy's) — 287
Kincade, Minnie — 291
Kinchloe, Ed — 88
Kinchloe's Hay & Grain Feed Store — 103
King —
, E. B. — 152
, Heath — 298
, Rev. Dr. Martin Luther Jr. — 258
Kinser, Mary Ann — 317
Kinski —
, Florence — 257
, Joseph — 271
, Mrs. Richard — 257
Kirby —
, Bud — 90
Building — 202

Kirby —
, Jean — 202
, Willard — 118, 121, 155, 223, 231, 275
Kirson's Dept. Store — 138, 165
Kloman, E. F. - Drugstore or Building — 42, 45, 46, 47, 53
Knotty Pine Coffee Shop 252, 270
Krage, Evelyn — 305
Kress Building — (see also S&H Kress) — 266, 295, 301
Kreticos —
, Jimmy — 161
, John — 111, 142, 161, 162, 169, 179, 185, 186, 188
, Mildred — 163, 209
Krisel, Theo — 52
Krisel's Bakery — 55, 73

LaFayette, Gen. Marquis de — 19, 114
Lakeman, Wm. — 13, 22
Landon — 162
Larcombe, Ray — 176
Latham & Greene — 28, 53
Lawrence, Robert de T. — 275, 289
Laws, Arrabelle — 119, 144
Leach, Thelma B. — 236
Lee —
, Fitzhugh — 59
, Gen. Robert E. — 37, 39, 233, 292
, Henry — 55
, Julian P. — 55
, Richard Henry — 4, 5, 7, 48
, Thomas — 2, 4, 9
, Thornton — 225
Travers' Furniture — 294
Lees, D. H. — 188, 193
Leeton Forest — 35
Leggat, Scott — 320
Lemmon, Rev. George — 13, 21, 23
Lerner Bros. Dept. Store — 165, 168, 173, 253, 301
Lewis —
, Dick — 90
, John L. — 201
, Sam — 147
, Wm. H. — 233

Library Annex — 305
Library, Warrenton — (also Fauquier Co. Public Library) — 75, 79, 81, 108, 109, 113, 121, 278, 285, 294, 295, 297, 301
Likly, John — 5, 48
Lincoln, President — 32, 68
Lindbergh, Charles — 118, 125, 151, 178
Lindsay, Mr. — 32
Lineweaver, J. W. — 290, 322
Linsay, S. C. — 286
Lion, Lewis — (see Lyon)
Lions' Club — 172
Little Folks — 93, 307, 322
Livery & Sales Stables of C. F. Galloway — (see Galloway)
Livery Stable, Warrenton Carriage Works — (see Warrenton)
Living Branch, The — 309
Lodge of the Sons & Daughters of Moses — 218
Long, Chaffraix — 141
"   , Huey — 154
Love, Congressman — 14
Lovell, Jim Jr. — 262
Luke, Sprat — 176
Lunceford —
, Adle — 163
, Edith Davenport — 122
, Ethel — 237, 238
, Robert — 77, 84, 90, 94, 114, 117, 119, 132
, Thomas R. — 28
Lyon —
, Elkon — 28
, Louie (Lewis Lion) — 53, 56

Mack's Pastry Shop — 255
Mac's Cabs — 206
Macre, John — 21
MADD — 301
Maddux —
, James H. — 42, 45, 63
, James K. — 55
, Thomas — 6, 7, 251
Madison —
, Carrie - and Barber Shop — 318

Madison –
, Charlie - and Barber Shop – 55, 88, 91, 102, 202, 225, 250, 318
, Lee – 225, 251
Magill, Dr. Buckner – 158
Mahone, Gov. Billy – 59
Mahoney, Bernie – 231
Main Thing, The – 272, 319, 322
Manassas Battle – 32
Manor of Leeds – 2
Mansfield, Jill – 271
Marble Yard – 55, 62
Market House – 20, 23, 38
Marr –
, John – 31
, John Q. – 28, 31, 203
Marriott –
, Henrietta – 290
, Richard H. – 120, 200, 206, 210, 230, 231, 238, 305
Marshall –
, Charles – 56
, Douglas – 287
, John and Statue – 6, 22, 30, 59, 227, 228, 229, 230
National & Trust Co. Bank – 139
, Thomas – 6
, Wm. – 230
, Wm. C. – 52, 112, 230, 256
Marsteller, Phil – 157
Martin –
, Carroll – 290
, Ed J. – 71
, Mable Rider – 117, 144
, Nancy – 203
, T. I. – 139, 182
Martyn, Ben F. – 57, 62
Masonic Hall (Masons) – 23, 42, 47, 67, 263
Massie, G. Herbert – 120
Matteo, Mary – 255
Matthew –
& Fewell – 117
, Mr. – 133
Maxheimer –
, Albert – 151, 176
, Blinky – 133
, Shirley – 133
Mayflower Restaurant – 161, 162, 163, 171, 172, 185, 186
Mayhugh, Dick – 250

Mayhugh, George – 301
Maynard, Ken – 155
McCarty, Mason – 84, 264
McClanahan –
, Mabel – 290
, Mrs. Robert – 248, 256
, Raymond – 256
, Robert Photo Shop – 248, 260
McClellan, Gen. George B. 34
McConchie, B. F. – 52, 55
       ", Ray – 255
McDonnell, Austin – 145
McIntosh –
Clothing Store (John) 127, 173
, Mrs. Lucy L. (John) – 127, 156
McIntyre, Major – 97, 102, 124, 128, 137
McKee – 138
    ", Ralph – 157
McKinley – 64, 66
McLearen, Ernest L. – 161
McPherson, Gen. – 174
Mead, Bishop – 12
Meade – 36
Meadow Outdoors Foundation – 308
Meadowville – 160
MEDEVAC – 305
Melchers, Gori – 76
Melrose – 26
Memēre's Quality Bakery 130, 135, 180, 294
Memorial Park – 99
Menefee, Mr. – 54
Mercer, Charles Fenton – 19
Methodist – 14, 24, 25, 27, 30, 39, 40, 45, 80, 85, 89, 296, 306, 309
Mexico –
, Chihuahua – 171
, City – 171
Meyers – 90
Miller, Polk – 155
Millner, 1st Sgt. M. G. – 294
Mills & Roche – 66
Mills, Rachel – 256, 269
Minter –
, Margaret – 136
, Nina – 136
, Randolph T. – 136
Minute Men – 6
Mitenger's Pump – 170
Mix, Tom – 119, 158
Moffett – 48

Moffett –
, Blair – 226
, Frank – 150, 162, 212
, H. R. – 67, 68
, Nelson – 175, 193
Mondale, Walter – 309
Monroe, James – 19
Montgomery –
, Dorothy – 95
, Ian – 109, 263
Ward Catalogue Sales Agency – 258, 295, 311
Monument to Service Men 198
Moore –
, Billy & Billy Jr – 168
, Dorothy – 212
, Thomas L. – 19
Morgan, Wm. Eating house and home – 52, 65, 73
Morse, Samuel F. P. – 23
Mosby –
, John – 35, 36, 52, 91, 241, 279
Monument – 93, 98, 100, 256, 263
Square (Plaza) – (see also Public Square)
Moser Funeral Home – 222
Moses Hall – 218, 286, 288, 289, 309, 319
Moss, Lucian – 120
Moving Arts Center – 293
Mt. Zion Church – 208, 231, 235, 261, 263
Municipal Building – 61, 65, 80, 89, 143, 273, 275
Muntz Television – 209
Myer, Mr. – 174
Mytinger, Jacob – 44

National Variety Store – 112, 301
Natural Food Store – 307
Neavil, George – 1
Neavil's Ordinary or Tavern – 3
Nelson –
, Bill – 307
, Joseph H. – 10, 55, 56, 57
, Rev. G. – 65
Nelson's Auto Accessories & Parts – 146
Neptune Lodge – 206
Nesbit – 152

Nevill, Tim – 260
New Baltimore – 117
New Baltimore Journal – 53
Newby, Mrs. – 174
Newton –
  Bros. Circus – 166
  , Mr. – 244
New Warrenton Restaurant 150, 174, 186, 187, 217
New Warrenton Theater – 97
New Waterloo Court Condominum-Office Building – 303
New York – 171
New York Ninth, The – 34
Neyhart, Dorothy – 177
Nichol, H. R. – 152
Nina's 5 & 10¢ Store – 222
Nixon, Richard M. – 259, 272, 277
Noland, Barbara – 290
Nordix Farm – 135
Norris –
  , Ann E. – 286
  , Septimus – 12
  Tavern – 20, 21
  , Thaddeus – 14, 18, 19, 24
Northern Virginia Shopping Center – 234
North Wales – 183
Nusbaum –
  , Aaron – 54, 62, 74, 140, 154
  & Anderson – 74

O'Bannon –
  , Presley Neville – 11
  , Silas – 296
O'Brien, Harry – 92, 119, 227
O'Connell –
  , Blanche – 118, 182
  , Daniel – 301
  , Joseph Martin – 82, 84, 87, 88, 90, 92, 93, 94, 112, 119, 310, 317
  , Mrs. J. M. – 201
Odd Fellows Hall – 23, 24, 27, 47, 48
Olde Town Wood Chop – 289
Olde Towne Paint & Wallpaper Center – 277, 288

Old Gaol Museum – (see also Jail) – 246, 269, 291
Old Timer – (see Louise Evans)
Old Town Gallery – 290, 306
Old Town Handcrafts & Collectibles – 321
Old Town Warrenton Day (Spring Festival) – 295
Olinger, Ashby W. – 306
Olympic Flame – 308
Opera House – 91
Orange –
  & Alexandria R. R. – 26, 28
  Court House – 20
Ostrow Building – 209
Ostrow, Johanna & Walter 209

Padgett, Dempsey – 307
Palladium of Liberty, The 14, 38
Pappas –
  , Cleora – 313
  , Ernest – 150, 160, 162, 163, 167, 174, 179, 186, 187, 189, 196, 204, 218, 221, 318
  , Gus – 190
  , Virginia Painter – 207, 217, 318
  , Wm. – 150
Painter, Virginia – 174, 186, 189
Paint Shop, The – 288
Palmer –
  , Meade – 264
  , Robert E. – 248, 260
Paregal, Goldie S. – 147
Parker, Mrs. H. A. – 77
Parkinson, Mr. – 59
Parks & Recreation Board 273, 281, 285
Parlagreco, Stefano – 310
Patterson, Mrs. – 136
Pattie –
  Building Store – 109, 131, 163, 209
  , C. M. – 64, 89, 164
  , Dudley M. – 27
  , Horace – 53
  , R. M. – 80
  , T. Ed – 52, 64, 67, 81, 120, 161
  , William A. – 6, 26, 27, 38, 48

Patton, A. Woodrow – 236
Paul's Electric & Furniture 294
Payne –
  , A. D. – 53
  Bank – 63
  , Buddy – 291
  Building – 72
  , Capt. Alexander Dixon – 52
  , Dr. Winter – 38
  , James Nelson – 260
  , John Barton – (see John Barton Payne)
  , John Nelson – 260
  , Larry – 279
  , Louis B. – 176
  , Rice – 188
  , Richard – 5
  , Rossier – 273
P. B. Smith School – 294
Peace Corps – 313
Pearl Harbor – 182
Pearson –
  Elementary School – 294
  , Eva – 132
  , James – 233
  , Raymond – 109, 130, 163
  , Ron – 307
  , Virginia Ann – 170
Peirpoint, Gov. – 37
Penn, Clifton E. – 255
Penny, "Ollie" – 232
Peoples National Bank – 70, 80, 83, 161, 216, 222, 318
Peoples Pleasure Palace – 127
Perdum, Aubrey & Ruth Hart – 137
Persons, Forest – 312
Peyton, Yelverton – 5
Phillips, Kitty – 163
Phipps –
  Building – 210
  , Hubert B. – 206
Physician's Hospital – 182, 194, 215
Piccadilly, Ltd. – 318, 324
Pickett –
  , Ann – 10
  , George B. – 12
  , Martin – 6, 9, 10, 11, 14
Piedmont Cultural Arts Center – 309
Piedmont Environmental Council – 293

Piedmont Whig – 24
Pillory – 7, 19, 21
Pipenbring – 27
Pitt's Theater – 165
Planning Mill – 57
Poe, Allen – 190
Poehlman, George – 149
Pollock, Roberta – 35
Polo Field – 229
Pony Show – (see Warrenton)
Pool Room – 138, 159, 175
Pope, Henry V. – 21
" , Major Gen. – 34
Portnoy –
, Mollie – 300
, Ted (Theodore) – 179, 300, 301
Post Office – 55, 58, 63, 70, 96, 135, 153
Post, Wiley – 154
Powers, Francis Gary – 243
Prechtel, Don – 315
Presbyterian – 12, 24, 29, 35, 58, 91, 258, 289
Pretlow –
, Dr. – 232
House – 3
Price, Nancy – 230
Prickashikoff, Mme. – 188
Prince Wm. County – 2, 4
Prison – 7
Provost Marshall – 37
Public Square – 21, 26, 251, 257, 263, 264, 266
Public Square –
Cistern – 51, 52, 53, 59, 61, 77, 85, 87, 129, 130
Fountain – 86, 95, 117, 122
Well – 86, 207
Pumitia, Alice – 287

Quantico – 129

Rainbow Street Theater – 288, 293
Rainey, Speaker – 140
Ramey, Edgar – 70
Randolph –
, Mrs. A. M. – 172
, Mrs. Norman V. – 36
Rankin, Jimmy – 312
Reagan, Ronald – 297, 298, 309
Rec Hall – (see Fauquier Rec Hall)

Rector –
, Dan – 228
, W. E. Jr. – 141
Red Front Store – 156
Red Store – 3, 4, 6, 7, 9, 10, 18
Reed, Jim – 135
Remington – 59, 186
Revere, Paul – 6
Rhodes –
Drug Store – 167, 201
, J. W. – 167, 256
Rice, Mrs. Leo – 211
Richards –
, Col. J. D. – 114
, Mary – 119
, Paul C. – 84, 88, 264
Richardson, Evelyn B. – 224
Richie, Hunter – 157
Rider, Mabel – 117
Rindsberg, Abraham – 23, 27, 174
Rindsberg's Store – 23, 32
Risdon –
, Carroll – 171, 189, 270
, City – 127, 133, 156, 186
, Eddie – 123, 154, 155, 167, 171
, Home & Garden Center, Inc. – 270, 285
, Lucy L. – 127
Paint & Hardware – 171, 189, 270
, William H. – 137
, Willis – 270
Risque, Mr. – 181
Ritter, Frances Carter – 244
Rixey –
, B. F. – 45
, James M. – 44, 46
Rixley –
, John – 41
, P. M. – 76
Roadhouse & Bunch – 91, 99, 135, 136, 180, 222
Robb, Charles – 304
Robbins (Robins), Mrs. – 78
Robert E. Lee Restaurant 179
Roberts, Barnett – 272
Robinson –
, Albert – 75, 85, 88, 98, 119, 284
, Mary Lee Beach – 144

Robinson –
, Walter – 147
, William P. – 295
, William E. Jr. – 82
Rockerfellow, Nelson – 277
Rockwood Hall – 286
Rogers, Will – 154
Ronnie Poe's Olde Towne Texaco – (see Warrenton Supply)
Roop, Linda & Tom – 307
Roop's Refrigeration – 323
Roosevelt –
, F. D. – 136, 160, 162, 173, 177, 190, 191
, Theodore – 76, 131, 169
Rose –
, Alex – 63
, Kitty – 109
Rosenwald High School – 171, 210
Ross House – 239
" , Ruel H. – 27
Routt, James – 7, 9
Rowdy Hall – 55
Rowe, Gladys – 212
Rowzie, Reuben – 65, 108
Ruffner, Pres – 157
Rust, Dorothy Montgomery – 95

Saddle Shop, The – 248
Sadler, Sallie Wood – 67, 77, 86, 95, 179, 317
Safeway – 178, 273, 293, 299
St. Clair –
, Cornelia and store – 55, 62
, Dr. J. O. – 55
, Dr. R. R. O. – 62
St. James Episcopal Church – (see Episcopal)
St. John Catholic Church or School – (see Catholic)
Sanford –
, D. D. and store – 130, 135, 136, 290
, Mrs. D. D. – 222
Sanitary Grocery-Meat Market – 157, 171, 176
Sauer –
Building – 165, 168
, Charles M. – 176, 222, 232

354

Saunders –
  Boot & Shoemaking – 55
  , John A. – 22, 55
  , Thomas E. – 55
Scates, Lucille – 202
Schwab –
  , A. D. – 233
  , Anton – 109
  , Arthur – 56
  , T. R. "Dick" – 62, 85, 135
Scientific Skin Care Salon – 308
Scott –
  & Keith – 63, 64
  , C. W. (Dr. & Mrs.) – 125
  , Frances – 9
  , Robert Eden – 31
  , R. Taylor – 39
Sears & Roebuck – 219, 224
Sedam, Charlotte – 317, 324
Seidel, Robert – 290
Senecas – 1
Senior Citizen's Center – (see Shadow Lawn)
Shackleford –
  , B. H. – 307
  , Billy – 297
Shade Shop – 294
Shadow Lawn and Senior Citizens Center – 95, 132, 293, 294
Shaffer, S. S. – 53
Shah of Iran – 295
Sharp, Mrs. F. W. – 146
Shepherd –
  , Alan B. Jr. – 237
  , Wm. – 55
Shepherd's Butcher Shop 56
Sheppard –
  , Ed – 61
  , H. – 39
  , Ned – 71, 150
Sherman, Mr. – 216
Sherwin-Williams – 288
Shirley, J. W. "Pete" – 56, 80, 89, 123, 148, 152, 164, 166, 167, 183, 188, 191
S. H. Kress & Co. – (see Kress)
Shoe Center – 268, 299
Shumate –
  , Latham – 124, 145
  , Sidney – 120, 160, 184

Signal Corp Grill – 185, 301
Silco Cut Rate Store – 246
Silent Policeman – (see Dummy Policeman)
Silver Tower – 163, 169
Silvette, David – 198
Sinclair –
  , Cornelia, Kate, Louise 307
  , Jimmy Dr. – 151, 227
  , Mrs. William B. – 307
Singleton, Albert R. – 31
Skinker, Mrs. – 152
Sloane, George – 182
Smith –
  , Agnes – 5
  , Anne Brooke – 117, 287
  , Capt. Boyd – 98
  , Charles W. Marble Works – 47, 55, 74
  , Dick – 91
  , "Extra Billy" – 29
  , Gypsy Jr. – 90, 92
  , James C. – 29
  , John – 23, 29
  , Mary Amelia – 29, 54, 65, 124
  , P. B. – 187, 188, 205
  , Pearl Thornton – 256
  , Richard – 24
  , S. W. – 62
  , Thomas – 39, 125
  , William – 29
  , William Henry – 29
Snead, Judge – 251
Solar Corporation Building 299
Soldier's Lounge – (see U.S.O.)
Solid South, The – 84
Sons of Confederate Veterans – 153
Southern Fauquier Hunt Club – 236
Southern Railroad – 179
Sowers, W. S. – 223
Spain – 66
Spanish-American War – 66, 67
SPCA – 297
Spicer, Wm. – 6, 9
Spilman –
  , A. H. – 203
  , Edward M. – 29
  , Gen. Baldwin Day – 124
  , J. A. – 54, 59

Spilman –
  , John R. (Alderman) – 26, 41, 42, 57, 58, 62, 63
SPR Building – 310, 311
Springs, The – (see Fauquier Springs)
Sputnik I – 225
Square, The – (see Public Square)
Stable Door – 260, 301
Stafford –
  , Tom – 128, 138, 141, 155, 156, 157, 163, 176, 187
  , Tom Jr. – 163
Stag Annex – 55
Standard Oil Station – (see Warrenton Supply)
Statue Of Liberty – 321
Steeplechase – 43
Stephens –
  , Albert – 54
  & Jeffries – 42
  Building – 42, 45, 52, 54, 59, 62
  , Dr. J. H. – 42, 46, 54, 59
Stephenson –
  , Edward L. – 273
  , L. B. & Edna – 312
Stimson – 177
Stinson, Mrs. Wade – 283
Stitching Post – 322
Stock Exchange Building – 165
Stocks – 7, 19, 21, 291
Stokes, Wm. S. IV – 251
Stone, Charles G. – 184, 204, 231
Stoneman – 36
Strother, Wm. – 58
Stuart – 36
" - Mosby Historical Society – 316
Stuyvesant School – 85, 194, 218, 240
Suddith's Lot – 48
Sudduth –
  , E. J. – 137, 143, 186, 205
  , John D. – 172, 190, 203
  , Lawrence – 312
  Memorial Monuments 104
  (-Moser) Funeral Home 206, 222, 232, 283
  , Mrs. W. E. (Mildred) – 133, 190
  , Nellie – 67

355

Sudduth —
, Polly — 133
, W. E. — 205, 283
, W. E. — 104, 133, 205, 283
Sudduth's Funeral Home — 98, 133
Sullivan —
& Bro. — 63
, C. N. — 152
Surles & Associates — 299
Susquehannock Indians — 1
Swain, Johnny — 251
Swain's House of Style Beauty Shop — 318
Swanee Tavern — 178
Sweeney, Howard — 270
Sweeney's Shoes & Men's Wear Store — 307
Swift's School Room, Mrs. Harriet — 24, 27

Tavenner, C. A. — 38
Tavers, Grace — 176
Taylor, Elizabeth — 286
Taylor High School — (see William C. Taylor)
Teats, Bob — 312
Telephone Company —
Fauquier — 56
Fauquier & Upperville 54, 56
Piedmont — 74
Upper Fauquier & Warrenton — 72
Warrenton, Plains, Alexander — 54
Telephone Exchange, Warrenton — 72
Terry, Mary Sue — 314
Texaco Station — (see Warrenton Supply)
Thayer, Powell — 177, 198, 208
Thayer's Appliances — 177, 295
Thoma —
, Kathleen — 132
, John and Bakery — 73, 75, 88, 99, 100, 132, 161, 228
Thompson —
, Dick — 108
, K. A. Jr. — 212
, Lilly — 129
, Richard — 11, 14
, Sallie — 11
Thompson's Service Station — 152

Thornton —
& Burke's Drug Store — 195
& Willis — 151
, Dr. — 256
, Dr. John L. — 120, 158
, Edward C. "Ed" — 151, 176, 223
, John L. Jr. — 158
, Thomas C. 73, 78, 80
Thornton's Drug Store — 223
Thoroman, James — 317
Thoroman's Radio & TV Service — 253, 273
Thorp, Hallie — 122
Thorpe —
, Nina Minter — 222
, Richard — 159
Three Mile —
Island — 319
Switch — 26
Thrift Shop — 123, 171, 180, 274, 288
Tiffany —
, C. E. — 72
, Wallace N. — 145, 167, 173, 178, 184, 196
Timberlake —
, E. L. — 171, 190
, Harold — 145, 150
, James — 317
, Jim — 288, 319
Tiny Tot Day Care Center 272
Tolbert, Gen. — 287
Toll Gates — 87, 101
Tompkin, Louise — 239
Tongue —
, George and property 139, 140, 141, 143, 181
, Johnnie or Johnzie — 59, 181
, John Robert — 181
, Johnzie — 10
Town Duck — 295
Town Hall — 20, 40, 41, 45, 58, 59. 60, 80, 89, 120, 134
Trailways Bus — 188
Taver's (Travois) —
Building — 137, 162, 195
Furniture — 294
Travois, Lee — 162
Treese Nurseries, Inc. — 277

Treherne, Mrs. Thomas — 178
True Index, The — 38
Truman, Harry S. — 191, 198, 202
Tucker, Pat — 290
Turkey Run Church-St. Mary's Episcopal — 3, 6, 12
Turner —
, E. S. — 72
, Lee — 150
Turner's —
Saddle Shop — 48
Tavern — 14
Taxi — 215
Twain, Mark — 317
Tyler, Mrs. John Webb — 114
Tyson, Mr. — 135

U.F.O.'s — 251, 276
Uhlfelder — 44
Ullman —
Bros. — 157, 159
, Herman E. — 224
, Mrs. — 174
Ullman's Store — 69, 82, 123
UNICEF — 226, 228, 264
U.S.O. Club — 180, 189, 200, 208, 218
Utterback, A. W. — 47, 54

Valentine, J. — 5
Van Wegen, Ginger Anderson — 294
Venture Club — 240
VFW — 306
View Tree Mountain — 36, 77, 175, 212, 220
Village —
Flowers — 323
Inn — 137, 294
Square Dancers — 293
Virginia —
Gazette — 20
Inn — 162, 294
Museum — (see Fauquier Chapter of)
Stage Lines — 196, 206
Vision Quest Wagon Train 304
VISTA — 259
Vizzi, Mrs. — 139
Volney — 14

Voss –
, G. A. and store – 40, 73, 102, 127, 263, 269
, S. M. – 28
Wadlow, Robert – 173
Walden, John – 21, 241
Wall, Rev. Wm. – 29
Wallace –
, Benjamin R. – 22, 23
, James W. – 12
Wallach –
Building – 123, 264
, Richard – 123
Walraven –
House – 21
, Mrs. Jessie Caldwell – 72
Ward –
, Anna – 308
, Beckeley – 30, 48
, Grace – 30
, John – 41
, Mary Anne – 30
Warner –
, Daniel – 23, 256
, John W. – 286
Warren Academy – 6, 10, 24, 37
Warren –
, Gen. Joseph – 6
Green – 11, 24, 31, 38, 44, 45, 53, 63, 91, 120, 137, 138, 146, 157, 159, 234, 275, 311
Green Academy – 24
Warfield, Wallis – (see Windsor, Duke & Duchess)
War Prison Farm Labor – 190, 191
Warrenton – 11
Appliance Center – 202
Baptist Church – (see Baptist)
Bible Fellowship – 310
Cafe – 98, 109, 111, 129, 135, 142, 150, 162
Carriage Works – 84, 87
Christian Bookstore – 309
Daily Banner, The – 66
Fire House Craft Market – 297
Flag of '98, The – 23, 30

Warrenton –
Fruit Market Grocery Store – 175, 190
House – 48
Hunt – 55
Improvement Company 89, 92
Motel – 135
Pony Show – 101, 263
Republic, The – 24
Restaurant – 142
Review – 80
Rifles, The – 31, 43, 53, 74, 90, 92, 93, 94, 96, 97, 182, 198
Seminary – 12
Skating Rink – 75
Station – (see Depot)
Supply – 75, 87, 89, 93, 185
Supply Filling-Service Station – 104, 111, 118, 173, 272
Surplus – 322
Teen Club – 225
Theater – 122, 129, 130, 276
Times – 22, 84
Training Center – 220
Virginian, The – 86
Wholesale (House) Co. 221, 271
Yellow Cab – 260
Washington –
, D.C. – 12, 80
, George – 3, 4, 6, 14
, Mrs. W. H. – 112, 118, 131
, W. D. – 198
, William D. – 30
Waterloo –
Coiffures of Old Towne – 303
Mini-Mart – 311
Waterman's – 27
Waters –
, Catherine – 28, 29
, Williams – 26
Waters' Tavern-Hotel – 3, 9, 14, 28, 62
Watery Mountain – 59
Watson, Joseph H. – 23, 24, 51
Waugh, Fred – 124
Weaver, Janet – 36
Weedon, A. O. – 90
Weeks –
, Jack – 145
, W. C. – 64
Welcome Wagon – 243

Welfare Dept. – 165, 277
Welton, Michael – 21
Wesley Chapel United Methodist Church – 314
Western –
Auto – 224, 233
Union – 149, 156, 162, 181
Weston, Mr. – 197
What's Cooking – 310
Wheat, First Securities – 295, 301
Whig, The – 24
Whipping Post – 7, 19, 21
White & Smith's – 38, 40
White –
, Charles M. – 54
, J. – 62
, Judge C. M. – 78
, Mayor – 56
, Mr. – 141
Sulphur Springs – (see Fauquier Springs)
, Willard – 93
Whitmore –
, Bessie Woodzel – 119, 135, 144
, Joseph A. – 187
Whittier School, John Greenleaf – 38
Wilder, L. Douglas – 314
William C. Taylor High School – 212
Williams –
, Bob - 172
, Forest – 167
Willis' Drug Store – 151, 156, 167
Willis –
, Thurston – 85, 133, 151, 155, 203
, Tom – 203
Wilson, Woodrow – 89, 97
Winchester – 4, 5
Windsor, Duke & Duchess 120, 181, 319
Winmill –
, Allen Townsend – 165, 188
, E. W. – 125
, Mr. – 114
, Mrs. Robert C. - 127, 188
, Viola T. – 283
Wise Golden Buys – 323
Withers –
, Daniel – 12
, John B. – 39, 52
, Thornton – 42

357

Wolfe, Stanley — 148, 317
Woman's Realty Building (Exchange) — 114, 188, 202, 207
Wood —
, Capt. Lew — 92, 182
, Daniel P. — 60, 80, 86, 171, 176
, Fannie — 37
, Jerry — 271
, Josephine — 170
, Sallie — 67, 77, 86, 95, 179
Woods, Judge William — 156
Woodward, William — 310
Woodzell —
, Alice — 156
, Bessie — 119, 135, 144
, George — 131
, Samuel — 203
World Vision — (see Vision Quest)
Wray, Steven — 308
Wyer, John P. Drug Store — 55, 62

Zerega, Jimmy de — 167
Zieger —
, Clifford P. — 160
Field — 164

X-15A-2 — 249

Yates —
, H. C. — 39, 40, 44, 54, 63
, L. C. — 63
Store — (see Five Points)
Yeatman, George E. — 22
Young Men's Christian Association — 74
Youth For Understanding 294
YWCA — 97

1987-1995 REFLECTIONS

Activity around Court House Square seems to have increased the past nine years. Although some organizations have moved their meetings to one of the several shopping malls, many are held both day and night in The Square area, especially the John Barton Payne Building. Two new places are the five story office building at 98 Alexandria Pike-1987, and in 1989 next to the First Baptist Church, their Family Life Center with its name changed to honor Rev. Joseph Penn who died January 1995. The Wherehouse Youth Center opened in 1993 on Third Street to help young people of the community. Restaurants have come and gone on Main Street and surrounding it.

A few old businesses closed and others took their place. A new shop, Sarah Belle's opened, 1995, in the private residence at 110 Main. Several "Old Timers" died including; in 1989 Carroll Risdon and Tom Hutchison, 1991 Wallace Tiffany, 1993 H.B. Carter and 1994 James Austin. In 1995 Lucy Blackwell Jones who died in Colorado, was honored in a ceremony at the Old Jail Museum, that is now open full time except on Mondays.

Many new organizations have been formed, but because of store closings, in 1988 Friends of Warrenton and The Partenship For Warrenton were formed with one goal being to revitalize downtown. Warrenton joined the Virginia Main Street Program, too, so new activities came into existance.

In 1988 the first "Evening Under The Stars" with big band music and dancing in The Square occurred and continues. Money was raised to restore street lights. The Old Courthouse has had special lighting to show off its features and it's planned for other buildings also. 1990 had utility poles of Main Street decorated as palm trees for Tropical Madness entertainment and children building sand castles, but that lasted only two years. A Roaring Twenties program and stores adding Sunday hours while extending week day hours was planned but didn't work. There was an Easter celebration this year, having "strolling", an egg hunt and other things. 1991 and the years thereafter had a Northside Festival in Eva Walker Park. 1992 saw a Halloween Happyfest beginning with breakfast at the John Barton Payne Building, parade, games, and races. 1993 and following years, a wine festival, "In Good Taste" was held. "Business After Hours", an open house for shoppers, was tried but not continued. The Christmas celebration has changed from Santa coming by firetruck on first Saturday in December to beginning 1988, Santa appears Friday night by horse drawn carriage in a parade while musicians play and fairy tales are some activities. Next day Santa is again in a parade. Each weekend of December has planned entertainment with shopping. 1993 had First Night Warrenton debuting to see in the New Year.

Among Old Town standbys are the Bluemont Series each summer with music and dancing on Warren Green Hotel's lawn, the May Spring Festival- Warrenton Day- was 17 years old in 1995, the Memorial and Veteran's Day parades. 1991 was the last Volunteer Fireman's Carnival parade due to security, safety, and cost of maintenance. The planned parade that year for support of the Gulf War troops happily turned into "Welcome Home" to them. A parade that didn't come to The Square began at the Sheriff's Office and went along Keith Street to the new Visitor's Center where the Chamber of Commerce is now.

Several VIP'S visited over the years, among whom were US Rep. French Slaughter, Vice Pres. Quayle's wife Marilyn, Sen. Robb, Gov. George Allen and the biggest excitment was in 1993 when Bill Clinton and Al Gore came through town on their way to Washington. An Old Town Inaugural Welcome was given them.

Of course crime continues. Crack cocaine came to town, a Bible was stolen but returned at St. James Church, a man was robbed and beaten on Alexandria

Pike as well as a drive-by shooting there, an assult was near the Post Office, a lady was hit by a car on Main Street and there were some break-ins. Even a large snake was run over and killed on Main Street in 1993. After a heat wave a heavy rain storm came. It was thought the snake had been in a drain. In 1990 a gasoline deposit was found under the Old Courthouse, being ten feet deep, floating on the surface of the water table. It was determined to be from Olde Towne Texaco and was cleaned up in 1993.

In 1988 pickets were on The Square to protest the Western By-pass meeting. There were many debates about Disney and Wal-Mart coming to the area before being rejected, however K-Mart opens 1996 at The Village Shopping Center and Wal-Mart is still trying. The Lottery caused discussions, too, but went into operation in 1988, as did the 911 system in 1995. The recyling program is in effect, too. The 17 year locust cried loudly in 1987, but the gypsy moths came quietly, so each year planes spray them. Many pigeons were found dying in Old Town in 1988 due to an exterminator's drug in the corn they ate.

The past was remembered, 1987, in the Bicentennial celebration of the US Constitution's 200th Anniversary in the Old Courthouse and the diggings in the Old Jail Museum's exercise yard where 19th century items were found. The Fauquier Veteran's Memorial was dedicated on Hospital Hill, 1993. Guess John Marshall might have had a laugh. In 1990 a lady lost a bet and had to sit in his statue's lap for a photograph. It's located in front of the Juvenile and Domestic Relations Courthouse. In 1995 a bride and groom had their picture taken on its steps, and Main St. was featured on the cover of a brochure published by the National Trust for Historical Preservation.

Many many things have happened around The Square. As someone said, "It's a nice place-still a charming little town having much appeal."

BUSINESSES NORTH SIDE MAIN STREET
#7- Cub Run Antiques (closed about 1990)
and Courthouse Antiques
1990- Courthouse Antiques (moved to #52-1994)
1994- Flowers By Teresa
#11- The Stable Door
#13- Door to apartments above
#15- Fauquier Pharmacy (closed 1993)
Vacant
#21- F&M Bank-Peoples
#29- H.B.Carter (relocated to #45)
1989- became a mini-mall
Farrar's Men's Wear
From Any Angle
Tutto Bene (closed)
All In A Row (closed)
1994- Earthly Paradise
A.L. Morency Fine Arts & Specialties
1995- Rust-Dust-& Must Shop (moved)
#31- Town Duck
#33- Dental Office
#35- Ivy Basket
#37- Risdon Paint & Hardware (closed 1988)
Divided store- apts. above
1988- PIP Printers & Piedmont Title Agency
1989- Southern Financial Federal Savings Bank
1993- PIP renamed Old Town Printing
1994- Back In The Woods
#41- Hurst Jewelry (closed 1992)
1994- Sportshack
#43- Carter's Furniture Store (closed 1988-Storage)
1994- New Leaf Bookstore
Fauquier Artists Alliance above
#45- H.B.Carter & Co. Department Store
#53- Post Office
#61- Piccadilly, Ltd (closed 1994-reopened at #80)
Jay Katzen Campaign Office
1995- Sonshine Pictures (also remodeled to
include #63)
#65- C&S Florists
#67- The Shoe Store
#71- Wise Golden Buys (closed)
1989- Custom House (closed)

      1990- Framing Matters (moved to #81B)
      1991- The Purple Plum Gifts & Antiques
#73- Creel's Jewelry (closed 1989)
      1990- Sadrolashrafi's International Food & Deli
#75- Charlott's
      1990- Sadrolashrafi's Oriental Rugs
      1995- Snowden's Oriental Rugs
#77- Rhodes Drugstore
      Rhodes Gift and Orvis Shop (above)
      1995- also Rhodes Fly Shop
#79- Rhodes Lunch Counter
      1989- Main Street Pub (closed 1989)
      1992- Uptown Cafe (closed 1992)
      1992- Old Town Cafe
#81A- Village Flowers
#81B- Custom House & Framing Matters (closed)
      1994- Tradewinds II (moved)
      1995- Antiques & Accents
Presbyterian Church
#103- Eicher's Flowers & Gift Shop

BUSINESSES SOUTH SIDE MAIN STREET
#20- Wheat, First Securities
      Caprice Cafe- below
#22- Jimmie's Old Town Market
#24- Madison's Barber Shop
#26- Warrenton Surplus (moved)
      1988- Loveladies Antiques (moved to #36C)
      1991- The Thorp Collection
      1993- The Clothes Horse (closed 1995)
      1995- Decked Out
#28- Apartments above
#32- Sweeny's Shoes (closed 1993)
      Displays of town, activities, real estate
#34- Stitching Post
      1995- Jay Katzen Office
#36- National Variety Store (closed)
      Divided store, made staircase down separate-
#36A- 1992- Merry-Go-Round
#36B- 1990- New Leaf Book Store (moved to #43)
          and Organic Harvest
      1994- Amish Windmill
#36C- 1991- Loveladies Antiques (moved to #52 1994)

      1995- Hunting Horn
#40- Hutchison Travel Bureau
#44- Cardinal Cake and Bake Shop
#46- Thrift Shop
#48- Christian Science Reading Room
#50- First Church of Christ (moved to Jackson St.)
      Apartments
#52- Furniture Interiors (closed 1994)
      and Upper Level Antiques
      1994- Loveladies Antiques (To Lee St. 1995)
      1994- Courthouse Antiques
#56- Apartments above
#58- Edgar Snowden Oriental Rugs, Ltd (moved to
                       #75-1995)
      Vacant
$64- Tally-Ho Gallery (closed)
      1992- A Touch of Williamsburg (closed)
      1993- Frame Craft
#66- Dove Cote Studio (closed)
      1991- Bill Fendley Insurance
#68- Roop's Refrigeration (closed)
      Antique Shop (closed)
      1992- Frame Craft (moved to #64)
      1993- Mane Salon
#70- SPR Building- Offices and shops
#78- Dollar General Store (To Town Center Mall 1993)
      Divided building
      1995- Fabric Emporium
#80- 1995- Piccadilly, Ltd.
#82- O'Connell & Mayhugh PC
#88- Commercial Cabinetry (closed)
      1990- The Clothes Horse (moved to #26 1993)
      1993- Just Write (closed)
      1995- Evergreen: Gardens & Wildlife
#90- Realty Company
      Virginia Gold Cup Association
#92- Blue Ridge Hardware (closed 1996)
#100- Surles & Associated, Ltd

COURT HOUSE SQUARE
Old Gaol Museum changed to Old Jail Museum
#14- John Marshall Building, now Juvenile &
                Domestic Court
#10- Fauquier National Bank, now Fauquier Bank

www.ingramcontent.com/pod-product-compliance
Lightning Source LLC
Chambersburg PA
CBHW071951220426
43662CB00009B/1091